"The most factual writing by any author on the Shoshone Nation."

Raymond D. Yowell
Western Shoshone Citizen

"I wholeheartedly support the truth as written in Mr. Gale Ontko's series, *Thunder Over the Ochoco*. This writing is most exciting, factual and represents the Shoshone oral history as close as could be expected. He represents our heroes as no other could—dog soldiers such as Red Wolf, Wolf Dog and Has No Horse, men who played such important roles in our history and culture.

Jack C. Orr (Dogowa)
Citizen of the Western Shoshone Nation

Also by Gale Ontko:

THUNDER OVER THE OCHOCO

AND THE JUNIPER TREES BORE FRUIT

Volume V

GALE ONTKO

Illustrations by Gale Ontko

— A Maverick Publication —

ISBN 0-89288-276-X

Library of Congress Catalog Card Number: 93-18698

On the cover:
The Pursuit by H.W. Hansen
Courtesy of Bill and Dorothy Harmsen Western Art Collection

For additional copies of Gale Ontko's books, contact:
Maverick Distributors
P.O. Drawer 7289
Bend, Oregon 97708
541-382-2728

Published and printed by Maverick Publications, Inc.
P.O. Box 5007   Bend, Oregon 97708

DEDICATION

ANDY ONTKO
Trapper, stockman, hard-rock miner
and businessman who knew almost everyone
in eastern Oregon by their first name.

IN MEMORY OF

Andrew Gale Ontko

Born: August 18, 1927
Died: July 2, 1998

TABLE OF CONTENTS

PART VII
And the Juniper Trees Bore Fruit

APPENDICES

PREFACE

Some say that I am not a schooled writer and they are correct. Perhaps this lack of formal journalism enables me to write from the heart without outside influences affecting the final result. Whatever, it is my sincere wish that this work has given the reader a new perspective and respect for the land called Ochoco. If so, then I have accomplished my goal as a recorder of history.

For years I had doubts that *Thunder Over the Ochoco* would reach its intended destination but with luck it just might happen. However in response to complaints that it took me longer to write the history of central Oregon than it took the pioneers to settle it, I have only one comment. There were a lot more of them than there was of me. Sometimes an author bites off more than he can reasonably chew in a short span of time. Now that I have struggled through five volumes of *Thunder Over the Ochoco* I suppose it is right, maybe even proper, to acquaint the reader with the writer and the Ochoco he grew up in. In previous volumes others have given some glowing reports which I sincerely appreciate but now is the time to part the willows and plunge into the stream of thoughts. Most likely the best way to do this without going under is to let the driftwood float with the current. I may get caught in a whirlpool but eventually I should reach calm water. So here goes.

The ranch where I grew up and still own has been in the family for five generations. Constructed in 1871, the two-story log cabin I called home was the first house to appear in the Upper Ochoco Valley just three years after a brace of Gatling guns ripped the heart out of Has No Horse's big Shoshoni encampment which sat on what is now Ontko land. For a time in the 1890's this property belonged to U.S. Congressman Newt Williamson who, along with Oregon Senator John Mitchell, was a key player in the Oregon land fraud trials better known as The Looting of the Public Domain. I remember Mr. Williamson as a dignified old gentleman who carried a cane topped with Scissors Creek gold. This gold-headed walking stick is now on display at the A.R. Bowman Memorial Museum in Prineville, Oregon.

Many have asked what inspired me to record events. Blame it on my Grandmother Koch. At a very early age, she gave me a diary with strict instructions to "write in it!" This was at a time when the most earth-shattering event you could witness was the passage of an aeroplane maybe once in three or four years if you were lucky, had sharp eyesight, good hearing and wasn't caught napping. Anyway, I thought it might be wise to complete the diary as best I could in one year or most likely I would never receive another present from grandma. So, I started writing down everything I saw or heard including what the neighbors said or did. Once they caught on, I wasn't too popular especially with an old gentleman who lived down the creek. He was a U.S. Land Commissioner who had spent a little time in federal prison on a timber fraud charge. As it turned out, I shouldn't have worried about not receiving another gift from grandma. Every year without fail, I got another diary. By the time I was ten years old, I was the best traveling source of information in the Upper Ochoco Valley. Come to think if it, my mother also had a hand in my writing delinquency. Not only was she a school teacher but she authored *Through the Golden Gate of Yesteryear: Life on the Upper Ochoco 1907 through 1918* which is much more peaceful reading than *Thunder Over the Ochoco*. Actually, if I could have inherited my mother's writing talent I might have penned a best seller but let's face it, I ain't that gifted.

Somewhere in there, my folks decided I needed a music education. Now it just so happened my grandparents owned a huge upright concert piano. Why, is anyone's guess since no one in the family could play it but that was soon to change. The neighbors all gathered (probably hoping that piano lessons would keep me out from underfoot), loaded the two-ton monstrosity on a hay wagon, transported the thing down through the meadow to the lower ranch and I got stuck with eight years of classical music lessons before I convinced all concerned that wasn't my calling.

There was a sawmill and logging camp on the ranch. Every evening it was my job to pack a couple of gallon jugs of milk over the hill and deliver them to the cookhouse where I would spend hours listening to the old horse loggers spin yarns and of course, take notes. Another source of interest was the mining camps and I was well acquainted with them. My Grandfather Ontko was a hard-rock miner from Pennsylvania who homesteaded at Suplee in the Paulina country where I was born. Grandfather Koch discovered the only gold in the Ochoco Valley that wasn't connected with the rich Scissorsville strike of 1873. Both my father and uncle worked in most of the quicksilver mines in central Oregon and my step-grandfather, who was a close friend of Death Valley Scotty, made the initial discoveries of most of the quicksilver mines in the West—from the famous Horse Heaven Mine in central Oregon to the Champion Lode in northern Nevada.

In the early 1930's Grandmother Koch built the well-known Log Cabin Service Station and Store on the old Mitchell highway and my parents operated it for many years. I honestly believe every person in eastern Oregon stopped there at one time or another and they were a wealth of information. "Ya wanna hear the story about old so-and-so? Well by gawd I'll tell you." It might not have been all truthful but at least it was something instead of nothing to go on.

There were also Indians who drifted through the country. For years, an old couple arrived every fall and camped in a grove of trees on the lower ranch. Dave and Rose Chocktote were assigned to the Klamath reservation but I suspect they never stayed there. Dave spent the year wandering throughout eastern Oregon visiting the haunts of his youth. He and his wife traveled by wagon with a saddle horse hitched to the back and made their living trading buckskin gloves, slippers, jackets and rawhide riatas for whatever handout they could get. Incidentally, their products were in great demand and their needs were quite basic. Perhaps a sack of oats for the horses; maybe a bag of potatoes or other garden produce; and if really lucky, some kind soul would throw in some salt, sugar, flour or coffee to supplement their meager supplies.

One evening I was hunkered down by the campfire listening to Dave reminisce about a friend who had lived much like him—traveling around the country—before his death several years in the past. After sitting in silence for some time, Dave again spoke: "Dead Deer was a brave *pahah nuck* (old man). He die like a dog soldier. White guys call him Mike Deer Gut." End of story. Deer Gut isn't a very pleasing name but us palefaces weren't too complimentary about Indians at that time. I guess it was because Indian attacks were still fresh in the old timer's minds. According to them, it had only been about 25 years since the last good battle had taken place on the Oregon-Nevada border. By "good battle" it meant some injuns had gotten what they deserved. Anyway, I never gave Dave's story another thought until some 30 years later. While lost in the corridors of research, I stumbled upon the name of Shoshoni Mike Daggett. Mike Daggett . . . Mike Deer Gut? Could be. It was worth a look which led to some interesting results.

And then there was White Eagle—a real character. He claimed to be Shoshoni but I imagine he would be whatever one might want. White Eagle was a professional wrestler and always visited the ranch on his periodic rounds throughout the West. The main Prineville event, and the bout which drew the biggest crowd, was a match between White Eagle and a local lad who wrestled professionally under the name of Cowboy Breese. When those two tangled you got your money's worth and depending upon who you talked to at the time—Chief White Eagle or Cowboy Breese—it was a toss-up as to who was the better grappler. It just so happened that White Eagle's wife—an English girl—was a cousin to the gentleman who married my mother's cousin.

In the 1960's an Indian friend of my father spent several summer vacations on the ranch. He roamed the country from the John Day Valley to the High Desert searching for clues to his past. Not realizing I was intimately acquainted (because of my job) with every hump and gully between the Columbia River and the Klamath Basin, he shared more information than he really intended to . . . some of which shall remain where it belongs—in the depths of my mind. This big warrior was a professional football player for the L.A. Rams.

Gosh! If you've stayed with me this long, you have to be as interested in central Oregon history as I am. I hope you enjoy Volume V and gain a better insight into this area's turbulent past. Pleasant reading and many thanks for putting up with my ramblings.

Gale Ontko

REMEMBRANCE

Sixty years—'twas a meadow then,
and the deer roamed wild and free;
Sixty years—I see it again
as it appeared to me.
The old trail ran where the barn stands now;
The trail was here before the plow,
And we worked horses and milked a cow,
In the day that used to be.

A noted writer once commented: "Any journalist who has done investigative reporting knows how difficult it is to verify the testimony of interviewees, to determine the accuracy of what they say and finally to put it all together into a coherent whole." He spoke the truth. I soon discovered I was treading on thin ice when delving into the vigilantes and the resultant central Oregon range war. Some who talked, when they realized I was taking notes, refused to give any more information. Others, who had met some of the tougher elements at gun-point, told me many interesting things. Keep in mind that it is not hard to hide something unpleasant from history. People don't lie. They simply leave out parts that they don't want publicized.

For the main part, *Thunder Over the Ochoco*, Vol. V, is the memory of those who lived it. To mention just a few is to neglect the many who helped on this volume for the list becomes a litany of the old timers of Crook, Grant and Harney Counties—which includes the later counties of Wheeler, Jefferson and Deschutes.

Some of the names who added a wealth of information to this volume are best given in Hazel Smith Denton's *Memories*.

Deep in my heart is a memory
Of days so long ago,

Remembering good times with friends we know
When we all lived on The Ochoco.

Lookout Mountain and The Ochoco
Are sacred names to me,
If I had my choice, next to Heaven,
That's where I'd want to be!

Most of the people have gone,
And everything has changed so,
But still, it's home and I love those names
Lookout Mountain and The Ochoco.

The Blevins, the Kochs and the Tollidays,
The Smiths, Staleys, Youngs and Cornetts,
The Keetons, Johnsons, Laniuses and Ontkos,
Are friends and neighbors you just don't forget.

The Higgins, Morgans, Russells and Hindermans,
The Taylors, Davises, and Louie Beirl,
Farquar McRae and Julius Cornez,
Each one lived by the Golden Rule.

The Fullers, Lakins and Herefords,
The Millers, Martins and Dills,
Art Champion, the Werths and Leaches,
Good times memories linger still.

Places change,
People come and go,
But, if you're like me, you treasure
Those days on The Ochoco!

Thank you, Hazel, for allowing the use of your thoughts and thank you pioneers of the Ochoco—Shoshoni and American—for letting me share your heartaches and your joys. It will never be forgotten.

I would also like to thank all of those who, over the years, took the time to call or write and offer encouragement in my efforts to record the history of the Ochoco. It was their confidence that kept me going. Without that I may never have reached the goal I set out to attain.

Gale Ontko

INTRODUCTION

I am interested in seeing things saved that are disappearing. People are inclined to forget things if somebody doesn't put them down in a book.

Bernard C. Winn
Hobby Makes Grist For Book

The Shoshoni wars were but a flashy prelude compared to the seething unrest Prineville held in store. Situated in the heart of the vast unknown, she became the queen of Oregon cow towns and the mistress of one of the richest cattle domains in the Old West. Isolated from the rest of the state by a major mountain range and miles of virgin prairie, her wilderness empire fast became the mecca for every hunted man west of the Great Divide.

Shunned by all civil authority, Prineville became a law unto itself. As conditions became more and more desperate, large companies organized to protect the range only to see thousands of cattle and hundreds of thousands of sheep rushed to the Blue Mountains each year. Soon the range became crowded to the limit and King Grass could not be denied.

Under the gentle guidance of Judge Colt and a hangman's noose, a vigilance committee was formed: an organization which ruled the 10,000 square miles of cattle country and the town of Prineville with an iron hand. Word leaked to the outer world that no stranger dared settle in Crook County and the national press took up the attack with blazing headlines.

Thoroughly miffed, Prineville's representative stormed the state capital. A fiery individual bearing the impressive title of Colonel William Thompson, he was quick to inform state officials to "keep your blasted nose out of Prineville's personal affairs." Vigorously upholding the actions of the vigilance committee, Thompson coined central Oregon's most publicized battle cry when he voiced this warning to all who would oppose the vigilantes: "If these depredations do not cease. . . the juniper trees will bear fruit!" Still on the warpath, the "madcap colonel" challenged Harvey Scott, editor of the Portland *Oregonian* and a United States senator to a duel in the lobby of Salem's Chameketa Hotel, plunging Prineville's private conflict into nation-wide scandal.

What followed is one of the most disgraceful chapters in Oregon history. *Vigilante* became a word whispered with fear and contempt as mob rule and violence hovered over the land. Six-shooters roared in the night; ranchers disappeared never to be seen again; the range reeked with the stench of rotting bodies; and the juniper trees bore fruit! Only under threat of martial law did the land barons who perpetrated Oregon's devastating range war submit to the Federal Reserve Act of 1906.

Crook County was to enjoy four years of tranquillity before rifle shots once more echoed across her borders. In the rugged confines of the Deschutes River canyon she became a witness to the last great war of its kind fought within the continental boundaries of the United States—the battle of the railroad giants.

These were the troubled years when only the strong survived. An eternity of bloodshed set to the background music of death. What began as a concerto of sorrow keyed to the monotonous roll of the war drums . . . the sodden thud of an arrow caressing human flesh . . . the dull rumble of an army howitzer increasing the tempo with canister and grape would end with the muffled staccato of a hundred hoofbeats in the night . . . the soul-tearing shriek of a man dragged to death down Prineville's main street . . . the plaintive bleat, augmented to a roar as thousands of sheep plunged to their death . . . the sullen rhythm of hammer against railroad spike driven still deeper by the electrifying splat of a rifle bullet. This crescendo of desolation would witness the grand finale of . . . *Thunder Over the Ochoco!*

THUNDER OVER THE OCHOCO

AND THE JUNIPER TREES BORE FRUIT

Volume V

PART VII
AND THE JUNIPER TREES BORE FRUIT

PART VII

AND THE JUNIPER TREES BORE FRUIT
1881 — 1916
(a period of conflict pitting neighbor against neighbor)

My enemies call me the "mad-cap Colonel."
So be it! But if these range depredations do not
cease—the juniper trees will bear fruit!

Col. William (Bud) Thompson
Secretary, Ochoco Livestock
Association

Yes, the new occupants would cleanse the land. The Ochoco was now gaining momentum on the road to progress—if not by choice, then by rule of gun and rope. A group of vigilantes—later they chose to be known as sheepshooters—ruled the 10,000 square miles of sheep and cattle country with brutal force. Judge Lynch's reign in Crook County, fueled by one needless act of mob violence, generated a lawless spirit that soon burst out of control. This account is not intended in any way to reflect upon their descendants who are far removed from the sins of the past and are now respected citizens of the community. Its purpose is to clear the record for innocent men who were victims of the vigilantes. These men too left families who deserve at least as much consideration as the offspring of their slayers. What follows is one of the blackest chapters in Oregon history.

In my day as cattleman in Crook County, six-
shooters roared in the night, ranchers disappeared
never to be heard of again and the juniper trees
bore fruit!

James M. Blakely
Leader, The Citizen's Protective Union

3

CHAPTER 180

THE STYLISH '80S

*The towns had lawyers, doctors, shoemakers, tailors
and barbers. Town lots had jumped in price from
ten to hundreds of dollars. Everybody was making
money. Some more than others.*

Henry Villard
Oregon Economic Leader, 1880

Now the Ochoco was overwhelmed with new tribes called stockmen, miners, loggers, freighters, merchants and speculators. The mode of life would not be the same. Perhaps not better but certainly different than the days of wigwam and feathers. As one old-timer recalled—and he should know—Prineville had all the cow town brashness of its more notorious counterparts such as Dodge City, Kansas and Tombstone, Arizona.[1]

By 1880, U.S. population exceeded 50 million and Prineville's share was a bustling crowd of 400 prosperous and dignified townspeople who, in their eyes, were becoming just a shade sophisticated. These were the days when such gentlemen as Doc Holliday, Charlie Long, Clay Allison and Hank Vaughan were the tough characters of the Old West and the heroines were such un-retouched ladies as Big Nose Kate, Calamity Jane, Madame Moustache and Prineville's own Annette Tallman, a full blood Shoshoni and daughter of the Snake war chief, Tall Man who had taken the long count in the battle of '66.

Tall, willowy, bronze-skinned Annette lived in a cozy cottage down on the banks of the Ochoco—some prudes called it "Rotten Row"—within shouting distance of Joe Kelly's Last Chance Saloon on

---

1 Interview Art Michel, March 22, 1979. A turn of the century store-keeper, Art was still working at Erickson's Super Market (now Erickson Sentry) when he was in his nineties.

the corner of Fifth and Main. Actually, there were three cabins along the river occupied by Annette, Katrina Driggs and Penelope Sutton—three extremely good-looking young ladies who were also known as Naughty Nettie, Irish Kate and Bad Penny.[2] When this trio of femininity strolled up Main Street with their long, fashionable skirts dragging on the boardwalk, cowhands, miners, businessmen and homesteaders would gaze longingly at such an invigorating sight—and mothers would not allow their children to look at "such brazen hussies." The gentlemen called them "doves of the roost." In those days, West 5th Street was the "tenderloin district" and East 6th Street was known as "Brewery Lane."

Portland could brag that it witnessed a brilliant display of the newfangled Edison incandescent lamps when the steamer *Columbia* arrived from the East Coast with four 60-lamp dynamos in the fall of 1880 but Prineville could make a greater boast. Mail was arriving once a week from The Dalles by pony express and that was something unusual. More exciting, Main Street was illuminated by coal oil lamps and if this was good enough for Portland, it was good enough for Prineville—as Portland didn't have electric power until 1882. That same year, Prineville's fire department was born, consisting of a six-man operated, man-drawn pumper that was shipped around the Horn and 112 years later was still at the fire department in good working order. By 1886, this state-of-the-art fire engine was backed up by a 20-man pumper.

The citizens were also enjoying a lively flow of revenue. Beef prices were on the rise for the first time since 1873 and 58,000 head of cattle were trailed to Cheyenne for shipment to the eastern market. Gold was pouring out of Scissorsville at a healthy rate while timber harvesting was becoming big business. The only disturbing news came when President Hayes ordered the closure of Fort Harney. On June 14, 1880, the 21st U.S. Infantry under the command of Lt. Edward Farrow (the white pony soldier who had engineered the Shoshoni's final defeat)

---

2   It should be noted that for clearly apparent reasons the names of Annette, Katrina and Penelope will not appear anywhere in the records of the Baptist citadel of early Prineville. For all information concerning these ladies of questionable virtue, the author is indebted to several old timers who (although now gone) asked to remain unnamed and that request will be honored. Before speculation can run rampant, Penny Sutton was no relation to Charity Sutton, who with her second husband, Robert Wilson, moved to Prineville in 1877.

abandoned the post leaving eastern Oregon open to Shoshoni attack if they so desired.

By virtue of its leadership, Prineville was the fashion plate of the interior and fiercely proud of it. According to Joaquin Miller—world traveler—the most beautiful women he had ever encountered lived in the Blue Mountains of eastern Oregon and the local girls didn't take this compliment lightly. They strived to earn and keep it.

As one interested observer would put it, "When a researcher starts rooting back into the past trying to find out how people dressed . . . what they carried in their pockets . . . he runs into some of the darndest things." He knew what he was talking about.

All ladies were well-dressed but for the sake of enlightenment, let's follow the town courtesans on a shopping spree as these gad-flies did seem to get around a bit more than the general run of women in those days. Prodding the memory of those who professed to know, all were well-groomed and delightfully attractive but apparently Annette Tallman was a cut above the ordinary. Maybe it was her sedate upbringing at the Catholic mission in The Dalles where she received her classy name. One ardent cowboy would describe her as "having a face broad at the brow with high cheekbones that were not sharp but full and soft. Her hair had the shine of black velvet and her teeth were all the whiter for her full naturally red lips." He would further marvel at "the slender feminine appeal of her figure in a dark dress." He had spent a lot of months on the bleak High Desert.

Hugh Herdman, a smitten prospector from Scissorsville, would wax poetic:

> *From chin to brow your face, I trow,*
> *Commands me call you saint Annette;*
> *Howe'er at times in making rhymes,*
> *I write you down, Annette, coquette.*

It certainly wasn't any literary masterpiece but at least Hugh got his point across.

Then there was Sgt. Reginal Bradley, a career soldier who had covered central Oregon from Fort Watson to Fort Klamath. Bradley had his sights set on Irish Kate. In a reflective mood he would express his thoughts somewhat better than Herdman.

> *When I cease to notice a woman's charms*
> *I am quite ready for an Angel's arms.*
> *Until that time, may it never come*
> *God give me strength and keep me young.*

And apparently the Good Lord was listening. Sgt. Bradley penned those words at the age of 102.

Now, let's explore town. When shopping, the girls had the pick of four general stores—Johnson's, Sichel's, Hahn & Fried's and Breyman & Sommerville's—before spending an evening at the Glaze Opera House. Among other attractions at the local emporium of performing arts was the periodic appearance of the De Moss Family Concert Company advertised as the West's favorite entertainers.

At the start of the Shoshoni war James De Moss (a United Brethren minister) and his wife Elizabeth joined an Iowa wagon train bound for the eastern Oregon gold fields, arriving at the Grand Ronde Valley in the fall of 1862. It soon became common knowledge that the Rev. James in hand-to-fang combat was not above killing some wolves with a Bowie knife and that Elizabeth, on the trip west, had bested an Indian warrior in a tug-of-war over the possession of a dead fish. Aware of these feats of valor, the boisterous inhabitants of a mining camp now known as Baker City, Oregon convinced the De Moss family to file a homestead claim on the Powder River. By 1872, James, Elizabeth and their children were recognized as accomplished vocalists and musicians. Soon the De Moss "Lyric Bards" (as they were then named) were giving concerts in mining camps from Scissorsville, Oregon, to Silver City, Idaho; in army outposts from Fort Walla Walla, Washington Territory to Fort Harney, Oregon—and all the pioneer settlements in between.

George De Moss (James' son) would later note that "from Fort Boise we launched out into the great Shoshone desert." In their first public rehearsal given in the southern Blue Mountains of Oregon to a rapt Shoshoni audience James De Moss would comment: "If we can please the preachers at Walla Walla and with the same program please the wild men of the mountains, we surely ought to please the multitudes of the world." And so they did from Queen Victoria of the United British Kingdom to Czar Nicholas II of Imperial Russia to Tillman Glaze, proprietor of the Bucket of Blood, U.S.A.[3]

Also at the Glaze Opera House, Penny, Kate and Nettie could join Prineville's elite to be entertained by the popular songs of the '80s which included "Old Dan Tucker," "Money Musk" and "Turkey in the Corn" rendered by such gifted vocalists as Marcella Sunbrick, who did a number on "Sweet Genevieve," and Mary Gorden whose curtain stopper was "Come Where My Love Lies Dreaming." Then there was Emma Eames (born in Shanghai, China in 1867) who made a specialty of "Dixie." And if they were real lucky, Ernestine Schuman-Hienk on her tour of the gold camps might stop in and have the boys clapping in the aisle when she sang "Home to Our Mountain." Maria Gay's "Call Me Pet Names" was also a showstopper. Of course the old-timers—but not where their wives could hear—would swear nothing could compare to the time in Virginia City, Nevada when they saw Adah Isaacs Menken "ride nekked across the stage" in the melodrama *Mazeppa*. To them that was the premier sight of the West with the Glaze Opera House coming in a very poor second. Even Mark Twain, who had a fairly level eye in his head, saw her as a "whole constellation . . . magnificent spectacle . . . like a vast spray of gas-jets." Of course, he was a *Nevada News* reporter at the time and prone to exaggeration. After all, Adah was not naked—just wearing an opaque, skin-tight costume—but she left windrows of deliciously shocked and restless men from Boise to Salt Lake City gasping in her wake . . . but not at Prineville's dignified opera house. Fortunately Glaze also owned the Bucket of Blood, although he preferred to call it the "Singer Saloon."

One of the rousing attractions at Glaze's Bucket of Blood (not the opera house) was Big John Heenan (one of Adah's four husbands), the American heavyweight bare-knuckle champion whose conversation was limited almost entirely to oaths and who practiced his left jab on Adah. Once in awhile some dumb logger was foolish enough to stage an exhibition fight with Big John after which the logger licked his wounds in the brush and felt damn proud of himself.

---

3   For a complete history of the De Moss Family Lyric Bards see Elbert De Moss, *Sweet Oregon*.

Adah was no slouch in the ring either. One night in a Virginia City saloon she announced that she could box as well as any man and volunteered to put on the gloves with anyone willing. A rash miner stepped forward, and according to legend she knocked him out in the second round.

When strolling downtown, only old-fashioned Kate wore hoop skirts, for these contrivances had gone out of style as the Civil War ended. Penny preferred crinoline instead of the steel hoops to bolster her figure and tight corsets were coming into style. When the first settlers arrived between 1868-70, the bustle had been the rage but by the 1880s it was the barb. Petticoats were ruffled down the back for that well-rounded look and even had an extra-long ruffled detachable tail which must have served some purpose or another. As stated in fashion magazines in Harriet Markam's Millinery and Dress Emporium on the corner of Fourth and Main, "white ladies" wore suspender garters, generally attached to a long whale-bone corset. No mention was made as to what was proper for their "red sisters" but one guesses that Nettie was denied this added bit of finery.

It was claimed that Kate, Nettie and Penny—and certainly the other ladies—wore elaborate underdrawers of embroidered flannel which had been in style before the Civil War and for the country cousins on the upper Ochoco it was not indiscreet to wear long red flannel ones during the winter months. During the record-breaking cold snap of 1880-81, the town girls got their chance to find out how comforting they were.

From about 1875 on, Harriet's dress shop would stock such items as princess slips, though generally the preference for an upper undergarment would be a chemise, a corset cover, or a camisole covered by a balmoral skirt. Her customers could also invest in a paletot which was a kind of jacket with long sleeves and high neck, buttoning down the front like a military tunic or a sacque, which was a feminine version of a man's sackcoat with trimmings. Also available was the long sacque, which was a copy of the men's version of a cut-a-way coat. Mitts with finger ends removed were a must and Harriet stocked plenty of those.

A trip to one of the mercantile stores could produce a curling iron—heated on a wood stove or over a kerosene lamp—for the well-coifed look. Kid and cloth high-button shoes equipped with high or medium heels were the proper foot attire. "English Lavender" smelling salts were also very high on the list of purchases. Even in the late '60s and '70s for a mere dollar or so a girl could buy such female comforts as "Peerless Bust Developers" complete with exercises, but one thing she couldn't buy was face powder.

On the promenade up town, Kate might wear a calico dress, high-necked with only her own efforts and imagination to beautify it, which could turn out disastrous or humorous or delightful depending upon the mood. And usually she would be accompanied by some smitten young buckaroo, logger or miner. Some would have you believe that so long as these admirers had a six-gun strapped to their side, they were well-dressed. It couldn't have impressed the ladies less.

Neither would an escort be wearing his broad-cloth pantaloons neatly pressed—not unless he wanted the whole baggy-looking town to call him a "cheap John." Neatly creased trousers were a sure sign they'd just been bought ready-made from Breyman & Sommerville's general store on South Main and as such, they were taboo. You had your clothes made at Gormely's Tailor Shop on the corner of West Fourth and North Main or at least took the trouble to wash out all signs of creases.

Not only the necessities, but the good things in life had to find their way into the Ochoco Valley by horse power. Sixteen-horse freight wagons—sometimes three in tandem—rolled through Prineville daily, some carrying gold-laden ore to The Dalles for shipment to Tacoma, Washington; others carrying supplies to Lakeview, Oregon, Alturas, California and Winnemucca, Nevada. When the south-bound wagons arrived in Prineville, they had already been on the road 30 days and expected to take 10 more days just to reach Lakeview. In rough travel (winter snow and spring mud) a freighter figured for each 22 miles traveled it would take 36 hours. Water, or lack of it, was a big problem on the Lakeview run. One enterprising freighter kept his thirsty team going by giving them canned tomato juice to drink.

The stage stop was at the Prineville Inn, present site of the Cinnabar restaurant on the corner of East Third and Main. It was a rambling wooden structure run by a Chinese man who charged 50¢ a night for lodging and 25¢ for a meal. Transportation from Prineville to Shaniko was $15. However, if that was inconvenient, you could hire a team and wagon for $8 a day plus the board of the driver for the same trip.

Now, let's join Penny for a stagecoach ride to Shaniko. Most likely she would prefer a traveling dress of serge, very chic and her hat was usually a bonnet framing golden curls which fell to her shoulders. When Penny—her head held high—walked down Main Street it can be guessed that all male eyes focused respectfully on her and followed her progress with longing. She, being a tolerant queen of mankind, would accept this tribute from loyal vassals as a matter of course. Upon boarding the coach she most likely would be greeted by some gentlemen fresh from the eastern Oregon gold fields and these admirers would take note of such a pleasing subject. Probably they would depict Penny as "a sweet sixteen" using a popular western phrase of the time which could apply to any attractive lady no matter what her age. A passenger of Penny's perfect dimensions was so exceptional that one old timer was overcome just thinking about her. He swore he once rode the overcrowded Shaniko stage and had the privilege of sitting next to Bad Penny. "The unaccustomed pressure beside a man filled him at once with a mystical enthusiasm." No doubt. One thing for sure Penny would be in safe hands on her trips to The Dalles City. Her male companions being from eastern Oregon would travel with loaded firearms and at the drop of a hat would use them without hesitation against friend or foe. Incidentally, when making a coach run in the winter, all a passenger had to keep warm was a flask of liquor and a hot brick. For winter jaunts it's a safe bet that Penny would be wearing a crinoline hoop covered with a heavy wool balmoral skirt and her curls would be covered with a warm Parisian hat. One thing for certain, when traveling Penny would be stylishly dressed, for the most active spots in town were the stage station and hotel lobbies—usually full of the idle curious waiting for some kind of news to spread through town and seldom were they disappointed.

One tidbit passed along in 1881 concerned that modish Paiute, Princess Winnemucca, who was again drawing national attention. On December 5 of that year, Sally abruptly married Lt. Lewis Hopkins of Virginia. Tongues really started wagging. Not only was the gentleman a southern aristocrat—but heaven forbid, he was five years younger than Sally![4] Obviously the red wench had no shame. Where she met Lt.

---

4   The *Nevada Silver State*, December 8, 1881; the *San Francisco Chronicle*, December 8, 1881;; the *New York Times*, December 18, 1881.

Hopkins was open to discussion. Some claimed it was in Montana when Sarah was visiting her sister Elma. Others swore it was in the Ochoco during the Bannock War.[5] One thing for sure, Hopkins was a high-stake gambler not long for this world. Having spent as little time as possible in Sally's loving arms, he died of tuberculosis on October 18, 1887 at Lovelock, Nevada.[6]

Shortly after her marriage, Sally headed for Boston, Philadelphia and New York City, lecturing on the inequity of eastern Oregon Indian policy. This would make copy for Dillard & Company's *Prineville News* advertised as independent in politics with Republican inclinations. Unfortunately with a Democratic majority ruling the town, even such stimulating reporting as this couldn't maintain circulation and the *Prineville News* soon went broke leaving Prineville without a fourth estate from the latter part of 1881 to 1882—a critical lapse in public record. Then in 1883, Dillard was back in business but on November 11 of that year the *Prineville News* burned to the ground at a loss of $1,500.

But back to the stage station and the bits of gossip it could produce. In those days, pants were equipped with suspenders . . . "galluses" as the boys around town called 'em. One day a drummer (salesman) who dropped off the Shaniko stage, dusted off his Congress shoes and headed for Dick Graham's Longhorn Saloon. According to the locals, his galluses were stupendous—so wide and ruggedly built they gave the appearance of holding him down into his trousers rather than holding them up around him. The top of his pants hit him just below the breastbone. On the galluses' snaps, instead of the usual "Fireman's" it said "Hercules" which meant they were ordered special from the Hudson's Bay Company.

After leaving the Longhorn, the drummer sauntered into the Jackson House and expressed dismay at the condition of the hotel towels. Somewhat miffed by this insult, his host replied, "There's 26 men used that towel before you and you're the first one that complained." And so it went in the fair city of Prineville.

The livery stables also did a booming business. There were three within easy walking distance of the stage station—Henry "Shoe-Peg" Hamilton's on the corner of East Fourth and Belknap; Maupin & Perkin's

5   Patricia Stewart, "Sara Winnemucca," *Nevada Historical Society Quarterly*, No. 14, 1971, p. 31; the *New York Times*, December 18, 1881; the *Nevada Silver State*, December 1, 1881.

6   The *Daily Silver State*, October 20, 1887.

on the corner of East Second and Belknap; and the Glaze Livery Stable on the corner of West Second and Beaver, take your pick. But be forewarned, if you were headed out of town by stage, it was not uncommon for the four-horse coaches to upset which perhaps is the reason that livery barns two-horse rental carriages were so much in demand.

When riding out on the frontier, the ladies wore a sunbonnet—home-made, stiff-starched and stiffened still more with cardboard or light wooden inserts which were taken out when the bonnet was laundered. Luckily, they could make their own starch from the settlings of potato water and if that wasn't available, by soaking wheat in water, straining it and then pouring off the water after its starchy dregs had settled.

Never did they wear men's pants or ride astride. The Indian women, yes, but white ladies rode side-saddle. Maybe this explains why Naughty Annette had more fun—she wasn't bound by so blamed many rules. Anyway, the proper way to ride was for the equestrian to hook her knee over the padded horn sticking out of the left side of the saddle and she rode with both legs on the same side of the horse demurely covered with a dozen yards of riding skirt. Some women became expert riders and even had an extra down-covered horn for jumping. Others preferred the light, one-horse buggy which could be rented from a livery stable if you had no transportation of your own. It cost one dollar for an evening of joy-riding or four to five dollars a day depending on how far and how fancy you wished to travel.

They tell of the time when Nettie Scott, on a bet with a rancher, raced her buggy from the upper Ochoco into Prineville—a distance of 30 miles—thundering down East Third Street in the unbelievable time of two hours from ranch to town. Nettie spent the remainder of the day rubbing down and walking her prized trotting horse to keep him from dying of exertion.

When attending a social event, the ladies' escort most likely would be wearing a black broad cloth coat with vest to match which was high style. In fact, it was good enough for Hank Vaughan to wear when he challenged Charlie Long to a shoot-out in the Bucket of Blood Saloon. To top off this attire, he would be wearing nankeen trousers. Nankeen was a yellowish-brown cloth which wasn't exactly pretty.

For less formal attire, a sack coat was okay. This wasn't much different from the present single-breasted business suit except the lapels and top button were much higher giving it a military look. Across the vest would be a heavy gold watch chain with a large hook on one end and an oversized Waltham watch on the other. Or they might wear a "Dickens' chain" made popular by Charles with a toggle bar on one end and a key in the middle for the purpose of winding said Waltham watch. The watches would be enclosed in a hunting case and might be a B.W. Raymond, the famous railroad watch made by the National Watch Company which later became the Elgin National Watch Company of Elgin, Illinois.

Shirts would be linen, pulled over your head, with lots of tail and no pockets. If worn by George Barnes, Prineville's first attorney, the shirt might even have ruffles on the front. The collar turned down instead of up as in the 1860s and was set off with a silk bowstring tie with the ends tucked under the tips of the collar. The collar was most likely of paper made to be worn once and then thrown away. Although some of the upper Crooked River dandies got lots of mileage out of one of these collars when it really wasn't necessary. They came by the dozen and cheap too, from Montgomery Ward.

Montgomery Ward had started business in the early 1870's as "Grangers Supply House." Founded in 1867, grangers were the embattled homesteaders of the time and called themselves the Patrons of Husbandry or simply the Grange. A mighty and vociferous organization it was too and in due time would have one of its halls—Lookout Mountain Grange No. 741—perched on the Ochoco River voicing opinions. But according to some, Grangers Supply House wasn't as great as it advertised to be. The *Chicago Daily Tribune* on November 8, 1873 would warn: "Grangers Beware—Don't patronize Montgomery Ward & Company—they are dead-beats! This swindling firm may advertise 'Grangers supplied by the cheapest cash in America' with the utopian figures such as gold lockets for 1.50; 10 yards of poplin 1.75; 1 hoop skirt, 1 bustle and 1 hair braid for 1.00; gentlemen's toilet set containing razor, toothbrush, nail-brush, comb, hair-brush, lather-brush, razor-strap, shaving-box and soap for 1.00 but don't believe it. They're swindlers."

Apparently the *Tribune* got temporarily led astray believing propaganda circulated by Ward's competitors for on Christmas Eve 1873, the editor would print a retraction: "The November article was based upon what was supposed to be correct information but a thorough investigation by this office satisfies us that the article was grossly unjust." In fact, the *Chicago Tribune* encouraged not only farmers but "all persons, clubs or individuals" to deal with agents of the Grangers Supply House.[7]

Now, back to the upper Crooked River cheapskates with soiled collars. At Wards' you could order five boxes of collars—a dozen to the box—plus a pair of suspenders for one dollar; or you could pick up five real linen shirt fronts called "dickeys" for the same price. Dickeys tied around the neck and buttoned to the shirt at the bottom. George Roba would recall when the bottom button let go as it was apt to do, the dickey joyfully slapped you in the face.

You could even get steel flexible collars and cuffs in assorted enameled colors if you were so inclined. The celluloid collar which hit the market in 1872 was the brain-child of John Wesley Hyatt, inventor of the Hyatt roller bearing. The celluloid collar was pretty handy as far as cleaning was concerned but a sloppy smoker could darn near burn his head off if he dropped an ash or burning match head on them.

Speaking of smoking, tailor-made cigarettes—got the idea from Indians who rolled their tobacco in corn husks—were known even before the Civil War but were considered unmanly, unhealthy and wicked. Any Prinevillite worth his salt rolled his own, sniffed, chewed, smoked a pipe or cigar but no ready-mades. Up to World War I, they were shunned out West. Chewing tobacco—plug and twists—came out under such fancy names as Wedding Cake, Winesap, Star of Virginia, Rock Candy, Henry Clay and Daniel Webster to name but a few.

Shirt cuffs, hard starched and sometimes detachable, were worn with cuff buttons or links. You might not think bartenders were style conscious but they kept an eye out for guys wearing extra wide cuffs which not only dated them as being out of style—wide cuffs went out in the 1870s—but they were an extra added advantage to card sharps and a neat hiding place for an extra ace, derringer, knife or whatever the owner preferred. According to Henry Burmeister, one enterprising gent dropped a scorpion out of a cuff and promptly got a hole blown in his head in the

---

7   *Chicago Tribune*, December 24, 1873.

Stockman Exchange Saloon. This probably wasn't true but it shows possibilities as Al Swartz did get his brains blown loose in a card game at that establishment in 1882.

Hats and boots were the most expensive articles of men's clothing sold. These items were often paid for with $4 gold pieces called the "Stella" after the lady on the coin. Minted in 1880, some Stella's had flowing hair, some had coiled hair. Today the flowing-haired Stella is worth $9,000. Should you stumble upon a coiled-hair Stella, it is worth $11,000.[8] Not a bad return on a $4 investment.

The most expensive boots were hand-made and hand-lasted to your personal measurements at Selling's Harness and Saddle Shop and cost from$10 to $25. Ready-made boots at Hahn & Fried Mercantile you could get for $3 or$ 4, but nobody with an ounce of pride other than maybe a sheepherder or homesteader would be caught dead in a pair.

From 1871 on, the gents would be wearing a soft felt slouch hat with wide rolling brim—most likely black. Some wore Derbies and when out on the town even gunfighters wore high top hats. What made the real distinction between aristocrats (cattle kings) and commoners (saddle tramps) was the material from which the hat was made—fur or wool. The headgear of wool was for the poor man. But hat styles would change dramatically after John B. Stetson launched his trade in Philadelphia in 1865.

The first model to hit the West was the Boss. After it, came the Carlsbad, which was destined to become the cowboy style. Incidentally, "cowboy" was a loose term not generally used in the '70s and '80s. Next came the Buckeye with the extra wide brim and high crown worn un-dented. A Stetson cost $10 to $25 which was a considerable expense when a top hand's pay was $30 a month. But it was almost a lifetime investment since a Stetson refused to wear out.

With all the stylish folk wandering about, the upper Ochoco Valley was fast becoming quite the resort area. Warm sulfur springs on Wolf Creek were promoted as a very effective cure for rheumatism, gout or whatever malady was plaguing your body at the time. According to the *Howard News*, September 2, 1885, John Hereford's Wolf Creek Lodge was doing a booming business.

---

8   Fred Dickinson, "The five dollars worth $50,000," *This Week Magazine*, March 8, 1964.

Yes, Prineville and the surrounding area was coming of age and the growing pains were soon to take on ominous symptoms.

CHAPTER 181

THE RATTLESNAKE COILS

This country is settled up with a class of men that is good friends but bad enemies . . . .

Elisha Barnes
President, Ochoco Livestock
Association

The town mayor's cryptic warning to prospective settlers, in a letter dated April 21, 1882, was never delivered but the implied danger of meddling in Prineville's private affairs had reached fulfillment less than a month before.[1] The raw power of a select few had steadily grown following the discovery of gold in Belcher Gulch. Opposition to this movement was strangely silent. Perhaps from fear and perhaps not. It appears that the men who were not intimidated were concerned solely in protecting their own interests and the cancer took root. Aid in the fight for justice would come from an unlikely source. In the sunset of 1881, the notorious gunman, Henry Vaughan, drifted into Scissorsville, took a room at the Antler Hotel and bided his time gambling in Ryle Thompson's Pay Dirt Saloon.

Tempered in the smelter of Canyon City, Vaughan was no stranger to the Ochoco. Rumor had it that he was always welcome at Jim Blakely's big Willow Creek spread. Not a comforting thought to the livestock association for among other things, Vaughan was branded a horse thief and it was common knowledge that he was not adverse to shooting a man. Worse still, Vaughan and Blakely were boyhood friends born and raised just a few miles apart in the Willamette Valley. They had shared coffee

---

1   The original letter was found in 1942 between the walls of the Elisha Barnes house at 136 South Beaver Street, Prineville, Oregon. It is now on file at the A.R. Bowman Memorial Museum in Prineville.

and cattle drives, fought Indians side-by-side and wintered together in the worst the Ochoco could offer. Blakely would readily acknowledge that Vaughan was not socially acceptable but as he put it a half-century later, "Hank's been called a lot of hard names by the history writers but he was a good friend to me." Among other things, he was called a hard-bitten gunfighter, high-stake gambler, Indian lover and convicted murderer.

In 1865 (at the age of sixteen) Vaughan was roaming the gambling halls of The Dalles City when he met Dick Burton. Dick was every bit as wild as his older brother, Billy Burton, who—along with Henry Plummer—had just been hanged by the Montana Vigilantes on January 10, 1864. An explosive combination, Hank and Dick soon formed a loose partnership and headed for Idaho Territory to make their fortune. According to Vaughan his new companion neglected to tell him that the horses they were riding were stolen property. In the meantime Sheriff Frank Maddock of Umatilla County rounded up a posse and went after the horse thief. Vaughan and Burton were still in their blankets when about daylight the posse arrived. Somebody started shooting and when it was over, Dick Burton and Maddock's deputy Jackson Hart were dead and the sheriff had taken a bullet through the mouth extracting a few teeth along the way. It wasn't a fatal wound . . . it just disfigured Frank a little bit. For that, Vaughan spent a few years in the Oregon State Penitentiary.[2]

It seemed—at least to the locals—that Vaughan had no redeeming features. "My gawd," they exclaimed, "the man's married to a heathen squaw!"[3] They failed to note that she was the granddaughter of a Nez

---

2   At the time of the shooting Hank's father, Jacob Alexander Vaughan, was serving with the 1st Oregon Volunteer Infantry stationed at Fort Harney, then known as Camp Rattlesnake. Hank was sentenced to life in prison but after serving only 4½ years on his life term, Governor George Woods (who advocated a war of extermination against the eastern Oregon Shoshoni) granted him a full pardon. (Governor's Executive Documents, Records of the Secretary of State, Oregon State Archives, Salem.)

3   That was not exactly true. Apparently Vaughan had left his first wife, Lois McCarty, who he married in Elko, Nevada in 1875. Within three years he wed Louisa Jane Ditty in Pendleton, Oregon, without benefit of divorce from Lois. However when he took up with the Nez Perce woman he did obtain a divorce from Louisa in 1883. But his living arrangement with Martha Robie "the heathen squaw" wasn't quite legal either so in 1888—four years after leaving Prineville—Hank filed for a divorce from Lois which she strongly objected to. Hank finally won out and within days after obtaining his divorce from Lois McCarty he legally married his Indian lover. (Elko County, Marriages, Book No. 1, p. 84 dated May 8, 1875, Elko, Nevada; Umatilla County Court, Book of Marriages, page dated August 11, 1878, Pendleton, Oregon;

Perce chief and the widow of the respected Harney Valley businessman Henry Robie who, in his advanced years, found comfort in her arms before he expired leaving her a $70,000 inheritance and the reason for Hank's sudden interest in a Nez Perce woman.[4] With her financial backing Vaughan bought a ranch north of the Umatilla Reservation and went into the horse business. He then moved Martha onto the Umatilla Reservation in 1882 so she could take advantage of the proposed Indian Allotment Act which would qualify her to claim 160 acres of reservation land. With the luck of the cards, insofar as Hank was concerned, this act didn't become law until 1887.[5] So with his restless nature and nothing better to do, Hank was again haunting the eastern Oregon gambling halls.

On release, at the age of 33, Hank set up camp at the Pay Dirt Saloon but with the Thompson clan getting more arrogant, he drifted into Prineville gambling some and drinking plenty but he was staying for a purpose. Some six months before his arrival, Charlie Long—a fast-draw who bragged that he rode stirrup-to-stirrup with Billy Bonney in the

---

Umatilla County Circuit Court, Divorce Case No. 191-30, June 22, 1883; Umatilla County Circuit Court, Divorce Case No. 191-31, October 8, 1888; Early Marriages of Walla Walla County, 1862 through 1899, Washington Territory and State, Walla Walla, Washington.)

4 A.M. Robie, a retired colonel in the 8th U.S. Cavalry and a nephew of Isaac Stevens, first governor of Washington Territory, had made big money in the sawmill business. As early as 1867 his mill cut the lumber for the construction of Fort Harney. In 1877 he sold his 42,300 acre Diamond A ranch to Pete French. At the outbreak of the Bannock War, Robie and French were gathering Robie's horses off the ranch when the Shoshoni attacked. A few weeks later Robie died as a result of exhaustion from this desperate ride to the safety of Fort Harney but before he died he placed a $1,000 reward for the head of Pony Blanket. Maybe this was the reason for the Umatilla's interest in decapitating Pony Blanket. (See *Thunder Over the Ochoco*, Vol. IV, Chapter 169.) Robie's name has been variously spelled as Ruby, Rubey and Robsy. The Portland papers were partial to the Ruby spelling. The *Portland Standard*, December 23, 1881, would announce that "a little over a year ago he [Vaughan] married the widow of a man named Ruby." He hadn't but it shows that as early as 1881 Hank was known to be associated with Martha. Then on March 18, 1939, the *Sunday Oregonian* would quote Jim Blakely in an interview as saying "Hank was living with the widow of the respected Cyrus Ruby [Henry Robie], Colonel in the 8th United States Cavalry." The cavalry unit referred to was recruited in the Willamette Valley and never saw action against the Shoshoni due to a lack of enlistment. (See *Thunder Over the Ochoco*, Vol. III, Chapter 135, p. 331. For more on Robie see Brimlow, *Harney County and its Rangeland*, pp. 37, 57, 59, 78 and 81).

5 Called the General Allotment Act, this law would accelerate the loss of Indian tribal lands by granting tracts to individual Indians. The remainder of the tribal lands not selected by individuals were either opened for public settlement or sold for "the benefit of the tribe." Mainly because of this act the acreage of reserved Indian lands dropped from 138 million acres in 1887 to about 50 million acres by 1934 when further reduction was stopped. (*Historical Highlights of Public Land Management*, p. 38.)

Lincoln County cattle war—showed up as enforcer for the planned Ochoco Livestock Association. Vaughan knew that Blakely was a law-abiding man and may need help if things turned nasty. And so, Henry Vaughan—outlaw, squaw-man and ex-convict—pledged his guns to the decent citizens of Prineville. Blakely, who fought the association from the beginning, would give much credit to his old saddle companion: "I had a few friends but none of them stood by me better than Hank Vaughan."[6]

Caught in the middle of the initial thrust were the men charged with reporting daily events in an unbiased manner.[7] Prineville's first newspaper, the *Ochoco Review*, appeared in 1880. John Jeffery, editor and publisher, described the publication as a neatly printed 7-column folio independent in politics and devoted to the best interests of Wasco County. Dillard and Company's *Prineville News* was printed on both sides of an 8½ by 11 inch sheet of paper and for a time in its battle for survival was printed in Silver Lake, Oregon. By 1894, the embattled *Prineville News* would be absorbed by the *Ochoco Review*.

Appearing on the scene in 1880, the *Ochoco Review* was pushing Henry Dillard's *Prineville News* to the limit temporarily forcing it out of business by summer of 1882. With D.W. Aldridge as editor, John Douthit acting as sales representative and Star Mealey serving as reporter, the *Ochoco Review* was covering the controversial issues of the day and not everyone was pleased.[8] Others were secretly happy with the coverage. Among these was Jasper Johnson, local school superintendent.

---

6   Blakely interview, August 18, 1950.
7   Rumors persist that there are diaries still in existence written by those who rode with the Livestock Association—read vigilantes and sheepshooters. Supposedly these journals are sprinkled throughout with dastardly tales and the names of those who committed them. Don't you believe it. There were in fact such diaries and other incriminating documents but at the turn of the 20th century, this evidence kept pot-bellied stoves glowing red hot throughout the night. Those who participated in the ignition were trying to protect the innocent not the perpetrators of these violent acts.
8   Somewhere in the newspaper battles, the *Ochoco Review* was either absorbed by or changed its name to the *Crook County Journal* around the turn of the century. The author was able to obtain some highly censored copies that were printed during the sheep and cattle war with dates from the 1890's up to December 17, 1908. Not only were names blacked out but in many cases, whole sentences. In the 1960's, he loaned these copies to a student of history and when returned all dates from November 15, 1890 (*Ochoco Review*) up to December 22, 1904 (*Crook County Journal*) were missing. The only explanation being "I have no idea what happened. . . they must have gotten lost." The *Crook County Journal* published by A.C. Palmer was originally

In an effort to improve some youthful education, Johnson—in a deft political move—hired Aldridge to start classes at Mill Creek and ordered Dayton Elliott, Howard schoolmaster, into town to reorganize the Prineville public school system. At Elliott's request, Johnson called a meeting of the town fathers to discuss the question of levying a tax to build another school. This proposal was not looked upon with favor. The *Ochoco Review* took up the battle. In a blistering attack aimed at the "fat boys from the valley" who, in the editor's opinion, were growing rapidly rich in Prineville but didn't expect to remain long so therefore cared nothing for education, he fired a broadside. "The school levy was defeated and the school house was not ordered built because nearly every opulent mossback opposed the taxation." Aldridge further observed that "it is a common occurrence for any one of our general stores to sell in one day $1,500 to $2,000 worth of goods."[9] In short, the town wasn't exactly poverty-stricken.

Speaking of such matters, neither was the U.S. government hurting for land but after bilking the Indians out of millions of acres it was somewhat reluctant to part with any of its ill-gotten gains. In March 1881, Has No Horse again hiding out near Fort Bidwell and tired of being shoved around, petitioned the government for some land he could call his own. Concerned citizens pointed out to the secretary of the Interior that it might be a smart move to honor this request for it was feared that any effort to remove him to a reservation would trigger a repeat of the Bannock War. Interior Secretary Samuel J. Kirkwood was unimpressed. Fortunately Has No Horse was a patient man as his application wasn't granted until the passage of the Dawes Act on February 8, 1887.[10] However, within a few months after the 1881 rejection of Has No Horse's petition, Kirkwood was looking for a new job.

Another item of economic concern was the winter of 1881-82 when fortunes were made or lost at the whim of the weather. While the Ochoco Valley was experiencing a mild winter with only eight inches of snow in the upper valley which by the first week in February would be

the *Mitchell Monitor*. In 1903 it was taken over by S.M. Bailey.

9   *Ochoco Review*, March 4, 1882

10   At this time, Has No Horse and his wife Bessie were allotted the SW ¼ of Section 17, T.46N., R.17E. M.D.M. in the extreme N.E. corner of California. (Documents belonging to Patsy Garcia, Has No Horses' great-granddaughter.)

completely gone, the rest of central Oregon was not faring so well.[11] Taking advantage of the deep snow in the Cascades, the hide-hunters—Henry Birchtorf and Mort Venton—took off in December with a two-fold purpose; to trap fur-bearing animals and to wreck havoc among the starving deer and elk herds. Neither were cattle or sheep exempt from the skinning knife. Birchtorf and Venton alone could have financed a new school building. By January 1, 1882, they had delivered 4,000 pounds of deer hides to Fried & Sickel. Eleven days later on January 12, smoke rose in black plumes from the summit of Mt. Jefferson. According to the *Ochoco Review*, "the sight from here was a grand spectacle." At least Venton and Birchtorf couldn't be held responsible for this disruption of nature.

Overshadowing Mt. Jefferson's volcanic burp, a more violent eruption had shaken the town two days before. At the Silver Dollar, Vaughan was leaning on the bar sipping a beer when Charlie Long—a reckless 37-year-old gunslinger—walked in. Hank casually looked around, pulled a silk handkerchief from his breast pocket to wipe the foam off his neatly trimmed beard and at that instant, Long drew and fired. Vaughan took a .38 slug in his right shoulder, spinning him around and numbing his arm. In the following confusion, Long calmly walked out and disappeared down the street. The story quickly spread that Vaughan had offered his handkerchief to Long with the intent each would hold one end of it and shoot it out at arms length. Eye witnesses knew it wasn't true but the story stuck.

In an attempt to quiet the onlookers, Deputy Luckey arrested Long and the next day they headed for The Dalles. On arrival at the county seat, Long was bound over to the circuit court and released on $800 bail. Eleven days after the shooting, the *Ochoco Review* would report that Vaughan was able to be out on the streets again and on February 4, he rented a buggy and headed for The Dalles looking for Long.[12]

Out on the desert from Agency Plain on the eastern base of the Cascades to Wagontire Mountain west of the Steens, livestock were taking a beating. Ranchers reported sheep and cattle dying by the hundreds. With these men going broke, the Ochoco Valley stockmen were

---

11   *Ochoco Review*, February 11, 1882.
12   *Ochoco Review*, January 12, 14, 21 and February 4, 1882.

reaping the reward of their misfortune. At give-away-prices, Ewen Johnson was buying anything that could walk; John Luckey, Hank Breyman and John Sommerville formed a partnership and bought twelve hundred head of steers from Perry Reed, Al Lyle, Bill Gulliford and George Dodson. The Cecil brothers were forced to liquidate their entire herd to California buyers. To salvage a part of his herd, C. Sam Smith (part owner of the Silver Dollar Saloon) bought Jim Miller's Keystone Ranch on the upper Ochoco and in the process acquired Sheriff Luckey's interest in the ranch also. Smith soon spread to lower Crooked River, expanding his holdings to 8,300 acres of which 4,400 acres were Willamette Valley and Cascade Mountain Military Road Company lands. This acquisition would prove to be a costly mistake.

About the time Smith bought the Keystone Ranch, Jim Miller's brother, Joaquin, was taking Europe by storm. In England, Joaquin Miller who served for a time as editor of the Eugene *Democratic Register*, so charmed sedate Londoners that they named him "the Lord Byron of Oregon."[13]

His fellow Oregon editors were not impressed. After Miller's first book of poems was published in England, the editor of the *Albany Democrat* offered no congratulations. In a grouchy mood he wrote ". . . [Miller] has published a book of poems and become a man of fame in London. This fact makes me think no more of Miller but a lot less of Londoners."[14]

D.W. Aldridge, editor of the *Ochoco Review*, was a little more realistic when asked if he thought that London journalists were telling the truth about Joaquin's literary talents. "Lord no," Aldridge replied. "That would ruin us. News reporters should write something that everybody will read and state it so that nobody can remember what was written." Makes sense. Now back to the winter of 1881-82.

Bob Dorsey sacrificed his ranch to Seth Moore and Lew Hodges for $900. Joe Blakely sold 600 head of yearlings to a Santa Rosa buyer

---

13　Lord George Gordon Byron—the son of Captain "Mad Dog" Byron, a notorious libertine, and Catherine Gordon, a woman of erratic temperament—was one of the most important of the poets during the English romantic period and the most versatile. Among his outstanding works were "Childe Harold's Pilgrimage," a narrative poem; "Don Juan," generally regarded as his masterpiece; and "The Poisoner of Chillan."

14　Myers, "Print in a Wild Land," p. 190.

for a flat $24 a head. Ike Nelson, seeing a chance to make it big, sold his half-interest in the Prineville Livery Stable to Pres Perkins and Garrett Maupin for $1,800 to invest in cattle and it paid off.[15] One of the few small outfits who refused to sell was Luke Langdon perched in the snow-zone on the north slope of Grizzly Mountain. Besides shorthorns, Langdon was also raising blooded horses. Gambling on a break in the weather Langdon and his hired hand, Bill Harrison, took wagons into the lowlands on the Thompson brothers range where they cut and hauled wild rye to feed the starving cattle and horses in the hope of keeping them alive. Langdon would be successful in this attempt but in so doing he failed to endear himself with the Thompsons who were buying out every small rancher they could coax or scare into selling. An artist with a .45 Colt, Langdon was not an easy man to bluff.

Big-time operators, the Thompson brothers—Senator S.G. (George), Judge J.M. (John), Colonel William (Bud), and Duorey—were running longhorns from Antelope Valley into the lower Crooked River basin pushing dangerously close to Blakely's Willow Creek spread. They too had suffered heavy losses in the blizzard of '82 and were out to recoup their death toll. Leader of the clan was the flamboyant younger brother Bud, known throughout the West as a hot-tempered braggart and outspoken newspaper editor who settled any and all arguments with a gun. A slight-built man in his mid-thirties who packed a .38 bullet in his neck for more than 50 years, Bud honestly believed he towered above the rest of humanity and he wasn't shy about letting this be known. He was also a rabble-rouser. In a political payoff for his partisan viewpoint expressed in the *Salem Mercury*, Gov. LaFayette Grover commissioned Thompson a colonel in the Oregon Militia in 1872. Beyond doubt, Bud Thompson—pony express rider, Snake war veteran and friend of the international celebrity Joaquin Miller—was a force to be reckoned with in the settlement of central Oregon. The *Pacific Monthly* in direct reference to his mode of operation would note: "Crook County is filled with men who love to fight and always have. There is also no doubt that a certain outlaw spirit is still surviving from the days when the Vigilantes

---

15   The Prineville Livery Stable was located on the corner of East Second Street and North Belknap where the present Miller Lumber Company is now located.

really owned the County, allowed whom they liked to reside there and drove out whom they pleased."[16] And so it was.

The livestock men who survived the devastating winter were due for a pleasant surprise. By spring 1882, the cattle market was booming with cows selling at 89¢ a pound live weight. But if the economy was again booming in central Oregon, it wasn't doing so well elsewhere. The *Prineville News* received a bulletin from St. Louis stating that a Mr. Stephen Godo—because he was unable to support his family on $10 a week—was advertising for sale his six-year-old daughter for $2,000 and his eight-year-old son for a $1,000.[17] Also hoping to make a fortune, a local genius named R.H. Volrath invented a set of bed springs made entirely of wood. Neither the timber operators nor the town merchants took much interest in this new innovation. Of much more importance, at least to the citizens of Scissorsville, was the notification that the United States had banned Chinese immigration for the next ten years thus leaving a gap in the labor market.

Then to cause further financial speculation, Dr. Vanderpool—acting as veterinarian to the starving herds—revealed that he had discovered an underground river in the desert west of Bear Creek Butte, sparking interest of water development in that area.[18] He was not to reside in Prineville much longer.

The one thing the stockmen didn't want was more publicity about the desirability of the Ochoco. Within a week following Dr. Vanderpool's inadvertent announcement, a group of men met at the Singer Saloon on Saturday night, February 11, 1882 for the purpose of forming a livestock association.[19] Those who attended this meeting had something greater and more sinister in mind. It was a gathering of the big outfits—sheep and cattle alike—with strong and often identical financial ties to local business groups, timber operations, and the mining industry. Their enemies were the small producers—the 50- to 100-head cattlemen; the one-band sheepman; and any shoe-string operation that could conceivably present later competition. In the eyes of the high-stake gamblers, these penny-ante players were nits on the range to be discouraged from

---

16   Arno Dosch, "The War for Range," *Pacific Monthly*, February 1906, p. 157.
17   *Prineville News*, March 18, 1882.
18   *Ochoco Review*, February 2-25, 1882.
19   *Ochoco Review*, February 16, 1882.

coming into the Ochoco or to be run out if already present. This was the unpublicized purpose. The story released to the public was quite different.

To understand the full scope of what was to happen it becomes necessary to acquaint the reader with the underlying current of what would transpire. The eddies swirl from good to bad to good and like life itself, a fair conclusion cannot be based upon a single instant. What came into being was in a state of flux dependent upon the moment, the desire and the goal of the individuals playing out this drama on life's unexplored stage. It is not for us to pass judgment—only to record what happened—and as they said at the faro tables in Burmeister's Stockman's Exchange Saloon, "let the cards remain where they fall and the devil take the hindmost!"

The law abiding citizens gathered at the Singer Saloon were going to clean up the country by running out horse thieves, cattle rustlers, sod-busters and mining riffraff thus making the Ochoco a safe place for decent folks to live. Maybe they did scare away a few undesirables but there isn't a single record of their having caught or killed a verifiable law-breaker. That aside, the struggling small operators pitted against alternating droughts, gully-washers, killing frosts and harsh winters would find that nature at her cruelest was kind in comparison to the masked gunmen who painted the landscape with blood.

Those present at that fateful Saturday night meeting in February were Elisha Barnes, powerful political figure, prominent stockman and mayor of Prineville; George Barnes, tough young gunman who had recently been admitted to the Oregon State Bar Association and who—three days prior to this meeting—had formed Prineville's first law firm with Sam Richardson (soon to be appointed county clerk); Jim Lawson, member of the first emigration of 1868 whose duty was to provide a base of operations complete with unbranded horses, saddles and guns so those participating in raids would remain anonymous; and Col. William "Bud" Thompson, owner of six cattle ranches and killer of at least three men in gunfights.

Thompson gunned down his first victim in 1871 at the age of 23. Editor of the Roseburg *Plaindealer*, he got into an argument with the Gale brothers who published the rival *Roseburg Ensign* and in the process killed Henry Gale and critically wounded Tom Gale.[20] Before 1882 had drifted away, Harvey Scott, editor of the Portland *Oregonian*, would make the charge that any man Bud Thompson marked for death in central Oregon was destined for the grave. And Scott was in a position to know for Thompson once worked for him on the editorial staff of *The Oregonian*.

Ironically, the day after this meeting, the wife of Jasper Johnson (the embattled school superintendent) and the mother of four children died in a flaming cabin on Hay Creek. Cause of the fire unknown.

Two days later, Oregon celebrated its twenty-third birthday. John Harrison, a local ranch hand, had something better to celebrate. His wife had blessed him with a baby daughter. In a way, this little valentine helped ease the heartache of William Harrison, John's brother, whose wife had died of pneumonia three weeks earlier leaving him with a young son to raise. Then, four days after the birth of baby Harrison, "the honorable John Thompson" expired. No reason was given as to the cause of death.[21]

Within 24 fleeting days the fledgling livestock association would get the opportunity to test its well-oiled machine—an organization so well planned that for over a half-century many people were led to believe that the lynchings and shootings perpetrated by this mob served a just cause and were provoked by lawless acts which could not have been met effectively in any other manner. They would use Hank Vaughan as living proof that outlaws were tainting the land. Not only were the vigilantes backed by active members but they had the strong support of many silent sympathizers who were, in some respects, the more dangerous group.

In 1868, Andrew Warren and his wife Eliza Spalding Warren (the first white child to be born west of the Rocky Mountains) settled on Willow Creek. Their daughter, America Jane, married Joe Crooks who arrived on Willow Creek in 1872 with his brother Aaron. Joe was a soft-spoken rancher who minded his own business but not Aaron. In all likelihood Aaron, an influential man, took after their father John Turley Crooks, a schoolmaster who helped frame Oregon's Constitution. This coupled with strong family ties to the Rev. Henry Spalding—a prime mover in Oregon's early settlement—gave Aaron Crooks substantial

---

20   Kerolevitz, *Newspapering in the Old West*, p. 135.

21   *Ochoco Review*, February 18, 1882.

political clout which he wasn't above using to his advantage and the time for such action was fast approaching.

The trap was baited on a raw Wednesday morning, March 15, 1882. Aaron Crooks and his son-in-law, Stephen Jory, began surveying and blazing property lines on the north slope of Grizzly Mountain adjacent to Langdon's ranch. To date, all the private land claims in central Oregon had been filed under the 1862 Homestead Act . . . a piece of legislation which prompted Senator William E. Borah to comment: "The government bets 160 acres against the entry fee that the settler can't live on the land for five years without starving to death." Luke Langdon was willing to take his chances with starvation but he wasn't inclined to let some domineering claim jumper steal his property which—or so Langdon thought—was being attempted. For the past six months there had been hard feelings between him and Crooks over property boundaries. The General Land Office in The Dalles would later confirm Langdon's title to the property in question but for the moment, it was disputed territory. At the February meeting of the Ochoco Livestock Association, Crooks had been told to go out and claim "his land." On these instructions, Crooks moved onto Langdon's ranch. At noon, March 15, the surveyors leaned their axes against a big pine tauntingly within sight of Langdon's barn and rode home for dinner. This was a provocative—if not stupid—move on their part for Luke was known to be hot-tempered and a dead shot with pistol or rifle.

At daylight that morning, Bill Harrison—Langdon's horse wrangler—saddled up and rode into Prineville to pick up supplies and visit his motherless son who was staying with his aunt and uncle—Harrison's brother and sister-in-law. Around noon, Bill decided to have dinner with Annette Tallman. William Henry Harrison, a decent law abiding man was also a full-blood Shoshoni and had known Nettie from childhood.[22] On the way, he passed Jim Blakely's townhouse which sat only two blocks south of Annette's cottage. Well acquainted with Blakely's Willow Creek ranch, Harrison stopped to visit with Jim. Joe Blakely was also there at

---

22 Bill Harrison, his brother John and Annette Tallman (daughter of the Buffalo Killer dog soldier Tall Man and niece to Broken Knife) had been captured by the Warm Springs scouts on the John Day River in 1859. As prisoners of war, first at Fort Dalles where they received their Anglicized names, they were later held as slaves at the Warm Springs Agency. In keeping with the times, Bill was named for the ninth president of the United States.

the time. Across the street, Bud Thompson paused on his front porch to note the exchange of greetings.[23] It was well established that many townspeople knew the whereabouts of Bill Harrison on March 15, 1882 . . . a day that would be held in question for years to come.

Back on Grizzly Mountain, Langdon—packing a .45 Colt and a double-barreled shotgun—was waiting when Crooks and Jory came back to continue their survey. He quietly told them they were trespassing on his land. They chose to ignore him. In the argument that ensued Crooks drew his pistol on Langdon and Jory charged him swinging an axe. Luke shot and killed both men. Glancing up, he became panicked. A rider was approaching. Without thinking of the consequences, he jumped on his horse and lit out for Mill Creek where his brother George was cutting wood. This move would spark the grim series of events which brought the vigilantes to power. A cold, calculated scheme that paid off with the anticipated reaction—two men dead and another on the run.

Garrett Maupin—part owner of the Second Street Livery Stable and son of the man who killed Paulina—was out rounding up horses when he heard two shots. Riding over to investigate, he saw Langdon, heavily armed, riding out at a hard gallop.[24] He then discovered the bodies of Crooks and Jory and took off at breakneck speed for Prineville.

"Two men have been murdered," he yelled reining his foam-lathered horse to a stop at Kelly's Last Chance Saloon. The first men onto the street were Joe and Jim Blakely. While some dashed off to notify Deputy Luckey and form a posse, the Blakely brothers and Bill Harrison volunteered to ride out to Langdon's ranch and bring in the bodies of the murdered men. When they arrived at the scene of the shooting, no one had moved the bodies but Crooks' and Jory's wives who witnessed the killings from about one-quarter mile away had placed their aprons over their husbands faces. After the bodies were loaded onto pack horses, Harrison stayed at the ranch to look after the safety of Emma Langdon and the children and also to take care of the needed chores.[25] Meanwhile,

---

23 Blakely's house sat on the northwest corner of the intersection of West Fourth and North Claypool Streets. Thompson's house sat on the southwest corner of the intersection of West Fourth and Claypool Streets. Annette's cottage sat on the bank of the Ochoco River at the dead-end on the east side of North Beaver Street one block north of its intersection with West Fifth Street.

24 *The Illustrated History of Central Oregon*, 1905, p. 710.

25 Emma La Francis Langdon was a French-Canadian. Her and Luke's children were Mary,

the Blakely boys arrived back in Prineville late that evening with the dead men where a coroner's jury was selected to determine the cause of death. Being a mere formality, this determination didn't take up much time. Crooks had been shot twice with a .45 Colt having one bullet lodged in his right shoulder and the other having passed through his lungs. Jory in his axe charge had taken a 10-gauge shotgun blast in the chest with buckshot penetrating his brain killing him instantly. Once that was established, the verdict read: "We the jury impaneled to inquire into the cause of the death of A.H. Crooks and Stephen Jory find from the evidence that the deceased came to their death by gunshot wounds inflicted by Lucius Langdon.[26] It is apparent that no one else was considered a suspect.

By some twist of fate, another brother to Luke, Perry Langdon—a sheep shearer—was living in the Perkins House Hotel with Garrett Maupin. When Maupin galloped into town with the news of Luke's deadly attack, Perry, sensing the mood of the crowd, took no chances and left town that night. He was never seen in central Oregon again.

When Luke fled the death scene, headed for brother George's cabin, he had only one thought in mind and that was to borrow some money to go to The Dalles and turn himself in. In 1882, The Dalles was still the hub of government for central Oregon and Luke was gambling that if he could reach the county seat, he might have a chance for a fair trial.[27] Having been involved in a bitter lawsuit with Aaron Crooks and on the Thompson brother's blacklist for having cut rye grass on their range in January, Langdon was certain if he gave himself up in Prineville he would never live long enough to make it to The Dalles.

Daisy (Claypool), and Lambert (a gambler). All information on Lucius Langdon is from correspondence with Jax Zumwalt, great nephew of Luke, letter dated October 4, 1977; and Glen Langdon Jr., great nephew of Luke, letter dated September 12, 1977. Their information was contributed by a relative who wishes to remain anonymous. Glen Langdon Jr. was the grandson of George Langdon who was with his brother Lucius in Prineville just hours before Luke was killed.

26 The coroner's report was signed by: Dr.H.A. Belknap, J.H. Garrett, J.W. Page, S.S. Brown, C.A. Newbill, S.G. Wood. *Illustrated History of Central Oregon*, pp. 710-11.

27 Lucius Lambert Langdon came west in 1875. He married Emma LaFrancis on February 15, 1875 and took up a homestead claim in central Oregon in 1880 listing his mailing address as Cleek, Wasco County Oregon. This is the reason he was so anxious to get to The Dalles. Cleek post office was established in 1881 and was located west of Grizzly on The Dalles-Prineville stage road. "Crook County's Reign of Terror Blot on History," *Central Oregonian*, Centennial Edition, Thursday, October 28, 1982, p. 3B.

Playing a hunch that Langdon would attempt to contact his brother George, a posse which Sheriff Luckey didn't accompany, slipped out of town under the cover of darkness and headed for Mill Creek. Led by Bud Thompson, it would include Til Glaze, Sam Richardson, George Barnes, Bob Graham, and Charlie Long. It had been just a little over two months since Long had been bound over to the circuit court on an $800 bond for taking a shot at Henry Vaughan. The posse returned to town empty-handed insofar as Luke was concerned but they claimed they saw him run from George's cabin and they had confiscated his saddle horse and Winchester rifle.

Thompson's unsuccessful effort to capture Langdon would be described by Luckey in a letter to Sheriff Storrs at The Dalles. " . . . at one o'clock in the night they approached the cabin . . . saw a light but before they could surround the house the dogs gave the alarm . . . it was very dark and he [Langdon] got away . . . a runner was sent back to town and every available man able to bear arms turned out determined to get him if possible. They scoured the whole country and guarded all the avenues where it was thought he was likely to escape. J.M. Blakely and a party of men thought he would return home as the boys at Mill Creek had captured his horse and gun . . . ."[28]

Thompson would claim that as he, Barnes, Richardson, Glaze and Long—"men of unquestioned courage and discretion" as he put it—approached the cabin both murderers (Luke Langdon and Harrison) escaped in the snow. Then, "eleven men rushed out of the cabin after the two murderers" but, according to Thompson, he and Long leveled double-barreled shotguns and ordered them back inside. They knew only one of the men and that was George Langdon whom they immediately arrested.[29] If Thompson was telling the truth about taking George into custody, and there is no reason to believe he wasn't, the posse had no motive—legal or otherwise—to arrest young Langdon as he was cutting wood some twenty miles to the east when the shooting of Crooks and Jory took place. His only crime was being the brother of Luke Langdon.

---

28 Luckey's letter to Sheriff Storrs reprinted in *The Illustrated History of Central Oregon*, 1905, p. 711.

29 Thompson, *Reminiscences of a Pioneer*, pp. 169-72, published in 1912 when Thompson was editor of the Alturas, California *Plaindealer*.

To cloak their own actions, Barnes, Thompson and Graham would go to any length to make it appear that fugitives from the law had taken over the community. In fact, Thompson was doing his best to implicate Ewen Johnson in the cover-up. He would publicly announce that Johnson had found a cabin concealed in a fir thicket on Mill Creek in the vicinity of Stein's Pillar; that it contained both provisions for men and horse feed; and it had the appearance of having been used extensively . . . "but there was no visible trail leading to it!" This supposedly was George Langdon's hide-out. It was also claimed that Johnson lead the posse to the cabin the night of March 15 and then sent two of his sons—one to Scissorsville in the upper Ochoco Valley and one to Prineville—to alert the settlers that a gang of outlaws were hid out on Mill Creek. It is doubtful that Johnson even saw the posse and it is certain he had nothing to say about fictitious gunmen.

Many people silently believed that the ten strangers the posse encountered at the Mill Creek cabin were made up to support the charge that the Langdon's were part of an outlaw gang in order to justify the next act of violence. Suspicious from the beginning, Blakely questioned Charlie Long. Long, a hired gun who had nothing to hide, readily admitted that the unauthorized posse never saw anyone with the Langdon brothers. Nonetheless, Bud Thompson feigning belief in the outlaw gang theory wouldn't back down.

Several weeks before Aaron Crooks was encouraged to provoke Luke Langdon into action, the men who formed the livestock association were spreading rumors that desperate characters had congregated in the Ochoco Mountains where they advanced from petty crimes such as cattle rustling to "bolder acts embracing brutal and diabolical murder." Worse yet, according to the budding livestock association, the settlers were allowing it to happen. It's quite likely the decent element of central Oregon were smart enough to recognize what was about to happen and were hoping to stay out of harm's way. Some would not be so lucky.

In mid-January, word leaked out that Wayne Claypool—member of the first homestead party to breach the Ochoco in 1866—had witnessed a violent act of larceny but was refusing to discuss the incident with local authorities. Whatever he had seen aroused the curiosity of those who were promoting the idea that night-riders were inhabiting the land. Claypool was not so foolish as to talk, especially when Bud

Thompson—soon to be secretary of the Ochoco Livestock Associa-tion—tried to pump him for information claiming he'd have the law-breakers arrested. Perhaps he would have but it's apparent that Claypool didn't believe him. Offering no apology, Claypool told Thompson that "rather than appear against them [the perpetrators of the crime] I will abandon all I have and leave the country because if they don't kill me they'll destroy all I have." To make a volatile situation even more uncertain insofar as Claypool was concerned, his youngest son, Chester, was spending a lot of time on Grizzly Mountain with Daisy Langdon, Luke's daughter . . . not a smart move on Chester's part in view of the fury hovering on the near horizon.[30]

It is evident that Wayne Claypool, one of the most substantial citizens in the Ochoco Valley, was intimidated beyond any normal reaction. Within a week after Thompson contacted Claypool, D.W. Aldridge, editor of the *Ochoco Review*—on Thompson's request—made this meeting public. Why, is not clear but apparently it had some signifi-cance in the web of intrigue surrounding the formation of the vigilantes or "the committee" as they preferred to be called. No sooner had the newspaper hit the street when three men "all known to be thieves and desperate characters caught the editor, knocked him down, pulled out his beard and would probably have done him greater bodily harm had not Til Glaze interfered and stopped them." Supposedly Glaze's intervention in the scrap embittered the whole gang against him and Thompson.[31] In truth, the hit men were range riders employed by one of the big cow outfits and were operating under the direct orders of the livestock association . . . maybe even Thompson himself.

By March 17, the contenders in the main event were entering the ring. The fact that Blakely thought Langdon might return to his home on Grizzly Mountain was enough to convince Sheriff Luckey that he best lead a posse into the Bear Creek country on the chance that Langdon was headed for the California border and being an "Indian lover" might try to tie in with Has No Horse now hiding out on Warner (Hart) Mountain. With Luckey and all available riflemen charging into the rims south of town, other citizens who believed Luke may have returned home asked

---

30   Chester Claypool (who died at an early age) and Daisy Langdon were married in Prineville, Oregon in the 1880's.

31   Thompson, *Reminiscences of a Pioneer*, pp. 167-68.

Blakely to go after Langdon and arrest him. Jim didn't want to get involved in the affair because he was not a law officer and he thought it was the duty of John Luckey to take charge. In the end, the townsfolk won out.[32] So, with the backing of Hank Vaughan, Lucian Nichols (whose brother Frank was a member of the Oregon Legislature), Robert Smith and Jerry Schoolin, Blakely left Prineville at 4:00 p.m. and rode north toward Langdon's ranch.

As Blakely's group was mounting up, George Langdon arrived intending to accompany him to Grizzly Mountain. Earlier that day when Thompson's gunmen arrived back in town more rational minds came to the conclusion that there was no justifiable reason for George's arrest so he was released from custody and given back his revolver. As Langdon approached Blakely, Bill Foren (U.S. deputy marshall) sauntered out of Kelly's Last Chance Saloon and ordered Langdon to hand over his pistol. Giving Foren a cold stare, Langdon quietly told the marshall if he wanted his gun to come over and take it. A coward at heart, Foren was afraid to do it. At this point George decided to stay in town and keep an eye open for any plot that might affect Luke's safety if and when Blakely brought him in.

On the ride out to Langdon's ranch, Schoolin told Blakely that Buckskin Powers—Prineville's justice of the peace—had given him a warrant for the arrest of Bill Harrison. This seemed mighty strange but unknown to Blakely's party, the cover-up was already in progress. In his letter to Sheriff Storrs, Luckey would acknowledge the warrant admitting "they were trying to make Harrison an accessory after the fact." According to Luckey, Justice Powers issued the certificate of arrest because at the inquest Harrison gloated over the bodies of Crooks and Jory and claimed that it served them right, striking his breast and saying "Big Injin me!"[33] Both Schoolin and Blakely knew that Harrison had been in town when the shooting occurred and Blakely knew that he had been at the Langdon ranch when the inquest was held. So they agreed to ignore the summons.

It was getting dark when the arresting posse reached the Langdon ranch. When the men got within about 200 yards of the house a dog

---

32 "Early Day Sheriff Fights for Law," *Sunday Oregonian*, November 14, 1948.
33 *Illustrated History of Central Oregon*, 1905, p. 711.

barked. They saw a man mount a white horse in front of the house, jump over a ditch and gallop toward The Dalles-Prineville stage road. Vaughan took pursuit and covered him with a Winchester rifle but there was no occasion for gunplay. Blakely called out and the rider stopped. Recognizing Jim's voice he then rode up to the posse. It was Luke Langdon.

Emma Langdon, who was standing in the cabin doorway with two small children clutching her skirts, started screaming. Blakely called out to her and identified himself. The six men, including Langdon, then went into the cabin where Mrs. Langdon invited them to stay for supper. While she was busy with this, Blakely rode over and told the Crooks and Jory families that the posse had Langdon in custody and would take him into Prineville to stand trial for murder.

Neither Schoolin nor Blakely told Harrison about the warrant for his arrest. After supper, Harrison slowly put on his only red silk shirt, handmade boots and black Stetson—his Sunday best—and asked if he could accompany his boss and friend back to town. Permission was granted.

The guard posse got back into Prineville about 2:00 a.m. and sent for Sheriff Luckey to pick up their prisoner. It was now early Saturday morning, March 18. Shortly after the posse arrived at Hamilton's Livery Stable, Thompson and Luckey came into the stable office and put shackles on Langdon. The sheriff and Blakely then took Luke over to Sam Jackson's Culver Hotel (more commonly known as the Jackson House) had a good fire built and told Langdon to get some sleep on a bar room lounge. When Luke was brought into the hotel—a choice place to confine a supposedly dangerous criminal—George Langdon stepped out of the shadows packing a .45 Colt (some claimed it was Luke's) and said he would stay with Luke to ensure that no harm came to him before the legal proceedings scheduled for 10:00 a.m. that morning. At this time, two questions must be asked. If the civil authorities responsible for the community's well-being were operating within the law why were the Langdon's so worried about protection? Also what or whom were they afraid of? It becomes increasingly obvious that the Langdons along with Wayne Claypool, Ewen Johnson and perhaps a few others knew something the general public wasn't yet aware of and this knowledge definitely troubled them. Whatever it may have been, George stayed with Luke until nearly daylight. Then, against his better judgment, he rode out to Grizzly to escort Emma back to town for Luke's hearing.

Meantime, Luckey asked Blakely to help guard the prisoner but having been in the saddle for ten hours, Blakely wanted some sleep and declined. Although things were beginning to look suspicious none of the men who brought Langdon in thought that Harrison was also considered to be a captive. With U.S. Deputy Marshall Bill Foren present they believed it was safe for Harrison to remain with Luke when they turned him over to Foren and Luckey. Therefore, all of the posse members (except for Nichols who volunteered to help guard Langdon) went home. As further insurance that nothing would go wrong, Jerry Luckey, the sheriff's uncle and highly respected citizen, had been deputized to help keep order. By now a good many men were gathering around the Culver Hotel but no one, least of all Blakely's posse, thought that men like John Sommerville and Eugene Luckey, Gus Winkler and the Barnes brothers would be working up a lynching party. But it was soon confirmed when Winkler tried to talk Joe Blakely into joining the mob.

As the night dragged on, a reporter from the *Prineville News* burned the midnight oil preparing this glowing account to be slapped on the front page of the Saturday edition: "On Wednesday of this week occurred the atrocious murder of Crooks and Jory on Willow Creek by L.L. Langdon, who a few days after was captured together with W.H. Harrison an accessory and taken to Prineville where they were placed under guard at the Jackson Hotel . . . ."[34]

The reality that Langdon and Harrison were held in a hotel bar room brings up another thought provoking question. Why weren't they lodged in the security of the city jail? Over a year before Luke's indiscretion when the newly appointed city council was exceptionally pure of heart, the first ordinance passed had to do with the use of profane language.[35]

---

34 *Prineville News*, March 18, 1882 published by Horace Dillard. The newspaper office was located on West Third Street in the vicinity of the present Terry's Jewelry and Gift Shop.

35 The first Prineville city council met in a two-story frame building near the corner of Third and Main Streets on Monday, December 27, 1880 and took their oath of office before S.T. Richardson, justice of the peace of the Prineville precinct, Wasco County Oregon. The members were: Elisha Barnes, council president; F.E. Whitaker, A. Hodges, Josephus Wilson and Dan Richards made up the council. Minutes of the Prineville City Council 1880, p. 1.

It stated that anyone guilty of using profanity in any house or public place within the incorporated limits of Prineville would be deemed guilty of a misdemeanor and liable to a fine of not less than five and not more than twenty dollars. If the guilty parties didn't pay their fines before a certain time, they could be summoned to work on the city streets at the rate of two dollars a day. Since some gentlemen were not inclined to stop cursing or overly eager to subsidize the city maintenance program, the council took drastic measures. On January 1, 1881—only five days after the ordinance was enacted—the council let a contract to Charles Solomon for the building of a jail with room for a recorder's and sheriff's office. It was specified that the building was to be completed by April 1, 1881 and it was.[36] Yet neither Langdon nor Harrison would ever see the inside of it.

At daybreak, March 18, Prineville was jarred awake by the violent ringing of the school bell. Elizabeth Blakely jumped out of bed, dashed to the parlor window and saw a crowd milling in the street. Glancing toward the rear entrance of Graham's Longhorn Saloon—Dick Graham was the acting coroner—she shouted, "Oh no! They're carrying the body of a man in a red shirt!" Tight-lipped with anger, Jim exclaimed, "My gawd! That must be Bill Harrison!"[37] Now fully awake, Blakely spirited into the street totally unprepared for what he was about to encounter.

---

36   Minutes of the Prineville City Council 1880-87, pp. 1, 9, 13.
37   Blakely to Herb Lundy, Oregonian reporter, *The Sunday Oregonian*, March 19, 1939.

CHAPTER 182

THE RATTLER STRIKES

I feel conscious of having done my duty as a law
officer so there I let the matter rest . . . .

John L. Luckey
Prineville, Oregon, March 18, 1882

No one really knows if that statement is correct. A man from Albany, Oregon checked into the Culver Hotel around midnight March 17. He would recall that very late in the evening, he decided to go downstairs and see what night life was like in Prineville. As he approached the head of the stairway he came up to a man standing there with a six-shooter in his hand that "looked about half as big as a medium sized mountain howitzer." The gentlemen said, "Mister, wouldn't you just as soon go back to your room and stay there until morning?" The Albany visitor suddenly decided he did, very much, want to go back to his room and stay there until daylight. During breakfast, he learned there had been "a certain vigilante action in town a few hours earlier" and some unfortunate citizen had been ushered out of this world into the next in a rather violent manner.[1]

What happened between 2:00 a.m. Saturday morning when Blakely's posse delivered Langdon to the deputy sheriff and daybreak when the wild ringing of the school bell awoke the town is best described by Luckey in his official report to Sheriff John Storrs. Perhaps confession is good for the soul.

Luckey begins with the arrival of the posse.

> They all came to town together, Harrison, Langdon prisoners, arriving about two o'clock a.m. Blakely woke me up

---

1   Ned Norton, Centennial Edition, *Central Oregonian*, July 1968.

saying they had captured Langdon and wanted to turn him over to me. I went down to the stable office where they had him, put shackles on him, took him into the hotel, had a good fire built and told Langdon to take some sleep on the lounge. I sat down by the stove to guard him. The town was soon aroused; at least quite a number of men came in to see Langdon, as I suppose, through morbid curiosity. Mr. W.C. Foren, deputy U.S. marshall, came in and stayed with him. [No mention of George Langdon being present.] Harrison went to bed and about 4 o'clock got up and sat by the stove in charge of L. Nichols. At about 5 o'clock in the morning as I was sitting at the stove with my back to the front door, the door was suddenly opened and I was caught and thrown backward on the floor and firmly held, while my eyes were blinded and immediately a pistol was fired rapidly 5 or 6 times. I heard someone groan just about the time the firing ceased. Harrison was hurried from the room. I could tell it was him by his cries. I went to Langdon and found him dead. I looked around and a masked man stood at each door warning by ominous signs for no one to undertake to leave the room. So soon as they were satisfied that Langdon was dead they quietly left the room. At daylight I took some men and began the search for Harrison and found him hanging from a banister of the Crooked River iron bridge.[2]

To add further confusion as to what happened that fateful morning, Thompson claimed—which Blakely firmly denied—that the posse turned the prisoners (again the plural) over to him and he was helping guard them when twelve or fifteen masked men burst into the hotel barroom, killed Langdon and dragged Harrison away.

Thompson's account, which undoubtedly sheds some light as to what happened, doesn't support Luckey's official report. After all, Thompson was covering his own tracks. In keeping with his version of the event, the prisoners were being held at the livery stable when he arrived. Upon his request, Luckey and Foren had them moved to the

---

2   Luckey's letter to Sheriff Storrs at The Dalles dated March 18, 1882. *Illustrated History of Central Oregon*, 1905. Some of Luckey's descendants still live in Prineville. A great-great nephew and niece are also a nephew and niece to the author of *Thunder Over the Ochoco*.

barroom of the Culver Hotel where Thompson remained to assist in guarding the defendants. The deputy and U.S. marshall guarded the street door while Thompson kept watch on the back door. Langdon, shackled and lying on a couch, fell asleep. Harrison was sitting near Thompson when they heard the street door open. As Thompson turned to look four men burst into the lobby and threw the two law officers to the floor. At the same instant two men rushed across the barroom and leveled their revolvers at Thompson. The whole proceedings took place within five seconds. All were masked, even their hands being covered with gloves with the fingers cut off to better handle their weapons.

In another instant the room was filled with masked figures. Apparently every man had a place assigned him and in less than a minute every entrance to the hotel was blocked by armed guards. Thompson would then note: "As two men leveled their guns at me I put up my hands, and I want to say I stood at attention." At the same time two more men ran around the stove and as Langdon struggled to his feet one of them struck Luke with his pistol knocking him to the floor. Then in a frenzy, they emptied their revolvers into his body. It was later confirmed that Langdon was riddled with bullets from several handguns. Every vital organ including his lungs, heart and liver were pulverized. While this was going on other men placed a rope around Harrison's neck and as he was dragged out of the room he cried out to Thompson, "For God's sake save my life and I will tell it all" implying that he knew something about the murder of Crooks and Jory which he didn't. Thompson never saw him alive again.

Twelve men were left in the bar after the main mob had vanished. Not a word was spoken until Thompson asked permission to go to Langdon's body and straighten it out. This he was permitted to do and after about twenty minutes one of the masked figures give a signal and in an instant "all were gone, passing out through two doors." Keep in mind that this is Thompson's commentary . . . the acknowledged leader of the vigilantes. Thompson, himself, would never admit to any participation in the committee's activities—only to his role in the so-called livestock association. The way Thompson reasoned, just because he was in the Culver Hotel when Langdon was gunned down, it enabled "my enemies, especially the outlaw gang, to accuse me of being the head of the vigilantes." He would also bemoan the fact that Harrison's death gave

Harvey Scott an opportunity to declare in the *Oregonian* that Thompson was the chief of the vigilantes and if he gave the order could have "any man in three counties hanged."[3] There was no doubt in the minds of central Oregon residents that Scott was telling the truth.

Now for the third eye-witness account as to what happened in Sam Jackson's Culver Hotel on Saturday morning, March 18, 1882. Langdon's body was already getting stiff when Leo Fried—local businessman and soon to be part owner of the big Prineville Land and Livestock Company—dropped in at the hotel dining room for an early morning cup of coffee before opening his general store. According to him, things had calmed down and all seemed peaceful. Bill Harrison was sitting quietly by the stove sipping coffee and the guards were discussing Langdon's premature death. Suddenly Harrison interrupted their conversation with this comment: "Whatever Luke did, he was always good to me." Following that remark, the cluster of men who were milling about the hotel lobby—none of them masked—grabbed Harrison and dragged him outside as he pleaded, "For godsake, I got a little boy with no mother! I ain't done anythin' but work for Luke!" Neither the U.S. marshall nor the deputy sheriff made any attempt to stop them and it was Fried's belief that the men involved were members of the newly formed Ochoco Livestock Association. Once outside, a rope was placed around Harrison's neck and one of the men jumped on a horse and raced down Third Street with Harrison clawing frantically at the noose and dragging behind. Joined by other horsemen, the mob circled several blocks coming back down North Main; then they veered north on Beaver Street towards the back of the Longhorn Saloon before galloping west on Second Street toward the Crooked River bridge.[4] Harrison was already dead.

As a Shoshoni horse wrangler cashed in his chips on a muddy frontier street, the cards were being dealt to a beginner in the elegant

---

3   Thompson, *Reminiscences of a Pioneer*, pp. 172-74.
4   Old Timer Edition, *Central Oregon Shopper*, August 4, 1949, p. 3 col. 5. The first bridge across Crooked River was built in 1874. The lumber used in construction came from Bill McMeekin's sawmill located on the Ochoco River where the *Central Oregonian* office now stands. The bridge spanned Crooked River at what is now West Second Street about a block west of Deer Street. At that time Crooked River ran through what is now downtown Prineville merging with Ochoco River at a point a block west of the present Deer Street bridge. The old river channel is still visible marked by a three to four foot drop-off which meanders between Fairview Street and Main Street south of SE Second Street.

community of Hyde Park, New York. This new player in the game of life would find his niche in history as Franklin Delano Roosevelt, 32nd president of the United States.

By the time Blakely got dressed that morning, "the man in a red shirt" had been jerked down West Second Street where a crowd now gathered at the Crooked River bridge to morbidly stare at his battered body hanging on public display. Few people believed that Luckey couldn't identify any of the lynchers. It was also being questioned as to why the two law officers who knew that Harrison was not legally a prisoner didn't intervene as noted by Leo Fried.

For the sake of argument since Fried was the only eye-witness who claimed to have seen the faces of those who committed the act of violence, let's concede that Luckey was correct and the men were masked. The horse which dragged Harrison to death wasn't masked and it was generally known whose horse it was and who rode it. It so happened that the horse was one Jim Blakely had sold a short time before and the deputy sheriff had a strong personal reason to shield the rider.

For the remainder of the day, the townspeople shuffled about in muffled silence. Luckey would write: "The town is quiet today. Powers held inquest upon the bodies. I am not informed what the verdict in either case was. I feel conscious of having done my duty . . . ." To insure no one forgot what happened, splashed across the front page of the *Ochoco Review* was the reminder: "At about 5 o'clock in the morning a mob entered the barroom of the Culver Hotel, compelled the guard to stand aside, shot Langdon to death as he lay on a lounge and Harrison was roped and dragged to the Crooked River bridge from which structure he was hanged . . . ."[5]

Yes, Prineville was deathly quiet and for good reason but not for long. When George and Emma Langdon rode into town expecting to see Luke before his 10 o'clock trial, the pervading gloom was rent by a scream of pure hatred. Seeing Luke's tortured body still sprawled on the barroom floor, Emma La Francis Langdon's French blood came to a seething boil. Charging into Hahn & Fried's General Mercantile, she bought a .38 Colt, a box of bullets and stalked back to the Culver Hotel. Luke's wife was out for revenge. Entering the lobby, she fired a shot at

---

5   *Ochoco Review*, Saturday, March 18, 1882.

Luckey but being quite agile he ducked out the rear door and stayed hidden out in Maupin & Perkins livery barn until the Langdon's left town the following day. Following this episode, the townspeople were so frightened over what had transpired in the past five hours they wouldn't even help George and Emma prepare Luke's body for burial.[6]

When he thought it was safe to venture out, John Harrison removed his brother's body—now swaying ominously in an up-canyon wind—from the Crooked River bridge and with the help of Annette Tallman and Kate Driggs provided Bill with the essentials needed to enter the land of his fathers. Sunday morning, Langdon and Harrison were buried in unmarked graves on the bleak sagebrush covered hill north of town. For some unexplained reason, Aaron Crooks and Stephen Jory who were buried on Friday, were also laid to rest in unidentified graves.[7]

Soon after Emma Langdon tried her best to remove Sheriff Luckey's badge with a .38 slug, a new development was taking shape. As the day dragged on, a sinister group drifted into the Stockman's Exchange Saloon and the Ochoco Livestock Association transformed into the Ochoco Vigilance Committee dedicated to enforcing law and order in central Oregon . . . and feared by every honest citizen east of the Cascade Mountains. Known leaders in this organization were Elisha Barnes, Joe Hinkle, Bud Thompson, and Sam Newsom. How many followers they had is anyone's guess.

By Saturday evening, the Langdon's were aware of this meeting and George was certain that he was the next victim on the hit list. He tried to talk Emma into leaving also but having more nerve than good sense, she refused to be run off of her Grizzly Mountain horse ranch. the next morning after attending to Luke's burial, George gave Emma $300, took Luke's best saddle horse and lit out for the Columbia. Shortly after his arrival at The Dalles inquisitive truth-seekers asked Langdon if he had been run out of town by the committee. In all honesty, George

---

6   Testimony of Jax Zumwalt, great nephew of Lucius Langdon, letter dated October 4, 1977.

7   Prineville's boot hill is now a part of Juniper Haven Cemetery. The burial sites of Langdon, Crooks and Jory have never been listed in cemetery records although there are known unmarked graves in the old Prineville Cemetery which is now named Pioneer Cemetery, located in the southwest corner of Juniper Haven. William Henry Harrison's name or burial site aren't even acknowledged as being in the old Prineville Cemetery. Some would hint that Harrison was buried in the Grizzly Cemetery but there is no evidence—other than some unmarked graves—to support that claim.

admitted: "I would rather be a live coward than a dead hero and I left Prineville because the crooks there were too strong and too dirty for the small ranchers to handle."[8]

By mid-summer, George Langdon returned to central Oregon to check on Emma's welfare only to find out all of her horses had been stolen. With the help of the Blakelys and C. Sam Smith who placed their range hands at Langdon's disposal, the missing horses were retrieved. Seeing the futility of trying to operate the Grizzly ranch, Emma and her children returned to The Dalles where she later married John Archibald.

It wasn't long before other central Oregon residents were getting nervous as the Ochoco Livestock Association openly embraced a vigilante mode of operation. Frank Loeker put his brewery up for sale and headed for Washington Territory. Leo Fried sold his interest in the mercantile store to Moses Sechel and left for Portland. Realizing he should have kept his mouth shut about underground rivers, Doc Vanderpool took down his shingle and retreated to The Dalles.

And the actions taken by the committee may have been tormenting some people's conscience. Dick Graham, who was staying at his summer resort in Big Summit Prairie, got word to get back into town immediately. Brother Bob who was managing the Longhorn Saloon had abandoned the place and taken the stage for San Francisco. Without comment, Special Deputy Jerry Luckey headed over the Cascades to Eugene where he committed suicide.[9] Things were not going smoothly in the queen of Oregon cow towns. Adding more fuel to the 1882 summer of discontent, 23,000 head of sheep took the trail east leaving no forage for the big cattle drives to follow.

Only three summers had passed since the Shoshoni war machine laid waste to eastern Oregon. Now better news was in the offing for the empire builders. Word drifted up from California that another blight on the range was about to be eliminated. Bad Face, in an attempt to unite with Has No Horse, was reported to be dying in a remote mountain valley on the Oregon-Nevada border.

---

8   Testimony of Glen Langdon, Jr., grandson of George Langdon, letter dated September 12, 1977.

9   Letter to the author from Eugene E. Luckey dated June 10, 1988, Burns, Oregon.

CHAPTER 183

PAIUTE JUSTICE

*I had not thought to fashion sandals of the grave for
one so young. His father takes the little life-shoes to
bind on a slain enemy; Thus he will find our babe
in the Spirit-World and be his friend.*

Lilian White Spencer
Shoes of Death

If the Ochoco vigilantes needed further education in cruelty, they
could have taken lessons from the Paiutes. Has No Horse once observed
that for a people who would suffer almost any indignity from the white
men while steadfastly refusing to join their Snake brothers in combat
they had a peculiar sense of intolerance when it came to dealing with
their own kind. It always saddened him that his old partner-in-arms
married into the earth eater tribes.

Bad Face, whose Paiute wife witnessed her last sunrise at the end
of an infantry bayonet on the Malheur River, had been content to fend
for himself for the past 17 years. Then in July 1882, Bad Face—now over
90 years old—married a young widow with a year-old child confirming
Has No Horse's suspicion that he was senile.

Anxious to show off his new bride, the old warrior started out for
the Snake war chief's hide-out on Warner Mountain. On this honeymoon
trek, the enthusiastic groom overextended himself and fell desperately
ill before he reached Has No Horse's camp. A rider was sent ahead and
Has No Horse immediately came to the aid of his friend, traveling to the
place of sickness and ordering a sweat house built. By sundown a Paiute
shaman began working on Bad Face and he was expected to improve.
Instead, he settled into a coma which came as no surprise to Has No
Horse, who had little faith in Paiute healing powers. Unfortunately, his

own medical advisor and son-in-law, Wolf Jaws, was hiding out some-where in the Blues and unavailable for consultation.

The healing process stretched into late August and the distressed Winnemucca family sent for the services of Wovoka (The Cutter). Again disappointment. The Cutter was in one of his periodic trances and couldn't be disturbed but their plea for medical assistance alerted report-ers of possible front page headlines. However, by the time they located the Paiute camp and their stories reached the local papers, the news was a month or two late on what had transpired.[1]

Meantime, the old chief lay by the fire wrapped in a rabbit-skin robe with his feet buried in the warm ashes. Sometimes he would awake and during one of these moments he told Has No Horse that he dreamed his wife had caused an evil power to enter his body. As Bad Face's relatives hovered by his side their eyes moved to his young wife who huddled in a corner of the tipi becoming increasingly frightened. In the minds of the assembled Paiutes, the woman was guilty of her husband's illness.

Hoping to stall off any rash move, Has No Horse suggested she be taken to a nearby mountain spring and immersed in the cleansing water to be purified. Unaware that he was attempting to help her the girl, believing she was going to be drowned, found a rope and when no one was looking attempted to hang herself. The Paiutes were now certain that the woman was evil because she had not atoned for her sorcery by bathing in the spring and the attempted suicide proved her guilt.

A council was held and Has No Horse—knowing the futility of arguing with Paiute mentality and disgruntled with Mrs. Winnemucca's refusal to participate in a proven Shoshoni ritual for the exorcism of evil spirits—agreed the woman should be stoned. As darkness approached, she was stripped, forcibly bathed and then sprinkled with ashes. At least with this cleansing her spirit could ascend the Milky Way where she would meet her ancestors in a world where there were many animals to hunt. When night fell a circle of fires were lit on a nearby hill and the sentence was carried out.

---

1   *Daily Silver State*, September 27, October 8 and October 31, 1882 (Winnemucca, Nevada); Reno *Evening Gazette*, October 25, November 16, 1882.

The woman was tied by one leg to a stump while the Paiutes and members of Has No Horse's entourage joined hands and began a monotonous chant as they slowly circled their victim. She vainly tried to protect her child but the infant was torn from her arms by one of Bad Face's relatives and dashed head-first against a pile of rocks killing the child instantly . . . and the terrible dance continued.

At last, the lead dancer stopped near the woman, picked up a rock and smashed it into her back. She screamed and fell forward as a trickle of blood flowed from the gash. More rocks followed and after a few agonized moments a large stone crushed her head and ended the gruesome ceremony. Her body and belongings and those of her child were placed on a fire and consumed. The Ochoco vigilantes would have admired this final action.

With the death of Bad Face's wife, no one with the possible exception of Has No Horse, doubted but that he would miraculously recover. He didn't. The old dog soldier lingered on as a living skeleton until September 22 before his spirit ascended to the stars to unite with his martyred bride.

Sam Davis, editor of the *Carson City News* who was present at the end, would honor Bad Face in this unadorned eulogy: "He was as much a king as Alexander and also enjoyed the advantage of having died in Nevada. He turned his feet to the setting sun on Friday last and his immense moccasins shaded his face in dying moments. . . . " Davis had scooped the other newspapers.[2]

And so, while the citizens of central Oregon consoled themselves with the demise of Bad Face and washed the bitterness from their throats caused by the lynching of Bill Harrison another significant battle loomed on the western horizon . . . the debate for countyhood. The rowdy inhabitants of the Ochoco—due to their lax ways—were being taxed for the construction of a new courthouse at The Dalles City and that rankled.

---

2   Winnemucca's death, *Carson City News*, September 27, 1882. For some reason, the *Daily Silver State* in its October 31 edition claimed he died on October 21, 1882 and the Reno *Evening Gazette* didn't pick up the story until November 16, 1882.

CHAPTER 184

A COUNTY AND A MAN

In the end, the uneducated elect the quarter-educated who, in turn, receive in total confusion the conflicting advice of the half-educated.

Erick von Kuehnetl-Leddikn
National Review Reporter

By 1882 with Prineville sporting five saloons and gambling houses, Scissorsville two and the outlying towns at least one each, lawlessness was approaching epidemic proportions. It was soon decided that a few local authorities—also uncontrolled—would be in order and self-government became the issue of the day.

The first notes of the county symphony were heard in the late summer of 1880 when a concerned Prineville citizen wrote a letter to *The Dalles Times* warning of unrest in the Ochoco country.

> The question of the division of Wasco County is being generally agitated here. This question was discussed to some extent two years ago but at that time met with serious opposition, not only from your part of the county but from many of the citizens here. Now, however, there seems to be but one unanimous opinion and that is 'a new county of our own we should have, and that immediately!' Citizens of The Dalles hardly understand how little real protection or advantage to their part of the county our present organization is. Were it not for our local officers crimes might be committed daily and the criminals escape long before the arm of justice could be stretched across the 125 miles that intervene between us and the judgment seat at The Dalles. And as it is, the few cases that we are compelled to take to The Dalles for trial cost the county such enormous sums

that we are ashamed to make the balance against us any
larger and many offenses are allowed to shock the moral
sense of the community without any attempt to visit punishment upon the heads of offenders.[1]

It is strongly suspected that Bud Thompson, a "printer's devil" by
trade who had served on the editorial staff of the *Oregonian*, was the
author of this rousing message. There was just cause for complaint in
regard to the financial problems. It was common knowledge that Ochoco
taxpayers charged for transportation, housing, feeding and prosecution
of local felons had paid for the Wasco County courthouse. In fact,
property valuation had become so inflated that William Pickett—Prineville's reformed alcoholic—refused to accept appointment as
Wasco County assessor.

To further excite the imagination there was serious talk that the
Oregon Short Line en route from Salt Lake City would pass through the
Ochoco to the head of the Willamette Valley. This caused additional
unrest pitting the big livestock operators—who were adamantly opposed
to a railroad crossing their range mainly from fear of an anticipated
homestead rush—against the mining and timber barons who couldn't so
easily trail-herd their product to the eastern market. The livestock interests won out and the Short Line continued westward through Baker City,
Pendleton and The Dalles. However, before completion, unpaid railroad
workers stalled the construction train in Pendleton for weeks. In desperation, Capt. Henry Wagner was dispatched out of Fort Walla Walla with
a detachment of cavalry in an attempt to get things moving. Between the
threat of military force and the pleas of local officials the track was finally
completed in 1884.[2]

During this turmoil, John Hipple Mitchell—editor of *The Dalles
Mountaineer* and *The Dalles Times*—was losing his senatorial fight
against ex-governor LaFayette Grover. In the process, he almost killed
the bill for the formation of Crook County. Had it not been for the Hon.
Frank Nichols—Prineville's state representative—the measure would
have failed. The ensuing legislative in-fighting is a bit of political history
not generally known.

---

1   *The Dalles Times*, September 6, 1880.
2   "Centennial Countdown," *The Oregon Journal*, April 22, 1959.

Benjamin Franklin Nichols—ex-sheriff of Polk County; brother-in-law to Col. Cornelius Gilliam, commander of the Oregon Expeditionary Forces during the 1848 Yakima War; nephew to Stephen Meek, the mountain man who led the first wagon train across central Oregon in 1845; and brother to Lucian Nichols who was helping guard Luke Langdon the night he was murdered—would prove to be a formidable opponent. A druggist by profession, Nichols established Prineville's first drug store in 1877.[3] In Prineville, he began studying law and by 1880, being a staunch Democrat, he was appointed to Oregon's House of Representatives.

It was during this period that H.W. "Yallerdog" Roberts made the statement that to survive in Crook County, "a man had to be two things, a Baptist and a Democrat. He wasn't worth a damn if he didn't claim to be both."[4]

By mid-1882 gambling on county formation and the appointment of county officials was getting heavy and the ante was no two-bit pot. Betting (in an off-hand manner) was one way of swinging elections either by attempting to influence the choice or by actually buying votes. As high as $5,000 and $6,000 bets were riding on the outcome. Hank Vaughan, out of sheer contempt for the slate of proposed county administrators, lost a bundle.

Nichols was dispatched to Salem on the pledge to create a new political sub-division. Almost at the beginning of the session, he introduced House Bill #65, the intended birth certificate of Crook County. The measure passed the House by a large majority but was tabled in the

---

3   In the early 1900's, when railroad fever was sweeping through central Oregon, Nichols became convinced that the Corvalles and Eastern Railroad would go through Laidlaw (now Tumalo), so he sold his Prineville holdings and moved to what was then western Crook County. He settled by his close friend, Marsh Awbrey, for whom Awbrey Butte in Bend is named. One of the final times Nichols returned to Prineville was to take part in the cornerstone ceremony for the building of the Masonic Lodge in 1920. One of the oldest Masons in the state, Nichols was brought to Prineville for the ceremony by ambulance from a Bend hospital where he was recuperating from a broken leg. It wasn't long after the Masonic lodge ceremony that Nichols died in Tumalo at the age of 95. He is buried in the Masonic section of Juniper Haven Cemetery in Prineville. In Nichols honor, a portion of Court Street north of Ochoco Creek was named Nichols Street. However, in the 1950's the Prineville City Council changed the street's name to North Court Street to preserve uniformity.

4   As told by H.W. Roberts grandson, Fred Roberts September 1976. The early community of Roberts located in Birch Canyon some three miles south of the present Prineville Reservoir was named for the Roberts family

Senate without discussion. This was done to force Nichols to vote for Mitchell, which he refused to do.

About this time an opportunity occurred for the state treasurer to pay out $100,000 on the state's indebtedness and thus save a large amount of interest. Edward Hirsch, the state treasurer, with the sanction of the governor and attorney general, paid the $100,000. At this point, a bill was introduced in the lower house to legalize the act. Through Nichols' influence this bill was also tabled. Solomon Hirsch, senator from Mult-nomah County and brother of the treasurer, was quite anxious to get Ed off the hook and make this bill a law. He was also chairman of the committee on counties. Sol contacted Nichols and was told that the bill to legalize his brother's indiscretion would be passed after and only after the Crook County bill had become law. Consequently the Senate was forced to pass the bill creating Crook County in order to authorize the payment of the state indebtedness.[5]

On October 24, 1882, Crook was carved out of a remnant of Wasco County. . . a chunk of real-estate stretching from the crest of the Cascades to the John Day River. Six times as large as Rhode Island, four times bigger than Delaware, equal in size to the state of Massachusetts, and located in the geographic center of Oregon, it contained the largest stand of Ponderosa pine in the nation. Covering 9,000 square miles of gold, sheep and cattle country, Crook County was the wealthiest in the state of Oregon.

In 1885, it would add to its already sizable area a section of Grant County known as the Beaver Creek District. Many who witnessed this acquisition would see the day in 1899 when Crook would donate nearly 500 square miles of its original size to form Wheeler County and still later, suffering the pain of an unwanted pregnancy, give birth to the entire counties of Jefferson in 1914 and Deschutes in 1916 leaving the mother county in its present form.

There was a grand and glorious battle on the home front as to what name should be attached to their new county. Various groups were campaigning for such titles as Johnson, Claypool and Ochoco; but the most popular name offered was Crook to honor Maj. Gen. George Crook who opened the Ochoco for settlement. To meet county specifications

---

5   *The Illustrated History of Central Oregon*, 1905, p. 710.

for the nomination of his name, Crook had more going for him than the successful destruction of the Shoshoni war machine. Many army officers were granted opportunity to exercise their talents in Indian administration . . . Sheridan, Grant, McClellan, Crook and Howard are but a few of the generals who shave-tailed on the western frontier. Of this starred group, George Crook was the acknowledged master eulogized by the grizzled veteran, Gen. William Sherman, as "the greatest Indian fighter and manager of the army that the United States ever had."

Crook was born September 8, 1828—four years before Has No Horse—on a farm near Taylorsville, Ohio, the ninth of ten children born to Thomas and Elizabeth Mathews Crook.[6] Young George was apparently destined to stay on the farm but fate in the form of Robert Schenck—Whig member of the House of Representatives—intervened, or so Schenck told a reporter of the *Washington Chronicle* in 1883 when "his boy," Gen. Crook, was a national hero.

According to Schenck, he had to find a lad from the Third Ohio Congressional District to fill a vacancy at the military academy and remembered that his friend, Squire Crook, had seven boys so he sent word for him to come to town. "He came," recalled Schenck, "and I inquired if he had a spare boy he'd like to send off to West Point. After studying awhile, he said he didn't know but what he had." Schenck would continue: "The boy was exceedingly non-communicative . . . he didn't seem to have the slightest interest or anxiety about my proposal. After explaining the requirements and labors demanded by the military school I finally asked him, 'Do you think you can conquer all that?' His monosyllabic reply was, 'I'll try.' And so I sent him . . . ."[7] At the age of nineteen, George borrowed $115 from an army captain, bought the sparse equipment required and entered West Point Military Academy on June 1, 1848.

Cadet Crook did not offer a great deal of mental competition to his classmates. He was never appointed cadet sergeant or even a corporal but remained quietly in the ranks. Only in conduct was Crook an example to his classmates. He consistently ranked in the upper half of his class but then, George was too busy keeping his academic head above water

6   Crook, *Autobiography*, p. xx; Burke, *On the Border With Crook*, states that Crook was born at Dayton, Ohio, September 23, 1829.

7   *Washington Chronicle*, Washington, DC, files of 1883.

to indulge in the luxury of demerits. Not once in four years did Supt. Henry Brewerton find it necessary to grant permission to Cadet Crook to receive articles from home, a pleasure which most cadets enjoyed from time to time. His problem stemmed from extreme shyness. Needless to say, his best friend at that time, Phil Sheridan, was not so quiet. In 1852, Crook graduated thirty-eighth in a class of 43 thus becoming the lowest ranking cadet ever to rise to rank of major general in the United States Army. He was immediately assigned to the 4th Infantry Regiment based in Oregon where he engaged against the hostile Rogues, Yakimas and Snakes until the outbreak of the Civil War.[8]

When Crook left the Ochoco to enter the Apache Campaign, Gen. Howard would describe him as "a peculiar man six feet in height, never fleshy, of very light complexion with light hair, wearing when I saw him, a thin moustache." During the Snake offensive Crook had a blonde beard which naturally parted at the chin. These two parts of his beard were usually in braids during battle and drawn to the right and left.[9] Howard also noted that Crook was even more reticent than General Grant, carefully keeping all his plans and thoughts to himself. "He was very temperate in eating and drinking and he was so strong and muscular that he appeared never to be troubled with fatigue. He was indeed a favorite with the Indians and though terrible in his severity when they broke out and made war, and perhaps at all times distrustful of them, yet he believed in keeping his word with an Indian as sacredly as with a white man and in all his dealings with them was uniformly just and kind." Howard also observed that "The general had that art which few men possess, that of saying very little to you in conversation, being at the same time such an attentive listener that one was unconsciously drawn out in discourse." This was indeed high praise coming from the self-proclaimed Messiah of the Red Man.

Crook's reticent and unobtrusive character became his hallmark through life. "Probably no officer of equal rank" so claimed Capt. John Bourke, "issued fewer orders or letters on instruction. Crook carried this principle into every battle of his career and his men knew that in the hour

---

8   For more on Crook's career in Oregon see Harvey Scott, *History of Oregon Country*, Vol. II, p. 184 and Vol. V, pp. 223-25; *Oregon Historical Quarterly*, Vol. XI, pp. 56, 68.

9   As remembered by John Luckey who served as scout for Crook from 1866 to 1868 during the Shoshoni War.

of danger Crook would be found in the skirmish line not in the telegraph office."

Crook in an address to the West Point Class of '84 emphasized "that with all his faults and he has many, the American Indian is not half so black as he has been painted. He is cruel in war, treacherous at times and not overly cleanly. But so were our forefathers. His nature, however, is responsive to a treatment which assures him that it is based upon justice, truth, honesty and common sense; it is not impossible that with a fair and square system of dealing with him the American Indian would make a better citizen then many who neglect the duties and abuse the privilege of that proud title." Back in Oregon the administrators of a new county were doing their best to prove that final statement while loudly proclaiming they would never "neglect the duties or abuse the privileges" of self-government.

By 1882 General Crook was stationed in Omaha, Nebraska as commanding officer of the Military Department of the Platte. In 1885 when Grover Cleveland took over as twenty-second president of the United States, he placed Crook in command of the Military Division of Missouri and promoted him from brevet to the paid rank of major general, something President Hayes had attempted to accomplish in 1877.[10]

This was the man whose name was being considered for application to a newborn county in the heart of Oregon. The nominations finally narrowed down to two names and a twelve-man committee was appointed to decide whether the infant county would be Crook or Ochoco. It is doubtful that either warrior would want his name attached to the lawless area central Oregon was fast becoming. On the final ballot, the vote came out seven in favor of Crook and five for Ochoco. The general had won another battle with the Snake war chief.[11] The committee later admitted that they rejected Ochoco not because he overlooked the stoning

---

10   Crook, like many command officers who served during the Civil War, was reduced in rank at war's end. This was an effort by the War Department to save the government money. In 1868 when Crook was again advanced in rank to Major General it was a brevet commission which meant he had all the authority and responsibility of a three star general but received the pay of a Lt. Col., his last rank before being promoted to brevet Major General. And so, for the next 17 years, Gen. Crook was short-changed when his monthly pay check was delivered.

11   Other Oregon landmarks named for Gen. Crook are Crook Glacier on the south slope of Broken Top in the Cascade range and 7,834-foot Crook Peak in southern Lake County. During World War II, a landing craft was named *Crook County*. It operated in the South Pacific.

of a woman in the late summer, but because he and his mongrel followers were poaching cattle coming in to water at Andrew Jayne's well on the southern boundary of the newly formed political district.

Once the county was named, the struggle for county seat began. It was expected that Paulina, Mitchell and Scissorsville would present a threat but there were also such thriving metropolises as Willoughby, Ochoco, Cleek, Bridge Creek and Meadow in Big Summit Prairie vying for the honor. They didn't stand a chance when it came to a vote. Prineville stuffed the ballot box with its majority population and won hands down.[12] It seems odd that when the final count was tallied, the two top contenders—Scissorsville and Paulina—never registered a vote. Undoubtedly some election officials decided that a plebiscite from Scissorsville with its floating mining population was undemocratic; and Paulina—the suspected hideout of every desperado west of the Great Divide—didn't have a snowball's chance in hell of having its vote recognized.

Now, the real bid for power began. Newly elected governor, Zenas F. Moody (who didn't want people to know his middle name was Ferry) owed a political debt to the Ochoco vigilantes and the first installment was due. In office little more than a month, Moody began appointing county officials. Keep in mind that all appointments were not to take effect until January 1, 1883.

Bud Thompson's brother George became county judge; Sam Richardson, law partner of George Barnes, county clerk; Gus Winkler, manager of Selling's Saddle Shop and suspected member of the Harrison lynch mob, county treasurer; Dick Graham, owner of the Longhorn Saloon where Harrison's body was first put on public display, county coroner; George Churchill, a known vigilante sympathizer, county sheriff; Ben Allen, influential sheepman and Charles Cartwright, big-time

---

12   The vote for county seat was:
   Prineville: 467; Cleek (on Hay Creek): 85; Mitchell: 43; McKay Creek: 5; Cross Keyes (on lower Trout Creek): 2; Black Butte: 3; Mill Creek: 40; Carmichael (upper Willow Creek): 7; Meadow: 6; Willoughby (3 miles west of Grizzly): 16.
      Contrary to McArthur's definition in *Oregon Geographic Names*, pp. 797-98, which states that Willoughby suggests a play on the words *willow* meaning "willows by the creek," Willoughby was named for a family that settled on Willow Creek in 1872. In an interview with Warren Glaze (Til Glaze's son) in July 1968, he stated that Dr. Willoughby was a Prineville dentist in the early 1900's.

cattleman, county commissioners; and Sam Newsom, Indian hating veteran of the Yakima War, county assessor and county surveyor. According to some, the sponsors of these local officials were men with the blood of innocent victims on their hands . . . men who would attend Sunday services and smile as they dropped one or five dollars in the collection plate.

On December 5, 1882, six days after county organization and during the second session of the county court this august body appointed George Noland, another law partner of George Barnes, district attorney and Prineville mayor, Elisha Barnes, justice of the peace. Barnes first official act was to unite Barney Springer and Ann Todd in holy wedlock at the Occidental Hotel. There was more than love involved in this nuptial connection. While the Crook County debate was in progress, John Storrs—Wasco County sheriff who had coveted John Y. Todd's central Oregon holdings since 1878—filed a preemption claim on Todd's Farewell Bend headquarters ranch. In a swift move to counteract this application, Todd signed the Farewell Bend ranch over to his foreman, Barney Springer and then to cinch the deal Springer married Todd's daughter in a civil ceremony in Prineville. Then the county court, in an obvious effort to gain media support, appointed Star Mealey town constable and Henry Dillard—as sort of a consolation prize for his defunct newspaper—was given the job of county school superintendent.

There was also some unfinished business to take care of, namely taxes owed to Wasco County for the construction of a new courthouse. No problem. The Hon. Frank Nichols had done his homework. Buried in the act for creation of Crook County was an interesting clause. Section 6 would set forth quite clearly that "the County Clerk of Wasco County shall, within forty days after the passage of this Act, ascertain the proportions of the amount of money expended by Wasco County for building a court house in the year 1882, collected in taxes from the inhabitants now to be embraced in the County of Crook . . . and pay back the amount."[13]

However, the citizens of Wasco County had a more urgent matter to resolve than the loss of some tax dollars to their newly delivered offspring to the south. Vic Trevitt, a popular bartender and owner of the

---

13 *Illustrated History of Central Oregon*, 1905, pp. 710; *Oregon Special Laws 1882*, p. 178.

Mt. Hood Gentlemen's Club; a veteran of the Mexican, Cayuse and Yakima wars; and a prominent spokesman for Wasco County who served in the Oregon legislature as a member of both houses (where he undoubtedly crossed sabers with the Hon. Frank Nichols, father of Crook County), left The Dalles City in the fall of 1882 on a business trip to San Francisco. While there, he unexpectedly booked passage to that vast political subdivision in the sky. He was also a devout member of the Masonic Lodge.

Trevitt had often expressed the desire that upon his death he would like to be "buried among honest men" and to Vic the only honest men that he had met either west or east of the Cascade Mountains were Indians.[14] Therefore it was arranged that he would be buried on Memaloose Island. This island, located a few miles west of the mouth of the Klickitat River in mid-channel of the free-flowing Columbia, was one of the most noted Indian burial sites west of the Rocky Mountains.[15]

At the time Trevitt made his request he could not have known just how much trouble his demise would cause. By the time his remains were brought back from San Francisco in the late fall of 1882 the mighty Columbia was locked in ice from shore to shore. If Trevitt's friends wished to carry out his last request this unexpected delay would necessitate that his body be held in storage at a Portland mortuary where it remained for many weeks.

Finally the Columbia thawed and immediately the Masonic Lodge members prepared for what would become the most notable funeral conducted along the River of the West. In March of 1883, the newly commissioned S.S. Hassalo transported the mourners to the island under the gaze of curious Indians who had gathered to watch this latest whim of the crazy Americans. It would remain to be seen whether they approved or disapproved of this desecration of their sacred burial island.

With the mourners aboard the sternwheeler watching, the Masons built a brick cairn that would house the casket. This provided a base for

---

14   McCoy, *Melodic Whistles in the Columbia River Gorge*, p. 53.

15   The deceased were placed on wooden platforms which tended to collapse over the years and centuries of use covered this island with layers of bones and skulls presenting a grisly sight. Known to the Chinook Indians as the Island of the Dead and called Sepulcher Island by Lewis and Clark, this ancient burial ground can be seen from milepost 73 on both Washington Highway 14 and Oregon's Interstate Highway 84.

the 13-foot-high marble column—sacred to the memory of Victor Tre-vitt—which can still be seen today from both the Oregon and Washington shore. During construction of this massive pedestal the Indians watched in silence keeping their distance as the stone monument was hoisted onto Trevitt's burial platform. Whatever their thoughts were about the white men's intrusion it is significant that no more Indians chose to trust their dead to the hallowed grounds of Memaloose Island . . . a burial site they had used for centuries.[16]

Now back to Wasco County and its recent amputation. Effective as of January 1, 1883—some two months before The Dalles City bar-tender was laid to rest in an Indian burial ground—Wasco County would turn jurisdiction over to the newly appointed officials of Crook County. The vigilantes were now in control. Through the active and passive sympathizers they had secured political domination of county govern-ment and some would carry this power to extremes. Eight days before the vigilantes took legal control of the county's destiny, the flood-gates of hell were wrenched open by the raging torrent which engulfed the Ochoco.

16   McCoy, *Melodic Whistles in the Columbia River Gorge*, p. 53-55.

CHAPTER 185

PEACE ON EARTH

*Like the unrepentant adulteress woman, they had
eaten and wiped their mouths and they had said:
"We have committed no wrong."*

Proverbs 30:20
A Biblical Observation

Before the county battle simmered down, the rule of gun and rope
had already begun. If reporter Mealey had displayed any nerve, the
Ochoco Review for December 25, 1882 would have hit the street with a
blazing banner . . . A Good Day to Die! Followed by sub-headings like:
Notorious gunmen stage shoot-out in the Bucket of Blood; Local rancher
murdered in the Stockman's Exchange; Teenagers lynched two miles east
of town; Deputy U.S. Marshall dying of lead poisoning. But Star
Mealey   town constable pro tempore—wasn't a total fool so he left well
enough alone.

Sunday, December 24, was a day for joyous celebration. Unlike
the rest of eastern Oregon, Prineville was enjoying balmy weather and
the town was making the most of it. Highlight of the afternoon was a race
between some of the fastest horses in the Pacific Northwest and bets were
running in the thousands of dollars. One of the favorites was a little mare
owned and ridden by eighteen-year-old Charley Luster. Although he was
employed as a range rider by Al Swartz—who settled in the Ochoco in
1868—Luster was still considered a stranger in the community. As race
time drew near, young Luster bet two month's wages—$60, all the money
he had—that he would win. A short time later it was rumored that Luster
had been seen in deep conversation with Bud Thompson and Charlie
Cartwright. This shifted the odds three to one that Luster was going to
throw the race in favor of Barney Markam's thoroughbred ridden by
Luster's best friend, Sid Huston.

During the reported discussion between the jockey and Bud Thompson, Hank Vaughan and Charlie Long were in a card game getting on each others nerves. Vaughan—still nursing a grudge—took the three-to-one odds and bet Long that Luster would win. Later in the day, a flushed Luster came in winner by a length and ominous rumblings were heard throughout the crowd. Those who bet against the young range rider suddenly disappeared while the lucky winners headed for town and celebration.

By 3:00 p.m. Prineville was doing everything but observing Christmas Eve in a solemn and reverent manner. Over at the Baptist Church, Brother Powell was having a hard time getting even a few seats filled but maybe he was having problems seeing. The *Ochoco Review* once reported that "Uncle Johnny Powell mistakes a church call bell for a hand lamp and makes several efforts to light the thing with a match."[1] Perhaps the church was empty but the saloons were crowded to the saturation point.

Over at Kelly's Last Chance, Nettie Tallman was engaged in guerrilla warfare and outnumbered like her warrior brothers, she was fighting a losing battle, At the moment, she was facing a showdown with a flushed and determined Mossy Barnes—kid brother to George.

On the opposite street corner a scowling Al Swartz stomped into the Stockman's Exchange and cussed the "sonsuvbitches" who thought they owned the range.[2] At the bar, Charley Luster was buying drinks for the house and bragging that "no tinhorn politician tells me how to ride a horse race."

Three blocks to the south in the Bucket of Blood, two gunmen eyed each other warily as Katrina Driggs tried frantically to talk Charlie Long into taking her home. Sitting quietly at a back table was Vaughan's Indian wife. Close by, George Barnes—drinking heavily in a high stake poker game—eyed her with unveiled contempt.

---

1   *Ochoco Review*, February 4, 1883.
2   Raised in Salem, Oregon, Al Swartz, a family man, arrived in the Ochoco Valley with the first big wagon train of settlers in 1868. He owned a small ranch on Crooked River some eight miles south of Prineville near what is now called Swartz Canyon where he raised horses and a few longhorn cattle. His brother Ike Swartz, who came to the Ochoco Valley in 1872, was a logger. Another brother, Dave, also a logger, arrived in 1879.

Across the street, Deputy U.S. Marshall Bill Foren elbowed his way into the Silver Dollar growling that "nobody better get tough tonight or I'll buy 'em a one-way ticket up the hill." This was a reference to the cemetery north of town. Backing him was Gov. Moody's hand-picked choice for sheriff, George Churchill. About then Bud Thompson swaggered in, plunked his feet up on a card table and ordered Limburger cheese and beer. Sam Smith who was tending bar made the delivery. He had barely turned away when Thompson shouted, "This damn cheese is no good! I can't smell it!" Smith paused in mid-stride, turned deliberately and giving Thompson an icy stare snarled, "Dammit man take your feet off the table and give the cheese a chance." For the moment everything was under control.

A block to the north, Mayor Barnes was setting up drinks at the Longhorn and running competition to his son as he tried to drop his rope on Penny Sutton. To date, she had been somewhat successful in eluding the old boy. By now, "Uncle Johnny" Powell had found the church bell rope and was ringing in the holiday season.

Over on South Beaver Street, Susanna Barnes and her daughter-in-law, Ginevra, placed presents under the Christmas tree and prayed that their men would stay out of trouble this night, especially Mossy and George. They weren't worried about Bill for he was fairly level-headed and old Elisha was too crafty to get caught in any foolishness. Unknown to them, the thunderheads of violence were already building to gigantic size.

Word was being passed around that there was going to be a private party out at Bill Barnes' ranch two miles east of town and the guests of honor were Charley Luster and Sid Huston, rider of the losing horse.[3] While this request was being circulated, a more sinister invitation was being extended in the Bucket of Blood. Sam Smith—who had turned over bartending to his partner Henry Cleek—and Jim Blakely drifted into Glaze's saloon in time to see Bud Thompson in deep conversation with Charlie Long. It was a forgone conclusion that Long was being paid to gun somebody down. It was now about 4:00 p.m.

---

3 At this time, William and J.M. (Mossy) Barnes were living together. (*Illustrated History of Central Oregon*, 1905, p. 712). It appears that Bill was taking care of his somewhat handicapped younger brother.

Moments later, Long drifted up to the bar and offered to buy Hank Vaughan a drink. Vaughan quietly told Long that he'd drink with him after Long paid off his gambling debt. Long chose to ignore this remark. Stepping back from the bar, Vaughan said, "Charlie, let's settle things right now." At this point, both men walked to the middle of the saloon and commenced shooting.[4] By thumbing, gunfighters like Vaughan and Long could draw and hit what they were shooting at in a quarter of a second. Most fights were across a bar or a card table not over ten feet apart so the prime requisite was speed. At that distance you didn't need to aim.

Before Vaughan even stepped back from the bar, the saloon emptied. Only two men besides the gunfighters were left in the barroom . . . one hid behind a screen, the other—dead drunk—was laying on the floor between two whiskey barrels. Vaughan was packing a .44 Bulldog Colt and Long a .38 five-shot Smith and Wesson. In less than three seconds, ten shots were fired. A shade faster on the draw, Long's first bullet hit Vaughan in the forehead, traveled around his skull and came out the back of his head temporarily blinding him. His second shot got Hank in the left breast over the heart which ranged through his left lung and came to rest near his spine but he still didn't go down. With blood pouring down his face, Vaughan fired five shots, hitting Long three times in the left shoulder and once in the left arm. During this exchange, Long got off three more shots none of which hit their target. Then Charlie staggered behind Vaughan snapping his empty pistol at the back of Hank's head before going down. By the time the gun smoke had drifted to the ceiling, Long was laid out on a poker table to die. Vaughan was being watched for the same purpose.

A silk handkerchief—Hank's trademark—was now clasped over his heart as he stumbled out the saloon door and bumped into Sam Smith. He asked Smith and Blakely to help him up the street to Graham's Longhorn Saloon believing he needed the services of a coroner. Upon arrival, Vaughan announced that he was a dead man and invited those present to take a last drink with him. Martha Robie, who had silently followed Smith and Blakely into the Longhorn, took a long look at her common-law husband and tersely announced, "He won't die." Hank, his

4   As told by Jim Blakely, March 19, 1939.

head throbbing like a Shoshoni war drum, was not so certain. Stretched out on a pool table, he turned his bloody face towards Blakely and made a request. "Jim, take my boots off. My dad said I'd die with my boots on . . . so take 'em off." Blakely—no stranger to trouble and a man who packed several bullets in his own body—understood and honored Vaughan's last demand.

Meanwhile, young Dr. Belknap was working feverishly over Charlie Long. His left shoulder was completely shattered and one of the bullets, which Doc probed for but couldn't remove, ran upward from his arm and was lodged deep in his body. Long had defiantly lost the use of his left arm and at this time, it appeared he would soon die. On this depressing note, Dr. Belknap headed for the Longhorn where it was reported that for all practical purposes, Vaughan was already dead. After a long painstaking search, he removed the bullet from above Hank's heart and remarked, "With a constitution like his, he just might recover." Everyone doubted this diagnosis except Vaughan's Nez Perce companion.[5] With the help of Blakely and Smith, Martha loaded Hank in a buggy and took him home.

With the opposing gunmen now neutralized, the town returned to its celebration. Ike and Dave Swartz left the Stockman's Exchange and headed for their ranch in Crooked River canyon leaving brother Al in a friendly card-game with John Gray, Dave Stewart, Bill Cadle and Perry Read—all of whom shared contempt for the Ochoco Livestock Association. Swartz, who openly defied the vigilantes and was in constant danger of being ambushed, had taken a seat with his back to the wall where he could see anyone coming through the saloon door.[6] Around 10:00 p.m. he felt a wind on his back and asked, "Why's that window open? It's cold." Gray had just dealt a hand. Glancing at the cards, Swartz held three aces and discarded his other two cards. He then got up and closed the window. Returning to his seat, he looked at Gray and said, "hit me."[7] At

---

5   Hank did not obtain a divorce from his first wife, Lois McCarty, until October 8, 1888, four years after he left Prineville. Lois was a sister to the notorious McCarty brothers who—besides being rustlers—were involved in bank and train robberies throughout the West along with Butch Cassidy and the Sundance Kid. It is interesting to note that Billy the Kid's real name was Patrick Henry McCarty.

6   *Illustrated History of Central Oregon*, 1905, pp. 711-12.

7   Roy Gray, descendent of John Henry Gray, September 1955. At the time of interview, Roy, who was 75 years old, was working at the Alexander-Stewart sawmill in Prineville, Oregon.

that instant a gun exploded followed by the sound of tinkling glass. Swartz jerked erect, then crashed over the card table with a bullet in the back of his neck. He was dead before he struck the floor.

While Constable Mealy made a feeble but honest effort to conduct an investigation of Swartz's murder, Sheriff Churchill and U.S. Marshall Foren were conspicuously absent. Apparently something more urgent was demanding their undivided attention.

Earlier in the evening, jockeys Charley Luster and Sid Huston started back to the Swartz ranch with Ike and Dave but at the mouth of Dry Creek changed their minds and returned to town for another round of holiday drinks. This was poor judgment on their part.

After Long and Vaughan exchanged Christmas presents, the talk again turned to the afternoon race. The losers were in an ugly mood and the more they drank, the meaner they got. There was increased muttering that the Sunday race would be the last one Luster ever rode. Then someone started a rumor that "the damn Huston kid"—son of William Huston and a boy raised on Willow Creek—was planning to steal some of Bill Brown's horses. Since Brown was a member of the livestock association in good standing, this was equivalent to committing suicide. After a few more drinks, a committee headed for Swartz Canyon to dispense some justice. They didn't have to ride far.

A half mile south of the Prineville Club Hall on South Main, the social committee ran into the returning cowhands and invited them over to Bill Barnes' house for some Christmas cheer. On the way, they stopped at Marshall Foren's house for more whiskey.[8] Here, Huston became suspicious that all was not well and decided he and Luster would ride back into town. It didn't work and a fight ensued. Beat into submission, the jockeys were roped to their horses and taken to Bill's house. Upon arrival, they were forcibly jerked from the saddle and kicked inside where a kangaroo court was convened. The law firm of Barnes, Richardson & Noland would represent the "Prineville Racing Commission" with Judge Lynch presiding. The teenagers would serve as their own defense. As they were being dragged outside, Sid Huston yelled at Luster, "Fight, you sonuvabitch . . . they're going to kill us anyway!" Apparently this

---

8   William Foren's house sat approximately where 811 S Main is presently located. In 1996, the address was changed to 662 S. Main.

wasn't successful. From evidence later found at the scene, both boys were shot and were either dead or near death when the rope was applied to their necks.

On Christmas Day—some would call it "Red Noel"—Sam Smith and Jim Blakely were ridding up to the Keystone Ranch which Smith had recently purchased from Jim Miller. Some two miles east of town they discovered the bodies of Luster and Huston hanging in a big juniper.[9] From the blood, they could tell the boys had been shot in the body and then in the back of the head after they were hanged. It was a severe shock to Blakely who had known Sid Huston since he was a baby.[10] The sight of his body swinging from a juniper limb filled Jim with a burning hatred. When Blakely arrived back in town, he visited Vaughan—who had also known the Huston boy from the time he could walk—and told him of the killing. Hank swore he would live long enough to even the score. Outlaw and lawman—a lethal combination—would unite to make life uncomfortable for the vigilantes.

Unexpectedly, U.S. Marshall Foren didn't accompany the detail which rode out to bring in the bodies. The reason given was that Foren (who also served as town blacksmith) had been kicked by a horse the night before and couldn't get out of bed. It leaked out, however, that Sid Huston had shot him when the vigilantes attacked the boys. His curiosity aroused, Blakely checked and found a bullet hole in the side of Foren's cabin. No one was allowed to see the marshall and a few days later he died.

Within three days of the lynching, the *Ochoco Review* would report that the boys had confessed to numerous crimes after "a rope had been judiciously use on them" and had also revealed who their confederates were.[11] There was no mention of names but before January ended wholesale slaughter would begin. This boastful account was submitted by an anonymous correspondent—but beyond doubt it was Bud

---

9   This tree was located where the present Union 76 station and wrecking yard sit at the iui ' on of Barnes Butte Road and U.S. Highway 26.

10 Sidney Huston was born near Albany, Oregon in 1865 and it was there that Blakely first knew him. In 1871, William Huston, Sid's father, moved to the Ochoco and with his family settled on Willow Creek next to Blakely's big cattle ranch.

11 *Ochoco Review*, December 28, 1882. This article was believed to have been given the green light by temporary editor Henry Dillard who would soon take over as Crook County's first school superintendent.

Thompson. It claimed credit for the vigilantes, glorifying their performance and branding Al Swartz and the boys as being part of a gang that had been running stolen livestock out of the country. It also accused Swartz of defying the vigilantes which was most likely true. He was an outspoken man who had publicly denounced the cold-blooded murder of Bill Harrison. The puzzling aspect of this article is that Hank Vaughan—a known outlaw who shot his first man in Canyon City at the tender age of 15—was not mentioned.[12]

The violent lynching of Luster and Huston aroused the decent element of Prineville but most were afraid to even talk about the event let alone act upon it. There would be more killings before any response was forthcoming.

As for the rest of the United States, the new year was also ushered in with a bang when *Life Magazine*, Vol. 1, No. 1, hit the newsstands on January 4, 1883. Issued every Thursday at 10¢ a copy, it contained such timely articles as "The Ballad of a Bore," editorial cartoons, and numerous advertising. Ballyhooed as a "History of Our Times," it would appear in Baldwin's Main Street drugstore before February scaled the southern Blues.

---

12 Vaughan got out of this charge of attempted murder by reluctantly enlisting in the 1st Oregon Volunteer Infantry on January 2, 1865. Six weeks later on February 17, 1865, Henry C. Vaughan was found to be unsuited to military discipline. . . a nice way of saying that he was dishonorably discharged. (Wasco County Circuit Court, Criminal Case File No. 55-51, Oregon State Archives, Salem; Military Department Records, File No. 59-36 and 60-28, Oregon State Archives, Salem.)

CHAPTER 186

THE DAY OF THE HUNTED

Vigilantes hell! Murders and cowards, I call 'em. . . .

James M. Blakely
Crook County Rancher

The vigilantes were on a roll and gaining momentum. In an effort to justify their vigorous activities, the secretary of the Ochoco Livestock Association would graphically describe what transpired in the month following the Christmas Eve massacre.

"As time wore on," he would explain, "the gang again became more bold and many acts of outlawry were committed. It was agreed that no one should ride the range without notifying the Association. Copies of the [association] by-laws were sent to every stock owner in the county and all were asked to join. Along in January, about the 10th as I remember, a crowd of rustlers came to town, and after filling up with bad whiskey rode up and down the streets, pistols in hand, and declared they could take the town and burn it, and would do so if there was any monkey business."

The vigilantes—sticking to their story of an organized outlaw gang terrorizing the community—seem to have forgotten, or ignored, that the so-called "crowd of rustlers" were local cowhands who had ridden into town for a belated New Year's celebration and were bothering no one. There only crime other than refusing to pay homage to the newly appointed county officials was to be working for the wrong cattle outfits.[1]

Secretary Bud Thompson would continue: "That night there was monkey business. Three of the gang were hung to a juniper two miles above town, while another was shot and killed in town. [This makes eight men killed in less than a month.] The next morning notices were found

---

1   Blakely, interview, August 1950.

posted, with skull and crossbones attached, telling all hard characters to leave the country. There was then such a hegira [exodus] as has seldom been witnessed. Men not before suspicioned skipped the country . . . among the number was an ex-Justice of the Peace."[2] This was Buckskin Powers who was reluctant to serve a warrant for the arrest of Bill Harrison. It is not difficult to comprehend as to why people were suddenly looking for a healthier climate.

As a bleak January sun cast its feeble rays on the frozen bodies of the previous night's lynching, the residents of Crook County were stunned to find the following warning nailed to buildings, fence posts and trees:

Vigilance Committee.
To The People of Wasco County!

"Salus Populi Suprema Lex."[3]

Whereas, it became necessary for this organization to meet out summary punishment to the leaders of the thieves, robbers, murderers and desperadoes, who for many years defied law and order, and threatened the lives and property of honest citizens of this portion of Oregon, and as the late fearful tragedy at Prineville testifies that justice is slow, but sure, we promulgate this our pronunciamento for the purpose of justifying to the world, and particularly to the people of the State of Oregon, any future action which we may take.

We deeply deplore the necessity which called our organization into existence; but the laws of our State are so defective that as they now stand on the Statute Books, they all favor criminals going un-whipped of Justice; a retrospective view will show that in this respect we speak only the truth.

Having first lopped off the branches, and finally uprooted the tree of evil which was in our midst, in defiance of us

---

2   Thompson, *Reminiscences of a Pioneer*, p. 174.
3   A Latin phrase meaning: The Welfare of the People is the Supreme Law.

and our laws, we beg to be allowed to rest here, and be not forced again to take the law into our own hands. We are very loath to shed blood again, and will not do so unless compelled in defense of our lives.

A Warning

We are well aware that at the present time, a combination of the few remaining thieves, their friends and sympathizers, has been formed against us, and have threatened all kinds of vengeance against persons whom they suppose to belong to this organization. They threaten associations in every form, and that they will commit arson in such ways as will defy legal detection. The carrying out in whole, or in part, of each or any of these devilish designs against us, our property, or any good citizen of this county, will cause us to rise but once more; do not trifle with us; for if you do, we will follow you to the bitter end; and give you a "short shrift and a hempen collar." As to this, our actions in the past, will be a guarantee for our conduct in the future.

We trust this will have a good effect. We repeat, we are very loath again to take life, and hope we shall never more be necessitated to take the law into our own hands.[4]

January 1883   By Order of the Committee

Shortly after the appearance of this notice, Charlie Long—the association gunman—was back on his feet. He was now packing his useless left arm in a specially made leather sling compliments of Selling's Harness and Saddle Shop. As an added precaution, tucked in his left arm sleeve was a double-barreled .41 Remington derringer. For more than 50 years, this firearm, which came out during the Civil War, was a favorite hide-out weapon for men of violence on both sides of the law. Although its effective range was only on the order of 15 to 20 feet, that was more than sufficient when considering the damage its .41 calibre slug could

---

4 The original warning, which appears to have been written by an attorney, was shown to the author nearly 40 years ago by a person who will remain unnamed. Shortly thereafter many documents—if not all—pertaining to the vigilantes and range war were placed in a stove and burned.

do to a man sitting on the opposite side of a poker table. Knowing that Vaughan was also on the road to recovery, Long lit out for Washington Territory. It was claimed that Charlie often boasted that in his lifetime he intended to kill 12 white men in order "to have a jury of my peers in hell." However, he wasn't yet ready for another confrontation with Hank.

Since he hadn't fulfilled his contract with the livestock association, Long would receive no pay. He, too, was expendable. When Long arrived in Walla Walla, his conversation was as empty as his saddle bags but it was abusive. He immediately started bullying a young homesteader, threatening to take his ranch and run him out of the territory. This he did on a daily basis. In time these threats would produce a violent reaction.

Meantime, Vaughan rented a buggy from Henry Hamilton and took out after Long. He made it as far as Athena, Oregon, when the need for a stiff shot of whiskey overtook him. In the Athena Saloon a bunch of loggers were raising the rafters. After about the fiftieth "timber," Hank's patience grew thin and he told the bull of the woods to "shut-down the operation." In the shooting-scrape which followed, Hank's luck turned sour. His old .44 Bulldog misfired and a logger shot him about the same place where Long had beefed him. By the time Vaughan recovered from this episode he had lost the desire to go after Long and he returned to Prineville with Martha Robie.[5]

Martha, whom Hank affectionately called "Gus" was a stabilizing influence on Vaughan and often accompanied him on his legal and illegal horse and cattle excursions across eastern Oregon, Nevada, Utah, Arizona, Idaho, Wyoming and Montana. Maybe that's what kept him alive. Whatever, those who knew him said that Vaughan—a man with hot blood in his veins—was easy-going and likable when he was sober. But when drinking hard liquor that could change in the blink of an eye. It was during these drinking sprees that Hank would ride his horse into saloons and shoot glasses off the back bar or anything else that got in his way. After he got the hell-raising out of his system Hank would pay for any damage without argument. Clark Wood, a news reporter friend, would recall that when Hank was with ordinary citizens he was "happily harmless, a good natured, soft-spoken person of more than average height with splendid shoulders and engaging manner. Yet he always had guns

---

5   Blakely on both Long and Vaughan, August 1950.

under his long coat and a marvelous facility in producing them when the occasion seemed auspicious."[6]

Noah Brown, a night clerk at the Umatilla House in The Dalles City would describe Hank as "weighing about 165 pounds, erect and straight as an Indian, always fashionably dressed with neatly trimmed beard and hair, gentlemanly and courteous in manner. He was quite charitable [always ordering drinks for the house and buying expensive gifts for those he liked] and usually pleasant. He didn't seem to know the word fear and when in a state of intoxication or in a bad mood nothing daunted him."[7]

It wasn't so much that Vaughan was mean as it was that he liked excitement of any kind. He gave little thought to the pain his actions would bring to flesh and bone including his own. Luckily for him, Hank displayed a remarkable physical ability to heal from knife or gunshot wounds. Billy Mayo (Pendleton town constable) claimed he saw Hank stripped once and "he was a regular sieve . . . he had scars all over him where he had been shot or cut."[8]

During Vaughan's reign of terror, Jim Blakely (sheriff of Crook and Wallowa counties), Joe Blakely (sheriff of Gilliam County) and Billy Blakley (sheriff of Umatilla County) never found it necessary to arrest Hank. Sensible lawmen soon learned that the safest way to approach Hank when he was drinking was to do it unarmed. Umatilla County Deputy Sheriff Matt Taylor readily admitted, "I never carried a gun when I went to arrest Hank, I was afraid he would take it from me . . . I arrested Hank many times but never had any difficulty in doing it as I never attempted it when he was drunk."[9]

By the time Vaughan got back to Prineville from the Athena shoot-out a new development had taken place. Following Long's failure to carry out committee instructions, a request was circulated seeking the services of one or more "bounty hunters" to rid the Ochoco of unwanted predators. This offer would attract the attention of the more unstable elements of frontier life.

---

6 *East Oregonian*, March 27, 1948, Pendleton, Oregon.

7 *Wenatchee Daily Word*, December 18, 1922, Wenatchee, Washington.

8 *Spokesman Review*, August 16, 1913, Spokane, Washington.

9 Taylor, David M., "Recollections of Hank Vaughan," Works Projects Administration, General History 200.11, Umatilla County Biographies, Hank Vaughan, p. 2, Oregon State Archives.

On July 3, 1883 a riot exploded into raw violence at the Oregon State Penitentiary. During the outbreak, fourteen convicts took prison Superintendent George Cullins hostage and demanded that the gates to freedom be opened. This order was denied. However, after the superintendent received a few whacks with an iron bar, prison officials were willing to negotiate and the gates were opened. Although guards shot several of the fleeing men and some were recaptured, a few were available to the highest bidder and central Oregon looked like a good place to advertise. At least two of these criminals—perhaps more—may have arrived in Prineville.

On July 12—nine days after the prison break—two rough-looking strangers strolled into the Silver Dollar Saloon where Vaughan was sipping a beer. It soon became obvious they were trying to goad Hank into a fight but for some reason he wasn't taking the bait. After a few more shots of whiskey and some derogatory remarks, the drifters left the saloon and headed toward the livery stable. Vaughan leisurely finished his beer and he too ambled in the direction of the horse barn.

Over at Hamilton's stable another new arrival was in the process of renting a buggy. He intended to buy some land and go into the livestock business. Young Van Gesner, a Portland physician, had decided that there was more money to be made in raising sheep than there was in patching bullet holes. Time would prove him correct for sheep made Gesner a very wealthy man. But for the moment, his choice of Crook County as a base of operations—when sensible residents were vacating the area in droves—leaves room for speculation. Dr. Gesner was either a brave man, a damn fool or had an inside track with the Ochoco Livestock Association . . . take your pick.[10] As he and Henry Hamilton walked into the livery stable office to finish their business, the two unidentified gunmen disappeared into the livery barn.

A few minutes later, Hank Vaughan—now packing a double-action .41 calibre "Lightning" model Frontier Colt sporting an 8-inch barrel—stepped out of the glare of the street into the gloom of the livery barn and hell itself was jarred to its very foundations. The two mystery men stepped out of the shadows as Perry Read and Billy Circle, both of

---

10   Dr. Gesner would live in Prineville for a few years; then move to Portland for awhile; and again return to Prineville and take up residence. He died in Portland in 1931.

whom worked for Hamilton, and both of whom dove for cover. Within the next two seconds as bullets ricocheted off the walls, Vaughan shot and killed the nameless gunmen. With Henry Hamilton and Dr. Gesner as witnesses, the vigilantes couldn't deny that it was a pure case of self-defense.[11] And so, another scheme had failed but the committee wasn't giving up by any stretch of the imagination.

It's worth noting that when Vaughan's single-action .44 failed him at Athena, he was faced with a tough decision. In the 1880's most gunfighters (and Vaughan was no exception) preferred a single-action revolver when it came to betting their life on the immediate outcome of a shoot-out. Aside from the fact that the double-action was a new development which the gunmen didn't trust, in the hands of an expert the first shot from a single-action was a split second faster than one from a double-action and gunmen depended on that first shot. Because of this, they took a dim view of newfangled double-action handguns, especially those with a short barrel. However, the long-barrel weapon was acceptable. When it came to getting off more than one shot the double-action long barrel was just a shade faster than fanning a single-action and that fraction of a second could mean the difference between life and death. Vaughan's gamble to switch to the "Lightning" model .41 Colt paid big dividends in the Hamilton Livery Stable attack.

During the winter of 1882-83, two young cowhands drifted into the Crooked River Valley and began working for various cattle outfits breaking horses. While working for the Thompson brothers, they apparently did something to displease the brothers, for soon after leaving to work for the Hay Creek Company, Bud spread the word that they had told him their names were Tom and Frank Page but after talking to Peter French and Bill Brown, he recognized them as the "notorious Mogan brothers" from Nevada.[12] What they were notorious for was never mentioned. As far as the rest of the community was concerned, the Mogan's had never used an assumed name, they were hard workers, good

---

11   Henry "Shoe Peg" Hamilton's livery stable was located on the south side of East Fourth Street between North Main and North Belknap Streets in the present parking lot to the east of the Cinnabar Restaurant and Lounge; and across East Fourth Street from the BLM Prineville District Office. It was destroyed by fire in 1927.

12   Thompson would also claim they were a quarrelsome pair who "posed as bad men and were not long in involving themselves in trouble and were shunned by the better class of citizen." Thompson, *Reminiscences of a Pioneer*, p. 175.

horse breakers and minded their own business. Mike Mogan's wife was always willing to help with chores at the ranches where they worked and was, according to Celestine Miller, a young lady who "any woman would be proud to call daughter."[13]

Frank Mogan was the first to get into trouble. Thompson accused him of deliberately crippling a horse and demanded payment for the same. Frank refused to pay. Thompson brought suit and lost in a jury trial mainly because of Stephen Staats.

Staats, whose parents had a small ranch near the Farewell Bend spread, had taken a claim on the east slope of Powell Butte which butted-up against Sam Starr's big Red Cloud Ranch on the north side of the buttes. Even though Staats' claim contained the only good spring in the area, he and Starr got along very well. Earlier, Staats had openly accused the vigilantes of lynching Harrison. Therefore, it came as a surprise when in February he was appointed for jury duty with Judge S.G. Thompson presiding.[14] During Mogan's trial, Staats argued that a man couldn't be held liable for doing the job he was hired for which in Mogan's case was breaking wild horses to the saddle. The other panel members agreed. Lawyer Barnes had lost his first case.

By early summer Frank was working steady on Dick Miller's horse ranch on Mill Creek while Mike was riding circuit breaking horses wherever needed, figuring all was quiet. The committee didn't forget or forgive that easily but they had other business to attend to.

As spring settled on the Ochoco, ranchers were told they had to obtain permits from the livestock association before turning their sheep, cattle or horses out to graze. No permit, no grass. Out of fear most complied only to see more stringent rules applied. Each day, the enforcers grew bolder and bolder. Soon they were sending symbolic pieces of rope and threatening letters marked with skull and crossbones to special offenders. It didn't take much to be offensive. Perhaps the controlled use of water on private lands; maybe a fenced garden plot in some meadow; possibly a holding corral on the open range; or a small line-shack for the convenience of the herders. It made small difference what the real or

---

13   Elizabeth Miller Stanton, Celestine Miller's step-daughter, November 1938.
14   The summons was for February 6, 1883. *Illustrated History of Central Oregon*, 1905, p. 712.

imagined transgression might be just so long as it displeased the livestock association.

Without doubt, some who received warnings were stock thieves but for the most part they went to men whose only wrongdoing was to oppose a member of the vigilantes or to question some association rule. If the recipient didn't take the hint, he would next be seen slowly twisting in the breeze for it was now the season when juniper trees bore fruit . . . the hanged and bullet-riddled bodies of men who ignored the invitation to depart. The rule of gun and rope had begun. Before Crook was separated from Wasco County, Wasco was supplying one-third of the criminals sent to the Oregon State Penitentiary.[15] No longer was Wasco's overcrowding a problem. With the so-called decent element of Crook County in control, it was the local cemeteries that were running out of space. Completely out of character, Bud Thompson was uncommonly quiet about this stormy chapter in his long and turbulent life. In his *Reminiscences*, he barely mentions what transpired as if hoping it would die a natural death—a wish that refused to be fulfilled.

Jason Elder would note in his diary: "My Father, a horse rancher at Lower Bridge, received a letter with a length of rope enclosed. His horses had been watering in the Deschutes River at Steamboat Rock and the Tetherow's didn't like it." Elder got rid of his horses. Others who received skull and crossbone warnings at this time were Bill Cadle, who had a small cattle operation on Wickiup Creek a few miles southeast of the Keystone Ranch; Bill Peck, a blacksmith, who made the mistake of shoeing homesteader's horses; and Lew McAllister, a hard-rock miner,who wasn't even running livestock. Each in his own way tried to abide by the rules.

Peter Davis, described as "a nice little fellow" who lived on a small ranch on upper Crooked River, wasn't so cooperative. He received a warning marked with a skull and crossbones which he tossed in the stove. A few days later, Kennedy Montgomery, along with his brother-in-law, Jim Blakely and son-in-law, Perry Read, were riding for cattle and stopped to visit Davis. They found a half-eaten meal on the table, a scorched pot of beans on the stove, the partly burned warning and all of his personal belongings but no "Shorty" Davis. Read, Blakely and

---

15 *Oregon Journal*, House of Representatives, 1864, pp. 35-53.

Montgomery spent hours looking for him or his body, with no success. Davis had simply disappeared never to be heard of again.

No one was immune, least of all an Indian. In May, Gene Luckey, Jack Tetherow and George Cline were rounding up strays on lower Crooked River when they came upon a small band of Shoshoni. Like wolves, Indians were a determent to the range. When the riders got back into town, they boasted that "we got 'em all" and just to make sure none escaped, the cow hands "shot 'em between the eyes" before sinking their bodies in a big bog-hole. Some seventy years later when cleaning out a spring on the Flower's ranch on lower Crooked River, fourteen skeletons were found buried in the spring . . . each with a bullet hole in the skull.

Choosing their victims with caution, the vigilantes were careful not to place their own necks in jeopardy. When the grazing permits went into effect, George and Bill Barnes stopped Blakely on the street and reminded him that he had overlooked getting one. Blakely exploded: "I was born in this Oregon country and I'll be damned if anyone is going to tell me when I can go out after my own stock!"[16] The Barnes brothers didn't press the issue which was just as well. Blakely immediately dispatched a rider to The Dalles to pick up guns and ammunition—two Frontier model .41 Colts and three .32 calibre Smith & Wessons—which he gave to his cowhands with orders to "shoot to kill!" He fully expected to receive a skull and cross-bones notice but with his brother Joe and Hank Vaughan backing him, Jim was ready. Soon, another fast gun would quietly join his ranks.

Shortly after the dismissal of Charlie Long, the word went out that the livestock association could use some hired guns. The committee having strong political ties to the Willamette Valley, the request was circulated from Eugene City to Portland and even found its way into the state-approved penal colony in Salem. Of the various applicants, the Whitley brothers came highly recommended. They were tough and not overly concerned with the finer points of the law which, under certain aspects, could prove to be quite useful.

Somewhere along the course of events, Til Glaze had come under committee suspicion. Being a business owner, he was smart enough not to choose sides but though he never spoke out against the vigilantes

---

16   Blakely, *The Sunday Oregonian*, March 19, 1939.

neither did he go out of his way to support their cause. More to the point, not only was Glaze an ex-lawman but he had some strange ideas on community activities. On the plus side, he was the proprietor of the infamous Bucket of Blood, a praise-worthy endeavor; on the minus side, he insisted on referring to the saloon as "The Singer," a wimp of a name if there ever was one. Glaze also organized a city concert band and encouraged the pursuit of cultural arts by building an opera house on North Main Street. In short, Tilman Glaze was a man not to be trusted.

In early March, Glaze announced he would be making a business trip to Dallas passing through the state capitol on the way. The cards were falling into place. Glaze was known to have a violent temper and when aroused would react with little thought as to the consequences. Given the right incentive, nature would take its course. If the Whitleys were as good as claimed, they could eliminate a source of irritation, gain a proper reputation and become a valuable asset to the livestock association's rules enforcement committee.

When traveling, Glaze packed a model 1851 Navy Colt—a .36 calibre cap and ball six-shot revolver. A little out-dated for the times but in the hands of the right man it was a deadly weapon. As anticipated, shortly after Til's arrival in Dallas, he entered one of the local saloons and got into an argument with the oldest Whitley brother . . . a man who walked with a pronounced limp caused from a Snake arrow in his left leg some twenty years earlier while riding army dispatch on the Applegate Trail. Strangely, the Whitleys were friends of the Langdons, having crossed the plains in the same wagon train in the 1850's.[17] It is guessed that they were told—or led to believe—that Glaze had had a hand in Luke's death. Whatever, when the gun smoke cleared, three Whitleys were dead. From that moment on, Glaze fondly referred to his pearl-handled Colt as "Old Whit." In later years, his son would explain. "My Father was not a killer and never used his gun in any way but to defend himself."[18] That is probably a true statement but Til was never known to side-step a gunfight even when it could have been avoided.

Hanging the Navy Colt in plain view behind the bar, Glaze was now another member of the community that the vigilantes would stay

---

17 Glen Langdon, Jr., letter dated September 12, 1977.
18 Warren Glaze, July 1968. The author had the good fortune not only to see Glaze's Model 1851 .36 calibre Navy Colt but also to hold it in his hands.

clear of. On his return to Prineville and still in a mean mood, Glaze told Blakely, "If you ever get one of those skull and crossbone warnings, bring it to the saloon and we will tack it up on the wall and I'll put a hole through the center with Old Whit."[19] Blakely never received one but it wasn't long before he knew he was a marked man.

Shortly after Davis disappeared, Sid Stearns and his cousin, Billy Pengra (ranchers from the upper Deschutes River) were making the 40 mile round trip into Prineville for supplies. Billy's father (Sid's uncle) was Byron Pengra, military road builder and railroad promoter who had been the main backer in attempting to drive the Nevada branch of Central Pacific's rail line through central Oregon . . . a plan which failed. Central Pacific was successfully blocked by the Ochoco and Harney Valley Livestock Associations even though Pengra personally packed the battle to Washington, D.C. Backed by Oregon railroad tycoon Henry Villard, the ranchers made certain that no iron rails would cross the center of the state.

Between 1880 and 1883, Villard's Oregon Railway and Navigation Company operating out of The Dalles was laying track west into Portland and east—hugging the south bank of the Columbia River—to join with Northern Pacific which was jamming west out of Bismark, North Dakota to complete Oregon's transcontinental railroad link with the Atlantic Coast. When Northern Pacific posed a threat to the livestock association's drive for isolation, Villard put the knife to their throat in rough and tumble frontier fashion. He quietly bought controlling interest in Northern Pacific with $8 million "received from friends."

In late 1883, the final spike was driven in the wilds of Montana with Ulysses Grant present at the ceremony. Within three months, Villard's railroad empire collapsed and he returned to his native Germany but no iron tracks bisected the center of Oregon. However, his "eastern immigration bureau" sent 30,000 people to Oregon as new settlers and that was not greeted with thunderous applause by certain gentlemen in the new county of Crook.[20]

---

19 Blakely, August 1950.
20 Henry Villard, born in Bavaria, Germany, immigrated to the United States in 1853. He entered newspaper work in 1858 and reported the famous Lincoln-Douglas debates. Under his guidance, construction of the first transcontinental rail line to Oregon was completed in 1883. For more on Villard see: *Memoirs of Henry Villard, Journalist and Financier*. 2 Vols., 1904.

On the other hand, Pengra—as surveyor-general of Oregon in the 1860's—had secured a large land grant by act of Congress and by 1883 was running a big livestock operation in eastern Oregon. It was with his financial backing that Billy Pengra and Sid Stearns filed preemption land claims on 160 acres each within the present city limits of where Bend, Oregon now sprawls in semi-glorious splendor. Because of his political clout, Byron Pengra was exempt from vigilante harassment even though he had invoked their ire with the railroad scheme.[21]

As Sid and Billy approached the rim where the trail plunged into Prineville valley, they saw a man riding like his life depended upon it. Close behind were a dozen horsemen. Then a rifle shot reverberated across the flat. Leaving Pengra to bring the wagon, Stearns made a wild ride into town and reported what they had seen and heard.

Sheriff Churchill couldn't be bothered with this news. He was too busy overseeing the construction of an addition to the existing jail which, when finished, the *Prineville News* would note "as a matter of sad information, Prineville is going to have a genuine skookum house."[22] Out of curiosity, Moses Sichel and Blakely decided to ride out and check on what was happening. Upon the flat southeast of Powell Butte they spotted about twenty vigilantes standing around something on the ground.

It was Steve Staats. The whole top of his head had been blown off. Blakely noticed how the men milling around Staats' body were looking at him and talking quietly among themselves. Glancing nervously at Sichel, he whispered, "I'm going to get out of here!" and took off at a

---

21 Bryan J. Pengra married Charlotte E. Stearns in Illinois in 1849. They came to Oregon and settled in Lane County in 1853. Pengra founded and edited the *People's Press* of Eugene in 1859 and by 1865 was promoting the town of Springfield as the western gateway to his military road from the upper Willamette Valley to the Owyhee River. (Corning, *Dictionary of Oregon History*, p. 194.)

22 *Prineville News*, December 8, 1883. The Prineville jail stood where the present Senior Center parking lot is located between North Main and North Belknap Streets facing East Second Street. In the Chinook jargon *skookum house* means a "prison;" *skookum tum-tum* means "brave;" and *skookum* by itself means "strong or strength." (*Dictionary of the Chinook Jargon*, published by J.K. Gill & Co., 1889, p. 50)

gallop toward town with Sichel hot on his heels.[23] Sheriff Churchill made no attempt at investigation and were it not for friends, Staats' body would have been left on Juniper Flat to rot. As it was, Staats' closest neighbor—Sam Starr, owner of the Red Cloud Ranch—gave his own ten-year-old son Chester the sad task of riding to Bill and Emma Staats' ranch near Farewell Bend with the news of their son's death.[24]

As Blakely and Sichel approached the outskirts of town, a group of men milling around the Crooked River bridge hurriedly mounted their horses and galloped away. What they were up to was never disclosed but Dorothy Lawson McCall (mother of the future governor Tom McCall) would recall that when she first moved to the McCall's lower Crooked River ranch at the close of Crook County's range war as many as six bodies had dangled from the bridge beams at one time . . . a disturbing revelation for a New England bride.[25]

Within days following Staats' murder, Blakely got a chance to ruffle the committee's feathers. Elisha Barnes, who had been appointed Justice of the Peace by the County Court, had formed a partnership with William Gird, a well known Corvallis horse breeder who was running thoroughbreds on the John Day River near Mitchell. In the summer of 1883 they were grazing horses on Combs Flat. When dividing up the herd, the partners used a 67 brand putting the 67 on the stifle for a Barnes horse and on the shoulder with the same iron for a Gird horse.

One morning, Nathan Gird—William's son—rode out to Combs Flat to get a fresh mount. Everyone agreed that Nate was a nice young fellow but the vigilantes were looking for an excuse to get him, mainly because Nate was more popular with the townsfolk than Elisha's loud-mouthed son, Morris. Anyway, Gird got his rope on a 67 horse and broke its leg. Unfortunately, it was a Barnes horse but Nate said he didn't know that until after he had roped it. He then shot the suffering animal and returned to town.

In the meantime, George Barnes found the horse, cut out a piece of the hide with the brand on it and when he got back to Prineville had young Gird arrested and bound over to the grand jury. Any chance of a

23 Blakely, *The Sunday Oregonian*, March 26, 1939.
24 *History of Crook County*, p. 233; Virgil Starr, September 1963.
25 Dorothy Lawson McCall, June 1968.

fair trial in a court dominated by vigilante sympathizers was doomed from the start. Also, after what happened to Harrison, it wasn't safe to let him spend the night in jail. Knowing this, the Blakely brothers emptied their pockets and came up with $300 to post a cash bond for his appearance in court the next day with the stipulation they would hold young Gird in their custody until court time.

That night, Jim sent Billy Combs up to the flat with instructions to cut patches of hide off the dead horse both on the stifle and the shoulder. The following morning when court convened with Judge George Thompson presiding and lawyer George Barnes prosecuting, Blakely got himself appointed as Gird's defense attorney.

Looking at Barnes, Jim asked, "Who knows where the brand comes from?"

George was quick to reply, "I do. I cut it off."

Blakely held out for more proof so the court appointed Joe Blakely and Jim Lawson as representatives for each side to ride out to Combs Flat and fit the patch of hide Barnes had entered as evidence onto the dead horse.

"It wouldn't fit anywhere," Lawson reported when they got back. "There's hide cut off both the stifle and the shoulder."

"That's a damned funny thing," Barnes said but that settled the case. Judge Thompson had to release Nate. Sensibly, Nathan Gird left Prineville that afternoon for the Willamette Valley and didn't return.

Within days of the Gird outburst, another eruption occurred several thousand miles to the west which made the lethal activities of the vigilantes look like the efforts of a single maggot attempting to devour a buffalo herd. At 10:02 a.m. on August 27, 1883, the island of Krakatoa exploded. Eleven square miles suddenly collapsed creating sound waves audible 300 miles away with the volcanic dust dimming central Oregon skies causing brilliant coloration's of sunrise and sunset for the next three years. The ensuing tidal wave—reaching a maximum height of 130 feet—killed upwards to 36,000 people.[26] The vigilantes could envy such potent power as that.

---

[26] *Smithsonian Magazine*, Vol. 24, No. 12, March 1994, p. 29. The island of Krakatoa lies between Java and Sumatra in the Sundra Strait which connects the Java Sea with the East Indian Ocean.

Even with glowing sunsets, Blakely's court victory was fleeting. About the time Nathan Gird was run out of town, Dick Miller loaned his two best horse trainers to other ranchers. Frank Mogan was breaking horses for the Meyer & Brown Livestock Company based in Rabbit Valley and Mike Mogan was breaking wild ones for Jim Lawson, Miller's ex-father-in-law. In July, Mike rode into town for supplies. While there, he stopped at the Longhorn Saloon where he got into a poker game with Mossy Barnes. Mossy was losing heavily. Finally, he won a hand. Half drunk and in a mean mood, Barnes accused Mogan of shorting the pot by six dollars. Mogan thought he was kidding until Barnes pulled a gun. In a quiet voice Mike said, "Why Mossy, you wouldn't shoot . . . ." and at that instant Mossy pulled the trigger.

Mogan was hit bad but he slowly stood up, walked across the street to the livery stable and buckled on his gun. Half-way back to the Longhorn, he collapsed in the middle of Main Street . . . Mike Mogan had taken a .44 calibre slug through the lungs. While one man rushed to get Doc Sites, others packed Mike into the saloon and laid him out on a pool table to die. Dr. Sites did the best he could but there was no chance to remove the bullet. Mike refused to stop breathing so they packed him up to the Occidental Hotel and a rider was dispatched to Mill Creek to notify his wife.

About sundown, Bud Thompson rode into town and spread the word that ever since George Barnes had served as his attorney in the lawsuit against Frank Mogan, whenever Mike came to town, he would "abuse" George's younger brother. On this occasion, according to Thompson, "the poor frightened boy," on seeing Mike in town, "went home, secured an old cap and ball revolver, came back to the street and shot Mogan in self-defense"[27] Those who witnessed the event knew this was an outright lie. No one, least of all Mossy, was questioned as to what actually happened.

The day after the shooting, Blakely went to the hotel to see Mogan. Mike told him, "Jim, I hope to God I get well. I know who done this and I'll take care of them fellows. That was Bud Thompson's gun that Mossy used. I saw it often when I was working for him." Mike never got his

---

27   Thompson, *Reminiscences of a Pioneer*, pp. 175-76.

wish. He died a few days later and his body was taken to The Dalles for burial.

There was no doubt in anyone's mind that if Mike should die, Frank Mogan would even the score. So, immediately after the shooting. Mossy was rushed out of town to Til Glaze's Swamp Ranch on the far western boundary of Crook County.[28] There, he stayed hid-out for days. In fact, Mossy Barnes was never arrested. The killing was ruled "justifiable homicide" on the grounds that Mike owed Mossy six dollars and refused to pay.[29] But the cold-blooded murder weighed heavily on Mossy's mind. A week after Mike's death, he was showing signs of insanity. A few days later, Mossy Barnes, age seventeen, attempted to commit suicide. Twelve more tormented years would pass before he found relief. In January 1895, James Morris Barnes died by his own hand.[30]

For the next couple of months with the vigilantes lust for blood temporarily sated, life in Prineville was relatively quiet. But not for long. One day after press time and eleven days before Thanksgiving, fire broke out in the *Prineville News* office and before the flames subsided all buildings in the block between West First and West Second Streets were destroyed including the Occidental Hotel.[31] For a time, the Glaze Opera House and Glaze Livery Stable across West Second Street were threatened. One block to the east, Garrett Maupin's livery stable survived the fire but his brother's saloon in Antelope went up in flames two weeks after the Prineville inferno. During this combustible period, Nancy Johnson gave birth to her ninth child, James Ewen Johnson, said to be the first white child born in the newly created Crook County.

By December 8, 1883, D.W. Aldridge was back in business, publishing his paper in Silver Lake and reminding all concerned that he

---

28 The old Glaze cabin sat about a mile south of the present multi-million dollar Black Butte Ranch development northwest of Sisters, Oregon. Joe Glaze, Til's brother, also had a cabin in this same area and it was he who took care of Til's large horse herd.

29 *Illustrated History of Central Oregon*, 1905, p. 712.

30 Blakely, *The Sunday Oregonian*, March 26, 1939; *Central Oregonian*, Centennial Edition, Thursday, October 28, 1982, p. 3B, col. 3. In keeping with the secrecy of the times, his obituary saved by a relative for these many years, lists the cause of death as apoplexy.

31 This is the block bounded by North Main and North Beaver Streets where the present Elk's Club and parking lot are located. Some accounts claim the blaze started in the kitchen of the Occidental Hotel which is a likely spot but it appears the newspaper office was the guilty culprit.

"WANTED—ALL WHO OWE US to step up and settle now. Money is scarce and material must be replaced."[32] Damage to Aldridge's printing press and other equipment was estimated at $1,500. If nothing else, Aldridge had style.

He would also mention that Billy Circle had salvaged 1,000 pounds of nails from the ruins of the Occidental Hotel and with Charlie Maling's planing mill turning out some of "the finest lumber we have seen in this place" delivered to Power's Cabinet Shop (apparently Buckskin had slipped back into town) the block was going to rise from the ashes. Billy Circle would rebuild his inn and under the proprietorship of Dan and Mary Richards rename it the Circle Hotel.

If 1883 blasted its way through central Oregon with all the gusto of Dr. Gatling's celebrated weapon, the rest of the globe seemed quite relaxed. In Italy—although incurring no celebration—a baby christened Benito Mussolini was born. As Adolph Hitler's right-hand man, he did command some recognition during World War II. To offset this increase in population, the famed German composer Richard Wagner died with his boots off. And back on the Atlantic slope, Buffalo Bill Cody was organizing a Wild West Show complete with Donald McKay, the old Shoshoni war veteran whose Snake remedies were guaranteed to cure the ills of the afflicted.

---

32   The *Prineville News*, December 8, 1883.

CHAPTER 187

AND TO ALL, A GOOD NIGHT

This thing called me, it often seems
ain't mine a little bit,
It's just a part of someone's schemes,
and I ain't ownin' it.

Arthur Chapman
Cow-Puncher Philosophy

Ten days after the *Prineville News* first hit the street after the November fire, a gentle snow drifted down Third Street. A gaunt, haggard man buried deep in thought turned his shuffling horse up Main Street. On his furrowed face was etched the lines of tragedy. Six months ago his brother had fallen in the dust of this same street, his lungs blasted out by a .44 Colt held in the hands of a psychopathic teenager.

Twice within the past two weeks, Frank Mogan had received the grim warning of the livestock association signed with the skull and crossbones. Mogan had foolishly accused the vigilantes of deliberately murdering his brother, denouncing them as cowards. Worse yet, Bud Thompson was scared to death that Mogan might come after him.

Thompson had made certain that he was out of town the day Mike Mogan was fatally shot and for very good reason. Even Thompson would acknowledge that "the other Mogan brother affected to believe that I had given the revolver to the boy and had told him to use it." Those who witnessed the shooting knew that young Barnes was packing Thompson's ivory-handled .44 Colt. Still professing his innocence, the colonel would state, "I explained to Frank the absurdity of the charge but he still held a grudge against me for discharging him and made many threats against my life. He declared he would kill me if he had to lay behind a sagebrush and shoot me in the back. Still I paid no apparent attention to the threats, being satisfied he would never at any rate face me."[1] For all of his bravado, Bud Thompson was living in dread that the day would arrive when he had to make a stand against Frank Mogan.

The shooting of Mike Mogan had occurred on a muggy afternoon in July. At the time Frank had been breaking horses for Mike Brown in Paulina Valley. When the shocking news reached him, Frank was determined to ride into Prineville and kill not only young Mossy Barnes but also "that sonuvabitch who put him up to it . . . Bud Thompson." But he didn't. It didn't help his state of mind that Thompson had accused him of killing horses when he broke them to the saddle, a charge that George Barnes had tried his very legal best to make stick. In his profession, Frank could ill-afford such a reputation.

At the time of Mike's death, he swore vengeance but Martha Mogan, his sister-in-law, and his boss Dick Miller talked him out of it—and he knew they were right. "Don't lower yourself to their standards," Miller advised. So he burned inside and watched Mike's killers roam the streets of Prineville like little tin gods.[2] Beside, he had to protect his bride, a sad girl who had every right to be worried for tragedy was no stranger to this woman. She had been Mike's wife—a widow at age 22, she now belonged to Frank. They had been married only two weeks and in that time, Frank had received two warnings to get out of the Ochoco country. Obviously someone was afraid that he was going to settle in Crook County now that he had a wife and Frank Mogan could pose a dangerous threat to vigilante rule.

"Good evening, Mr. Mogan, doing your Christmas shopping?" The greeting jarred Frank back to reality. Yes, it was December 18, 1883, just six days before Christmas. Mogan gazed into the well-scrubbed face of little Lizzie Miller and slowly the cloud lifted.[3] "Merry Christmas, Miss Miller," he smiled.

Certainly tonight was no night for black thoughts. He hitched his horse at Johnson's Mercantile and walked in. Fifteen minutes later he emerged with a package containing a dress, complete with amber hairpins and a bottle of English Lavender Smelling Salts, a present for his

---

1   Thompson, *Reminiscences of a Pioneer*, p. 176.

2   As remembered by Elizabeth Miller Stanton. Elizabeth, the daughter of Richard Miller, knew the three Mogans very well. All information in this chapter on Frank and Martha Mogan, unless otherwise noted, was given by Elizabeth Miller Stanton, November 1938.

3   Elizabeth Miller Stanton's step-mother was Celestine Johnson Miller.

wife. Mogan then rode back up the street and reined in at Joe Kelly's Last Chance Saloon. One drink and then he would head for home. As he stepped through the bat-wing doors he saw John Combs and Jim Blakely sitting at a card table in earnest conversation with Dave Stewart. Joe Blakely, Mike Brown and Sam Starr were standing by a pool table. He was in good company. The drink was warming . . . straight whiskey. Mogan stood at the bar, his elbows resting on the counter top, again filled with memories. So deeply was he engrossed in thought, he didn't hear the gentle swish of the saloon doors as Bud Thompson entered, flicked the snow from his mustache and stared grimly at Mogan's back. Silent as a mountain lion stalking its prey, Thompson closed the distance between him and Mogan. A hushed silence fell over the saloon. The muted strains of "Joy to the World" drifted up Main Street from the Prineville Club hall (four blocks to the south) where the annual Christmas program was in progress. As eight-year-old Lizzie Miller closed her recitation with "Merry Christmas to all and to all a good night" a gunshot echoed down the snowy street.

Mogan, still preoccupied with his thoughts, stared into his half-empty glass. Then it happened. Coldly, methodically, Thompson drew his .44 . . . the same gun which had killed Mike Mogan. Deliberately he brought the muzzle up and the spell was broken as a heavy calibre slug ripped into the back of Frank Mogan's neck and all but severing it at the shoulders. Mogan was a dead man when he hit the sawdust covered floor. Thompson then emptied his gun into Frank's limp body.[4]

In the awkward hours that followed, Dick and Tine Miller packed the grim Christmas greeting to Martha Mogan and before daylight, she arrived in town to claim the body of her second husband murdered in full view of a dozen onlookers. One of the eye witnesses had this to say: "I was in Kelly's saloon on December 18, 1883 when Bud Thompson walked in and killed Frank Mogan. Frank was standing with his elbows on the bar and his hands at the sides of his face. He [Thompson] walked up behind him and shot him in the back of the neck. It was cold-blooded and cowardly."[5]

---

4   "Crook County Vigilantes," *The Bulletin*, Bend, Oregon, June 10, 1984.
5   Blakely to Herbert Lundy, *The Oregonian*, Sunday March 26, 1939; "Early Day Sheriff Fights for Law," *Central Oregonian*, Prineville, Oregon, August 4, 1949, p. 3.

Thompson was not only quick to justify his action but gambled that witnesses to the crime would be so intimidated they would keep their mouths shut . . . and for the moment they did. Bud would claim that on the evening of December 18, he was called to Hahn & Fried's general store to attend to some business. It was just after dark and while there Mollie Nichols, Judge Nichols' daughter, told him she had overheard Frank Mogan tell one of his friends that he had come to town to kill Bud Thompson and would not leave until he had accomplished his purpose. As a consequence, Thompson believed this threat was going just a little too far, so, "I determined to settle the matter one way or the other at our first meeting. The test came sooner than I anticipated. On seeing me, he attempted to draw his gun but was too slow, and fell with more than one bullet through his body." Honesty was never one of Thompson's stronger qualities.

Sheriff Churchill went through the feeble motions of an investigation and the evidence was turned over to the grand jury. It becomes quite obvious that Thompson wasn't the least bit concerned about being found guilty of murder in any degree. In his own swaggering way, Thompson would boast, "The committing magistrate [George Churchill] at my request, placed me under bonds to appear before the Grand Jury. The announcement caused an uproar among the throng with which the court-room was packed, and I was compelled to go among them and explain that it was done at my especial request. I wanted the matter to come up in the Grand Jury room and so told the people. Attorneys from every part of the State volunteered their services to defend me free of charge. I wrote to them, of course thanking them, but told them I had no use for attorneys, as the matter would never go beyond the Grand Jury, and there it ended, the District Attorney, Mr. McBride, proving my strongest witness." If Thompson was telling the truth, and he may have been, it gives some idea as to how powerful the vigilantes actually were in the state of Oregon. Not surprisingly, the Crook County grand jury found "not a true bill," thus sparing George Thompson the embarrassment of sitting in judgment over his little brother.[6]

What is surprising is that Martha Mogan—every bit as tough as her departed husband—did not give in and she brought civil suit against

6   "Early Day Sheriff Fights for Law," *Central Oregonian*, August 4, 1949.

Thompson for "damages to personal property" which rankled the colonel no end. He quickly hired George Barnes to defend him and even the brilliant mouthpiece of the Ochoco Livestock Association couldn't bring in a "not guilty" verdict. The jury awarded Martha Mogan a judgment of $3,600 to pay for the loss of two husbands in less than six months time but it was a shallow victory. Thompson refused to pay and no one cared to take up the cause even for a 22 year old widow . . . and so yet another murder went unpunished in Crook County—but not unnoticed.

Adverse publicity was filtering to the outside with dire repercussions. Filled with sarcasm, surrounding neighbors were referring to the inland empire as "Crook"—as in corruption and criminal character—to describe Crook County. And the mood of the local citizens was beginning to change from mortal fear to open retaliation.

CHAPTER 188

A RATTLESNAKE
WITHOUT FANGS

So justice overtook me, you all can plainly see.
My soul is doomed forever, throughout eternity.
It's now I'm on the scaffold; my moments are not long.
You may forget the singer—but don't forget the song.

"Bad Companion"
A Cowboy Ballad

During Thompson's trial someone (perhaps reporter Aldridge) leaked the story to the outside press. In a fit of rage, Thompson charged *The Oregonian* with publishing "distorted and untruthful statements" regarding the murder of Frank Mogan which he still insisted was self-defense. The editor's unflattering exposé goaded Thompson into making his notorious threat that he would kill Harvey Scott (editor of *The Oregonian*) on sight.

It was Bud's belief that Harvey Scott held a personal grudge against him because Thompson happened to be in Salem when Senator James Nesmith beat Scott half to death with his cane. Thompson swore that his meeting with Nesmith in the Chemeketa Hotel was accidental but "Scott never forgave me, nor did he in fact neglect any opportunity to lambaste me after that."[1]

Aside from what happened in Salem, the murder of Frank Mogan was bringing the Crook County cauldron to a seething boil. On January 19, 1884, just 29 days after Frank had been placed in his grave, Kelly's blood-stained Last Chance Saloon exploded into flames. Before the fire was extinguished most of the buildings on Main Street between East

---

1   Thompson, *Reminiscences of a Pioneer*, p. 124.

Third and East Second were destroyed. Besides Kelly's saloon, Bushnell's Harness Shop and Glaze's Livery Stable were turned into rubble at an estimated loss of $10,000.[2] Less than two months before, all the buildings on Main Street between West Second and West First had been incinerated in the 1883 Occidental Hotel blaze.

The cause of this latest conflagration was a mystery but the embers were still glowing when John Combs, Jim Blakely and Sam Smith received an invitation to appear at the grist mill on the Crooked River at the west end of town. There they were met by Dave Stewart, Charlie Pett (Stewart's Scissors Creek gold mining partner) and Clay Neese, minister of the Union Church. That night they conceived the idea of forming a citizen's protection union and within a few days enlisted Hank Vaughan, Kennedy Montgomery, Perry Read and Joe Blakely for anti-vigilante operations. Their goal was to seize administrative control of Crook County.

Vaguely aware that there was something suspicious about these nightly meetings, the vigilantes contemptuously referred to Stewart's protective union as "the Moonshiners" and it was by this name that they became best known. The Moonshiners devised a code so they could send messages to those they trusted. The county was divided into three sections and organized politically so the Moonshiners could take over county government when Crook held its first election on June 2, 1884. Blakely took the immediate area around Prineville north to Antelope and west to the crest of the Cascades. Dave Templeton—ex-49er, town druggist and big livestock operator—organized the south end of the county from the upper Deschutes River to the G.I. Ranch and Paulina Valley. Andy Lytle—veteran of the Shoshoni wars and cattleman in the Grizzly area—took the east section of the county through the Ochoco Valley, Scissorsville, Big Summit Prairie and north from Mitchell and Ashwood to the John Day River.

It was hard work trying to brace up the backs of folks who had been terrorized for two interminable years . . . and the vigilantes weren't

---

2   The 1884 files of the *Central Oregonian* lists a Wilson Saloon destroyed in the January fire. Prior to 1884 only two Wilsons are mentioned as having settled in the Prineville area: Robert Wilson in 1877 and J. Wilson in 1880. There is no record of a Wilson Saloon. It is possible that one of these Wilsons was working as a bartender at the Last Chance Saloon during the 1884 fire.

just sitting idly by either. George Barnes let it be known that the Moonshiners too would be reduced to ashes. To survive, the citizen's protective union needed credibility and they needed it now. Joe Blakely, without telling anyone, decided to provide that confidence. In late April with Hank Vaughan covering his back, Joe paid Bud Thompson a visit at his headquarters ranch.

As a note of interest, Thompson's ranch was located east of the Hay Creek headquarters ranch. Hay Creek operated the largest sheep-shearing plant in eastern Oregon. There, tens of thousands of sheep were sheared annually using the Australian method whereby the sheep were driven onto the second floor of the barn, clipped and then shoved down a chute to the ground below. Because of his close proximity to Hay Creek Company, Thompson owned a very valuable piece of property.

When Vaughan and Blakely arrived at Thompson's house, Joe quietly gave Bud a choice: get out of the county immediately or confront him at the end of a blazing gun . . . face to face and right now! There was no way that Thompson would accept the final offer. Blakely then told Bud that if he didn't have a good enough saddle-mount to make the trip, brother Jim had a horse he'd be more than willing to sell for that purpose. Thompson took the suggestion. That same day, he bought a horse from Jim Blakely, sold his ranches to Amos Dunham at a financial loss and the following morning struck out across the desert for Lakeview.[3] The citizens of Lake County held no desire to harbor Crook County's fugitive so Thompson rode on to Alturas, California.

In this wide-open frontier town, Col. Bud Thompson launched a stormy career as editor of the *Alturas Plaindealer*. A highlight of those days would include the mob-lynching of five cowhands from the Pit River bridge. Thompson called them "the Hall Gang." This happened not long after the fiery colonel charged them with robbery and warned in his paper that "if these depredations do not cease, the juniper trees will bear fruit."[4] So once again, the infamous central Oregon battle cry echoed across the land.

With another one of their ace gunmen out of the way, the vigilantes' power was slipping and they were desperate. In a meeting at the

3   "Crook County Vigilantes," *The Bulletin*, Bend, Oregon, June 10, 1984.
4   Thompson, *Reminiscences of a Pioneer*, pp, 181-82.

Longhorn Saloon, the committee concluded that Sam Smith, John Combs and the Blakely brothers—suspected ring-leaders in the Moonshiner movement—were getting dangerous. In an effort to retain control of the county, the Ochoco Livestock Association started issuing mass warnings, the bulk of them directed at the Blakelys and Ken Montgomery.

On Friday, May 2, 1884—in an effort to bolster Andy Lytle's recruitment—Jim Blakely toured the upper Ochoco Valley ranches and mining camps of Scissorsville and Howard. The next morning he rode over the Ochoco Mountains to Mitchell, notifying that end of the county that the situation in Prineville was reaching the critical stage. Tone Cannon, who was friendly with the vigilantes, alerted Jim that he best be on guard for he was a marked man. This warning was confirmed when Blakely arrived back in Prineville Monday evening. Sunday, while he was out of town, Gus Winkler cornered Perry Read in the Bucket of Blood Saloon and told him if his uncle Jim didn't watch his step, he would "be going up boot hill feet first one of these days."[5] Friends who had attended the livestock meeting that same evening told Blakely that Winkler had repeated his threat there.

On Tuesday morning May 6, Blakely retaliated. The way he put it was, "And then came the day when I buckled on my gun to kill a man." Not surprisingly, Elizabeth Blakely didn't share her husband's determination to enter the rattlesnake's den and said so. A stubborn man, Jim took his wife's hand and softly told her, "You ain't goin' to stop me this time. I'm goin' to take care of that Winkler." So saying, he strapped on his .41 Colt and walked uptown.[6]

The first person he encountered was George Barnes. Barnes quickly got his hands out in the open and said, "Jim, I ain't got anything against you." "George," Blakely replied, "tell your boys, especially Gus, I'll meet 'em at Dick Graham's in a half hour." He then picked up Hank Vaughan, the Wagner boys, Sam Smith and John Combs (all dead shots) and returned to the Longhorn. The saloon was empty.

While the rest of the men returned home, Blakely moved slowly up Main Street heading toward the Jackson House when he spotted his quarry. Winkler was standing on the front steps of the hotel talking to

---

5   Blakely, *The Oregonian*, March 26, 1939.
6   "Early Day Sheriff Fights for Law," *Central Oregonian*, August 4, 1949.

Moses Sichel. Nervously he stood his ground as Blakely strolled by without speaking and crossed Third Street to Sichel's store but didn't enter. He then turned around and slowly headed back toward the Jackson House. By then, Winkler knew Blakely was looking for him.

Sichel jumped off the porch as Winkler ran through the hotel lobby, out the back door and hid in the outside toilet. Blakely followed, shouting "Come out of there, Gus with your hands filled!" Slowly, the toilet door opened and Winkler came out but not with a gun. Instead, he had his hands high above his head. Blakely made him walk back through the hotel lobby and onto Third Street. By now a crowd had gathered. "The stage is gone this morning," Jim told Winkler, "but it leaves again Wednesday morning. You better get on it because you won't get out of here alive if you don't." Winkler took the stage and went to The Dalles.

The Blakely's acts of defiance (both Joe and Jim) gave the people some much needed hope. Those who had been shrinking in the corner suddenly came forth and voiced their support of the Citizen's Protective Union. In a last ditch effort to quell this revolt, George Barnes issued a blanket alert that the vigilantes would destroy the Moonshiners.

Two weeks after his showdown with Winkler, Blakely went to The Dalles. In the Cosmopolitan Hotel lobby he met Tom Buchanan, driver of The Dalles-Canyon City stage and nephew of the only bachelor to become president of the United States.[7] Buchanan was interested in Luke Langdon's property on Grizzly Mountain for he planned to settle in Crook County (which he did in 1887) and run competition to the Yancey brothers' freighting outfit. During this conversation, Gus Winkler, who had been running Ben Selling's Prineville Harness Shop and was well-acquainted with Buchanan, strolled by. Noticing Blakely wasn't wearing a gun, he loudly announced that "it was a damned good thing," implying that if Blakely had been wearing one, he would have shot him.

Blakely went up to his room, buckled on his gun and located Winkler in the George Allen Saloon. Walking up to the bar, Blakely looked around the room and announced, "Come up everybody and have a drink on me except that fellow there," and he pointed to Gus.

---

7   James Buchanan, 15th president of the United States (1857-1861) shocked the nation when he invited his 26-year-old "mischievous romp of a niece" Harriet Lane to serve as White House hostess. It was said that of all the First Ladies, few were as popular as this polished young woman. (Margaret Brown Klapthor, *The First Ladies,* pp. 38-9)

Winkler walked out. Five years later, Blakely again crossed trails with Winkler when he trailed a herd of cattle to Fort Walla Walla. At the fort, Winkler stuck out his hand like an old friend and said, "Howdy, Jim." Much as he hated to, Blakely shook his hand.[8]

By the time Blakely got back to Prineville from The Dalles, Dave Templeton and Andy Lytle had organized nearly 80 men who were willing to face the vigilantes in a gun fight. As Blakely stepped off the stage, George Barnes greeted him with the boast that he and his bastard organization would be broken before the week was over. The first county election was just seven days away.

That night a vote was taken by the Protective Union and everyone was ready for the showdown. At noon the following day, Jim Blakely, Joe Blakely and Hank Vaughan strapped on their guns and strolled down Main Street. Behind them, with blood in their eyes, marched 75 ranchers, loggers and miners armed with Winchester rifles. The vigilantes were barricaded in the Singer Saloon, perhaps thinking Blakely wouldn't fire on Til Glaze's establishment. They were wrong.

"If you think you can stop us," Blakely yelled, "come out shooting!" The Moonshiners could see the vigilantes peeking out of the saloon windows but none made a move. Getting madder by the moment, Blakely begged them to come out and fight. Then the Moonshiners stormed the saloon. With 78 guns pointed at their collective heads, the best the vigilantes could do was surrender without firing a shot.

On June 2, 1884 in the first general election held in Crook County, the so-called Moonshiners captured the ballot box winning all county offices. Jim Blakely beat George Churchill by 206 votes to become county sheriff. His good friend and supporter, John Combs, running as a Republican came in last. Fred McBride, a new lawyer in town, made a clean sweep for district attorney. This is the same McBride who Thompson claimed was his key defense witness in the shooting of Frank Mogan. It would appear that once again Thompson had lost sight of the truth. George Barnes didn't receive a single vote for that position.

Prineville News editor Dave Aldridge became the county's first elected school superintendent. Bill McFarland, ex-Colorado cavalry trooper, civil engineer and teacher at the Mill Creek school, was elected

---

8   Blakely, *The Oregonian*, March 26, 1939.

county surveyor. A.G. Palmer, Mitchell newspaper reporter and one time law clerk for Circuit Judge A.S. Bennett, was elected county clerk. Dr. James Sites, first accredited doctor to arrive in the Ochoco country in 1868 and who because of failing health gave up his practice and went into the sheep business, was elected county coroner.

For some unknown reason, George Thompson (who declined to run for county judge) won a seat in the state senate by a slim margin of 35 votes over Commissioner Charlie Cartwright. Apparently the voters believed that Bud's brother was less of a threat than Commissioner Cartwright. And, to round out the score, Frank McDonald beat the Hon. Frank Nichols (father of Crook County) by 136 votes to become county judge.

The vigilantes were down but they weren't out. Within ten years they would again be on the prowl under a different name. As the Crook County Sheepshooters Association, they would dispense misery in lethal doses. Although a strong undercurrent still existed, it seldom surfaced for a decade and life would be peaceful in the Ochoco. If for no other reason, as *The Oregonian* would wisely note, it was because "the situation in central and eastern Oregon was such that fugitives from justice could flee in no direction without colliding with a nemesis bearing the name Blakely, adorned with a sheriff's badge or draped with a judge's robe." This was a true observation.

The Blakely boys gained a reputation when they broke the vigilante's stranglehold on the Crooked River country. With Jim serving as sheriff of Crook County, Joe was elected sheriff of Gilliam County; Billy was sheriff of Umatilla County; and George was the district judge at The Dalles.[9] In the poker game of crime, its tough odds to beat four of a kind. Although a risky business, law enforcement must have been a healthy occupation for the Blakely brothers for all lived to be over 90 years old. Jim was 100 years old when he died on January 24, 1953. He outlasted Hank Vaughan by 60 years.

---

9   Jim Blakely later served as sheriff of Wallowa County from 1904 to 1908; Joe Blakely later became chief of police in Pendleton, Oregon; William (Billy) Blakley, who spelled his name different from his brothers, was elected to the state legislature in 1902; and George Blakely was the first licensed pharmacist in Oregon. (McCarthy, *A History of the Oregon Sheriffs 1841-1991*, p. 47.)

A fitting obituary for the gentlemen who took the law into their own hands was offered by the *Illustrated History of Central Oregon* in 1905. It would state it in simple terms: "Some ex-members of the vigilantes live in Crook County, honored and respected citizens; some have left the county; some have committed suicide; some have gone via the 'booze route,' and some have gone insane." May they all rest in peace.

The one banished to northern California would soon become enmeshed in his old habits. Since his reckless actions would involve other fugitives from the Ochoco—not only the "madcap" colonel himself, but a possible missing person from the Prineville area and a known native son and daughter—it is a story worth telling. Ironically, it would be called the Lookout Lynchings . . . reminiscent of the 7,000 foot flat-topped mountain which Thompson saw weekly, maybe even daily, on his jaunts from Prineville to his Willow Creek ranch.

CHAPTER 189

ALL HANGIN' IN A ROW

If a historian were to relate truthfully all the crimes, weaknesses and disorders of mankind, the reader would take the work for satire.

Pierre Boyle
French Philosopher

In order to set the stage for the approaching Lookout tragedy, it is necessary to go back a few years and revisit some earlier inhabitants of the Ochoco. In 1866, Little Rattlesnake, chief of the Pit River Shoshoni, drifted into the Ochoco Valley for a meeting with Has No Horse and Paulina. While here, during the ceremony of the Love Dance (a Shoshoni ritual as common as the Rain, Sun, War and Scalp dances) Pisha (Little Mouse), a Pit River maiden, was given in marriage to Weedzewa (Iron Mouth), a Big Lodge warrior. In keeping with Shoshoni custom, Iron Mouth went with his bride's family to the Pit River area where both he and Little Mouse fought in the Battle of the Infernal Caverns in 1867.[1] Soon afterward, Little Mouse was taken captive and confined on the Klamath Reservation where she was given the Christian name of Mary Pisha. In 1869, following Gen. Crook's defeat of Little Rattlesnake in the Battle of Devil's Garden, Iron Mouth and Little Mouse, who had escaped from the Klamath reserve, set up camp on Fall River near Fort Crook in northern California, which at the time was under the command of Capt. Henry Wagner.

Col. William Thompson of the Oregon Militia and Capt. Wagner of the 1st U.S. Cavalry had crossed swords during the Modoc campaign. Since they didn't see eye-to-eye on battle tactics, it follows that Thompson in his memoirs would depict Wagner as being quite indulgent

---

1 See *Thunder Over the Ochoco*, Vol. III, Chapter 141, "Hell's Cave."

in his appetite for sexual pleasure. Whatever, back at the Shoshoni encampment on Fall River, Iron Mouth was getting bored with inactivity. By all accounts, the Big Lodge soldier was a hurricane on the battlefield but when it came to spousal engagements he was about as impressive as a blacksmith's punctured bellows. After taking out his frustration on Little Mouse, he abandoned her and their two infant sons and rode north toward the Ochoco for a reunion with his old comrades in arms. Iron Mouth was killed on Pony Blanket's suicidal push from Silver Creek in central Oregon to the Columbia River in 1878.

Shortly after the Weedzewa family break-up, the displaced Prineville vigilante—who claimed to know—slyly noted that Capt. Wagner "began to cast eyes of favor on the comely young Indian woman," meaning Mary Pisha.[2] Thompson would then infer, that among other duties such as protecting the settlers from Shoshoni attack, Capt. Wagner was supposed to civilize the Indians. Therefore, it was only a matter of time before he carried out orders by protecting and enlightening Mary Pisha in his private quarters. This arrangement was agreeable to Mary "who preferred the favor of the white chief to that of her dusky husband."[3] Already, Thompson was laying the foundation for Mary Pisha's character assassination by implying that she left Iron Mouth instead of the other way around.

Perhaps because of his tawny girlfriend, Wagner's sentiments lay with the Snake war tribes and he was often on friendly terms with Has No Horse, even to defending his actions during the Modoc and Bannock uprisings.[4] On the other hand, he had no use for the Paiutes, specifically Sarah Winnemucca who married his second in command, Lt. Edward Bartlett, an officer Capt. Wagner especially hated. And it was Wagner who served the warrant on her brother Natchez, arrested him and delivered him to Fort Alcatraz in 1874.[5] Being a warrior himself, Wagner held

---

2   Direct quotations, unless otherwise noted, are taken from Thompson, "The Lookout Lynching," *Reminiscences of a Pioneer*, p. 178-86.

3   Prior to Thompson's banishment to northern California in the spring of 1884, he had known Capt. Henry Wagner since Wagner's arrival on the West Coast in 1867.

4   See correspondence from Capt. Henry Wagner, 1st U.S. Cavalry to Assist. Adj. Gen., March 11, 1878, Letters Received, Office of Indian Affairs, Oregon Superintendency.

5   Hopkins, *Life Among the Piutes*, pp. 200-01; Reno, *Nevada State Journal*, February 12, 1873; *Daily Alta California*, San Francisco, January 30, 1874, p. 1, col. 3.

no sympathy for Sarah's pacifist teachings or the way the majority of the Paiutes accepted them.

The captain and his Shoshoni companion had barely set up house-keeping when the War Department ordered him to take command of the desolate outpost of Fort McDermit on the Oregon-Nevada line. With the Modoc War hovering on the horizon and the Snakes ready to revolt at any moment, this was not an ideal assignment. The Indians lurking around Fort McDermit—dependent upon where they camped—were accountable to one or the other of two government agencies which seldom agreed on any issue. Under the usual arrangement, Paiutes milling around the parade ground begging for a hand-out fell under the jurisdiction of the Nevada Indian Superintendency; militant Snakes camped less than a mile to the north, backed by the Santa Rosa mountains and waiting for an opportune time to attack, were subject to the Oregon Indian Superintendency. In such an unstable environment and well aware of the Snakes unpredictable reaction to one of their own living with a white man, Capt. Henry Wagner—who honestly respected Mary Pisha—thought it prudent to leave her at Fort Crook. Mary Pisha thought otherwise. Being discarded by two men was not very comforting to her peace of mind and ultimately would fuel the gossip which dogged her for life. Wagner, doing his utmost to make certain that Mary and her children would be taken care of, won out and in so doing negotiated a unique marriage contract.

Sgt. Calvin Hall, a cavalry trooper out of Fort Harney whose term of enlistment had expired, owned a ranch on Pit River near the little town of Lookout, California, located some 56 miles south of the Oregon line and about 28 miles west of the Infernal Caverns where Mary Pisha had fought side-by-side with the dog soldiers. Trooper Hall, a trusted friend, had served under Capt. Wagner in the Shoshoni war. Now, his old commanding officer proposed a more serious assignment. If Hall would take care of Mary and tend to her needs, Wagner would give him a small portable sawmill which the government had sent to Fort Crook to cut lumber for soldier's quarters. The arrangement was agreeable to Hall so the trade was made. Thus, the woman, her children and sawmill passed to a different ownership. Hall would adopt Mary's sons, giving them the names of Frank and Jim Hall. In due time, a daughter was born to this union and she too would be called Mary.

Over the next several years, if you care to believe Thompson, Mary Pisha Hall had numerous but fleeting love affairs. Keep in mind that Thompson—like the majority of western settlers—had a very low opinion of Indians; an even lower one of white men married to Indian women; and in the minds of the residents of both Modoc County and Crook County a Shoshoni-Snake was the most despicable of all. It seems that only a select few were concerned about Mary Hall's alleged romantic escapades. This constant defamation of character had the appearance of being premeditated. Calvin Hall always spoke highly of his Indian wife and those who knew her did the same.[6]

By 1886, two years after Bud set up camp in Modoc County, he was stirring up trouble. Mary Hall again gave birth to a son whose father, according to Thompson, was a wanted man named Wilson. He would hint that Wilson was a known horse thief in central Oregon. It is certainly possible that Thompson knew Wilson. Wasco County records show that in 1877 a man named Wilson filed a homestead claim in Crooked River Valley. Sometime between that date and 1883 his name disappears from county records. Most likely—as many others did during that boisterous period—Wilson fled central Oregon before he became a "seed-pod" on a juniper tree. That aside, Mary's youngest son, soon to be known as Wilson Hall, was marked for extinction from the day of his birth for he would never live to witness his 16th birthday.

A sense of *déjà vu* was beginning to emerge in Modoc County, California . . . a parallel to Crook County, Oregon that is almost uncanny. As time wore on, the Hall boys were blamed for all the ills that befell Modoc County from vandalizing the local schoolhouse to cattle killing and the mutilation of horses. Thompson, the editor-publisher of the *Alturas Plaindealer*, was using the newspaper as a means to agitate the public. He was concerned that the Halls were "the terror of the neighborhood," but he was also confident that these conditions would not last for long. With the *Plaindealer* serving as his mouthpiece, Thompson would write, "When the law fails to protect life and property, I have always observed that men find a way to protect them." The seeds for vigilante justice were now planted. Soon they would germinate.

---

6   A search of Modoc County records would confirm this. Alturas, California, September 16, 1963.

By 1898, the Crook County range war had engulfed Lake County and was threatening to slop over into northern California. Dr. Shearer, a wealthy Modoc County stockman living close to the Oregon line would light the fuse of dissension when he hired some Klamath Indians to harvest his hay crop. According to Shearer, the Shoshoni Frank Hall had a complaint against the Klamaths and proceeded to cut their wagons and harnesses to shreds with an axe. Unfortunately for Dr. Shearer, neither he nor anyone else could prove that Frank Hall "committed the dastardly act." No problem. Being a good friend of Bud Thompson, Shearer made the newspaper editor aware of this crime and other acts of larceny which he was satisfied that "Frank Hall was guilty of performing." Here was the ammunition and Thompson was quick to fire a broadside. "I wrote," he said, "an article for my paper detailing the grievances of the people of that section and ended by predicting that, unless it was stopped, juniper trees would bear fruit." A year and a half later Thompson's prediction came true, only it was the Pit River bridge and not the juniper trees which produced "berries."

Throughout all this furor, Calvin Hall was able to keep his step sons free of the law which not only says something about his promise to Capt. Wagner but could also indicate that they were more innocent of wrongdoing than some would like to believe. Then, in 1900, a stranger arrived in the little town of Lookout some 35 miles southwest of Alturas. The rumor soon spread that he was a notorious gunman named Yantes and Thompson let everyone know that "Yantes took Mary, the Indian woman, away from old man Hall and lived with her on a ranch he had located." Naturally, Yantes added to "the boldness and reckless conduct of Frank and Jim Hall and the half-breed boy Wilson Hall." What Thompson didn't reveal was that "Mary, the Indian woman," was not Mary Pisha Hall but instead was her daughter Mary Hall Lorenz.

Following several more months of agitation things came to a boil. In May, 1901 a burglary was committed and a warrant was issued to search the Hall and Yantes homes where supposedly several of the stolen articles were found. This led to the arrest of the "entire gang" or as Thompson put it, "the two white men, the half-breed boy and the two Indians were held under guard." While waiting for the grand jury to issue an indictment, the district attorney's office instructed the special prosecutor brought in to try the case to dismiss the charge of burglary and rearrest the men for petty larceny.

During this legal maneuver, the five defendants were being held under guard in the barroom of the Lookout Hotel. When word leaked out that they would be tried on the lesser charge, the editor of the *Alturas Plaindealer* took up his pen and entered the fray. Informed sources swore that Yantes and the Halls had "made threats of dire vengeance upon those instrumental in their arrest." Obviously justice had to prevail as everyone knew that "the Indians and Yantes were desperate men, and to turn them loose would be equivalent to applying the torch to their homes, if not the knife to their throats." This essay produced the desired result. The rule of gun and rope was about to begin.

At 1:30 a.m. on the morning of May 31, 1901, masked men burst into the Lookout Hotel; took the prisoners from their guards at gunpoint; dragged them down the moonlit street behind galloping horses; and hung all five, including 15-year-old Wilson, from the railing of the Pit River bridge. The news spread like wildfire and created intense excitement from Seattle to San Diego. The major West Coast newspapers in two-column headlines told of the killing of a whole family. "An old man," wrote a reporter for the *Sacramento Union*, "his three sons and his son-in-law were ruthlessly hung for a petty crime . . . the stealing of a few straps of leather." That commentary said it all.

Northern California, painfully aware of the vigilantes reign of terror in central Oregon during the 1880's and the increasing violence of the current central Oregon range war, was quick to react. Before the Modoc County vigilantes could gain a toe-hold, special law enforcement officers were rushed into the area with the warning that should local residents cause any trouble, the California National Guard would be sent in. Judge Post, assistant attorney-general for the state of California, also arrived in Alturas to prosecute known members of the lynch mob. He was accompanied by his personal body guard, the noted gunfighter Danny Miller. This would cause Thompson to go into hysterics likening Miller (but not where he could hear) to "a rat terrier following a mastiff" while the special law enforcement personnel became "head hunters." The investigation would not go smoothly.

At least twenty unidentified men took part in the lynching but over a span of seven months, the grand jury was able to return indictments on only five suspects.[7] Most of the witnesses to the crime refused to testify even under the protection of martial law. During the long, drawn-out hearings, the three defense attorneys—G.F. Harris, E.V. Spencer and John E. Raker—took turns going to jail for contempt of court and, in a courtroom brawl, Miller drew his .44 Colt and attempted to shoot lawyer Raker. At another point during the hearings, Miller pistol-whipped a young man named Russell whose brother operated the now infamous Lookout Hotel where the mob violence took place. Before this legal farce was over the tax payers of Modoc County would hand over nearly $40,000 in entertainment fees.

Finally on January 4, 1902, Mary Lorenz—at the risk of her own life—signed a warrant for the arrest of 15 men involved in the May lynching of her father, brothers and common-law husband. Within six days, these gentlemen were lodged in the county jail and charged with five separate counts of murder. Defenders of the accused were quick to blame the arrests on alleged fraudulent declarations of guilt made by John Hutton and Claude Morris. Their claim was that detectives hired by the state forced Hutton to turn state's evidence on the promise of a lesser charge than murder in the first degree; and that they plied young Morris with whiskey until he got so drunk he unknowingly signed an affidavit of guilt. Then, according to local sympathizers, the lawmen threatened Morris with perjury if he recanted his confession. On this assumption, the Lookout hangmen went to trial.

Old Mary Pisha was not allowed to testify because she undoubtedly would be narrow-minded in her interpretation of legal proceedings. That said, the celebrated trial began. With little deliberation, the Modoc County jury returned a verdict of "not guilty" for all who were charged with murder and that same day, the prisoners were quietly discharged from jail two and three at a time. One jury member would admit that the character of the prosecution's witnesses was enough to sway their votes in favor of the lynch mob. After all, these testifiers were nothing more than "Indians, half-breeds and disreputable characters of every shade and degree."

---

7   Those arraigned were: R.E. Leventon, Isom Eades, James Brown, John Hutton and Claude Morris. Thompson, *Reminiscences of a Pioneer*, pp. 182, 184.

These "creatures," as the *Alturas Plaindealer* would call them, may have been disreputable and they may have been Shoshoni but they weren't stupid. By the next morning following the not-guilty verdict, all of the state's witnesses had left the county. According to Thompson, "during the night they fled and scattered like a covey of quail." Being sensible people, they got out of Modoc County before they too became decoration on the Pit River bridge. All that remained was Attorney-General Post and his gunman Danny Miller. After a leisurely breakfast, they boarded the Sacramento stage "and were seen no more."

Thus ended the tragedy of the Lookout Lynchings. Thompson would express sorrow. "It [the trial] accomplished nothing save to blacken the character of our citizens and cause the outside world to look upon us as outlaws and desperadoes." Somewhere in that observation is a profound truth which seems to have eluded the colonel. In 1912, he would question if those "who now possess this land of plenty ever give a thought for those who conquered the wilderness and made it a fit and safe abode for the millions of civilized men and women who now enjoy its blessings." Fortunately for the empire builders, they seldom do.

The lawless movement south of the Oregon border—like its Crook County predecessor—was a long time in dying. Ninety-three years after the infamous Pit River bridge lynching, enlightened residents of Alturas—when told an undesirable citizen was moving into their community—warned the state of California that vigilante justice was "alive and well" in Modoc County.[8] And thus time marches on.

8   Jeff Bernard, Associated Press Staff Writer, *The Bulletin*, Bend, Oregon, March 18, 1994.

CHAPTER 190

A LULL BETWEEN STORMS

If they just went straight they might go far;
They are strong and brave and true;
But they're always tired of the things that are,
And they want the strange and new.

Robert W. Service
The Men That Don't Fit In

About the time Joe Blakely was inviting Bud Thompson to vacate the country, Chester A. Arthur, described as a "dignified man with clean-shaven chin and side-whiskers who looked like a President," decided to visit the Shoshoni on the Wind River Reserve. Prior to President Arthur's visitation, President Grant—recognizing Gourd Rattler's contribution to Manifest Destiny—presented him with a silver mounted saddle in appreciation for his loyalty to the cause. It was at the presentation ceremony that the old chief made what was claimed to be his most famous statement:

> Do a kindness to a Frenchman [white man], he feels it in
> his head and his tongue speaks; do a kindness to an Indian,
> he feels it in his heart. The heart has no tongue.[1]

When President Arthur arrived on the reservation in 1883, Gourd Rattler exhibited the same stubbornness as Has No Horse when it came to social contact with the White Father. Upon that occasion he refused to go with other Shoshoni leaders to greet the President. Instead, dressed in his best attire, Gourd Rattler stayed in his lodge and waited for Arthur to call upon him . . . which the twenty-first president of the United States did.

---

1   Trenholm and Carley, *The Shoshoni*, p. 258.

Back on the home front, as the citizens of Crook County settled down to some quiet living other events were taking place. Before the summer of 1884 had passed, they would be clamoring for the latest best-seller, *Huckleberry Finn,* written by their old Nevada neighbor, Mark Twain. Over in the backwoods of Missouri, the Trumans were celebrating the birth of a son, Harry S., a backwoods urchin who no one suspected—least of all old squire Truman—would become the thirty-third president of the United States.

By fall, Crook County was trailing thousands of cattle into Montana replacing the buffalo and fortunes were being made. On the northwest corner of Third and Main, the stage station was being remodeled into the Prineville Hotel under the managership of Perry Poindexter who in 1888 opened a first-class restaurant and would eventually build his own hotel.

The Poindexter Restaurant Menu

BREAKFAST AND SUPPER

Porterhouse steak	20¢	Pig's head	10¢
Sirloin steak	15¢	Calf's head, pickle sauce	10¢
Beefsteak, Spanish style	10¢	Bass, baked or fried	10¢
Hamburger beefsteak	10¢	Fried Smelts	10¢
Roast Mutton, mint sauce	10¢	Oyster stew	20¢
Pig's feet, sautéed	10¢		

3 eggs, fried, boiled or scrambled .... 15¢

Hot cakes, Flannel cakes and Corn batter .... 5¢

DINNER

Chicken soup	5¢	Potato soup	5¢

THE DAILY SPECIAL

Assorted cold meats	15¢	Veal Chops in batter	10¢.

All 15 cent orders and upwards will be served with Butter free of charge.
Bread and Potatoes with Meats and Fish free of charge.

Charlie Maling, foreseeing a construction boom, built a shingle mill (the first in Crook County) on McKay Creek in 1885 and did a thriving business. Charlie Solomon started a wagon shop to keep up with the demand for new vehicles. Charlie Pett, tired of working in the flour mill, sold his interest to Dave Stewart and went to mining on Scissors Creek. Another split came between Henry Cleek and Sam Smith. Smith gave up his interest in the Silver Dollar and joined forces with Henry Burmeister in the Stockman's Exchange. Mitchell, also on the move, saw the construction of a new refreshment parlor. In the summer of 1885, Robert and Katie Misener opened the Water Spout Saloon, running stiff competition to Bill Cranston's den of impropriety.

Up in Umatilla County a couple of old Prineville cronies were having a spirited reunion. Hank Vaughan staggered into the Weston Dance Hall and proceeded to dispense justice Ochoco style. City Marshall Barney Prine could foresee that if someone didn't look out for the best interests of the community there was going to be hell to pay. So, being a big man with the strength of a blacksmith, Barney—taking off his own pistol for safety's sake—took Hank's gun and wouldn't give it back until he went home and sobered up. Knowing his limitations, Hank obeyed and another crisis was averted.

During this burst of activity, huge fires—sparked by vigorous land clearing operations—were raging from Lakeview to Klamath Falls and filling the country from the Deschutes to the John Day with smoke and competing with Krakatoa's glorious sunrises. In the upper Ochoco Valley a swarm of crickets were devastating the crops. En route to the Mayflower Mines, Til Glaze and family passed through an army of crickets that covered the landscape from hillside to hillside. Anne Glaze would recall that "the wagon left its tracks outlined in the black horde."[2]

On Big Summit Prairie another plague was taking over. While the white folks were preoccupied with annihilating each other during the first half of the decade, Has No Horse and a remnant of his tribe quietly took up residence on the south side of Big Summit Prairie. The big cattle and sheep outfits had been grazing the prairie since the latter 1870's but it wasn't until the spring of 1885 that people became a problem perhaps due to a recent act of Congress.

A year after the fact in the attempt to control the activities of cattlemen determined to keep "nesters" off the land, Congress by the Act of February 25, 1885, make it unlawful to use any force, threats or

2   Anne Glaze, *Crook County News*, August 4, 1939, p. 4.

intimidations against settlers on the public domain. The act also declared it illegal to fence areas of the public domain in order to prevent or obstruct settlement.

That year saw the Elliott, Merritt, Lowery, Nelson, Province, O'Kelly, Puett and Mulvahill families arrive; along with bachelors Anderson, Connell, Childers, Dudley, Powell and Schmidt.[3] Of this latter group William John Schmidt was the most colorful.

Best known as "Summit Prairie" Schmidt, he had a claim in the upper Ochoco Valley between what is now the Ontko Ranch and Ochoco Ranger Station where he proudly owned one horse and two cows. Laying claim to another 1,600 acres in the prairie, he worked this modest herd into forty horses and 350 cows. On marrying Sarah Lowery Swift, he became determined to build a fancier house than that of his brother-in-law Ed Merritt which would take some doing. Merritt's large two-story house with double inside stairways and upstairs dance hall rather overwhelmed neighbor Has No Horse's willow-woven big lodge.

Undaunted, Summit Prairie Schmidt laid to. For a man who'd parlayed one horse and two cows into a fortune and who, by 1911, would drive a sparkling new Cadillac up Canyon Creek into the prairie, it was all in a day's work. When finished, Sarah's wedding present—a two-story structure with winding staircase and interior finished in mahogany wainscoting—was the showplace of the high country. It even put Dick Graham's lodge and summer retreat for the townsfolk to shame. Besides that, all this construction kept Bill Childers—who erected the first sawmill in Big Summit Prairie—in business and seemed to have little effect on the pride of Jim Anderson, who covered the exterior of his cabin with flattened five gallon cans.

With all this activity, especially the begetting of children, it soon became necessary to construct a school house. Miss Ella Katherine Miller, daughter of the original owner of the Keystone Ranch and a young lady who called Joaquin Miller "Uncle," was chosen for the job of school teacher.

---

3   First of the Big Summit Prairie settlers to suffer a fatality was Rufus (Sam) Nelson who also owned a ranch two miles southwest of Mitchell. Nelson was killed on a horse drive to Nebraska in 1889.

Snow-bound for half of the year, the locals had to provide their own entertainment. John Elliott's thirteen-year-old daughter, Lydia, would write:

> The snow in winter was quite deep and we had fun sleigh riding to one another's houses enjoying singing games and feeds. One time I rode to the top of Round Mountain and had a picnic lunch on top . . . saw lots of game. There were bears, deer, foxes, grouse, native pheasants, sage hens and hundreds of cranes.

> The Indians would camp up there in the spring and hunt deer and the squaws would dig camas, a small bulb that grew plentifully there. They would cook it, then dry it and grind it on rocks, then make cakes and bake them on hot rocks—that was most of their bread.[4]

It is obvious from Lydia's notes that for a pleasant change, the Ochoco settlers and the Shoshoni were existing in harmony. In that high mountain solitude cooperation was the greater part of survival and both factions were pleasantly surprised. This mutual trust would not be shattered until the 1890's and then through no fault of either neighbor.

In June 1885, at the start of the Summit Prairie invasion, things were made lively in Prineville with the reappearance of the *Ochoco Review*. This time under the editorial pen of George Barnes and the investigative reporting of John Douthit. Advertised as bright and breezy, it started out as a folio—a single sheet of folded paper—and blossomed into a quarto in 1887 thus doubling its original size.

It appears that Editor Barnes was out to deal his old adversaries some light-hearted misery for the August 1 issue of the *Ochoco Review* was loaded with interesting tidbits of information. Following are a few examples of Douthit's fact-finding accounts.

> James Blakely was driving around town one day this week with lace curtains on his buggy. [For this foolishness the shocked citizens of Crook County voted the sheriff out of office.]

---

4   Lydia Elliott O'Kelly. John O'Kelly, her son, shared this with the author, June 1973.

The local bankers, Mr. Howard and Mr. Baldwin, also received their share of abuse. According to Editor Barnes:

> Joe Howard exhausted all his skill as a salesman trying to sell a California fat man a bottle of anti-fat. The Californian said if Joe and Tom Baldwin's forms were an example of what the medicine would do for a man he was afraid to try it.

Til Glaze's brother didn't escape unscathed either. *The Ochoco Review* would dutifully report:

> Joe Glaze beat up on a guy and was hauled into court. The case of the state vs. Glaze was a failure. Joe didn't assault or batter to the violation of any laws. A jury decided it was no crime to hit a man when he connects disagreeable adjectives with your name.

The *Review* would also note that Billy Todd "knows where to get a good bargain." It seems that Todd rode all the way over from Mitchell to Prineville just to buy six bits worth of sugar. That probably wasn't all that he came for. Henry Burmeister and Sam Smith had just installed new barroom fixtures and the Exchange was being advertised as the finest saloon in eastern Oregon. Because of this, according to Barnes, "our boys have caught on to the Colorado style of asking a friend to drink. Instead of saying 'let's smile' they say 'let's irrigate.'"

However, Editor Barnes failed to see the humor when Taylor Hill, a Kentucky publisher, subscribed to the *Ochoco Review* because he "had a need for some wrapping paper."

By the end of August, the *Review* would report: "John Howard, 19-year-old son of General O.O. Howard, suicided with a pistol in Yellowstone Park one day last week. It was said a love affair was the cause of the act." It would also document a non-love affair.

About a week after young Howard's mishap, Ed Evans (proprietor of the Ochoco Brewery) got into an argument with ex-vigilante Bill Brown and ordered him to get out of town. Brown left but about eight o'clock that evening, after tipping a few at the Exchange, he wandered back into the brewery. Evans, also under the influence, lunged behind the bar, grabbed a sawed-off 10 gauge shotgun and attempted to blast Brown into the Ochoco River. Fortunately a more sober patron knocked the barrel aside and the blast missed Brown's head and gave the horse king another day in the sun.[5]

Then came the brutal winter of 1885-86, followed by a summer drought and a second devastating winter. Throughout the West stockmen reaped their just reward as millions of cattle and sheep perished. This weather, coupled with overgrazing in the 1870s and early 1880s, crippled the livestock industry for the next thirty years and precipitated the sheep and cattle wars.

As New Year 1886 charged in on the heels of a howling blizzard, Portland bragged that it had 144 saloons and all were doing a booming business. This gave Prineville pause for thought and within eighteen months she too would provide more liquor establishments for her thirsty offspring. Under Sheriff Blakely's protective gun prospective land-owners were pouring in by the droves from the Willamette Valley. In fact so much traffic was flowing over the Santiam Trail from Eugene, Salem, Albany and Corvallis that Robert and James Smith (grandsons of Captain John Smith, the Indian agent) took up a claim on Squaw Creek and constructed a general store, boarding house and livery stable. This was the founding of the town of Sisters.

Once again county elections were hovering on the horizon. Two years of peace and prosperity had brought the usual complacency. On June 7, 1886, Crook voted out all the county officials who had effected this pleasant change. It now had John Newton "Newt" Williamson with ranches strung from the upper Ochoco to Bear Creek Butte and key player in "the looters of the public domain" for sheriff; George Barnes who took an unholy interest in circuit court activities for district attorney; W.S.A. (Bill) Johns, a slick local attorney for county judge; and Linn Woods of unknown credentials for county coroner. But that wasn't all that Crook County did. Along with the rest of the state electorate, they voted in Oregon's most liberal governor, Sylvester Pennoyer, a radical Democrat who credited his strong victory on a stand against Chinese labor. The citizens of Crook County would soon regret this choice when one of Pennoyer's first acts in office was to attempt to establish a state income

---

5   *Ochoco Review*, September 5, 1885.

tax on all incomes over $1,000. Not a pleasant outlook for the richest county in the state.

While Oregon's male population was exercising their right to vote, the army—goaded by complaints from concerned citizens—was busy rounding up stray Shoshoni. Caught in the net was the old Lohim warrior Yellow Jacket and some Tussawehee refugees belonging to Has No Horse's once powerful tribe. These unfortunate souls were herded into northern Nevada and confined on the Western Shoshoni Reserve in Duck Valley.[6] With the exception of Has No Horse and his few companions hidden on Big Summit Prairie, the Ochoco was now purged of its native inhabitants.

Within a year of his election defeat, Blakely sold his ranch and by 1888 had moved to Wallowa County where he established a 2,000 acre spread and went into cattle ranching on a large scale. In 1902 he was elected sheriff of Wallowa County. Jim celebrated his 100th birthday on July 31, 1952. Six months later, he died at his daughter's home at College Place, Washington on January 24, 1953 and was buried at Enterprise, Oregon.[7]

Jim Blakely made his last appearance as grand marshall of the Crooked River Roundup in August 1951. When the 1953 Crooked River Roundup was held, Blakely's favorite Palomino was led at the head of the parade with an empty saddle in tribute to the man who tamed the Crook County vigilantes.

As soon as Blakely turned in his badge, the Oregon City stage en route from Canyon City to the Willamette Valley was held-up at the Union Creek Crossing in the rugged Blue Mountains of Grant County. The outlaws made off with the Wells Fargo express box containing $1,000 in gold. This was just the first in a series of robberies that were to follow.[8]

About the time Blakely arrived in Wallowa County in 1888, another significant event was to take place north of the Columbia River.

---

6   By the early 1960s, descendants of this group made up about 50% of the Western Shoshoni Reservation's population of 740. (Harris, "The White Knife Shoshoni of Nevada," *Acculturation in Seven American Indian Tribes*, p. 105; Trenholm and Carley, *The Shoshoni*, p. 267.

7   *Oregon Journal*, January 24, 1953. Every newspaper in the Pacific Northwest published his obituary.

8   "Centennial Countdown," the *Oregon Journal*, April 24, 1959.

Hank Vaughan had ridden up to Ellensburg, Washington on a business deal with Ben Snipes, The Dalles banker and Wasco County cattle king. Whatever this meeting entailed is unknown but a short time later Hank was indirectly involved in a matter which eventually ruined Snipes financially. During this undisclosed visit with Snipes, Vaughan came face to face with Charlie Long . . . their first encounter since the 1882 shoot-out in Prineville. As a reminder of that confrontation Vaughan had a permanent scar on his forehead near the hairline and a bullet lodged next to his spine while Long had a useless left arm.

The story circulating around Prineville was that Charlie Long was dead. It was believed that shortly after he arrived in Walla Walla Long kept bullying George Smith, Jr. (known as the Okanogan Kid) until the young rancher was convinced that his life was in real danger. Getting a revolver, Smith waited for an opportunity to waylay the notorious gun-man. It came in late March 1883. As Long came strolling down the street, the Kid hid behind a half-open door. As Charlie walked by, Smith stepped out behind him and blasted Charlie in the back of the head killing him instantly.[9] Obviously this wasn't true. What apparently happened was that young Smith made Long a partner in his ranch operation in an effort to protect his own neck. Long may have forced Smith into doing this.

Long and James "Popcorn Jimmy" Muldowdey, a faro dealer, were sitting in the dining room of the Oriental Hotel when Hank and Dave Correl, a professional gambler and gunman, walked in. Hank and Dave placed their hats on a rack and as Vaughan turned around looking for a vacant table his eyes met those of Long. At this moment other hotel guests hurriedly got out of harm's way. After starring at each other for the better part of a minute Long greeted Vaughan and at the same time Hank advanced toward Charlie's table and extended his hand apparently willing to let the past be forgotten. Charlie accepted his hand and the two with their friends sat at the same table and ate a hearty meal. An uninformed observer would have thought them to be old friends. Both men were in town for several days and while they didn't associate with each other neither did they start a gunfight.[10]

---

9   Interview with Richard Long on July 3, 1959. Long, a direct descendent of Charlie, honestly believed this is what happened and basically he was correct. Smith did kill Long but at a much later date and it wasn't with a gun.

10   Nash Brown interview, *Wenatchee Daily World*, Wenatchee, Washington, December 19, 1922.

Back in central Oregon Fred Goulet, inspired by a display of electric arc street lamps he saw at Astoria in 1885, decided to illuminate the lower Ochoco Valley. With this in mind, Goulet had a small dynamo shipped into Prineville from Chicago and opened the Electric Saloon on August 7, 1886. This glaring display would cause a temporary trade decline in the old rough and tumble establishments. Not to be outdone, Bill Pollard opened the Pastime Saloon and by July 30, 1887, Ed White (captain in the 1st Oregon Infantry) would be advertising his new Deer Horn Saloon with the catchy phrase of "Come Early, Come Late, Come Often."

During Prineville's saloon building craze, Katrina Driggs was upholding her end for adverse publicity. When Charlie Long skipped town in 1883, Irish Kate went with him to Walla Walla and eventually ended up in a Spokane sporting house. While there she made an unfavorable impression on the city fathers. It seems that Kate burned down "the entire city of Spokane" or at least that's the way a breathless reporter for the *Seattle Post-Intelligencer* would put it. According to him it all began on a Sunday afternoon on August 4, 1889.

Kate, who had been drinking in Sam Wolfe's Saloon, went up to her room to fix her hair. She was heating a curling iron in the glass chimney of a kerosene lamp when a drunk wandered in wanting to purchase her services. He was in the mood to play but Katrina wasn't and when she said "no" they began to scuffle. In the ensuing wrestling match the lamp was knocked over and started a fire. An open window provided a good draft and some lace curtains sped the growing fire on its way. Before the flames were extinguished almost all of the downtown area of Spokane lay in smoldering ruins. Thus goes the life of a working girl.

However, the indiscretions of a fallen Prineville dove wasn't the only newsworthy topic to excite the citizens of Prine's village. The most disconcerting was when Has No Horse and his warriors periodically set up camp within sight of Prineville's city limits. The present site of Les Schwab's tire shop on East Third Street was known as Indian Town. On July 3, 1886, the *Ochoco Review* would report a warm-up to the July 4th activities. "Today, the Indians experienced one of their old tribal practices of killing one of their doctors who failed to cure a patient. The Indians pronounced it a just act as they believe an unsuccessful doctor is not fit

122

to live. This, we believe, is the fifth medicine man they have killed within the last five years." This news item would indicate that Has No Horse—in open defiance to the vigilantes—had been using this campsite on the Ochoco River since 1881.

By 1887, the profit-making outlook for the livestock, mining and timber industries of central Oregon was looking bleak. However, in a roundabout way Congress was trying to make the situation appear a little brighter at the expense of reservation Indians. The 1887 General Allotment Act would reduce tribal lands by granting 40 acre tracts to individual Indians who chose to accept them but there was a downside to this generosity. If they didn't do so, the remaining tribal lands not applied for would either be opened to white settlement under the land laws . . . or sold to the highest bidder. This was supposed to benefit the tribes. That same year saw Gov. Pennoyer create the first government board to control business and with his ambitious help, the big labor unions were gaining a foothold in Oregon and worker strikes were becoming common. When President Grover Cleveland complained of Pennoyer's high-handed intervention in private affairs, the governor sarcastically replied, "If the President will attend to his business, I will attend to mine."

During this political harangue the Kam Wah Chung Trading Company owned by Ing "Doc" Hay and Lung On set up headquarters at John Day to serve the Chinese miners of the eastern Oregon gold fields as a mercantile and medical clinic for herbal remedies.[11] It would also take on the duties of a religious and social gathering place. At the same time the Kam Wah Chung Trading Company was being organized, hundreds of workers—many of them Chinese immigrants—toiled high in the Cascades on one of the most ambitions projects in state history—undoubtedly with the blessings of Gov. Pennoyer.

In February 1887 as the Oregon Short Line puffed across the Northern Blues manned by a work engine called "The Shoshoni," iron tracks were inching ever closer toward the Queen of Oregon cow towns. The Oregon Pacific Railroad founded in 1880 had made its start at

---

11   As a young lad, the author was personally acquainted with Doc Hay who by the 1930's was blind. His medical concoctions were mighty potent smelling but they were very effective. For more on this phase of eastern Oregon history see *A View of Gold Mountain: Letters From the Kam Wah Chung Trading Company*, offered through the Oregon Council For the Humanities, Portland, Oregon.

Yaquina Bay on Oregon's rugged coast intending to knife through the heart of central Oregon's cattle country in its attempt to connect with Union Pacific lines at Boise City, Idaho some 600 miles to the east. If successful, the company would give Oregon its first cross-state rail link. Iron horses snorting across the range were not something eastern Oregon ranchers wanted or needed to round up livestock and herd them to market . . . and the stockmen had deeper purses than either the mining or timber interests. As the rails got dangerously close to Crook County's western border, investment money suddenly dried up. Col. T. Egenton Hogg—founder and promoter of the Oregon Pacific Railroad—for lack of financial support was forced into bankruptcy. Once again plans to bisect the Ochoco with bands of steel were thwarted.

However, the Oregon Pacific Railroad—along with the Mayflower Mining Company—introduced a Chinese population to Crook County. Not nearly as many as lived in the John Day country but enough to leave their imprint on central Oregon history. The forerunners of these Oriental pioneers were the Doon brothers, Ah and Moy, who came to the United States from China and landed in Prineville at the height of the great Snake uprising. Apparently they were aware of the dog soldier's penchant for Chinese scalps. Having no desire to run the Shoshoni gauntlet to Canyon City and perhaps encouraged by a fellow countryman, Ng Ah Tye who had struck it rich in the Scissors Creek gold fields, the Doons settled in Prineville working as house boys and cooks. At the time, Ng Ah Tye—called by the townsfolk Mr. N.A. Tye—was operating a gift shop on Main and Third.

By the depression year of 1887, the Doon brothers had saved enough money from their meager earnings to open a small restaurant next door to the popular Electric Saloon. At first mistrusted by the citizens, they soon gained a reputation for being thrifty, industrious and trustworthy. So much so that in 1889 when O.C. Culver gave up the lease on the Jackson House Hotel—owned by Benjamin Allen, wealthy stockman and president of the First National Bank—Allen leased it to Ah and Moy Doon. Although many citizens respected the Chinese businessmen it soon became obvious that others strongly resented their success believing that Tye and the Doons should be kept in a lowly position because of their race. This resentment came to a head when it was made public that Ah Doon planned to open a general merchandise store in direct competition with Hahn & Fried who were financially backed by a large Portland firm. Vigilante justice would be swift in coming to the "heathen chinee."

Shortly before daylight on a raw winter morning in December 1892—a favorite month for vigilante activity—the Prineville stage started on the first leg of its journey to The Dalles City some 120 miles to the north. Not wishing to disturb the sleepy passengers already on board, Ah Doon, carrying a large sum of money, climbed up to the high seat beside the driver to begin a long business trip to San Francisco. The first scheduled stop on The Dalles City run was the Hay Creek Headquarters Ranch north of Grizzly Mountain where breakfast would be served. Both men were looking forward to that pleasant interlude on what promised to be a disagreeable trip weather-wise.

About three miles west of town near the old army post of Camp Steele, the stage had to ford McKay Creek and then climb a short hill. Slowed by the creek crossing and half-frozen mud, the stage was barely moving when it reached the top of the incline. Out of the gloom packing all of the force of a dynamite blast in the Mayflower tunnel came the harsh command: "Hands up!" Jerking his team to a stop, the driver jammed on the brakes, peered through the gloom to see who was giving the order, raised his hands and yelled, "Take it easy, boys, the strong box is empty!"

Suddenly, a tall, thin masked man flanked by two masked horsemen emerged from the darkness with six-guns pointed at the driver and his passenger. In a quiet voice, the apparent leader replied, "We don't want your damn money. We're after the slant-eyed chink." The lanky outlaw then rode up to the coach, stepped from his stirrups to the wheel hub, then to the wheel rim and roughly grabbed Ah Doon, throwing him to the ground. Ah Doon, struggling, kicking and yelling landed in the arms of the other two men who had dismounted. As they held him in a death grip, the big man unbuttoned the squirming victim's overcoat and removed a scarf from around Ah Doon's head uncovering his long, glossy queue coiled on top of his head . . . the highly prized war trophy of a Snake warrior.

Obviously the men knew—as did the dog soldiers—that a Chinese man's pendent braid of hair on the back of his head was sacred to him and the worst thing that could happen, short of death, was to lose his queue. While his tormentors held him, their leader pulled Ah Doon's braided hair to its full length and committed the ultimate indignity to the helpless little man. With a razor-sharp skinning knife, he severed Ah Doon's queue at the scalp. That done, he jerked the pitiful fellow's fancy silk shirt from his trousers, held it taught and slit it into ribbons. For some unknown reason, the supposed road agent made no effort to search Ah Doon or take his money. Not surprisingly, the stagecoach occupants were as quiet as snowflakes falling on a mountainside during this operation.

After slicing Ah Doon's shirt to shreds, the knife wielder drew the sharp blade lightly across the Chinaman's throat and warned: "Don't come back to Prineville. If you do, the next time it will be your head that's cut off!"[12] The masked men then mounted and galloped away. It was never known who committed this brutal act but it was believed that the tall man who did the talking was a stranger while the two silent men were local citizens who were afraid their voices would be recognized. This most likely was a true assumption.

If nothing else can be said for Mr. Doon, he was a man of rare courage. Continuing on to San Francisco, he ordered supplies for the Chinese mercantile store and—in spite of his fear and grief at the loss of his dignity—returned to Prineville. When the business opened, Ng Ah Tye was hired as store manager. Since most of Prineville's citizens were offended by the cowardly treatment suffered by the harmless little man, the Doon brothers fared well in their new venture.[13]

Even so, there were still those who thought it quite hilarious to heckle the gentleman from the Orient. Ng Ah Tye would even the score with one wealthy stockman who took great delight in selecting a 10¢ item and then handing him a $100 bill in payment. One day Tye accepted the bill, went to the back room and returned with the change . . . all in silver dollars! By the time said rancher loaded a couple of canvas bags full of silver on his horse, he didn't think it was so funny.[14]

---

12 The scene of Ah Doon's tragedy—the low hill just north of Pine Products on Lamonta Road—was for many years known to local residents as "Doon Hill."

13 After spending many years in Prineville, Ah Doon and Moy Doon returned to China. An occasional letter to Prineville friends indicated that they were prospering in China also. Some of the local people who knew them well were Millard and Berniece Elkins, Rhonda Dake, Warren Glaze and Dolly Hodges Fessler.

14 As remembered by Rhonda (Hoover) Dake, who was the Crook County Pioneer Queen in 1980.

However Ng Ah Tye and Ah Doon fared much better than some of their countrymen who were searching for gold in a remote eastern Oregon canyon and whose fate the citizens of Wallowa County were able to keep secret for 108 years. In the spring of 1887, Chea Po, with a group of Chinese laborers, established a mining camp for the Sam Yup Company in Hells Canyon. In late May 1887 near the mouth of the Imnaha River at least 31 Chinese prospectors were ambushed and killed by a gang of horse thieves aided by local ranch hands and a 15-year-old schoolboy.[15]

Supposedly in an attempt to rent a boat from the Chinese to ferry some stolen livestock across the Snake River to Idaho (with robbery in mind), these men opened fire with high-powered rifles on ten unarmed miners. The shooting continued all afternoon until the killers ran out of ammunition. During the Deep Creek slaughter one wounded miner was beaten to death with rocks.[16] This blood-bath continued into the following day. Eight other Chinese who happened along by boat were killed In Robinson Gulch and thirteen men were shot at the nearby Dug Bar Camp. Even though the Chinese didn't speak English it appeared that some of the wounded were tortured in an effort to make them disclose where their gold was hidden. The horribly mutilated bodies were then dumped into the Snake River where they washed ashore as far away as Lewiston, Idaho some 60 miles downstream and Penawawa, Washington a hundred miles downstream. All had been shot; some bodies had axe wounds; and one corpse was found with a severed head and an arm wrapped in a coat tied to his belt.

As one historian would observe: "The brutality of the Snake River atrocity was probably unexcelled whether by whites or Indians in all the anti-Chinese violence of the American West." He was wrong. On May 19, 1866, the Snake war chief Paulina and his dog soldiers—doing their share to eliminate the "yellow peril"—attacked and killed 150 Chinese

---

15 Accounts vary on the number of dead but records found in the Wallowa County courthouse by David H. Stratton, a retired Washington State University professor, list 31 dead in diplomatic exchanges between the U.S. State Department and the Chinese government.

16 This was determined by a special agent of the Chinese Consulate in San Francisco who was sent to Lewiston, Idaho to investigate the crime in 1887. Those killed at the Deep Creek camp were: Ah Jim, Ye Lee, Wy See, Hop Sing, Hea Lee, Sing Heim, Heap Gee, Lee Bate, Hcim Lim and Hee Yee.

laborers en route to the silver mines in Idaho surpassing the Hells Canyon death toll by 119 souls.[17]

Like many events in eastern Oregon history the Hells Canyon slaughter was kept from the public view. As David Stratton (who did extensive research on the subject) would note it didn't show up in Oregon history books; there's no historical plaque where the murders occurred; the Oregon Historical Society *Quarterly* hasn't published an article on it; and *The Oregonian* never had a full story although it did print a partial account in 1888.[18] Obviously someone alerted the Chinese Consulate in San Francisco within weeks—perhaps even days—of the Wallowa County murders and a safe bet is that it was the Kam Wah Chung Trading Company headquartered in John Day, Oregon no more than 150 miles from the scene of the crime. Meanwhile the citizens of Wallowa County could see no reason to pursue this unfortunate incident any further.

In 1887 as special agents stalked the streets of Lewiston, Idaho; as Chinese merchants took Prineville, Oregon by storm; as President Cleveland and Governor Pennoyer went after each other's political throats with intent to destroy; and as the Oregon Pacific Railroad took to the Cascade crest like a wind-broken logging horse, Sid Stearns decided to move ranching operations from the upper Deschutes to the Crooked River. Bear in mind that less than four years had elapsed since Stearns had been placed on the vigilantes' endangered list. Leaving nothing to luck, Stearns would cover his back quite adequately. Joining forces with the powerful Prineville financiers Joe Howard and Tom Baldwin, he started a large cattle operation with headquarters on Crooked River some four miles south of town.

. Life being somewhat lonely in Crooked River canyon, Stearns headed over the Cascades and on November 15, 1887 married Frances Day. The honeymoon trip back to the ranch was not the most ideal. Just short of the Warm Springs Agency it got so cold that it snapped the wagon axle. The new bride had to stay with "Mrs. Nigger Brown who was a beautiful Spanish girl" until the wagon could be repaired. Nigger Brown, whom she never got to meet, worked for Howard, Baldwin and Stearns

---

17 For a full account of this slaughter see *Thunder Over the Ochoco*, Vol. III, p. 315.

18 In an article dated September 3, 1888, *The Oregonian* states that "the killers got some gold probably worth from one to two thousand dollars." Later estimates moved the total up to as much as $50,000. Most likely somewhere in between these two estimates is the correct amount.

on the construction of Stearns' dam on Crooked River. No dummy, Sid was smart enough to take his bride to the impressive Farewell Bend ranch first but the day for introduction to Crooked River was fast approaching.

Full of high expectations at being the head mistress of a cattle empire, Frances would lament, "I will never forget the first time I went to look at the Crooked River ranch. I told Sid he'd have to hog-tie me to take me to such a God-forsaken place where the sun never shone except at noon and full of rattlesnakes and coyote dens in the rimrocks." Frances Stearns was to spend the next fifty years of her life there and raise a family of eight children.[19]

Fannie was also afraid of Indian attack and for good cause. Only four months before her wedding, a band of Utes under Colorow—the 300-pound Comanche friend of Has No Horse—were moving through Colorado when on August 9, 1887, game warden Joseph E. Burgett, backed by a posse, attempted to arrest the Indians on the charge of violating Colorado game laws. It seemed that the Utes were not getting their meat in the proper season. They resisted and three Indians were shot. Burgett's posse then retreated and joined forces with a second posse led by Sheriff James C. Kendall who was trying to serve civil warrants on two of Colorow's warriors wanted for horse stealing. To Colorow, the serving of a warrant was the same as a declaration of war.

The governor of Colorado petitioned Gen. Crook for federal troops—a request Crook refused to honor. The outcome being that a troop of Colorado State Militia joined Burgett and Kendall and the fight was on, resulting in the death of three soldiers. According to Gen. Reardon of the militia fifteen Ute warriors were killed or wounded, 300 to 400 horses and 2,500 sheep and goats confiscated. U.S. troops would report that the militia killed four Indians, two of whom were girls and one, a small boy.[20]

This action would not improve domestic relations with Prineville's Big Summit Prairie neighbors. Upon receipt of this latest disruption in Shoshoni affairs, Has No Horse became highly agitated

---

19 Frances E. Stearns, "Indians and Rattlesnakes are Feared by Pioneer Woman," *Crook County News*, August 4, 1939.

20 *Colorado Governor's 1887 Report of the Ute Difficulties*, p. 61; *Secretary of War Annual Report 1888*, pp. 171-72.

which in turn made Crook County occupants rather uneasy. Prudently both sides held their peace.

Six weeks before this renewed Indian excitement, George Barnes bought out the *Prineville News* in June 1887 and effectively put it out of business. While this penny-ante transaction was taking place a high-stake game was in progress. Tom Baldwin, backed by state Senator Sol Hirsch of Multnomah County and Ike Fleichman, a wealthy Portland merchant, organized the First National Bank of Prineville with $50,000 in capital assets.[21] The bank soon ended up under the control of Tom and Harold Baldwin.

With this transfusion of working capital, Sheriff Williamson petitioned the County Court for a new house of detention. They listened. On September 8, 1887, a contract was entered between the Crook County Court and the Pauley Jail Building & Manufacturing Company of Portland to construct a county prison for the sum of $4,200. The contractor moved swiftly and by November 17, the new guardhouse was completed, accepted, paid for and awaiting occupants . . . which were not long in arriving.

While bids for the new jail were being let in September, Dr. Cass Cline, Prineville's first dentist, wandered into town. Since he only got 50¢ a tooth for extraction, he soon began supplementing his dental practice with horse-shoeing. That didn't pay to well either, so he fitted up a wagon with his dental equipment and, together with his family, called on the outlying ranchers to care for their dental needs.

A horse shoeing dentist was not the only oddity to arrive in Prineville in 1887. Henry George came out of the East preaching the gospel of national ownership of the land. The Willamette Valley politician, Sylvester Pennoyer, thought it was a capital idea. In his book on the single tax, Mr. George claimed that private ownership of land was the foundation of all misery and poverty among white men. Had he arrived in Prineville four years earlier he would have decorated a juniper tree. As was, the local residents just laughed him out of town.

---

21 Major stock holders were: Tom Baldwin, Henry Hahn, Ben Allen, Leo Fried, Mose Sichel, A.H. Breyman, Charles Cartwright and John Sommerville. Other stockholders—Ike Mills, Sid Stearns, Alma Lipman and Ed Jordan (representing eastern timber interests)—reads like a roster of the old timers of central Oregon.

For some reason, 1888 got off to a slow start and not only in the Ochoco but worldwide. Other than Benjamin Harrison winning the presidential election things were calm. Russian composer Rimsky-Korsakov did find time to crank out "Scheherazade" and England got rather excited when Jack the Ripper dispatched six London ladies to a safer world. However, by mid-January Oregon in general and Multnomah County in particular had another worry to occupy their thoughts. In fact, a two-fold concern. Foremost, what in heaven's name had they elected to pilot the ship of state? And second, why did the citizens of Portland spend more time in the outhouse than they did conducting business affairs? This last malady had been traced to drinking the sewage-polluted water of the Willamette River.

Once detected, a bill had been drafted to correct this unsanitary condition in which the good folks of Portland desired to obtain clear, pure water from the Bull Run River. The only impediment to this proposal was they had to get permission from the state to do so. No problem. It passed the legislature hands down. That's as far as it got. The governor vetoed the bill.

According to spokesmen from the governor's office, Pennoyer had determined the tax-exempt bonds required to finance this worthy endeavor "were unconstitutional" and besides that, construction of a reservoir on the slopes of Mt. Hood would most likely disturb the environment. Ecology had never even been of minor concern to Oregon in the past. Senator Tongue lobbied valiantly to uphold the veto but, thankfully for the diarrhea-ridden Portlanders, the state Senate overrode Sylvester's veto on February 7, 1889.

Across the mountains on the pristine central Oregon range some discouraging words were also being heard. Those "damn sod-busters" were polluting the wide-open spaces with barbed wire. "Lighter than air, stronger than whiskey and cheaper than dirt" is the way Warren "Bet-a-Million" Gates described his invention. It may have been the ultimate in modern technology for the homesteader but barbed wire held no appeal to the livestock industry which placed it in the same unwanted category as poison parsnip. Foreseeing the evils this instrument of the devil would bring to the community, T.F. McAllister took off on another tangent.

Back in 1879, Clark Rodgers—already fed up with overcrowding—hitched up his team, hauled logs from Grizzly Mountain to the

Deschutes River rim and rolled them down some 1,500 feet to the bottom of the canyon. In a small cove at the base of The Plains of Abraham (newcomers call it The Island), he constructed a 10 x 12 foot log cabin, cleared a chunk of ground and began growing fruit trees imported from The Dalles. On the plus side, Rodgers was not plagued with visitors. On the minus side, it was not easy to make trips to Prineville for supplies and the mail. So, in 1888, Rodgers traded the cove orchard to McAllister for a house and lot in Prineville. To satisfy central Oregon's growing demand for fresh fruit, McAllister and his hired hand, Billy Boegli, planted more apple, pear, cherry and peach trees to start a thriving business. In 1905, Boegli bought the cove and kept it for the next 35 years.[22]

At the same time Rodgers and McAllister were negotiating a trade agreement, the federal government—perhaps belatedly aware of Rodgers' logging operation on Grizzly Mountain and apprehensive about his close proximity to the Warm Springs Reservation—decreed that thou shalt not trespass on Indian lands. The real purpose of this act was to minimize illegal cutting of timber. The reason given to the public was to prevent intimidation of Indian occupants. Actually, Congress couldn't care less about its welfare recipients and would soon verify that reality.

Over on the Oregon-Idaho border several things were happening. In April 1888—nearly a year after thirty-one Chinese were murdered in Hells Canyon—some men were arrested for stealing horses. It soon became apparent that they were more than common horse thieves when Frank Vaughan (Hank's cousin), a teenage gang member who was present at the killings, turned state's evidence in exchange for immunity from prosecution.[23] Six men were charged with the first ten murders on Deep Creek. During these negotiations three of the accused escaped from the Wallowa County jail and fled the county.[24]

---

22 In the early 1940's, Boegli sold the property to the state of Oregon which made a park out of it. From the day of the first visitors, The Cove Palisades State Park—now laying at the bottom of Lake Billy Chinook—was a popular recreation spot.

23 Frank Vaughan was the son of Enoch Vaughan who had a ranch on the Imnaha River. (*An Illustrated History of Union and Wallowa Counties*, pp. 64, 568.)

24 Those charged with murder who escaped were: Bruce Evans, J.T. Canfield and Homer LaRue. Evans lost himself in the Big Hole country of Montana, leaving a wife and family behind; LaRue was killed in a poker game in California and Canfield went to Kansas where he spent time in prison. (David H. Stratton, *Essay on the Massacre in Hells Canyon*, 1983.)

In a bail hearing held on April 16, 1888 the remaining three charged with murder—Hiram Maynard, 15-year-old Robert McMillan and Hezekiah Hughes—were released on $800 bail because "30 citizens and taxpayers" contended that the evidence was insufficient to hold them in custody. This finding would almost guarantee their acquittal in a criminal trial.

Some four months later on September 1, 1888—after a two-day trial in the Wallowa County Circuit Court at Enterprise, Oregon—Maynard, Hughes and McMillan were found innocent of any wrongdoing. Records of the trial, if they existed, are still missing. According to one historian its unlikely that the jury wanted a guilty verdict because the accused were apparently well-known and at the time Chinese were held in such low regard that this murder didn't qualify as a serious crime. George S. Craig, a witness to the 1888 murder trial had this to say: "I guess if they had killed 31 white men something would have been done about it.[25] Ironically soon after the trial McMillan died of diphtheria at the age of sixteen.[26]

While this glitch in the American justice system ran its course another miscarriage was in progress a few miles east. As 1888 inched toward summer, an old Snake pacifist who had "seen the light" was being groomed for a mission beyond his limited capacities. Known to his tribesmen as Small Heart because he was not much good in battle, he was called Tyhee by his white admirers. *Tyhee* was the Chinook jargon word for chief. Since "chief" had expressed a desire to live like a white man, Idaho officials decided to send him to the hallowed halls of Congress to settle a family dispute between the Lemhi and Banattee Snakes. All Tyhee had to do was convince the lawmakers that the two tribes should have a separate reservation as the reluctant Lemhis were refusing to be corralled on the Fort Hall Reserve with the Robber Snakes and this was the reason for Idaho's present concern. Not looking forward to another great Snake uprising, Idaho was gambling on "Chief's" eloquence to bring about peace within the Shoshoni ranks by petitioning

---

25 "The terrible secret of Hells Canyon," *The Oregonian*, August 15, 1995.

26 According to an 1891 newspaper account. Robert McMillan made a deathbed confession to his father, Hugh McMillan, admitting that he and Frank Vaughan were among those armed with repeating rifles and revolvers who fired on the Chinese from two sides of Deep Creek Canyon.

Congress to restore the Lemhi Valley Reservation which it had abandoned by executive order in 1879.[27] The only thing Tyhee accomplished was an expense-paid trip to Washington, D.C.

In June, while Tyhee toured the eastern states in a railroad box car, Crook County's political front was in a state of flux. Sheriff Newt Williamson advanced to the Oregon House of Representatives and M.R. Ellis, appearing out of nowhere, defeated George Barnes to become Prineville's district attorney. John Combs, who had picked up only nine votes in the 1884 election, was elected sheriff but his hands were tied from the start.

And down in Nevada, the humble son of the late powerful Snake medicine chief White Man "died for a time." Even burning fire-brands applied to his bare feet could not make him twitch. Had he been a lesser man, the Paiutes would have buried him on the spot but, since Wovoka (The Cutter) had a habit of dying, they thought perhaps they should wait a few days which proved to be a wise decision. During his stay in heaven, The Cutter talked with God who told him he should return to earth and tell the Indians—among other things—to stop drinking whiskey and cease fighting with the white men. God also gave him new words for the old spirit dance songs. The Indians were to sing these words as they danced and to make certain they mastered the updated dance steps, the prophet made them practice for five consecutive nights. The Cutter assured the people that if they followed his instructions, used a sacred paint he prescribed and faithfully performed the Ghost Dance, wondrous things would happen. The most important event being that all white men would disappear from earth and dead Indians would return to life.

As the Messiah craze gained momentum, the Snakes at Fort Hall—forgetting their family feud with the Lemhis—became the intermediaries between the Paiute prophet and the plains tribes. There's no doubt that the residents of eastern Oregon were becoming increasingly nervous with Has No Horse lurking in the nearby shadows. As it turned out, they had nothing to fear from him.

December, in its blustery romp across the western states, would inoculate the Paiutes with scarlet fever which punished one and all with

27   Steward, *Basin Plateau Groups*, pp. 40-45; *Report of Commissioner of Indian Affairs 1879*, p. 54.

equal vigor. Showing no partiality, the man who talked with God would receive his share of scarlet rash and peeling skin.[28] By the end of the month, dozens of fever-ridden victims had joined with their ancestors in the Milky Way and death was knocking on Wovoka's door. Then, on New Year's Day 1889 as a blazing sun (the first seen in weeks) approached mid-day, an awesome thing happened. The western half of the United States was plunged into darkness lasting for more than an hour when the sun went into total eclipse.

To the Paiutes—as it was to all native Americans—the sun was a living being. Now some sky monster was intent on devouring it. While panic stricken Indians from the Great Plains to the Grand Canyon fell down in prayer, the residents of Crook County lighted coal-oil lamps and turned up the wicks to blacken glass chimneys so they could better view this unique event. The white brothers had figured out what was happening but in the lodges of the Sioux, Cheyenne, Shoshoni and Arapahos an ominous hush had fallen.

The old Paiute warrior who had discovered this battle in the sky gave vent to a screaming war whoop, dashed into his lodge and grabbing a rusty shotgun, began blasting away at the creature in the sky. Others joined in the battle. Whatever was attacking the sun had to be frightened away. But in spite of heroic measures the earth grew darker minute by minute as the monster continued to bite greater and greater chunks out of the dying sun.

People, now more terrorized by the space battle than they were of scarlet fever, dashed to The Cutter's sickbed begging him to do something—anything but evil would triumph. Soon the total blackness of night had shoved out the glory of day. Never did The Cutter pray with more sincerity or with more fear. With the complete and total death of the sun, gunfire and drumbeats turned to human wails of utter despair as Wovoka went into a deep sleep. For an hour the Paiutes would mourn the tragic death of their greatest, most beneficial friend. And then, from the very side which the sky-devil had first attacked there came a faint glimmer of light. As the glow of heaven slowly came back there was no

---

28 While cutting logs for David Wilson, a Nevada rancher, The Cutter was stricken with scarlet fever the first week of December 1889. In the cold weeks that followed The Cutter fought his battle of life almost alone. Paiutes refused to go near his makeshift wickiup in the snow. Bailey, *Wovoka The Indian Messiah*, pp. 86-87.

doubt in anyone's mind that Wovoka had saved the sun. The Cutter, in his own words, would swear, "When the sun died, I went up to heaven and saw God. God told me to come back and tell my people they must be good and love one another, and not fight, or steal, or lie. He would also reveal that Jesus, shrouded by clouds, was on earth."[29] Wovoka would now serve as the left hand of God.

Word of this miracle soon spread throughout the West and The Cutter's reputation as a man touched by God was established for all time. In the Indian's collective mind, the Paiute dragon slayer would stand on an equal footing with the biblical prophet John; the 16th century French visionary Nostradamus; and the current Nez Perce psychic Smoholla. All sensible Indians on the North American continent would pay homage to this holy man in the Nevada desert. All that is with the exception of two—the opposing war chiefs of the 1852 Shoshoni schism.

Shortly after the New Year's Day eclipse, Has No Horse rode into the Merritt ranch in Big Summit Prairie and expressed skepticism over The Cutter's periodic visits to the Milky Way. An admirer of Wovoka's father, a highly respected Snake medicine chief, Has No Horse blamed The Cutter's flights to the spirit world on the influence of his Paiute mother and the fact he had drank too deeply of Nevada's alkali-polluted waters. Less than four day's ride from the Paiute messiah's sagebrush tabernacle, Has No Horse made no effort to be redeemed by the anointed one but he did hint that believers could help to bring about one of The Cutter's prophecies—the disappearance of the white man.

Equally unswayed by The Cutter's divine revelation, Gourd Rattler would ask Hank Brownson, a Wyoming rancher, what he knew about "This new prophet we hear about in the West. The Sioux believe him but we do not know what to think."[30] In short, Gourd Rattler wanted to know if the white men thought that Wovoka was "truly a great medicine man." He, like Has No Horse, had his doubts.

---

29 "All evidence indicates that Wovoka claimed two definite and great religious experiences, the most profound one however being at the time the sun died. In our conversation he stated that it was about two years since he had visited heaven and received the great revelation but that it was about four years since he had first taught the [ghost] dance to his people." Mooney, *Fourteenth Annual Report of the Bureau of Ethnology II*, p. 772.

30 Washakie to Hank Brownson, February 25, 1892, Hebard Collection, University of Wyoming Library.

No so with the remainder of the Indian population west of the Mississippi River. Among the hundreds who came by foot, by horseback, by train to receive Wovoka's blessing and learn the ways of the Ghost Dance were the revered medicine chiefs Short Bull and Kicking Bear of the Sioux; Sky Walker of the Kiowa; Porcupine of the Cheyenne; Curley Headed Doctor of the Modoc; Medicine Crow of the Crow; and Little Wolf of the Comanche. Weather-wise, this search for divine guidance would be a bleak pilgrimage. Not only some bronze warriors but several white gentlemen would wonder if The Cutter's visitations in heaven had disturbed the Snow Spirit.[31] It would seem that it had.

With the Indian population hovering on the brink of extinction, interior Oregon was opened for an influx of ranchers who recognized the great potential of the desert country east of the Cascade range. These men, lying claim to huge tracts of land, drove in herds of cattle from Texas and fattened them on native grass. Other stockmen would import thousands of head of sheep and blooded horses to compete with the cattlemen in the rapid depletion of the range.

For the first two decades following the sheep and cattle invasion, the winters were open and livestock foraged year around. Hay was harvested only for saddle horses and barnyard stock. Then came the summer of 1888 and one of the worst droughts on record. Water holes and streams dried up. Many sheep and cattle died and those that survived went into winter in terrible condition. A mild winter would have been hard on the animals but the winter of '88-89 was like no other in the history of the Pacific Northwest. Lew Sarett—a writer exploring the possibilities of a winter storm—would aptly describe what was soon to transpire. "A rancher sleeps under the stars with an icicle gripped in his hand, somewhere tonight where the grim-lipped peaks brood on a haggard land." And so it was.

In November the first storm swept down from the Arctic. Over the next few months storm after storm bringing freezing cold and snow surged across the inland empire. Raging blizzards drove the settlers out of Big Summit Prairie as snow piled up six to eight feet deep. Most of the stockmen ran out of hay and had to drive their starving herds out to

---

31   James Mooney, who knew Wovoka, claimed that the Indian Messiah never wavered in the belief that he had actually visited God in heaven.

the high desert where they cut down juniper for them to eat. As winter dragged on the hunger-driven animals began stripping bark from willows along the streams to survive. In some areas, the damage done to stream-side vegetation would never heal. Only a few horses—who pawed away the snow until they found bunchgrass—managed to stay alive. As a last resort, the horses chewed on each other's manes and tails in a pitiful effort to forestall death.[32] Cattle and sheep died by the tens of thousands as the devastating winter known as the "Great Equalizer" continued without abatement. Ranchers went broke. Some attempted to rebuild from scratch. Others never even tried. They sensed that the day of the sheep and cattle baron was drawing to an end.

By January 6, 1889—just five days after God told Wovoka to get back down to earth and attend to business—all navigation on the upper Columbia came to a standstill. Ice covered the broad, free-flowing river from bank to bank. The Columbia from Portland to the Pacific was choked with floating ice and the Willamette was covered with two inches of frozen water. The ocean-going *S.S. Oregon* made the run from Astoria to Portland but took 55 hours to do so.

A three day blizzard in the middle of January took hundreds of human lives in a dozen western states. Only Wovoka's friend in heaven knew how many devout Indians froze to death on their trek to the wind-swept wastelands of northern Nevada to meet their savior. Perhaps more than died during the hellish Christmas season slaughter at Wounded Knee less than two years into the future.

During a winter white-out on February 25, 1889, the Oregon Legislature—snow bound at the state capital and lacking something better to do—gave birth to massive Harney County. Jake (W.J.) Johnson, a Crook County cattleman and one of old Ewen's sons, would be appointed deputy sheriff of the new subdivision. Carved out of the southern portion of Grant County this most recent offspring of the state would see to it that Deputy Johnson earned his pay. In a feud between the two frontier towns perched in this remote corner of Oregon a fierce political battle erupted when armed night riders stole the county records from Harney City and delivered them to Burns.

---

32 As remembered by Lydia Elliott O'Kelly whose family was forced out of Big Summit Prairie down to the upper Ochoco Valley to survive.

In spite of Sheriff Johnson—or maybe because of him—Burns would become the official county seat in 1890. Attempting to stay clear of this local controversy, the sheriff rode into southern Crook County, rounded up 500 head of frost-bitten horses on Gerry Mountain and drove them to one of the few available markets not ravaged by the arctic storms of '88-89 . . . South Carolina some 3,000 miles to the east. This would keep him out of the public's eye for the remainder of the year.

At the same time Oregon touched pen to the Harney County Treaty, Congress founded the Department of Agriculture supposedly to cure all the ills of the winter's storm. President Cleveland, in one of his last official acts before Ben Harrison took over the reins of command in March, appointed his staunch political ally, Norman J. Colman, to head the new cabinet-level post.

Meanwhile, Luther Gillenwater, crowding into the grass-depleted Crooked River Valley, was starting to become a nuisance with his sheep herds. He eventually got the message and moved over to Bridge Creek when Wheeler County was liberated from Crook in 1899 but not before he mysteriously lost an awful lot of sheep.

The early spring of 1889—blessed by the formal opening of the Paris Exposition featuring the newly completed Eiffel Tower—would see more bureaucratic shenanigans. The federal government (maybe as punishment to the weather gods) purchased most of the remaining lands held in Indian trust from tribal elders who knew not what they were doing; renamed this chunk of real estate Oklahoma Territory; and exposed it to the mercy of homesteaders. On signal at noon, April 22, nearly 50,000 settlers stampeded into Indian territory and another 70,000 square miles of native hunting rounds went up in dust. Historical records will confirm that between 1864 and 1890, almost 100 million acres of the western United States that had been assigned to the American Indian "in perpetuity" were lost to them forever.

Fortunately for the stockmen, this last blow delivered by the foster parents against their unwanted children had the desired effect of intimidating the snow spirit. Perhaps this deity realized that it was a futile effort to fight Manifest Destiny. Whatever the circumstances, the winter of 1889-90 was considered serene. However, 1890 was no landmark in the history of Crook County or the state of Oregon.

For some strange reason, Oregonians elected Sylvester Pennoyer for a second term as governor. Perhaps they couldn't believe his first term in office. A former advocate of slavery; openly opposed to Chinese immigration; and promoter of government control of private enterprise, many thought the wheels of Pennoyer's mind had slipped a few cogs. Considered to be "peculiar, eccentric and demagogic" by his conservative contemporaries, Oregon was now facing some ripsnortin' good times.[33]

---

33   For more on Oregon's 8th elected governor see *The Dictionary of American Biography*, Vol. XIV, p. 445 and Corning's *Dictionary of Oregon History*, pp. 194-5.

Has No Horse

Courtesy Patricia Garcia

Ocheo outside his wickiup—Paiute tribe. That is Red Willow (Tom Ochiko) standing next to him. Has No Horse's oldest and only surviving son. Copied by Delancey Gill of the Bureau of American Ethnology 1906, photographer unknown.

Sheep grazing on the head of the Ochoco River around 1900.

Courtesy Andrew Gale Ontko

A sheep herder's camp in the Ochoco Mountains.

Courtesy Andrew Gale Ontko

A band of sheep in the upper Ochoco Valley in 1905. They are grazing next to the established deadline.

Courtesy Andrew Gale Ontko

Joe Nedroet and Sam Ritter, early day range riders. Photo taken in 1906.

Courtesy Andrew Gale Ontko

The first home in Prineville of Prince and Ethel Glaze. Prince is the son of Til Glaze, the owner of the Bucket of Blood Saloon.

Del Sturdivan's homestead in the low desert east of Redmond, Oregon. Photo taken in 1907. Present location of the Redmond Airport.

Courtesy Andrew Gale Ontko

A typical homestead shack during the early 1900 homestead rush.

Courtesy Andrew Gale Ontko

From bluffs like these in the lower Deschutes canyon opposing railroad construction crews rolled boulders down on the laborers below.

The upper Ochoco River when
it was still a river in 1910.

Courtesy Andrew Gale Ontko

Crooked River Bridge, 330 ft. long, 304 ft. high, the highest single arch
span in the United States, Dalles-California Highway, Oregon

Crooked River Bridge, 330 ft. long, 304 ft. high. When it was completed it was
the highest single arched span in the United States, and remains one of the highest
railroad bridges in the country.

The lower Deschutes Canyon scene of the last and most expensive railroad battle in history.

The lower Deschutes Canyon where the redwood giants battled for supremacy.

Two young ladies meet on Prineville's main street, 1902.

Early ice cream parlor in Prineville.

Early day advertising at Lower Bridge west of Terrebonne. Painted in 1910.

Photo by Virginia Bennett

Henry and Ella (Sturdivan) Koch

Courtesy Andrew Gale Ontko

Stacking hay for winter feed with a Jackson Fork in the upper Ochoco Valley. Circa 1908 (top). Mowing hay for winter feed in the upper Ochoco Valley (bottom).

Courtesy Andrew Gale Ontko

Driving the unofficial golden spike when the Oregon Trunk Railroad reached Redmond, Oregon on September 30, 1911.

Courtesy Andrew Gale Ontko

Street scene in Redmond, Oregon. Circa 1911.

Top: A prospector's cabin at the Blue Ridge mine near Big Summit Prairie.

Middle: The second school house on Big Summit Prairie.

Bottom: Grave of Garret Maupin, son of Howard Maupin, and the man who found the bodies of Crooks and Jory, the first men killed during the vigilantes reign of terror.

A typical sheep corral constructed on the head of Garden Creek, a tributary of the Ochoco River, was in use from the late 1890s to the mid 1950s.

H.H. WHEELER

For whom Wheeler County was named, first president of East Oregon Pioneer Assn., also U.S. Mail carrier from The Dalles to Canyon City, was attacked near this spot by Indians, was wounded, mail looted and coach destroyed. Sept. 7th, 1866. Memorial erected by East Oregon Pioneers.

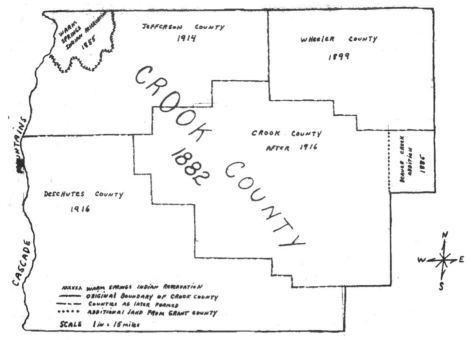

Map drawn by Gale Ontko.

Mary Jo Estep survived the last Indian massacre in the United States, but died within an hour after receiving the wrong medicine at a nursing home.

Associated Press 1988 photo that appeared in The Bulletin, *March 17, 1993*

CHAPTER 191

HE RIDES THE MILKY WAY

We are sending you to that Great God.
Tell Him that we, who invented forgiveness
do not forgive;
That we, who invoke faith would not believe.

Fred Donaldson
Gray Wolf

As Governor Pennoyer introduced 1890 to his constituents, the U.S. population was struggling to stay at 62+ million. The Indian nations were struggling just to stay alive. To date hundreds of thousands of native North Americans had died because of European contact. And the literally countless deaths would not stop here. The Indian population of the United States would sink to an all-time low of 250,000 people within the next ten years.

On February 16, 1912, Gen Nelson A. Miles in an address to the cadets at West Point would comment:

> History can show no parallel to the heroism and fortitude of the American Indian in the 200 year fight during which they contested—inch by inch—the possession of their country against a foe infinitely better equipped with inexhaustible resources and in overwhelming numbers. Had they been equal in number, history might have had a very different story to tell.

This statement—which could apply to the Shoshoni alone—was issued by a pony soldier who had wielded a cavalry saber against the thrust of a feathered battle lance held by such warriors as Buffalo Horn, Geronimo, Joseph and Sitting Bull. He knew what he was talking about.

In contrast to the Indian's dwindling numbers, the 1890 census would show that Oregon—in a ten year period—had gained another 139,999 souls boosting the population to 313,767. Portland alone now had 72,000 citizens consuming 10 million gallons of polluted water a day from the Willamette River. Prineville's stable population in 1890 was pushing 500 and the outlying communities of Paulina, Mill Creek, Sisters, Howard, Farewell Bend, Meadow, Mitchell and Grizzly could easily double that number. With Mayflower gold and Oregon King silver pouring into the area, money flowed like water. Before the decade passed five new saloons graced the streets of Prineville operating day and night seven days a week and it was not uncommon to see $500 to $1,000 on a poker table at any given saloon.

The terrible winter storms of the latter '80s had put a crimp in the sheep and cattle industry and horses were now the big profit makers. One carload of horses shipped to British Columbia in 1890 brought $125 a head as opposed to $30 a head for cattle. With horse prices sky-rocketing, horse equipment was in great demand. Saddler Smith—known throughout the West as the king of saddle-makers—would craft a custom made saddle for $35. If it was silver mounted, the price would jump to $45. Major horse producers were the Johnson brothers guided by old Ewen; Gene Luckey with strong ties to the city founding fathers; Joe Howard and Sid Sterns backed by the First National Bank of Prineville; Newt Williamson directing operations from his congressional seat in Washington, D.C.; Guyon Springer, the first man to cross the English Hackney with the Standard Trotter; Barney Markam, thoroughbred horse breeder; and Bill Brown, the acknowledged horse king of the American West. Added to this list were Dr. Belknap specializing in draft horses and Til Glaze who was raising famous race horses like Wasco and Fox on his Black Butte ranch west of Sisters.

It was now profitable to make stage runs twice a week from Prineville to Paulina and Grayce Wilson—daughter of the town butcher—would shock the community when she hired out to Buchanan's freight line as stagecoach driver making tri-weekly deliveries of mail and supplies to the upper Ochoco gold camps.

New business establishments were popping up all over. Among them was Gid Humstead and Jack Curtis' new Ochoco Restaurant. Even though their grocery bill ran as high as $90 a week, the restaurant was netting a $200 profit. Inadvertently, Gid married a Dillon girl—daughter of a sheepman—and was told to get out of the country. No dummy, Humstead sold his interest in the cafe to Charlie Prantz and departed for parts unknown.

As the second day of spring settled over the boisterous streets of Prineville, the *Ochoco Review* would headline a sad bit of news. The man known to the Shoshoni as Gray Wolf and the patron saint of Crook County had taken the sundown trail to the stars. Gen. George Crook died at the Grand Pacific Hotel (his Chicago residence) on March 21, 1890. Crook was only 61 years old when the final call to duty came. The cause of death according to Dr. McClellan, his attending physician, was heart failure. The real cause, according to the men in his command, was the wear and tear on a naturally powerful constitution brought on by the severe mental and physical strain of incessant work under most trying circumstances.

Among those sending condolences were the citizens of Crook County and their expressions of sympathy were read from the floor of the United States Senate by Senator John Mitchell of Oregon. No western town could better appreciate the importance of Crook's military campaign against the Indians than Prineville which, but for him, may never have gotten such an early start on the central Oregon frontier.

Ohio had given him birth; the banks of the Hudson River had heard his recitations as a West Point cadet; western Oregon witnessed his first feats of arms; West Virginia welcomed him as the intelligent and energetic leader of the army which bore her name; and eastern Oregon along with most of the western states owed him a debt of gratitude for his operations against the hostile Indians which infested their borders rendering life and property insecure.

The sudden death of Gen. Crook was a severe blow to Indian management throughout the West. The Indians knew it and their words and acts testified to their respect for the man known as "Gray Wolf" and "Three Stars." Expressing the sympathy of all Indians, Red Cloud of the Sioux spoke these words to Father Craft, a Catholic missionary. "General Crook came. He, at least, had never lied to us. His words gave the people hope. He died. Their hope died. Despair came again."

Although Gray Wolf was relentless in battle, the Indians were well aware that they had lost their only American ally in the final struggle for survival. Early residents of Crook County would recall that the Shoshoni in Big Summit Prairie built a huge fire, painted their faces black and mourned all night long.[1] Eight hundred miles to the south the Indians near Fort Apache sat down in a circle, "let their hair down, bent their heads forward on their bosoms and wept and wailed like children."[2]

Interment was at Oakland, Maryland, March 24, 1890. Three Confederate soldiers who formed part of the detachment that took Crook prisoner and sent him to Libby Prison—one of whom was his brother-in-law, James Daily—requested permission to attend the funeral services as a mark of respect for their late foe. On November 11, 1890, Crook's body was transferred to Arlington Cemetery, Virginia, escorted by two companies of United States Cavalry.

By December 1890, Indian troubles—sparked by Wovoka the Paiute prophet—reached their final, bloody anti-climax at Wounded Knee, South Dakota; a blood-bath Crook would have been able to prevent. Captain Bourke, who was awaiting the publication of his book about the general, commented briefly, "Now that he is dead and we have taken to slaughtering women and sucklings with Hotchkiss guns, the nation feels that it has lost one of its greatest sons."[3]

Once again the Ochoco lost another of its pioneers and a new decade loomed darkly on the horizon. The old vigilantes were returning to power as the Crook County Sheepshooters Association . . . this time with ample justification. Unfortunately, as before, their authority became dictatorial. If someone got in the way of a .30-.30 bullet—and many did—courts were not always impartial when it came to dispensing justice. Juries, when not stacked in favor of the guilty, were intimidated as masked riders from Crook County swept into Lake, Grant and Wheeler counties shooting sheep; driving them over cliffs; killing them by any means available. The winter of '88-89 may have been the great equalizer but the Winchester rifle—growing in popularity—was proving to be equally effective.

---

1 As remembered by the Elliott, O'Kelly, Elkins and Merritt families, all of whom—except the Elkins—lived in Big Summit Prairie at the time of Gen. Crook's death and were neighbors to Has No Horse and the last remnant of the Snake War Tribes.

2 Bourke, *On the Border With Crook*, pp. 486-87.

3 John Bourke to Charles Scribner (father of the New York publishers), June 8, 1891.

CHAPTER 192

WHISPERS OF DISCONTENT

Old Satan dreamed in his fiery bed,
That he was kind and God was dead;
That Oregon was a sunny state,
In which to find himself a mate.

Roy Leonard
Ochoco Sheepherder

In early May 1890, Dave Rowan bought Fred Goulet's Electric Saloon and renamed it the Dew Drop Inn. A favorite hangout for cattlemen, it was doing a thriving business at the gaming tables. Bear in mind that gambling—barred during Blakely's tour of duty—was wide-open in Prineville despite laws against it. Six month's flow of gold and silver had gushed over the rapids of Rowan's poker tables when, on November 13, some misguided soul tried to burn the Dew Drop down. Whoever it was, he was in deep trouble.[1] The emerging new rulers of Crook County didn't take kindly to such nonsense.

Six years before when the vigilantes had their heads stomped into the dusty wagon ruts of Prineville's Main Street it was believed they were writhing in their final death throes. Hardly. Like the deadly reptile they personified, the vigilantes uncoiling body was to inflict more wounds before the 19th century sun would set.

In 1890, the sea of grass—parched by the winter of '88-90—was evaporating and range war loomed just beyond the horizon. Old members of the vigilante group took a new lease on life, eyed one another as to livestock preference and aligned their gun sights on a fresh target . . . each other! They joyfully chose up sides and began plinking at former

---

1   *Ochoco Review*, November 15, 1890.

allies and God have pity on the small operator who got caught in the cross fire.

The cause for this latest bloodshed had its beginning some fifteen years in the past. During the 1870s it had become the accepted practice to winter all livestock in the lower valleys. Then as soon as the weather and grass permitted the animals were driven to the high country for spring and summer feed. This way the big outfits found it unnecessary to raise hay as animals had forage enough to carry them year around and ranged out the entire time feeding on the thick bunch grass, timothy and heavy stands of native meadow fescue that grew everywhere. This brought on the first big slaughter of sheep and cattle when Has No Horse's war machine—in its death throes—killed thousands of sheep, cattle and horses from Harney Valley to the Columbia plateau.

Federal laws which seemed to have no apparent bearing on what was about to happen in central Oregon were passed in 1890. California saw the formation of three national parks—Sequoia, Yosemite and Gen. Grant—with the implied threat of government regulations controlling the use of public lands. Then with little forethought Congress, by act of June 12, 1890, saw fit to authorize the cutting of green timber on the Menominee Indian Reservation in Wisconsin. This was the first federal law allowing timber harvest on Indian lands but certainly not the last. This act in itself posed no threat to private industry but more was to come.

Before another year would pass, Congress authorized the president to withdraw and reserve forested public domain to assure protection of timber lands and upland watersheds. Enforcement of this act would lay in the hands of the Department of Interior. Timber companies were not overly pleased with the outcome but were hardly worried. As for the livestock men, they could see no cause for concern at all . . . a complacent position they would soon regret. To round out national intervention in the use of public lands, John Douthit (a major stockholder in the Scissors Creek gold strike), was appointed federal magistrate to hear mining disputes and settle them on behalf of the government. The red tape of bureaucracy was drawing ever tighter and without doubt, Governor Pennoyer was in seventh heaven.

In 1881 the first big bands of sheep were pushed into the northern Ochoco ranging from the South Fork of the John Day River into Big Summit Prairie. Even so, for the next twelve years there were only six bands of sheep grazing the entire summer range between Lookout Mountain and Spanish Peak. The only worries then were to trail the sheep to the summer range; keep the bear, wolves and coyotes out of them; and then trail them back to headquarter ranches in the fall.

Cattle were left to graze on their own strung out from the headwaters of the Deschutes to the head of Crooked River filling every creek bottom in between. Large companies were organized and as the livestock continued to increase conditions became more desperate. Thousands of cattle and hundreds of thousands of sheep were rushed to the Blue Mountains as soon as the grass began to grow. The range became crowded to the limit.

During the lull, life continued as usual in Crook County. On May 14, 1890, Billy Foster—one of the cattle kings—drowned under mysterious circumstances while attempting to cross the flood-swollen Crooked River on horseback. By mid-August Jim Miller was nervously expecting the appearance of his wayward nephew who had recently escaped from the Oregon State Penitentiary.

The *Albany Democrat* would report: "Hal (Harry) Miller, Joaquin Miller's son, was in the city Saturday on his way from the State pen to points unknown. He was discovered and recognized by Policeman McClain who attempted to catch him but he ran like a deer. McClain fired two shots but failed to bring down the jailbird who made his escape and went toward Lebanon in which direction he was seen Sunday. The chase in Albany was quite an exciting one."[2] If Hal made it to Uncle Jim's ranch no one turned state's evidence and so it went in the Ochoco.

Soon to make local news was Wovoka's latest proclamation. In 1889, while the sun was "dead" during an eclipse, the young Paiute mystic had a vision of better things to come. A year later on November 22, 1890, George Barnes—writing in the *Ochoco Review*—was poking fun at The Cutter's prophesy of the Indians rising from the dead to inherit the earth. "The only good Indians," according to Editor Barnes, "are dead and even if they do have a Messiah to lead them, they can't do much damage!" Has No Horse, who held little faith in Indian pacifists, was inclined to agree with George. Others thought differently.

---

2   *Albany Democrat*, August 30, 1890. Hal Miller was Joaquin's son from his marriage to Theresa Dyer, his second wife. Joaquin's first marriage to a Shasta girl produced one daughter, Cali Shasta Miller.

The Sioux were taking Wovoka's revelation very seriously and a number of Americans were downright nervous that the Sioux could do some damage. In a state of sheer panic a warrant was issued for Sitting Bull's arrest for his part in Wovoka's Ghost Dance religion. On the bitterly cold night of December 14, 1890, U.S. Indian police attempted to serve the warrant and in the process Sitting Bull took a rifle slug in the head. This was just the introduction to a new strike against the Indians.

Among the army officers destined for the western command was one General McKeever. A desk officer, he had been removed from West Point and sent to the Dakotas for Indian duty. He was not happy with this disciplinary action and spent much time brooding over his fall from grace. After Crook's death, he was sent to the Pine Ridge Indian Agency. Perhaps this assignment was his Christmas present from the War Department. Whatever, 'twas the season to be jolly.

Three days after Christmas 1890, army troops moved in on the Pine Ridge Agency where about 350 starving Sioux were camped on Wounded Knee Creek. The next morning, shortly after dawn, men, women and children were butchered on the frozen plain . . . raked by bullets from four rapid-fire Hotchkiss guns. New Year's Day 1891 saw a burial party pry frozen bodies from their icy shrouds and dump them into a common grave. Included in the mass interment were four babies who were still alive. Everyone involved in the Wounded Knee mass murder was trying to keep it suppressed. It didn't work. Gen. McKeever leaked the news to the press and the *Ochoco Review* picked it up. Acting on a hot tip, the *Review* would report that when the secretary of war found out who the guilty culprit was, McKeever was discharged from the service under somewhat less than honorable conditions.[3]

Meantime, the Pacific Northwest—especially the infant state of Washington which had just been admitted into the Union on November 11, 1889—was overjoyed that a bearded 5 foot 6 Indianapolis lawyer, commander of the 70th Regiment of the Indiana Volunteers and Presbyterian elder was coming to visit. His name was Benjamin Harrison and he was not only the 23rd president but also the first to visit Washington upon statehood. The city of Tacoma was so excited it had four welcome arches quickly built to span the streets along the parade route. One arch

---

3   *Ochoco Review*, February 7, 1891.

was of native iron; one held 1,060 sacks of flour and 640 sacks of grain; another was an arch of coal; and one of heroic beams cut from Douglas fir logs.

As these mighty arches were being hurriedly tossed together, thousands of people down in Oregon stood in a driving rain on the morning of May 6, 1891 at the Eugene railroad station to welcome President Harrison to their city. A delegation had even caught a basket of mountain trout from the McKenzie River to present to the distinguished guest. But no one in Eugene ever saw the president. He had given orders the night before that he was not to be awakened until just before reaching Salem, toward noon.

State Rep. T.T. Geer, who was aboard the presidential train, said there were "exclamations that were not especially laudatory of the president" when the train pulled out. Perhaps the chief executive snubbed the people because he was in turn given the cold shoulder by Gov. Sylvester Pennoyer, who refused to meet Harrison at the Oregon-California border. According to Pennoyer the governor of a state was "a bigger man" officially than the president of the United States. "The states are sovereign" Pennoyer contended, "while the federal government is but the creature of the states."

The president made amends for his Eugene faux pas when he remarked in Salem, as the rain continued to pour, "My fellow citizens, I have just come from the land of sunshine, roses and irrigation to a country where it is evident that the Lord himself takes care of the crops." It rained throughout Harrison's one-day tour, which included stops at Salem, Chemawa, Oregon City and Portland.[4]

The following day, "Kid Gloves" Harrison (as Pennoyer called him) arrived in Tacoma where it was still raining. His Washington visit was so breathlessly anticipated that the Tacoma *Daily News* ran an ardent headline on the day of Little Ben's arrival which simply said: "He Draweth Nigh." And the welcome arches were waiting.

When the carriage loaded with dignitaries passed under each arch, the president would say, "Admirable! Admirable!" As they approached 15th Avenue and the mightiest arch of all, the president asked Mayor George Kandle, "What is this Mr. Mayor?"

---

4   "Centennial Countdown," *The Oregon Journal*, April 29, 1959.

"Timber!" yelled his honor in the ancient logging holler and in obedience to his command the log structure crashed to the ground . . . fortunately a couple of days after Harrison passed under it. By now, the president was accustomed to mishaps on his western tour.

Shortly after President Harrison's near miss on a soggy Tacoma street, the *Ochoco Review* on July 4, 1891 would announce that: "Geronimo, the desperate outlaw in the southwest was killed about 30 miles from Benson, Cochise County, Arizona Territory. A reward of $3,000 had been offered for him." By now, Wovoka—blamed by the American public for the massacre at Wounded Knee and fearing arrest—was hid-out somewhere in southeast Oregon's Trout Creek mountains.

The old Indian freedom fighters were quickly fading away. On October 16, 1891, Sarah Winnemucca died at her sister's house in Monida, Montana. One of the last passages Sarah had written in her autobiography contained the words, "Alas, how truly our women prophesied when they told my dear old grandfather [One Moccasin] that his white brothers, whom he loved so much, had brought sorrow to his people."[5]

To celebrate Sarah's demise, George McCoy, ex-Indian agent who was running sheep on Hay Creek moved into the Mitchell country which may not have been a smart move. On December 17, 1891, the Crook County range war was declared when masked sheepshooters burned out Henry Trent on the west branch of Bridge Creek followed by John Fopiano's death on Waterman Flat. Jim Wilson, his brother-in-law, took over the Fopiano sheep spread in the wake of mounting hostilities. And Luther Gillenwater, who had slipped his sheep herds over the mountains from Crooked River to Bridge Creek for safety's sake, was having second thoughts about the wisdom of that move.

By 1892, Prineville was ready for the big time. If Portland and Fred Goulet's saloon could have electricity so could Prineville. A contract was given to William Gates to light up the town and by mid-year, he did just that. The entire plant weighed 200,000 pounds and the Yancey brothers contracted to haul it from the Moro railhead for 1½¢ a pound.

---

5 Hopkins, *Life Among the Piutes*, pp. 258-59. For One Moccasin's vision of a beautiful relationship between his "white brothers" and native Americans see, *Thunder Over the Ochoco*, Vol. I, pp. 107-113.

The contract called for seven round trips to Moro with two ten-horse teams. Each round trip took nine days and by following the old pony express route, Steve and Jesse fulfilled the contract on schedule. To celebrate the occasion, Prineville general stores were advertising something new. Soda water with a crimped metal cap instead of a cork. It delighted women and children alike.

While the Yancey freight wagons inched over the pony express trail, Joseph Hubner, a native of Germany who was partial to sheep, saw the error of his thinking and traded them off to a befuddled Gillenwater for cattle. In fact, small operators were switching from sheep to cattle or from cattle to sheep—dependent upon who their neighbors were—in droves.

Across the Ochoco Divide Mitchell citizens, still miffed at being overlooked for the honor of county seat of Crook, were beginning to agitate for their own colony. On the final day of December 1892, the *Antelope Herald* would report, "We understand that a petition is being circulated in the Mitchell Country praying for the organization of a new county out of a part of Crook and a portion of Grant thus entitling either Mitchell or Waldron to a county seat." So the matter was launched without much success.

It was probably a good thing for depression struck the nation in 1893 and Crook County shared in the hard times much to the delight of Gov. Pennoyer. He continued to delight his followers and annoy most other people. When the depression hit, he abandoned the party which elected him to office (no tears lost) and embraced the Populist Party—something akin to Socialism—preaching the doctrine of free silver to all and again defying President Cleveland by proclaiming Thanksgiving Day a week later than that fixed by the president.

Back in Crook County there was little to give thanks for as all construction came to a halt. Wheat in eastern Oregon was selling for 25¢ a bushel and men were riding the trail idle and hungry because no one was hiring. Cattle prices were dropping to the point where there was no market, resulting in bank closures. Seven Portland banks closed their doors in one day and the Prineville Bank was swamped by apprehensive citizens who demanded gold coins to fill their purses. It was established that half of the real property changed hands because of foreclosures and sheriff's sales.

One of the worst hit was Ben Snipes who had built a cattle empire stretching from central Oregon north to the Canadian border and from the crest of the Cascades east to the Rockies. His herds numbered into the tens of thousands—even Ben himself never knew exactly how many cattle he owned—and he had made a fortune driving bunchgrass-fattened steers north over the Caribou Trail to the mining camps of British Columbia.

His first setback came during the terrible winter of 1881-82 which brought one snow storm after another, followed by freezing rain and bitter cold. It was estimated ninety percent of the cattle carrying Snipes S brand died. Old timers in Prineville remembered Ben saying at that time: "They call me Cattle King. Well, I've very likely got more dead cattle than any man in the world, but I'm still a very live cattleman. I have cattle. They're skinny and weak. Many may yet die, but some will live. I accumulated more cattle than all the rest and I can do it again." And he rebuilt his herd by buying all the cattle he could get his hands on.

Snipes had returned to his former greatness when again he was brought down by the financial panic of 1893 which occurred shortly after a daring bank robbery that already had depleted his personal assets. Snipes owned a bank in Roslyn, a mining town in central Washington. On September 24, 1882 customers going into the Ben E. Snipes & Company Bank were greeted by armed outlaws ransacking the establishment. At the time, Hank Vaughan was living in Pendleton, Oregon. Although Pendleton was 175 miles southeast of Roslyn, from the beginning Hank was a prime suspect in the case. This suspicion was reinforced when a professional gambler told Snipes he had seen a half-breed Indian, who he knew was one of Vaughan's most trusted gang leaders, looking the bank over a couple of days before the robbery. Then, to add substance to the gambler's tip, a stockman friend of Snipes claimed he met two strangers a few days after the robbery headed toward the Columbia River and one was riding an off-color horse with Vaughan's brand on it.[6]

---

6   Cal Hale, a rancher from Heppner, Oregon was said to have been riding the off-color saddle horse. A few hours before law officers arrived at Hale's ranch to check the horse, Hank Vaughan was supposedly seen in the horse pasture with a Winchester rifle where he disposed of the evidence. It was also said that Hank even took the precaution to skin the animal so as to remove the incriminating brand. Then Hank with five Cayuse warriors disappeared into the most inaccessible part of the Blue Mountains on an extended hunting trip. Meantime, even without evidence, Hale was found guilty of bank robbery and served several months in prison

Perhaps he did but undercover agents could never produce enough evidence to implicate Vaughan in the crime. In fact, Vaughan was never directly connected to any bank robberies but he was accused of being the mastermind of several.

In an attempt to save the Snipes empire after "the Great Roslyn Bank Robbery" and the depression of 1893, 21-year-old Ben Snipes Jr. struck out for Alaska telling his father, "If I strike gold, we'll be in fine shape." But the ship he booked passage on—the *Lady Jane Gray*—was lost at sea. Mary Snipes refused to give up hope and for the remainder of her life she set a place at the table for her son and kept a night-light burning. Old Ben went to Alaska to search but found no trace of the *Lady Jane Gray*. He returned to central Oregon broken in spirit and bankrupt.

As Snipes began his search for the *Lady Jane Gray*, a new western land rush was in progress. On a sizzling September day in 1893 a volley of gunshots sent more than 100,000 people surging across imaginary lines in the largest scramble for free land the world had ever seen. They came on foot and horseback, in wagons, on bicycles and by train, hoping to stake a homestead in the fabled Cherokee Strip, 7 million acres that were home to buffalo and Indians.[7]

At noon September 16, 1893, the sound of cavalry guns opened the 226-mile-wide Cherokee Strip to homesteaders. Trains packed so full that men rode on rooftops and hung from the sides, puffed southward from Kansas. To keep it fair, the trains could move only at 5 mph, as fast as a horse could run. By evening, tent cities had sprouted on the plain and the 40,000 to 50,000 lucky participants were lined up at nine land offices to register their claims. For the Indians, it was analogous to the German holocaust. For two notorious gunmen of the Pacific Northwest, 1893 would also prove to be a disaster.

After surviving years of broken bones in bullet-ridden bodies, time would finally catch up with Hank Vaughan and Charlie Long. On May 30, 1893—three and a half months before the Oklahoma free-for-all—a fatal accident occurred in Pendleton, Oregon closely followed by a bloody encounter near Okanogan, Washington. . . two tragic events

---

before more evidence surfaced and earned him a pardon and his freedom. (Ballou, *Early Klickitat Valley Days*, pp. 61-62.)

7   At the time of the land rush, the Cherokee Strip was home to the Osage, Pawnee, Kaw, Ponca, Tonkawa, Otoe and Missouri tribes.

which foretold the passing of an era in the American West. To fully grasp the significance of these incidents it is necessary to delve into the leading player's shady past.

CHAPTER 193

BULLETS ARE A GUNMAN'S BEST FRIEND

> *. . . when the fight was over Robert Tulloc lay dead with eight bullet and buckshot wounds in his body. Hank Vaughan had a bullet hole in his head but refused to die . . .*

> **The Weekly Arizona Miner**
> October 19, 1877

And so it came to pass that once again Hank would survive another shoot-out.[1] As the *Prescott Arizona Miner* would put it: "Such men seem to be hard to kill." At about the same time that Vaughan was gunned down in Prescott, Charlie Long, another hot-blooded Oregonian, rode into Santa Fe, New Mexico looking for excitement.[2] In 1877 two big cattle outfits were squabbling over which one would fulfill government contracts to supply reservation Indians with beef. On February 18, 1878 this quarrel erupted into the Lincoln County War. Long quickly signed on with the Murphy-Dolon faction where his gun for hire backed that of

---

1   Those in the posse were: U.S. Marshall W.W. Standefer, Yavapi County Sheriff Ed F. Bower, Town Constable Frank Murray, John Earb (a rifleman) and W.H. McCall who claimed he could identify Vaughan as having killed a man on the Texas border. This was U.S. Marshall Standefer's second encounter with Vaughan. It was Standefer who escorted Hank to the Oregon State Prison in 1865. (Bancroft, *Popular Tribunals*, Vol.., I, p. 715; Report of Superintendent of Commissioners of the Oregon State Penitentiary, Senate Proceedings, Messages and Documents 1865.)

2   In a letter from Leah Menifee dated July 7, 1961, she states that Charlie Long and his brother were on the Elliott wagon train which become lost in central Oregon in 1853. (See *Thunder Over the Ochoco*, Vol. II, *Distant Thunder*, Chapter 73.) Their parents had died of cholera en route to Oregon and the orphan boys were raised by James Howard, a Lane County minister. A great grand-daughter of Howard thought Charlie was shot and killed by Hank Vaughan in Prineville. Leah Menifee's great grand-parents were members of the 1853 wagon train.

Henry McCarty. . . now going by the name of Billy the Kid.[3] Another branch of the clan, the notorious McCarty brothers, were Hank Vaughan's brother-in-laws by his first marriage to Lois McCarty. Within four fleeting years, Long and Vaughan would trade bullets in Prineville, Oregon's Silver Dollar Saloon.

However, when Hank wasn't helping the McCarty boys steal horses and rob trains, he managed to avoid serious trouble while having great fun annoying lawmen at every chance. Neither was he always the target of their vexation. Pledging his gun to support the respectable citizens of Prineville was only one example of his complex nature. Some saw him as a gunman, a horse thief, a gambler and a drunk. Others, like Jim Blakely who knew him personally, remembered Hank as a jokester, a storyteller, a man of his word and a gentleman. All recognized his energy, ambition and leadership.

When Henry Villard arrived from Germany and took over as president of the Northern Pacific Railroad in 1881, he became acquainted with Vaughan. Villard's pet project was the linking of a transcontinental railroad to the Pacific Coast and Hank gained his powerful support by supplying the construction crews with hundreds of horses—stolen or otherwise. Vaughan also took a liking to railroad travel and not always with robbery in mind. In fact he was gaining a reputation for causing train robbers to re-think their occupation.

Shortly after Hank teamed up with his rich Indian girlfriend and a year before his arrival in Prineville, Hank and Martha (who often traveled with him) boarded a Northern Pacific coach bound for Spokane Falls, Washington. Hank was peacefully dozing when three men entered the railroad car and announced their intentions to relieve every passenger of their belongings. The instructions were simple: "Stand up, put your hands above your head and you won't get hurt." Then, while two outlaws stationed themselves at either end of the coach, the third went down the aisle collecting the traveler's valuables in a grain sack. Martha, sporting plenty of expensive jewelry, was in such a position that when Hank gave her a signal she moved his gun belt around so he could drop his hand and grab his revolver. When the single action Colt was in his hand, Vaughan

---

3   Billy the Kid's parents were Patrick and Catherine Devine McCarty. They had two sons, Joseph and Patrick Henry, the boy who grew up to be the famous "Billy the Kid." (McLaughlin, *An Encyclopedia of the Old West*, pp. 301, 335.)

started shooting. The holdup men lost their nerve and departed the train leaving the loot behind. Giving his fellow riders a baleful stare, Hank's sole comment was that it didn't seem right for a whole carload of men to let three thieves take advantage of them.[4]

Even though Hank helped the railroad at times it didn't mean that he—or more specifically his gang—was free from suspicion. But lawmen like the Blakely brothers who knew Vaughan intimately maintained that if you put your trust in Hank he would never let you down.

An early day passenger on the run between Ritzville and Spokane, Washington would tell of another time when Vaughan intervened for the railroad.[5] It seems that two men decided to board the train without paying any fare. According to the witness, "They were as tough as I ever saw. Both had Colts guns and swore they would ride or hurt someone." What transpired is best told in his words:

> . . . it was in the summer time and Hank was trying to take a "snooze" as he called it. When the conductor came through collecting fares the two bad men refused to pay. The conductor tried to explain that it was his duty to collect the fare and if they did not pay he would put them off. This was the conductor's mistake. The bad men swore by all that was holy that all the Northern Pacific employees from St. Paul to Tacoma could not make them pay fare or put them off. They flourished their guns and the passengers on the car were terror-stricken.

When Hank saw that the conductor was getting the worst of it, he took a good stretch, yawned several times and quick as a flash struck the largest fellow over the head with his own silver-plated gun, took him to the platform of the car and kicked him off. Everyone expected the other desperado to kill Hank, but he began to beg for mercy, but Hank took him by the collar and—well, I never saw a bad man get the drubbing that this fellow received. Hank was the hero of the hour and everyone wanted

---

4   Blankenship, *And There Were Men*, p. 232.
5   At the time, the author's great-grandfather, W.J. Sturdivan, was the town Marshall in Ritzville.

to be the first to shake his hand. Hank kept the two guns as mementos of the occasion.[6]

Six months before this run-in with the ticket cheaters in 1882, Hank and Martha arrived in Prineville. The *Ochoco Review* on December 3, 1881 would announce that Vaughan and his new companion, Martha Robie were living at the Jackson Hotel. "They had all evidence of wealth. Mrs. Roby-Vaughan wore diamonds of the first water and Hank had a pocket full of gold twenty-dollar pieces that he won shuffling cards."[7]

H.W. Fairweather, superintendent for the western division of the Northern Pacific, discovered a unique trait in Vaughan's character which many people—especially law men—were already aware of. One day Fairweather received an anonymous tip that Hank was planning to hold up the railroad pay wagon on its run from Spokane to Pend Oreille, Idaho with $200,000 in gold on board. In a smart move, Fairweather showed Hank the warning and offered to pay him $50 a day to ride as shotgun guard. Hank accepted and there was no attempt at robbery. As Fairweather later observed, "To put Hank on his honor was to win his allegiance."[8]

So for a time Hank was a hired gun for Northern Pacific and was known to have urged some undesirable gentlemen—by the means of bullets—to get out of town. For these displays of virtue Henry Villard was said to have given Vaughan a lifetime pass to travel any time on the Northern Pacific railroad. Hank would make good use of it. The abuse he had inflicted on his body over the years was catching up with him. Broken bones and gunshot wounds including at least one bullet from Charlie Long's Navy model Colt—which was still lodged near Hank's spine—caused him to travel south to soothe his aching body. By 1891, Hank had spent time at the Paso del Robles mineral springs in California and journeyed east to the Arkansas hot springs where, as a reporter for the *East Oregonian* put it, "Hank wished to try a health restorative."[9] But all he gained from this excursion was a little temporary relief.

---

6   Lue Vernon interview, *The Spokesman Review*, February 5, 1899.

7   This bit of information would be reprinted in *The Dalles Chronicle*, July 22, 1926.

8   *The Spokesman Review*, January 29, 1911.

9   *The East Oregonian*, January 5, 1891. Vaughan again visited Paso del Robles in the winter of 1891-92 and *The East Oregonian* of March 20, 1892 would report ". . . he feels like a new man."

These healing trips were being financed by Martha's settlement with the U.S. Government over horses lost to the hostile Shoshoni during the 1878 Bannock War.[10] The quest to find relief for his aching body may not have been very successful but apparently it did make Hank feel in a law abiding mood. On Christmas Day 1891, *The East Oregonian* reported that three men were creating a disturbance in the Blue Front Saloon. With assistance given by Hank Vaughan, Marshall Morgan arrested them. So Hank was again back in good form.

One of Hank's favorite hide-outs was located in the Wallowa Mountains of northeastern Oregon on the upper reaches of the Minam River. He had learned of the area from his Indian friends and it was here that he established a holding spot for stolen horses at what is now called Red's Horse Ranch in the Eagle Cap Wilderness. Even today it is accessible only by horse trails or by air.[11] Needless to say, with Hank's reputation early residents avoided this area at all costs. This is where Hank disappeared after the Roslyn bank robbery.

In late May 1893 when Vaughan emerged from his self-imposed exile his saddle mount was in bad need of new shoes and Hank was in need of a drink. So he rode into Pendleton and his first stop was the blacksmith shop where he had his horse shod in preparation for another ride into the mountains to round up cattle. While waiting for his horse, Hank stepped into Mrs. La Fontaine's Quelle Restaurant for lunch. Later he collected his horse but before leaving town he made the rounds of his favorite saloons. At about 5:30 in the evening, Hank stepped out of the Bureau Saloon located in the Transfer Hotel—better known as the Villard House—put spurs to his mount and rode furiously down Main Street toward the railroad depot. This breakneck speed was not unusual as it was said that Vaughan could lean from the saddle at a full gallop and pick

---

10 Office of Indian Affairs, Letters Received, 1887-1907, No. 13337-E, May 13, 1889, National Archives, Washington, D.C.

11 In 1946, Red Higgins (a Portland firefighter) bought 80 acres of land along with the old ranch house in what is now the Eagle Cap Wilderness and turned it into a popular retreat for Hollywood stars (Hank would have liked that.) Burt Lancaster is said to have helped lay the concrete floor of one of the buildings and legend has it that John Wayne was flown into the ranch aboard a DC-3 almost too big for the runway. Now in government ownership, the horse ranch has deteriorated for years under Forest Service management and they refuse to spend any money in renovation. ("Federal agency sits on once famous guest ranch," *The Bulletin*, Bend, Oregon, September 3, 1997.)

up a coin off the street . . . not only could but often did when he had been drinking heavily. He wasn't showing off this time.

Clark Wood, who was standing in front of Charley Reese's cigar store on Main Street said when Hank thundered by he was riding straight in the saddle. With disbelief, he saw Hank's horse lose its footing and fall sideways, pinning its rider beneath him. Many believed the horse caught a calk of its new shoes in the railroad tracks causing it to fall and throw its rider head-first into a pile of rocks. By the time witnesses to the accident arrived, the faithful horse had gained its footing and was standing motionless with Hank's foot still hung up in a stirrup.

Under the glaring headline, HURT AGAIN, *The East Oregonian* for May 31, 1893 would read:

> He was picked up, bleeding, dust-covered and insensible, his right eye nearly forced from its socket by striking the rocks and it looked for a time that the man who appears to have nine lives had at last been the victim of his own recklessness. He was taken to the Transfer House . . . and it was hard to say how his injuries would terminate. This morning, however, he rallied in good shape, and remarked, almost cheerfully: "It's pretty hard to kill me off."

During Hank's sixteen day struggle with death *The East Oregonian* would report that Hank received constant care from his family and friends. One of those friends who expressed great concern was none other than Charlie Long. All the old animosity had been forgotten and Charlie now looked upon Hank as someone to be admired. Charlie had his heart set on giving Hank some flowers to cheer him up but he couldn't find a florist shop mainly because Pendleton didn't have any. Being a determined man, Long entered a milliner's store and bought ten dollars worth of artificial flowers which he placed in a basin of water and sent up to Hank's room. Although he and Vaughan had shot each other more than once in Prineville's private war, in Long's mind it had been done in the line of duty and he held no grudge against Vaughan who was also doing his job. They just happened to be on opposite sides of the issue.

From the start, the press kept a running account on Hank's progress. Following are excerpts from *The East Oregonian*, the *Spokesman Review* and *The Dalles Times-Mountaineer*. For some unknown reason the only eastern Oregon newspaper keeping a low profile was the *Ochoco Review*. Perhaps publisher Barnes was afraid that Vaughan might recover. This is what the others had to report:

> *May 31* Vaughan is hurt somewhat about the chest, and may have a cracked rib. His eye is badly damaged but it is thought that he will not lose it.

> *June 5* Hank Vaughan is regarded by his physicians to be in pretty serious condition . . . and part of the time has been flighty and irrational . . .

> *June 8* Hank Vaughan took a turn for the worse . . . physically he is strong, his mental condition does not improve.

> *June 13* Hank Vaughan . . . lies in a condition of almost stupor and is unable to recognize those at his bedside.

> *June 14* Hank Vaughan's condition is considered quite critical. His throat seems paralyzed and he is unable to swallow.

> *June 15* A surgical operation was performed today for the relief of Hank Vaughan . . . three hours were consumed in the task. It is impossible to say at present whether he has a chance for recovery; yet Hank Vaughan has passed through many bad experiences, none of which an ordinary man could survive.

That evening *The Dalles Times-Mountaineer* broke the sad news: "This afternoon Dr. McKenzie of Portland assisted by Drs. Vincent, Smith and Guymon performed a surgical operation upon him [Vaughan] but he never rallied and died at 9 o'clock this evening . . . his skull was fractured and 12 or more pieces of shattered bone were removed . . ."

The East Oregonian on June 16, 1883 would tell the world in screaming headlines: "Hank Vaughan Dead—The life of one of the wild West's best known characters is ended." That said it all. Perhaps that is the way it should have been. The passing of Henry C. Vaughan also saw the passing of the frontier West. In his short but turbulent 44 years, Hank was a part of it. Now with a new and progressive generation clamoring for law and order Hank could not have long survived the restraints of civilization.

Vaughan was said to have killed 13 men "for business or for pleasure" and he carried the scars from that many bullets in his own body. As the solemn funeral precession carrying Hank's last remains left the Transfer House hotel, Hank would get the last laugh which would have delighted him. En route to the cemetery a runaway team crashed into another buggy, wrecking it and tangling up the horses as the impact launched seven Pendleton dignitaries into the dusty road. Hank was buried in an unmarked grave in the Olney Cemetery along the road to Pilot Rock, south of Pendleton, Oregon.[12]

The dirt hardly had time to settle on Hank's grave when Charlie Long joined him at that big horse-holding corral in the sky. After visiting Hank on his deathbed, Long returned to the Okanogan country of north central Washington where his ranch operation in partnership with George F. Smith, Jr. wasn't running too smoothly. It was known that Long threatened to kill Smith on several occasions, and it was also known that Charlie was mainly bluff. Smith, known as "The Okanogan Kid," thought he had a reputation to uphold but he was also scared to death of Charlie's fast draw. Eventually Smith saw his chance. He slipped up behind Charlie and killed him with an axe. Long was 48 years old at the time of his death.

Two men who lived by the gun and weathered a storm of bullets were now gone. It seems ironic that one was killed by a horse and the other was felled with a bloody axe. To celebrate these mishaps, the town of Mitchell, Oregon incorporated with a population of 50.

.   As years go, 1893 was not one to be celebrated. It came in with a ruinous depression; hit the midway mark with the exit of two colorful gunmen; and left with a bang when a boiler on the steamship *Annie Falon* exploded on the Snake River run. Captain Boughman saw his companion in the pilot house beheaded in the disaster. The new year of 1894 gave no indication of being any better.

---

12   Cemetery Records, City Hall, Pendleton, Oregon. Martha "Gus" Vaughan was 88 years old when she died in 1930. Her body was cremated and the ashes taken to Idaho to be placed beside her first husband, A.H. Robie. (*Athena Press*, March 28, 1937.)

CHAPTER 194

DISCOURAGING WORDS

Oh give me a home where the buffalo roam,
Where the deer and the antelope play,
Where seldom is heard a discouraging word,
And the skies are not cloudy all day.

"Home On the Range"
A Cowboy Ballad

The newborn year, baptized in the soiled waters of massive flooding, swept into Oregon cradled on the crest of an inland tidal wave. The Columbia backed up the Willamette River to a height of 33 feet—15 feet above flood stage—soaking most of downtown Portland in a 24-day overflow that caused an estimated $2 million in damage. The raging Ochoco River inundated the upper valley from hillside to hillside covering the meadows with debris as it ripped ranch buildings off their foundations and deposited tons of Ochoco topsoil on the streets of Prineville. Not to be outdone, an ice-choked Crooked River suddenly released its pent-up energy wiping out the Prineville flour mill while removing the Second Street bridge as it changed the river channel to its present location west of town.

During a pause in the flood, a new bridge (which required a different approach) was hurriedly constructed to keep up the flow of Prineville-Lakeview traffic. Then, following the February ice jam, a late spring run-off gushed down Crooked River in June. County Judge Bill Booth ordered Ed Harbin—the metal worker—to go down and inspect the new bridge. The bridge was doing fine but the newly constructed grade under Mesa Rim (now called Viewpoint) and the only approach to the south end of the bridge was not doing so well. During the examination a Silver Lake freighter came along and Harbin refused to let him cross the bridge. In a huff, the freighter walked back into town and complained to the judge. Mad as all get out, Judge Booth came back with the freighter and demanded that Harbin let him pass. Harbin wouldn't budge. But the judge overruled and the freight wagon passed over. The heavily loaded wagon was about 50 feet from the bridge when the grade collapsed taking some 30 feet of the south approach along with it down Crooked River.

Because of heavy traffic, the judge issued an order to replace the bridge immediately. Teams and men were sent to Mill Creek where they hewed out two logs for stringers; loaded them on logging wagons; and within the week traffic was again crossing over the silt-laden river. That done, Harbin and Harold Baldwin took a contract to rebuild the old Willamette Valley and Cascade Mountain Military Wagon Road bridge at Tetherow Crossing which also washed out during the spring floods. It took two years to complete the job, but its small wonder since the construction crew rode back and forth from Prineville daily, not on horseback, but on . . . bicycles!

Due in part to the spring flooding, freight charges became so exorbitant that the roads leading from Mitchell and Prineville to Shaniko were paved with wool. The *Antelope Herald* would report, "We are reliably informed that the citizens of the Hay Creek community are grading and repairing the public road with wool, preferring to utilize it in this way rather than haul it to The Dalles and lose money on it. Those loads were emptied into a mud-hole near Hay Creek last week and covered with earth."[1] The depression of 1894 was also playing a hand in this.

With the increase of livestock due to the depressed market, the range became overcrowded. In order to control feed and water, stockmen began to accumulate land under the government land laws by purchase, by political manipulation, by intimidation and by other means not necessarily legal. This was practiced to such a degree that the Blue Mountains and High Desert became virtually controlled by a comparatively few men formed into large companies. For example, the Prineville Land and Livestock Company, the Hay Creek Company and the Pacific Livestock Company (the Oregon branch of Miller and Lux) acquired title to very large holdings which gave them a great advantage over the smaller local stockmen.

---

1   *Antelope Herald*, April 9, 1894.

Beyond doubt, a great deal of fraud was practiced in securing title to the land. Final certificates were received for homesteads on lands situated high up in the mountains and deep in the desert where it was impossible to make a home or comply with the homestead laws. It has been stated that the Pacific Livestock Company secured title to many claims by directing their cowhands and other employees to locate homesteads on tracts of desirable grazing lands or springs and paying them $50 and expenses for their trouble and ranch. Big Muddy and Hay Creek were doing the same with their sheep herders and camp tenders.[2]

Lake-states timber companies were also busy securing vast holdings in the most valuable timber stands. Small land owners were either bought off or frightened out of the country and it was whispered that in a few cases homesteaders strangely disappeared. Shevlin-Hixon was gobbling up the upper Deschutes while Booth-Kelly took over the Ochoco. Every private landowner on the upper Ochoco sold timber rights to Booth-Kelly for 50¢ an acre. In turn, the big timber corporations leased grazing rights to the big livestock operations. During this period, the Oregon Western and Colonization Company was formed to dispense hundreds of thousands of acres of land granted to the wagon road companies by act of Congress. Dozens of settlers were told the land they had lived on for a quarter of a century no longer belonged to them and the ensuing battle cry would echo through the halls of Congress.

In spite of these setbacks, the Crooked River community was still expanding. Paulina faced competition when, on October 31, 1894, Suplee became another frontier outpost in the southeast corner of Crook County. This unique name was suggested by Charles Darling to honor his mother's maiden name and was accepted by Charlie Bernard and Joel Abbott, the founding fathers.

---

2 Similar practices were still being used as late as 1929. Mixed in the considerable holdings of the Mills Land & Livestock Company was a small amount of public land. One of the partners, Orrin Mills, had his wife's grandmother, Cora Agusta Cline-Telfer, file a homestead on the land. For appearances sake, Cora outfitted the crude cabin—which the company provided—with a skimpy selection of canned goods and hung a few old dresses in a corner. In an attempt to make it look like Cora was "proving up" on her land, she would visit the cabin, usually staying only overnight. This went on for about a year. Then Mills Land & Livestock Company took over the land. Everyone was happy. As remembered by Cora Peck-Morisette who visited the cabin with her grandmother during the summer of 1929 and retold to the author on April 20, 1995.

About the time Suplee was being named, a scattering of gun shots erupted on the Oregon-Idaho border and central Oregon settlers forgot all about battling among themselves. The Snakes had lost patience with white hunters who were shooting wild game merely for their hides and throwing away the meat. Earlier Dick Washakie—Gourd Rattler's son—complained that white men, trespassing on Indian allotments, were slaughtering game year around. By contrast the Shoshoni, sentenced to the narrow confines of the Wind River Reserve, hunted but once a year. He also questioned if the white men had the right to hunt on the reservation but because of his father's obsession with keeping the peace, the Shoshoni didn't interfere.[3]

The old dog soldier, High Head—one of the signers of the 1855 treaty at The Dalles and who had ridden shotgun guard for Has No Horse—was not bound by such foolish restraints. In November 1894 as the ranchers continued the slaughter of deer and elk, High Head and his hungry braves retaliated by waging war on the settlers cattle to get some meat. The stockmen in a state of panic called for army assistance. The cavalry galloped out of Fort Sheridan, Wyoming to put down this last Indian uprising deemed serious enough to require the dispatch of United States troops while two companies of 17th U.S. Infantry were transported by rail to Boise City.[4] High Head, somewhat overwhelmed by this reaction to a survival party, explained to his followers that they couldn't do much against 400 soldiers so they drifted quietly back to the reservation at Pocatello, Idaho.[5]

Two months before High Head had convinced himself and some undernourished Snake dog soldiers to declare war on a herd of shorthorns

3   Dick Washakie's testimony on the wanton slaying of wild game was entered into the U.S. Court of Claims as Case No. H.219, "Shoshoni Tribe of Indians, Petitioner v. The United States of America, Defendant."

4   Frederick W. Fraske, a litter bearer with Co F, 17th U.S. Infantry—at the age of 87—became the last survivor of the Indian Wars when in July 1961, 96-year-old Joseph Seufert of Auroria, Illinois died. "Indian War Survivor Spry at 87," *The Oregon Journal*, November 6, 1961.

5   Nicholas Kalama, High Head's grandson, a World War II veteran, cattleman and logger became chief of the Warm Springs Paiutes in January 1975. Kalama, born on the Warm Springs Reservation September 24, 1917 was 68 years old when he died October 30, 1985. He was survived by his wife of 38 years, Viola Wallulatun, sister of Chief Nelson Wallulatun of the Wasco tribe. For several days reservation flags flew at half-staff in memory of Nick Kalama. "Tribe Mourns Chief's Death,"*The Bulletin*, Bend, Oregon, October 30, 1985. The author had the honor of attending a tribal council meeting with Nick Kalama.

another Ochoco warrior was on the prowl. Til Glaze, owner of the famous racehorse Wasco (known as a money winner), had been hitting all the sporting events on the West Coast. Now he had his sights set on the Harney County Fair. On September 5, 1894, with Wasco in tow, he and Lorin (Jack) Parker rode into Burns prepared to do some heavy betting. Bud Howard, notorious gunman and another high-roller, was also in Burns planning to do the same thing. Gambling on the favorite horse to beat Wasco, Howard lost to Glaze and it didn't please him in the least.

Late in the evening of September 5, the three men met in the Tex Saloon. Bitter resentment flared and a group of onlookers scattered for safety from the trio's flashing guns. Eight shots rang out. When the gun smoke cleared, Parker—supporting Glaze in the duel—remained unhurt but Glaze was mortally wounded and Howard was dead. "Old Whit" had spoken again.

The coroner's jury brought in two separate verdicts; one stating that Glaze came to his death by means of a weapon in the hands of Bud Howard; the second read that Howard also died of gunshot wounds. The weapons causing such wounds being in the hands of Til Glaze and Jack Parker at the time said weapons were discharged. Tried and convicted of manslaughter, Parker was sentenced to seven years and six months in the Oregon State Penitentiary.

Charlie Byrd, editor of the *Burns Herald* had this comment on said shooting:

> All three parties engaged in this disgraceful and wholly uncalled for tragedy are well known in sporting circles in this state and other places. Bud Howard was known to be a dangerous man when provoked and Til Glaze was known to have been a man of the same stripe and when angered was a terrible man to abuse and browbeat all who crossed his path. John Lorin Parker, on the other hand, is not considered bad and from an acquaintance with him, we would take him to be inoffensive and generally courteous and very well behaved young man but when drinking we presume, like most others who indulge in that curse, strong drink, he says and does things a sane man would blush to think of.

We are truly sorry for the young man that he allowed himself to be drawn into this trouble and God knows, we hope it will be such a lesson to him that he will eternally vow and keep the pledge to leave the cursed stuff alone that results when taken into the stomach in crazing the brain and not only him but all others here to take warning and be a man and not let the brutish instincts which are common to the human family get the mastery.[6]

From his rambling, it would appear Charlie had sampled "the curse" before taking pen in hand . . . anyway, it's food for thought.

The last bullet fired from the gun that killed Bud Howard was shot by the mortally wounded Glaze. After Til's death, his son Warren kept "Old Whit"—a .36 calibre Navy Colt—under glass locked in a Prineville bank vault.

Glaze and Howard had barely been laid to rest when masked riders rode into Lake County and shot a Silver Lake merchant. It took three bullets to kill him. A jury friendly to the Crook County Livestock Association ruled his death a suicide although he'd been shot in the back. Shortly thereafter, a big Christmas celebration was planned. On Christmas Eve nearly 200 people from southern Crook and northern Lake counties crammed into a second story hall in Silver Lake and the festivities began. During the course of the evening someone accidentally knocked a kerosene lamp to the floor and the crowd panicked. In the struggle to escape, the overloaded stairway crashed to the ground and forty-three people perished in the blazing dance-hall.[7] It was enough to sober everyone for a year. No doubt about it, Christmas was a bad time for both Indians and white citizens of central Oregon.

The most excitement for 1895 originated and ended in the Mitchell country. Perhaps because they were predominately sheepmen, another effort was mounted in January to create the county of Sutton from parts of Crook and Grant with Mitchell as county seat. This proposal was fought out on the floor of the state legislature but the Mitchellites dream of separation again fell through and so ended a second attempt in two

---

6   The *Burns Herald*, September 6, 1894.
7   Veva Marietta Louise Buick Poorman, the last survivor of the Silver Lake fire on Christmas Eve 1894 died in Syracuse, New York on March 29, 1993 of natural causes. She was 98. She was buried in the Belcrest Cemetery, Salem, Oregon on April 6, 1993.

years to obtain a divorce from Crook County. Then to add insult to injury, Jim and A.G. Palmer (first elected county clerk of Crook) purchased the plant of the *Mitchell Monitor* and removed it to Prineville where the newspaper business wasn't too successful. George Barnes saw to that.

Perched on Crook County's northern border, Charlie Clarno—having lost faith in Mitchell's attempt at freedom—was seeing his own dream come true. Clarno, who operated a ferry on the John Day River, loved to experiment with boats. Over the years, he had saved enough money to buy a steam boiler and in 1895 built a miniature sternwheeler. Measuring 40' x 10' x 10' with a 3' x 3' pilot house just large enough for his head and shoulders, Clarno launched his craft on the John Day River 109 miles upstream from its junction with the Columbia. Charlie was soon making money charging $1 to cross the river in his new vessel. Soon people were coming from 100 miles in all directions to take an excursion on the *John Day Queen* for a 12-mile run above and below Clarno's landing. Sometimes it wasn't all fun as paying passengers were often obligated to help cut wood for the boiler's furnace.

It wasn't long before the river trips became big business. Clarno had a pipe organ (played by his sister) specially installed on deck and moonlight cruises including all night dances were in great demand. In fact, a trip on the *John Day Queen* became one of the more important social events of the gay nineties. The *John Day Queen* was also used for rescue service and as a passenger ferry until a bridge was built across the lower river in 1897. Actually, the river could be forded during low water but to make a buck Charlie warned all newcomers about nonexistent quicksand. Local residents and stage drivers never bothered with the ferry except during the spring run-off.

After the bridge was completed, Charlie sold his ranch and moved to Portland where he and his brother operated the Jefferson Street Hotel. In 1900, he decided to bring the *John Day Queen* down to Portland to operate as a pleasure craft on the Willamette River. There was only one problem—below Clarno's ranch the river dropped only 10 feet in four miles then in the next mile it plunged 40 feet lower over Clarno rapids. Unlike the steamer *Shoshoni*, the *John Day Queen* wasn't up to the task.[8] She crashed into the rocks and sank. The boiler was bought and raised

---

8   For more on the *S.S. Shoshoni*, see *Thunder Over the Ochoco*, Vol. III, Chapter 100, pp. 85-6.

from the river by a Dallas farmer to be used to power an irrigation pump. It made it as far as Shaniko where it rusted away in a wool warehouse. So ended the cruise of the *John Day Queen*, the only steamer to navigate the John Day River.[9]

In November 1895—as Mitchell's elite cruised the moonlit river aboard the *John Day Queen*—fire bugs appeared a few miles south of Clarno's ranch torching haystacks as they went in an attempt to put sheepmen out of business. On Cherry Creek, James Connally saw 180 tons of hay go up in smoke in a matter of minutes. Other sheepmen lost equal amounts of winter feed as five ranches were burned out in a matter of weeks.

To the unconcerned bystander the central Oregon range war is difficult to comprehend. It had all the primal instincts, not only of self-preservation, but self-achievement. In the minds of those involved—powerful cattlemen and equally powerful sheepmen—it was not a malicious act but more like heads of state enjoying one another's company while their countrymen slaughtered each other. High-rolling speculators, the big-time operators habitually faced each other across the gambling tables and the odds in this new game of chance were no different except that the stakes were human lives.

Before you judge, just remember that is the way the cards are dealt in the charade of life. The deer and the wolf may drink together but when the wolf becomes hungry the battle is on and may the best and strongest survive. Out classed? Hardly! Many a mule deer buck has gored his opponent into the dust . . . and many a wolf has torn the mule deer to shreds. The scale is unbalanced only in weakness and it was not meant for the weak, the sick, the unwary to be victors. Sylvester Pennoyer would argue against that concept—George Barnes, Jim Blakely or Til Glaze would not.

And so, the owners and managers of the large livestock outfits wined and dined together while their employees shot each other. With this in mind, ride into the Ochoco during its savage tenure under civilized domination.

---

9 *Oregon Journal*, June 5, 1938; *The Dalles Optimist*, August 14,1958; "The John Day—Landlocked Queen," The Commission of Public Docks, Portland, Oregon, 1967.

CHAPTER 195

CLOUDY SKIES

We would thank the Oregonian and the Governor to attend strictly to their business and not meddle with the settlement of the range question in our province . . . .

Corresponding Secretary
Crook County Sheepshooters
Association

On January 1, 1897, the population of Crook County stood at 3,212. By January 1, 1898 it had increased to 5,000. In an off-year election it appears that citizens of the Bridge Creek area, in an effort to slip through the political back door, had done some heavy campaigning. Robert Misener, a Mitchell saloon owner, was voted into the state legislature representing the county of Crook. It's hard to believe he wouldn't promote Mitchell's pet project . . . but for some undisclosed reason, once elected he didn't.

During the year it was estimated that 320,000 sheep; 40,000 cattle; and 10,500 branded horses were fighting for grass; while 1,500 hogs, 250 mules and an unknown number of big game were competing for the same forage. It was inevitable that trouble would ensue. The continued trespassing of outside sheep owners on range the cattlemen had for years considered their undisputed domain could mean nothing less than war. The local sheepmen who had occupied this range for years respected the rights of the cowmen by keeping off the range grazed by cattle. And the cattlemen respected the sheepmen's rights. In fact most ran both sheep and cattle until the outsiders came and then each had to make a choice—sheep or cattle—but not both thus pitting neighbor against neighbor in a no-holds-barred struggle for survival.

171

The first split came in 1896 when the big IZ cattle outfit organized the ranchers in the Snow Mountain area—where Crook, Grant and Harney counties border—into the Izee Sheepshooters Association. From this start came the sheep and cattle war which was an organized attempt by the cattlemen to drive the sheep owners back from the country they called cow range. They would strike swiftly and brutally.

The Izee Sheepshooters covering everything from Beaver Creek to Bear Valley; and from Wolf Mountain south to Silver Creek were able to keep up with the sheep problem but not for long. Over the next few years four more groups were organized to aid in the extermination of range maggots. With the Izee boys riding shotgun, 1897 passed without much fanfare due in part to the discovery of gold on the Yukon River in 1896. This drained most of the manpower out of eastern Oregon including the laborers at the Mayflower Mine, which was still shipping gold ore by freight wagons and railroad cars to Tacoma, Washington.

Fresh from the eastern Oregon camps, some of the more colorful characters to arrive in Dawson City—the boomtown of Yukon Territory—were Nellie Cashman, Joaquin Miller, Jack Miller and Katherine Rockwell. Nellie Cashman would soon be idolized as "Dawson Nellie," the miners guardian angel. Joaquin Miller, the old Shoshoni war veteran, had been dispatched by the San Francisco *Examiner* to do on-the-spot reporting of the Alaska gold rush. Jack Miller, the Snow Mountain logger now going by the name of Jack Dalton, opened the famous Dalton Trail from eastern Oregon to Yukon Territory. And Katherine Rockwell became admired by the sourdoughs as "Klondike Kate, the Queen of the Yukon." Since Kate is—in some respects—a local girl it seems proper to make her acquaintance.

Born in Kansas in 1877, Kitty Rockwell grew up in the rowdy logging town of Spokane Falls, Washington Territory. By her own description Kitty was "a handsome girl with violet eyes and red-gold hair."[1] From infancy the young redhead was a lively, impulsive girl whose strong will was difficult to control. In desperation her mother enrolled Kitty in various boarding schools but that did little to solve the problem as Kitty was expelled from each one because of her outlandish

---

1   All direct quotes are attributed to Kate when she lived in Prineville, Oregon at the turn of the 20th century.

behavior such as dancing and flirting with older men. At one convent school Kitty managed to collect seven diamond engagement rings before the horrified sisters found out what was going on and made her return them all.

By 1890 standards, Katherine was far from being a proper young lady. Because she lived only for fun and parties, mother Rockwell decided to take her spirited offspring to New York City for a change of scene and some strict supervision. Things did not work out the way mama planned. In New York teenage Kate, under the name "Kitty Phillips," got a job as a chorus girl in a variety theater. Apparently metropolitan culture was not the solution to austerity.

Home again in Spokane Kitty completed her "finishing school" in the boxhouses of the rambunctious lumber towns.[2] While she preferred being an on-stage performer working the floor was more profitable. The now seasoned boxhouse girl wandered for a time through the mining and logging camps of eastern Oregon and Washington following new opportunities. It wasn't long before she ended up in Seattle, the sin capital of the Pacific Northwest.

Kitty Rockwell and Seattle took to each other immediately and soon she was working for Big John Considine—the undisputed king of the boxhouses—in his infamous People's Theater. It was claimed by those who knew that Big John dressed his pretty waitress girls in short red jackets, black stockings, fancy garters, red slippers and . . . nothing else! Attendance increased enormously until law officers modified his dress code.

Kitty did not stay long in Seattle because yet another adventure was beckoning her. Gold had been discovered in the Yukon causing the biggest gold rush in history and Kitty wanted to be right in the middle of it. If there was one thing the lusty redhead had learned in the rough towns of eastern Oregon it was that a girl could do quite well by mining the miners. So she headed for Dawson City to pan the boy's pokes and win their hearts. She was pretty and she was ambitious. At twenty years of age, Kitty was the most sought after nugget in the gold-crazed Yukon . . . an enticing temptress in flesh-colored tights studded with

---

2   A boxhouse was a small theater supposedly for variety stage acts but in reality a brothel. The girls operated out of tiny second and third-tier cubicles or "boxes."

glittering rhinestones who freely admitted to earning $30,000 a year.[3] Soon the sourdoughs were calling her "Klondike Kate, the Queen of the Yukon."

In later years while serving coffee at her Prineville donut shop and restaurant Kate—her violet eyes twinkling—would laugh: "When I arrived in Dawson in 1898 miners were paying a dollar a dance that lasted less then a minute and $15 for a bottle of wine." She would also recall that these lonely miners would shower gold dust at the feet of the dance hall girls and often paid as much as $750 just to be honored by their company. According to Kitty her most spectacular number was the Flame Dance. "I was draped in 200 yards of chiffon which I kept floating about me as I danced under a play of colored lights. That act wouldn't get a hand today but the miners went wild about it. They called me the Flame of the Yukon."

Kitty rode high on the gold rush sporting $300 hats and $1,000 gowns. But also during this time she began an intense relationship that was to end as one of the great tragedies in her life. In a moment of unbridled passion Kitty lost her heart to a crafty Greek boxhouse waiter named Alexander Pantages. On the promise of wedded bliss, she grub-staked him for five years while he advanced from drink server to wealthy theatrical magnate boasting lavish theaters from San Francisco to Seattle, and from Portland to Spokane. During his rise to economic power, the Greek jilted the Belle of the Yukon and married a girl from—in his words—"the right side of the tracks." Maybe he did and maybe not. Kate would later claim that Pantages' new consort was nothing more than another chorus girl and she didn't take this affront to her reputation lying down.[4]

It was during this lover's spat that a forlorn Katherine Rockwell arrived in the railroad rejected town of Prineville, Oregon and opened a restaurant on North Main Street next to Mother Thompson's cafe where she entertained old friends from the gold rush days.[5] Dressed in the latest

---

3   "Klondike Kate," *Echoes From Old Crook County*, p. 121.

4   Glaring headlines in every major newspaper from the Pacific to the Atlantic shouted to a breathless world: "Klondike Kate sues Alexander Pantages for breach of promise." However in a bitter legal battle Kate never collected the $25,000 suit. (*Echoes From Old Crook County*, "Klondike Kate," p. 121.

5   Kate's restaurant, located between 4th and 5th streets, was sometimes referred to as Woodcraft Hall. It is interesting to note that the devastating fire of 1922 which destroyed most of the

fashion Kate would impress the local girls with her expensive wardrobe. They had never imagined let alone seen such elegant gowns of silk, velvet and satin. She also caused a stir among the community ranchers one of whom admiringly stated: "Kate was the first woman I ever saw who could roll a cigarette with one hand."

In 1914 at the ripe old age of 37, Kitty Rockwell married Floyd Warner and moved to his one-room shack on Salt Creek so named because the newlyweds—in their rush to enjoy matrimonial bliss—had forgotten to bring salt with them on their honeymoon.[6] It wasn't long before Floyd again heard the call of the wild and abandoned Kate. She then filed a homestead claim near Hampton Butte in what is now Deschutes County and eventually moved to the booming sawmill town of Bend, Oregon. In Prineville Kitty was fondly known to one and all as "Aunt Kate." In the quasi-sophisticated city of Bend she was rudely called "our destitute prostitute."[7] On this scornful note let's return to the dusty streets of Prineville and the oncoming central Oregon range war.

---

town's business district spared Kate's restaurant. The old building stood for many years before being torn down in the 1960's.

6   A tributary of Bear Creek, Salt Creek drains a barren chunk of real estate some seven miles south of the Bear Creek arm of Prineville reservoir on Crooked River. The honeymoon shack was still standing in the early 1970's.

7   Her wealth from the far North having long since escaped her Kate worked at whatever cooking and cleaning jobs she could find in Bend to get by. But perhaps her luck would change. Some 30 years in the past during the Yukon gold stampede a little Norwegian by the name of Johnny Matson would come to Dawson City every fall. For the next four or five days he would just sit around and watch Kitty perform. Known as the Silent Swede of Dawson, he never gambled or drank. Johnny just sat and watched the beautiful dance hall girl for the little hard-bitten prospector and trapper had fallen love with the Belle of the Yukon. Thirty-one years would pass and no one knew, not even Kate herself, how much Johnny Matson adored her.

Then, in 1931 during a Yukon blizzard, the little Norwegian miner was thumbing through a soiled copy of the *Alaska Weekly* when he chanced upon the name and address of Klondike Kate. He wrote a letter telling her about the love he had for her and promised if she would marry him he would take care of her. Kitty's knockout looks were gone but it hardly mattered to Matson for she was still the girl he had dreamed of on the long, cold Yukon nights. As for Kitty, she dreamed only of sharing Johnny's pot of gold but when Kate finally met the silent Swede of Dawson things started popping. The courtship by mail lasted nearly two years and then in 1933 Johnny came "outside" and the legends were united in Canada. Some would claim this was a strange marriage and maybe it was but it was right for Johnny and Kate.

After the ceremony Matson returned to his Yukon claim searching for the rich vein of gold he had pledged to Kate while Kate returned to Bend glorying in her new name. Over the years they wrote letters and got together every spring but Johnny refused to move to Bend. Sadly, lady luck was not to smile on Johnny for he died in his little cabin on Matson Creek in 1946 still searching for Kitty's elusive wedding present.

Meanwhile, Mrs. Kate Matson became a profit making sensation. Her flaming hair was now

175

With gold pouring into the West Coast, the livestock market exploded. The year 1897 saw cattle dump $8.8 million into state coffers; sheep and wool $4.9 million; and horses would add another $3 million. Now flush with money, a group of prominent cattlemen, sheepmen and merchants—Sam Smith, John Edwards, Tom Baldwin, Leo Fried and George Barnes—joined forces like old buddies and in March rode down to Carson City, Nevada to see Gentleman Jim Corbett and Bob Fitzsimmons slug it out for the heavyweight boxing title.

Corbett, a West Coast boy, known as a stick of dynamite on a short fuse, was the big favorite and betting was heavy among the Prineville supporters. After all, Corbett had fought Big Pete Jackson to a 61 round draw; then decked John L. Sullivan in the 21st round for the heavyweight title of the world. Now he was pitted against a scrawny 165 lb. Englishman from Cornwall, Wales who held world titles in two weight classes and now was after his third.[8]

The Prineville boys figured they could make a killing as all the Nevada miners—most of whom were Cornishmen—were betting heavily on Fitzsimmons. The only taker in the Prineville crowd was John Edwards, manager of the Hay Creek sheep outfit. John Griffith Edwards, who claimed to be an English nobleman, was also a native of Wales. When they saw Fitzsimmons climb into the ring, the Prineville high-roll-

tinged with gray but she never missed a trick when there was a chance to garner some publicity—and she wanted to be paid rather exorbitantly for anything she did. Kitty toured the country and appeared on shows where she was often described as a "rough talking old gal." Many stories about Klondike Kate may stretch the truth at times but Kitty would have approved as she always liked to make a show of herself. Much to the irritation of the virtuous ladies of Bend, Kate became the darling of the Bend volunteer fire department. In fact the firemen made her an honorary volunteer presenting Kate with a membership card which she carried with pride.

At the age of 71, two years after Matson's death Kate married again, this time to a long-time friend, Bill Van Duren. When asked why she was marrying again at her age, Kitty laughed: "Why not? Time's running out. I was the flower of the north but the petals are falling fast honey." The Van Duren's settled in the Willamette Valley town of Sweet Home where Klondike Kate Rockwell of Spokane, Seattle, Prineville and Bend died in 1957 at 80 years of age. At her request, Kate was cremated and it came to pass that the girl from the frozen north was laid to rest on the parched sands of the central Oregon high desert. (Interview with Roy Matson who was working at the Champion Lode mine in the upper Ochoco Valley in the late 1930's; Meier, *Those Naughty Ladies of the Old Northwest*, p. 22; "Klondike Kate," *Echoes From Old Crook County*, pp. 121-122; *Little Known Tales from Oregon History*, Vol. I, pp. 74-76.)

8   At the time, Fitzsimmons held the middleweight title and light heavyweight title of the world. Robert Wallace, *The Miners*, pp. 108-09.

ers knew they had their bets won. "My gawd!" Sam Smith laughed, "Fitzsimmons looks like a cannon-ball on a pair of pipe stems."

It was St. Patrick's Day and news reporters were setting up strange looking cameras for the main event but hardly anyone paid much attention to this. They came to see a boxing match. Finally Gentleman Jim and the Cornishman squared off. In the 14th round, the guy who looked like a cannon ball on pipe stems knocked out Corbett to become the world's new heavyweight boxing champion. Other than Edwards, the Prineville fans returned home broke.

Within a few weeks, the Marquam Grand Theater in Portland would advertise Oregon's first motion picture show. The Fitzsimmons-Corbett fight had been recorded on film and prices to see this epic event ran from $5 for a box seat to 25¢ for a gallery seat.

Again, the sporting gents of Prineville took the stage to Portland for the 4th of July celebration to witness the world champion broadsword fighter, Russian Baron Ivan de Malchin take on the West Coast's best, Pvt. Earl Nelson of the U.S. Cavalry stationed at Fort Vancouver. The baron won. So did some Crook County gamblers.

Six months earlier, an ex-Ochoco resident's rowdy son wasn't so lucky. To celebrate the arrival of New Year 1897, young Washakie strolled into an Idaho saloon, got into a poker game and ended up getting shot. He was Gourd Rattler's second son to die in a tavern brawl. When word reached the old chief, he swore he would come down from the mountains, gun-down the first white man he met and continue shooting until he himself was killed. In a state of panic, Rev. John Roberts (a Methodist Episcopal missionary) hearing of this rushed to Gourd Rattler's lodge and offered to forfeit his life for that of the slain son. The chief refused his generous offer. Curious, he asked what medicine the Reverend possessed that made him so foolhardy. It must have been potent for at 3 a.m. the morning of January 24, 1897, Gourd Rattler became a Christian and was baptized into the Episcopal Church.[9]

When word trickled into Big Summit Prairie through the Indian grapevine that Gourd Rattler had seen the light, cousin Has No Horse was unimpressed. He now placed Gourd Rattler in the same category as The Cutter . . . slightly balmy. Neither did he believe in the now popular

---

9   Ziegler, *Wyoming Indians*, p. 10; Trenholm and Carley, *The Shoshoni*, p. 308.

Peyote Cult introduced into the Shoshoni family by the Comanches. In the last decade of the 19th century, Peyotism had become the accepted religion of most Shoshonean tribes.[10] In retrospect it seems a certain white gentleman could have benefited from some spiritual guidance as much as Gourd Rattler when it came to poaching his fellow man.

Toward the end of the year Pete French, branded as one of the worst land grabbers in eastern Oregon—observing the Izee sheep-shooters success with running off sheep herders—decided a few home-steaders were also crowding. On the day after Christmas he sallied forth to do justice. In an argument with Ed Oliver, Oliver—a shade faster draw—shot and killed French. The trial was held in Canyon City where Oliver was acquitted of a murder charge simply because the jury was made up of homesteaders.

In the excitement of Pete's unfortunate accident, news hound George Barnes—French's cousin—overlooked the arrival of an unrec-ognized celebrity in the fair city of Prineville. The widow Mary F. Jones who went to work for Joe Eliott was the granddaughter of Captain Meriweather Lewis who, along with Captain William Clark, blazed the trail to Oregon.[11]

Five days after French staked out the only 6' x 6' plot he could truthfully call his own, the new year of 1898 marched into central Oregon facing an uncertain future. Great plans were being formulated with ramifications yet to come. Some six months earlier, the Forest Reserve Act of June 4, 1897 assigned responsibility to the Department of Interior

---

10   The Indians of Mexico—called Barefooters by the Shoshoni—were the first to use Peyote, a powerful intoxicant and narcotic drug obtained from the dried upper part of the Mescal cactus found in Mexico and Texas; second were the Apaches and third the Comanches. (Stenberg, *The Peyote Cult*, pp. 143-45.) Quanah Parker, chief of the Comanches, who introduced it to other family members would say: "I'll say it is good medicine to use. I've been through the mill. White people usually call it mescal. Some say it is a drug; I say it ain't a drug. It is a herb .... Some people say it makes you crazy. I know it won't. I've been taking it over thirty years and still got my head." ("Alice Marriott gives Quanah Parker's 'Peyote Way,'" in *The Ten Grandmothers*, pp. 165-72.)

11   Mrs. Mary F. Jones died in Burns, Oregon of heart disease at the age of 71. She was born Mary Lewis, October 5, 1858, at Stewartville, Missouri. She was the daughter of Meriweather Lewis, son of Capt Meriweather Lewis, "The Pathfinder." Following the death of her husband, she came west and settled in Prineville in the late '90's. She lived in Prineville and Bend until January of 1929. A member of the Joe Eliott household, it was with Mr. Eliott that she came to Burns. She was survived by one son, Lewis Jones of Oklahoma City, four daughters, Mrs. Anna Bryant of Tacoma, Mrs. Bessie Frisbie of Jacksonville, Oregon, Mrs. Etta Smith of Milwaukee, Oregon and Miss Cora Jones of Bend. (Obituary, *Burns News*, February 8, 1929.)

for the administration, conservation and use of public forest lands. Designated national forest reserves, these large tracts were surveyed, managed and protected by the General Land Office. The Act also provided for mineral prospecting, location and entry of mining claims on forested lands. Early in February 1898—under the placer mining law—search for oil was included and Yellowstone Park was designated a timber reserve.

Between such activities as annexing the Hawaiian Islands, extending public land laws into Alaska and declaring war on Spain, Congress found time to create the Cascade Forest Reserve which, for the next two years, was closed to livestock grazing. This legislation was intended to alleviate the growing unrest in central Oregon's livestock industry. Instead, the federal government successfully dropped the spark which blew the lid off the powder keg. Sheepmen who formerly grazed the Cascade range were forced to look elsewhere for summer pasture. They saw the Blue Ochoco Mountains. In wild exaltation, herders pushed their bleating flocks onto cattle range.

The stampede of small operators into the Ochoco Blues may, in part, have been the direct result of a report made to the state legislature by the Hon. Newton Williamson on January 1, 1898. If taken at face value it appears to encourage more livestock owners to settle in Crook County. "I will make the statement truthfully," shouted Williamson from the House floor, "and without pretense of booming the county, that Crook has withstood the pressure of the recent hard times as well as any community on the Pacific Coast. There have been fewer business failures, less enforced idleness and want than elsewhere. This statement of fact simply proves the assertion that a stock raising country is the best country on earth *for a poor man.*"[12] Maybe so, but in the minds of the cowmen, the continued trespass of foreign sheep could mean nothing less than war.

Before snow-melt, sheepmen from five northern counties—Wasco, Gilliam, Umatilla, Sherman and Morrow—were rushing into the Ochoco Mountains each with an idea of getting the best camps to operate from. On the south, the same prevailed as sheepmen from Lake and Klamath counties grazed the high desert from Horse Ridge to Snow

---

12 *Illustrated History of Central Oregon*, p. 713. Williamson, a powerful sheep operator, was grazing several large bands in the Ochoco at this time.

Mountain. In so doing, they clashed with the big cattle companies of Crook, Grant and Harney.

Herders pushed their flocks to the doorsteps of the cattlemen, setting fire to the range when they left in the fall. It was usual for bands to mix with others and have to be separated five or six times during the grazing season. When mix-ups occurred it generally meant building a separating corral. Two of the more famous ones were Ochoco Corral in the Lookout Mountain area and Association Corral near Snow Mountain. When a corral was constructed it was always in demand and nearly always in use bringing thousands of sheep to this point and trampling out all vegetation as they passed. The rancher on whose range the corral was located would remove this nuisance with a match.

The sheep owners had no interest in the land other than to get by for one season and let the next year take care of itself. Damage beyond repair was being done. Grass, once so plentiful it seemed there was enough for all the livestock in the state of Oregon, was fast disappearing. Range management, if such was thought of, was to out-manage your neighbor and beat him to the grass if you could. It was not uncommon for herders to leave their sheep miles back on the trail as they hurried ahead to claim a favorite campsite so another outfit couldn't use it.

No area, however high the carrying capacity, could withstand the continued onslaught that the Ochoco was being subjected to year after year; but the rush for forage went on without abatement. No area in the United States so needed the healing hand of the conservationist as the livestock and big game ranges of the Ochoco. By the turn of the 20th century, the high mountain meadows and bunchgrass plateaus were little more than the bleached ribs of an overgrazed, often burned, eroded land.

It can be guessed that the fugitive Shoshoni hid out in Big Summit Prairie were appalled over this desecration of the country they once called home. As one old warrior would put it: "Continue to contaminate your bed and you will one night suffocate in your own waste."[13] The grass-hungry stockmen of central Oregon would prove this observation to be correct.

Hay Creek Co. was one of the first to gird for battle. Tom Baldwin—aware of the coming storm—placed his sheep operation under

---

13   Sealth, a Duwanish chief, in a letter to President Franklin Pierce, dated 1855

the iron fist of a combat veteran. John Edwards had been in range wars in Utah, Colorado and Wyoming. He was no greenhorn when it came to fighting for grass. In Wyoming, the man of English nobility had seen his flocks increase to more than 100,000 head of purebred sheep and it wasn't cattlemen who drove the tough Welshman from his Wyoming range. Homesteaders and their barbed wire fences sent Edwards to Oregon seeking new lands. In the interim he hired on as ranch manager for the Hay Creek operation which employed over 100 men.

Now, as the grass-starved summer of '98 headed toward armed conflict, Baldwin sold Hay Creek Company to Edwards, Charlie Cartwright and J.P. Van Houten. Within three years, Edwards took complete control of the sprawling ranch empire and was importing registered Rambouillets from the French government's own flock. Oregon Blue Boy, the ranch's prize ram nabbed a blue ribbon at the Chicago World's Fair. For the moment, all Edwards had to worry about was to protect his pureblood sheep from coyotes mounted on horseback.

As droves of sheep applied more and more pressure during the '98 grazing season, the Central Oregon Sheepshooters Association was formed in the Paulina area to back up the Izee Sheepshooters. By 1898, the all-powerful Inland Sheepshooters Association headquartered in Prineville was sweeping the Ochoco Valley range; followed in 1902 by the Crook County Sheepshooters Association based on Camp Creek; and in 1903, the Lake County Sheepshooters Association headquartered in Silver Lake which covered all grazing lands from the upper Deschutes River through to Wagontire Mountain in Harney County.

At the beginning—during the spring and summer of 1898—both contestants in the range war were having a bit of a problem recruiting foot soldiers as many young central Oregon hotbloods had galloped off to try their luck in the Spanish American War.[14] No big deal. The war was over by August 2, 1898 and the home guard was soon back in the local trenches gleefully plunking away at whatever fell into their gun sights . . . and those gun sights would come to rest on the most colorful figure the Ochoco has ever know.

---

14   On May 11, 1898, the Second Oregon Infantry (several of whom were Crook County lads) shipped out for the Philippine Islands where they gained national fame taking a conspicuous part in the surrender of Manila. At the same time, the battleship *USS Oregon* fired the first shot at the battle of Santiago helping to destroy the Spanish fleet in Cuba Bay.

CHAPTER 196

A BULLET FOR HAS NO HORSE

Booming from peak to echoing peak,
Thunder drowned out the gale's thin shriek,
While the only color the sky could show
Was an angry smudge . . . a saffron glow.

Ethel Jacobson
Mountain Storm

Central Oregon cattlemen would boast that the IZ organization was in excellent working order and they weren't exaggerating. Having become accomplished sheepshooters, the IZ boys were soon liberating the range from other unnecessary pests including a few stray Indians.

In the twilight of the 19th century, the word-artist Carrie Blake Morgan might well have described Has No Horse as being . . . a gaunt phantom of yesterday haunting today. And that would have been true but the aging Snake war lord still held that spark of defiance which he applied so often in the defense of his people. This overpowering drive for equal treatment may have launched the Man Who Has No Horse on what could have been his last vision quest.

In late September a small Shoshoni party rode out of Big Summit Prairie to gather food for the coming winter. Moving leisurely up Beaver Creek gathering roots and berries, they eventually drifted into the South Fork canyon of the John Day River. Here, they had the misfortune to blunder into a group of riders returning from a sheep raid in Paulina Valley. In a matter of seconds all—two men and four women—were killed, their bodies calmly tossed over a cliff into the river along with weapons and camp equipment. Their horses, having some value, were confiscated.[1]

To further promote goodwill some range riders stole ten of the best saddle mounts from a Shoshoni herd in Big Summit Prairie. His patience worn thin, Has No Horse, with six battle-scared veterans of an earlier time, took to the trail of the vanished ponies. The old dog soldier was in a foul humor when they camped for the night on Deer Creek, a tributary to the South Fork of the John Day River. John Hyde, an Izee rancher, happened to ride past their camp and the Shoshoni immediately accused Hyde of stealing their horses. During the argument, the Shoshoni—in typical Indian style—formed a circle around Hyde who panicked and spurred his horse through the cordon of warriors.

Late that evening Hyde galloped into Bill Officer's ranch shouting, "That old Snake sonuvabitch Al Ochiho tried to shoot me.!"[2] This was unlikely as he rode into Officer's ranch without a bullet hole in him and the Snakes were not known to waste bullets just for the sheer enjoyment of it. Anyway, Hyde gathered the Izee sheepshooters and by daybreak, they were on their way to pay Has No Horse a visit. Daylight was slow in coming on this overcast morning and the vibration of pounding hoofbeats was augmented by the echo of crackling ice on the frozen ground.

The Shoshoni had broken camp and were traveling up a tributary of Deer Creek—now called Dead Indian Creek—still on the trail of the stolen horses. Some thirty years ago in this same area, Has No Horse had fought the United States Army to a stand-still. It's hard to say what thoughts raced through his mind when both parties—approaching from opposite directions—broke clear of the timber onto a small meadow. For an instant, the two groups froze. In the lead was Has No Horse flanked

---

1   Interview, Sam Ritter, September 8, 1955. In the early 1900's, Ritter worked for a rancher who had more than a passing acquaintance with this incident.

2   In November 1869 Colonel Elmer Otis, commander of the Oregon Military District of the Lakes, recorded a meeting of "three great war chiefs" with him at Fort Harney. The purpose was to convince the remaining Snake bands to accept reservation living. Has No Horse was the only one to agree to move to Yainax on the Klamath Reservation. (Steward-Voeglin, *Paiute Indians III*, p. 263.) At the Yainax Agency, Has No Horse was given the Christian name of Albert, a name neither he nor his tribesman accepted. However, his grand children and their descendants would be known by the family surname of Ochiho. (Most likely the name "Albert" was bestowed by Oliver Applegate, Indian sub-agent at Yainax and later appointed general Indian agent for Oregon.)

by his sons-in-law; Wolf Jaws who had became his spiritual advisor following the death of Buzzard Man and Bloody Antler, veteran of more battles than the cattlemen had ever known. Has No Horse sensed that the end of an era had come.

As a Shoshoni war cry burst from his lips, the gray-haired war chief exploded into a full gallop and charged the sheepshooters, firing his rifle from the hip. Every man in the posse shot at the same time and Has No Horse was blasted from the saddle. They continued firing as his bloodied body crashed to the frozen earth. The old dog soldier had been hit in the left shoulder just above the heart and another rifle bullet creased his skull knocking him unconscious. During this exchange of rifle-fire, Bloody Antler blew a hole in George Cutting's head you could ride a horse through. That was his last act before going down in a hail of bullets. How many Izee ranchers bore scars from this onslaught was never revealed.

In a matter of seconds the sheepshooters—who claimed that 14 .30 calibre slugs had ripped through Has No Horse's body—were certain that they had wiped out the lone survivors of the once powerful Big Lodge and White Knife tribes. It was now 9:00 a.m., Thursday, October 13, 1898. Less than a year before this bloody encounter with Izee ranchers, Has No Horse had ridden into northern Nevada to visit The Cutter. By some quirk of fate, he met DeLancey Gill. Gill, wandering across the West photographing Indians for the Bureau of American Ethnology, would record for posterity Has No Horse standing by his dwelling, one of the famed big lodges of the Western Shoshoni nation.[3]

Sobered by the death of Cutting and believing the Snake warriors sprawled across the icy meadow were all dead, the sheepshooters called it a day and headed home. Bill Officer would later claim that he had taken no part in this affair but would admit that he was "not very far away when it happened."[4]

Meanwhile, Has No Horse—his head throbbing like a Snake medicine drum—struggled to mount his pony for the painful ride back to Big Summit Prairie. Once there, he faced the unpleasant task of telling

3   This photo, entitled "Ocheo's Wickiup," is on file with the Bureau of American Ethnology and appears in Schmitt and Brown, *Fighting Indians of the West*, p. 280.

4   W.D. Officer to Forest Supervisor Harpman, February 5, 1927. Ochoco National Forest files, Prineville, Oregon.

his daughter that her husband and brother-in-law had been shot to death. On this tragic note, Mourning Dove sent a rider to the Klamath Reservation to notify Rose Chocktote—married to the son of Black Buffalo—that her father and uncle had been brutally slain by bad white men and her grandfather seriously wounded.[5] Only two old warriors now remained from the glory days of the Snake war tribes. Has No Horse—old and growing frail—would never fight again and Gourd Rattler was blind.

It seems ironic that the heat-drenched valley which saw the birth of armed conflict between European invaders and Snake defenders in 1698 was less than 40 miles west of the ice-crusted meadow that witnessed its death in 1898.[6] Two hundred years of bitter resistance to an alien culture had finally came to an end.

With the central Oregon range war in full swing and getting more vicious by the day, Has No Horse and his wife decided to return to their government allotment east of Fort Bidwell. His sudden disappearance from Big Summit Prairie would add credibility to the sheepshooters' claim that they had killed him. Has No Horse never returned to his beloved Ochoco and it would be nearly 16 years before he again made news. . . this time it was his actual death in 1914 while serving a two year sentence in a Nevada prison.[7]

Apparently at the time of his arrest, the story given to the Indians at Fort Bidwell was that Has No Horse had to be taken to Reno, Nevada and placed in an old folk's home.[8]

---

5   As remembered by Rose Chocktote, wife of Dave Chocktote and daughter of Mourning Dove and Bloody Antler. When word reached them of Bloody Antler's death the Chocktote's returned to Big Summit Prairie. Rose's Shoshoni name was *Buliso*, meaning evening primrose.

6   See *Thunder Over the Ochoco*, Vol. I, Chapter 4, pp. 41-51.

7   In the documents of the settlement of his estate after his death in March 1914, five younger brothers and sisters were listed as being born between 1844 and 1867 suggesting that his mother remarried after the death of The Horse. Documents belonging to Patsy Garcia, Fort Bidwell, California, Has No Horse's great-granddaughter. Patsy is the daughter of Homino Ochiho, Harry Ochiho's son and a nephew to Tom and Dick Ochiho.

8   This is what Cato Teeman—son of Picking Up (Tibuood) and Suzie Burns—believed. Cato's family had been taken from Fort Harney to Fort Bidwell in California in 1879 and that is where he was born around 1913. At the time of the 1997 interview Cato thought he was about 84 years old. He could remember Dick Ochiho, Has No Horse's grandson and a great uncle to Patsy Garcia. In 1997 Cato was facing blindness. According to him, "I worked the quicksilver mines at Fort McDermit that's why my eyes are bad." As an afterthought he slyly added, "I was married three times I know of" leaving the impression that he may have had more than

Jimmie Washoe, raised as a Paiute on the Fort Bidwell Indian Reservation, tells a much different story. On a cold November morning in 1904, Jimmie was born in a cowhide-covered tipi perched high up on a rocky ledge where the water tower serving Lakeview, Oregon now stands. Jimmie's father, Yee Won, was a Chinese cook at Lakeview who also made bootleg whiskey. His mother, Bonnie Washoe, a Paiute girl, took quite a liking to Won's "white lightning" and visited the still rather often to get her fill of rye whiskey and other pleasures. Bonnie enjoyed her whiskey more than was good for her health and when Jimmie was about two years old she died in her sleep with her child by her side. After Bonnie's death, her husband, Charlie Washoe—who raised Jimmie—would not let Yee Won see his son. Because of this, the Washoe family was always on the move, covering all of southeastern Oregon from Lakeview to the Owyhee River.

When Jimmie was old enough, Charlie Washoe took him to the Indian boarding school at Fort Bidwell where Jimmie spent the next seven years. It was here that Jimmie Washoe met Has No Horse. "I remember old Chief Ochiko. He was gray-haired and stooped and used a cane to walk. He would walk around near the school and down by the store. He was a gentle man, soft-spoken . . . and why he's got a lot of friends. There was trouble with some school teachers. Some teacher was beating on the school boys and word got around as to what he was doing."

When Has No Horse found out that students were being struck with a stick of wood he paid the boarding school a visit. No one treated Indians that way especially the children and he so informed the guilty teacher. When the teacher, a burly man, attempted to bluff the old dog soldier by threatening him with the same treatment, Has No Horse knocked him down with his cane and began hitting the teacher the same way he whipped the children. Soon thereafter the sheriff arrived and arrested Has No Horse. Apparently he was charged with a federal offense as the old warrior was taken across the state line to Reno where he was

---

three wives. After leaving the mines, Cato moved to the Burns Paiute Reservation where his grandfather Iron Mouth, also known as Pete Burns, had been a chief during the Bannock War. "I live with three dogs. We have no electricity, no water. I have an outhouse. A nice lady comes to get me every couple of days and takes me into town [Burns]. They want me to move from here so they [the Burns Paiutes] can build a casino." (Interview with Jim and Peg Iler, July 1997.)

sentenced to two years in prison for assault with a deadly weapon.[9] He died in his cell in 1914. His body was quickly removed and cremated. Did he die of natural causes? No one will ever know.

Author Jean Dunnington, who wrote a short historical sketch on Has No Horse, might well have written his epitaph. She would note that there is an ancient Oriental curse condemning a person to live in a time of great social change. "Ochiho," she would continue, "was born in such a time and was caught up in its turbulence. In his lifetime he experienced the coming of the white man, the Indian wars that followed, and the struggle to adapt to a completely changed world." No one could state his life-span any better.

Following Has No Horse's retreat to Fort Bidwell, old Tobacco Root—one of the signers of the 1865 treaty at Fort Klamath—would try to hold the few remaining fugitives together in Big Summit Prairie. He wouldn't have to try for very long. The last of the Ochoco Shoshoni had an appointment with the spirit world much sooner than expected.

---

9   Testimony given by Jimmie Washoe to Jim and Peg Iler, July 1997. At the time of interview Jimmie was 93 years old and living in a cabin at Fort Bidwell which he had built for himself in 1935. In good health and possessing an excellent sense of humor, Jimmie said he wasn't certain if he would make a better Chinaman than he has a Paiute and thought that he may never know.

CHAPTER 197

SHEEP TICK

Think what you please, says he,
But I hereby set all sheepherders free.
For men in hell I will not keep
Who damn their souls by herding sheep.

Roy Leonard
Satan and the Sheepherder

New Year 1899 tried to slip in unnoticed but the merry-makers in eastern Crook County were not about to let that happen. Some two weeks before infant '99 toddled onto the scene, the *Condon Globe* announced Mitchell was once more attempting to gain its own identity. Again on January 11, 1899, R.N. Donnelly—Grant County's representative—re-introduced the original draft for country recognition and was met with opposition from the Hon. Robert Misener. On January 26, the county proposal was brought up for vote and defeated. It finally passed the House on Monday evening January 20 and all eyes were on the Senate. Besides asking for a large chunk of Crook and a portion of Grant, the bill called for a 27-mile wide strip of Gilliam. Eventually amending the bill to include only a 25-mile strip of Gilliam it passed the Senate on February 16 and Wheeler County was born. However, Fossil—not Mitchell—captured the coveted county seat. Perhaps they should have rejoiced.

As the *Antelope Herald* would put it, "the Mitchell country citizens have been praying for organization since 1892." That observation was made in 1898. Nearly a hundred years later as 1996 crept into the state's poorest and least populated county, the residents were just as fervently praying for dissolution. The unwelcome solution to their financial problem being suggested by state officials was that Wheeler County be split up between Crook, Grant and Gilliam counties from whence it came.

189

Back in 1899—referring to Mitchell's defeat for the county seat—George Barnes in the *Prineville Review*, February 25, couldn't resist rubbing it in. "The people of that section have wanted a new county for years. They have got their desire but it is a bitter dose for some to take." And they weren't shy about gagging. One Mitchell merchant, Bob Cannon, to ease the pain took over a placer claim in Miles Gulch known as the Polmyra-Trosper Mine and dug up a $500 nugget. At that point he could have cared less if Waterman Flat was the county seat.

Perry Lewis Keeton—who arrived with his mother in the Canyon City gold fields in 1864—was appointed sheriff of the newly formed Wheeler County by Governor Greer who was having his own problems.[1] Theodore T. Greer, a Republican, gained the dubious distinction of being his father's brother-in-law by marrying the younger sister of papa Greer's second wife. The Democrats didn't let that rest in peace. Sheriff Keeton had his work cut out. Serving from 1898 to 1905, he got in on the main thrust of the range war. To make his job more difficult, his good friend Elzey Stephens was foreman for Muddy Company—the big sheep outfit. By 1902, in an effort to get out of the line of fire, Stephens gave up his foremanship and bought Burnt Ranch.

After stirring up central Oregon's internal affairs, the 1899 state legislature took time out to set up annual fishing and hunting seasons. In 1893 the first fish and game warden (protector they called him) was appointed. In 1895, the legislature—not so busy with Crook County's problems—passed a number of game laws for him to enforce. One set a limit of 20 game birds that could be sold during a single season. This cut into the profit of some of the local peddlers but not for long. Enforcement was rather hit and miss.

Something had to be done about this lackadaisical attitude so the 1899 legislature reorganized things and passed some more laws closing the beaver season and elk season until 1904 which in that year was extended to 1910. Still caught up in the heat of preservation, the lawmakers set the first bag limit for deer. It was five deer of either sex with an open season from July 15 to October 31. The 1901 session set the first

---

1   Keeton's father had died on the plains en route to the eastern Oregon gold fields. Perry worked in the Canyon City mines before strapping on his gun to become sheriff of sheep-infested Wheeler County. He spent his last years living on his son Grover's ranch in the upper Ochoco Valley.

trout bag limit of 125 fish per day and a duck bag limit of 50 per day and 100 in any one week. Of course, all these hunting privileges required licenses which meant revenue for the state but this new-found prosperity didn't do much to help the "Protector" uphold his end of the law so poaching continued unabated.

Modern technology was also running rampant in '99. Pacific Northwest Bell would install a telephone exchange in Prineville making it the only town in central Oregon with long distance phone service. Although a little slow in arriving, one of the first messages received on this newfangled contraption was word of Donald McKay's death. The old army scout who acted as interpreter on the Umatilla Reservation had passed away on April 19. Some unkind souls would claim this communications link was established to speed up medical aid for the casualties suffered during the range war. No so but by January 1, 1900, 31 phones were being serviced by Pacific Northwest Bell's central office in Prineville.

Paulina ranchers were now making trips to Prineville twice a year for supplies. However, lacking Prineville's instant communications, an illness could bring a 60 or 70 mile ride to summon a doctor any day of the year. On the other hand, Mitchell—refusing to play second fiddle to that "cow town across the mountains"—convinced J.W. Donnelly, M.D. (brother to their patron saint R.N. Donnelly), to set up practice on flood-prone Main Street. By September 1902, Dr. Donnelly had figured out that prospecting for lead in some sheepherder wasn't a paying proposition so he left the country.

In 1899 another killer was riding the range . . . spotted fever! Unexplainably most of the casualties were sheep tenders. At the time it was unknown what caused this painful disease. Highly infectious, it was exacting a heavy toll in human suffering and death which would bring about a local medical breakthrough. George McKay, a prominent Crook County cattleman, would become indirectly involved in the coming research.

McKay was also into thoroughbred horses. He raised Oregon Beauty and Linus, two of the most famous race horses registered at that time. McKay would sell Oregon Beauty for $50. A few races later, she sold for $12,000 . Soon this new owner was offered $20,000 cash for the central Oregon racehorse—which he refused. Claimed to be the most beautiful horse on record, Oregon Beauty—whose mane and tail swept the ground—burned to death in a stable fire on Long Island, New York around 1904.

In the late autumn of 1898, George McKay married Leander Smith. Eight months later, she died an agonizing death caused by spotted fever. Dr. Belknap, her attending physician, puzzled over this typhus-like disease which began with severe chills, headaches, backaches, loss of appetite and general restlessness. These symptoms were soon followed by a sudden rise in temperature to 106° F or higher and within two to three days rose-colored eruptions changing to deep red spread over the entire body. Signs of this ailment had appeared as early as 1873 but it wasn't until 1899 that it reached epidemic proportions in the Ochoco. Doc Belknap correctly reasoned that it was caused by an insect bite—but what kind of bug remained a mystery.

After weeks of dedicated observations, he discovered and proved that spotted fever was caused by the bite of a poisonous tick usually transmitted from infected sheep to men. With the range dispute getting ugly, this finding didn't benefit the wool grower's cause. Once confirmed, Dr. Belknap devoted much time to the study of spotted fever. Working with Dr. Marsdon of Burns, he developed a serum to inoculate against the disease. By 1907, Dr. Howard Ricketts, a research scientist, had joined the investigation. Up until 1949, aside from Dr. Belknap's early serum, no specific treatment for spotted fever was available.

The sheep tick battle of 1899 didn't slow down county receipts. Prineville would report that Crook County ranchers brought in over $1 million in cattle sales. Then for some undisclosed reason, the sheepmen (perhaps to make a point) recorded their annual commerce in this unique manner: "Wool, which if divided among the voting population of 1,200, made $842 that came into the county for every male citizen over the age of 21." They could just as easily stated that wool production also brought in over $1 million—$1,010,400 to be exact—but they didn't. Gold, still pouring out of the Mayflower Mine, was the principal medium of exchange; while silver, used for small change, was always scarce for it was continually making its way back to the local shopping centers.

With all this prosperity, Crook County would give the impression of being at peace with itself. Animosity between cowherders and sheepherders had been limited to a few isolated quarrels but like a festering boil, the surface tension was about to rupture. The 20th century would slink onto the land like a rabid wolf . . . and like the wolf it would carry its madness to the waiting pack.

CHAPTER 198

THE SADDLE BLANKET BLAZE

Want more range? Simply fence it in.
Possession represents nine points of the law.
If fencing is too expensive, deadlines are
a most effective substitute . . . .

Henry Snodgrass
Range War Organizer

Before the year 1900 was shotgunned off the range, the bitterness of war spilled from the battlefront into Prineville's streets and saloons. Cattle drives rumbled through the mud and gravel of Second Street, then the main thoroughfare leading into town. Six-gunned cowboys tied their horses to hitching rails and strode the wooden sidewalks to shop in false-fronted stores. They also stopped often in the town's eight saloons. The resemblance to Tombstone didn't end there. Fights—especially with sheepmen—were frequent and sometimes they were settled with bullets.[1]

Although sporadic raids had been made on sheep outfits since 1894, they were disorganized attacks. With the formal organization of livestock associations it was now full-scale war and neutrality went unrecognized. The era of cattle kings, sheep barons and poverty-stricken homesteaders had begun.

Each cattle association had its special meeting place and kept close contact with the other units, setting up rules of conduct and designating areas of responsibility. One of the contact areas was less than six miles from the town of Paulina where a lone scrubby pine grew in the

---

1 As remembered by Art Michel who arrived in Prineville in 1900. *Central Oregonian,* March 22, 1979.

narrow bottom of Wolf Creek.[2] This tree became the notorious "Sheep-shooters Tree."

Another trysting spot was some eight miles east of Prineville at a log barn surrounded by corrals near the confluence of Mill Creek and the Ochoco River. Here horses, guns and other tools of the trade were kept in obscurity. This large shed became the main arsenal and supply depot for the other organizations. It was, as one old timer put it, almost like a military operation. A reporter assigned to cover the emerging conflict was less kind in his appraisal. "Crook County, Oregon," he would note, "is the center about which the range war revolves. This county is filled with men who love to fight, and always have. There is no doubt that a certain outlaw spirit in Crook County is still surviving from the days when the Vigilantes really owned the county and drove out whom they pleased."[3] He may have been right.

Very little has ever been known about the personnel of these alliances of which there were at least five. In later years, Bill Officer—testifying in a Forest Service hearing—would disclose much about the associations' secret operations.[4] According to Officer, the Izee Sheepshooters, being the parent organization, would send their representative, a Mr. Henry Snodgrass (undoubtedly an alias) to make arrangements and help organize the cattlemen which he was adept at doing.

The first meeting with the Crook County cattlemen was held in the latter part of July 1898 (less than three months before the attempted execution of Has No Horse) at the Sheepshooter's Tree east of Paulina with representatives from Prineville, Big Summit Prairie and Camp Creek in attendance. In 1948, Elsie King (reporter for the Portland *Oregon Journal*) interviewed a cousin of one of the men present at the Paulina meeting. Even at this late date no names were mentioned, simply referring to those in attendance as Mr. A, Mr. B, Mr. C, and so on. The speaker for the night was Mr. S, an Izee cattleman which is an obvious reference to Snodgrass, also an assumed name.[5] The participants were

---

2   This pine, some 24 inches in diameter, was located in T.16.S, R.24E.WM. near the center of Section 18.

3   Arno Dosch, "The War for Range: An outline of the present-day struggle between cattle men and sheep men," *The Pacific Monthly*, February 1906, p. 157.

4   W.D. Officer, Izee rancher to Ochoco National Forest Supervisor, Harpman, February 5, 1927.

5   What Elsie King learned from this man was published in the *Oregon Journal* under the heading

instructed to make certain they didn't arrive until after dark and to come either alone or in small groups of no more than three or four so as not to arouse suspicion. Usually "Snodgrass" would not arrive at these meetings until shortly before 11:00 p.m. After 40 or 50 men had gathered a huge bonfire was built and the guest speaker would outline the purpose of the meeting and the methods used in the killing of sheep. Early on, he would suggest that if there was anyone present who did not want to join the sheepshooting association it was time for them to leave, go home, go to bed and forget they had ever been there. The organizer would then call each man present and ask if they agreed to join.

Many joined out of fear of retaliation. Some, like Billy Congleton and Sam Courtney, upon finding out the full impact of what was to take place would decide perhaps it was not a good idea and leave. Others like Elias Davis would pay for their lack of interest. There was no escape.

The rules of conduct were simple. If during the course of a raid it became necessary to kill a herder or camp tender he was to be buried on the spot and nothing said about it. If one of the riders was killed, he was to be brought home for burial and nothing said about how it happened. If a member should be arrested or brought to trial for any sheep killing, the rest were to agree to go on the witness stand and swear he was not guilty in order to obtain an acquittal of the accused in court.

In an effort to separate sheep from cattle a "deadline" was established which ripped through the heart of the Ochoco in an almost unbroken line from Bear Valley in Grant County to the end of the Blue Mountains in Crook County. North of the line sheep were allowed to graze; south of the line was cattle country. To identify this line—which ran through timbered country—pine trees were marked by cutting a big saddle blanket blaze on the north and south sides of each tree along the entire route. At specified intervals a notice was also tacked to the blazed trees:

WARNING TO SHEEPMEN

You are hereby ordered to keep your sheep on the north side of this plainly marked line or you will suffer the consequences.

Signed Inland Sheepshooters

---

of "Oregon's Bloodiest War," dated Sunday, July 25, 1948.

This line was so plainly marked that until the 1960's—when heavy logging destroyed these historic markers—it could be followed without difficulty. There were settlers inside the deadline who owned sheep but having lived there for years were privileged to certain rights. Even so, they were extremely cautious and kept their flocks on home ground. However, some were not so lucky. Such was the case of Aleck Mackintosh, one of the biggest sheep operators in Crook County standing on par with Hay Creek and Big Muddy Company. Mackintosh, a good-natured Scotchman, lived inside the deadline, but being a newcomer, he wasn't allowed to run his own sheep on deeded land. As the deadline was being fixed there were a few bands ranging south of the line. These were notified to move to the north or sheep side of the range. In most cases the sheepmen moved but when they did not a committee paid the herder a visit. The herder was placed under guard, his gun taken away and he was forced to stand by and witness the shooting of his charges. After the killing the herder would be taken into a lava field, his shoes removed and then told that he would find his boots at his camp. If he didn't move back of the deadline and stay there, he would be shot.

In 1899, one of the first bands to get caught inside the danger zone was a band belonging to Bill Mascall. His herder, ignoring the warning, was grazing sheep south of the deadline between Crook and Wheeler counties on Battle Ridge. When the gun smoke cleared, Mascall had lost 1,000 sheep. On this same raid, the committee eliminated some of Ed Shown's sheep caught between Rager Creek and Beaverdam Creek at what was called Dead Dog Spring because his sheep dog was shot there. Today, its called Big Spring . . . a rather bland name.

The range war would now begin in earnest. Not only were sheepmen packing the customary rifle but their herders and tenders were equipped with semi-automatic .45 calibre handguns in defiance of the rancher's time-honored six-shooters. It's worth noting that throughout this conflict, cattlemen did not trespass upon sheep range. No self-respecting cow would eat grass polluted by a band of woollies. Neither did the slaying of sheep always take place on the cow side of the deadline. Sometimes if a herder disregarded the boundary and slipped over for a little feed on the cow side, he got waited on by the committee.

Grover Blake, one of the early forest rangers, would note that among the sheepmen some herders took pride in committing trespass or stealing grass from someone else. They felt that they were doing their employer a favor if they succeeded in grazing some range that was "over the line." Sometimes they were successful but often only succeeded in getting their employer in trouble. Also, when the forest reserve was set, forest service employees were constantly making reports to the ranger about trespass on the part of someone which upon investigation were often proven to be exaggerated, unfounded or deliberate lies.[6]

One herder, a raw-boned, red-whiskered Tennessean who worked for Keenan and Morrow, was continually sneaking over the deadline and swiping a little grass. He carried an old .45-60 Winchester and a .45 Colt and bragged that he could and would take his chances with the sheep-shooters anytime they wanted to give him a try. Young Keenan, his camp tender, was also armed with the latest rapid firing semi-automatic Colt .45 and was eager to test it on any cowboy dumb enough to get in his sights.

When these gentlemen crossed the deadline with sheep, they always kept wide awake with guns ready for action but one day while they were on their own side and the sheep were shaded up around camp, the committee arrived. The herder was taking a nap. The old Winchester was lying on the ground by his side and the Colt in its holster. The tender was snoozing by the camp wagon.

"Stick 'em up!" a voice shouted. As the big Tennessean awoke with a start, the muzzle of a Smith & Wesson took a patch of skin off the side of his nose and nearly poked an eye out. Meantime Keenan hid under the wagon and made no attempt to help his fallen comrade. An hour later when they limped back into camp barefoot, they found a note pinned to the tent: "You'll find your guns in the big hollow tree at the upper end of the meadow. When you count your sheep you will find them 500 head short. Signed, Inland Sheepshooters."

The Izee Sheepshooters, maintaining their contribution to the cause, would provide one humorous note to what was fast becoming a funeral dirge. A story slipped out of the IZ headquarters bunkhouse that some wished would have remained untold. It seems that a boy with a band of sheep—while coming around Funny Bug Butte on the South Fork of the John Day River—was forced to camp overnight on the wrong

6   Grover C. Blake, *Sowing the Seed*, p. 6.

side of the deadline. He knew he had no business there, and was half afraid to sleep, so he camped in the middle of his flock. Somebody got wind of the fact that sheep were across the line of demarcation and in the middle of the night half a dozen "wild young fellows made a demonstration." The boy was forced to make a run for it surrounded by a hundred yards of sheep on all sides. He headed down the canyon, at the lower end of which was a temporary cow camp, where several hundred cattle had been rounded up. According to some old timers, when that mad rush of sheep and boy struck the cow camp, they produced the wildest stampede that ever took place in Grant County. It took four days of hard riding to gather up the herd and the boy wasn't seen for a week.

This was about the only amusing incident to come out of the central Oregon range war. When a man is fighting for his livelihood its a serious matter and he doesn't take that threat lightly. Many small outfits in an effort to remain neutral switched operations, going into horses which for some reason had not become involved in the dispute. One of these was Henry Koch.

His story begins a few years earlier. Shortly after Washington Territory entered the Union on November 11, 1889, Hank—a young man of German descent fresh out of Brunnenthal, Russia—landed in Lind and began courting the town marshall's daughter, Ella Sturdivan. Following their marriage, William James Sturdivan—known to all as W.J.—moved to Ritzville, the county seat and became chief deputy under Sheriff Ed Gilson. The *Ritzville Times* would report that Sturdivan "was given a surprise farewell in Nelson's Hall that he will not soon forget." A kangaroo court was assembled and four men were delegated to arrest the marshall and bring him in. The officers found "the outlaw" on Main Street and after a lively tussle handcuffed and disarmed him and took him into court. After a mock trial, the handcuffs were removed and Sturdivan was presented with an "elegant gift of a gold badge" as a token of esteem by the citizens of Lind. As a sideline, the *Times* would further relate that "Miss Luida O'Neil won the gum chewing contest."[7] Don't ask!

Sturdivan had barely pinned on his deputy badge when he received word from an old friend—Frank Redmond who had taken a homestead

---

7   Washington *Ritzville Times*, January 13, 1905.

claim in central Oregon—that an irrigation project was being proposed on the Deschutes plateau and he best get in on the ground floor. Sounded good to W.J. so he and his son-in-law saddled-up and rode into war-torn Crook County. Sturdivan took a homestead claim some 19 miles west of Prineville but the barren country between Cline Falls and lower Crooked River, even with the promise of water, held no appeal for Hank.[8] Looking for greener pastures, he headed for the upper Ochoco Valley.

Koch had no problem finding what he was looking for. Congressman Newt Williamson was more than eager to get rid of his Ochoco ranch; and the adjoining property belonging to Aldon Knighten was also up for grabs. Both ranches lay along the deadline which should have warned Hank that he was awfully close to no man's land but he never gave it a thought. Shortly before Henry's arrival, Williamson's sheep shearing plant on Dixie Meadows—almost within rifle range of the big Keystone cattle spread—mysteriously burned to the ground; and Knighten had a quarter of a mile of fence line decorated with sheep carcasses.

Having no desire to run sheep, Hank returned to Lind, loaded his wife and daughter into a buggy, and accompanied by his brothers George and Jake, trailed 250 horses into the Ochoco war zone. George, not happy with the range situation, sold his interest in the horse herd to Hank and returned to Washington. Jake, being an adventurous sort, decided to work for Williamson herding sheep.

One day, Ella decided to visit papa and mama and dropped Hank off at the lower ranch to do some work. When she arrived back at the upper ranch a week later, she asked the hired man where Hank was. "Oh, he's been down at the lower ranch since the day you left." Ella thought it odd when he didn't show up that evening and went to check. It seems that the hired man hadn't told Ella the full story. En route to the lower ranch she met Hank's brother Jake who had some startling news.

Four days after Ella's departure to visit her parents, Hank had been working on the Dyer place, another piece of property he had purchased from Knighten's son-in-law.[9] Late in the afternoon, he returned to the

8   Sturdivan's homestead claim included the area where Redmond's Central Oregon District Hospital is presently located.

9   This parcel originally was owned by John Douthit, reporter for the *Ochoco Review* and a prominent figure in the Scissors Creek placer mining district.

Williamson ranch, took care of some chores and retired to the house. For the past several weeks a trapper who had been employed by the big sheep operators to rid the range of coyotes had been camping off and on at the lower ranch. A sinister looking gentleman, he was described as a "strange acting character with odd-looking eyes who could quote whole passages from Shakespeare." No one knew his name but because of his familiarity with the Bard of Avon everyone called him "King Lear." On this particular day he had entered the house and was sitting at the kitchen table nursing a bottle of whiskey when Hank stepped inside. Without so much as a greeting, King Lear jumped to his feet, grabbed his rifle, fired a shot into the floor at Hank's feet and yelled "Dance, damn you!" Apparently satisfied when Hank did a few shuffling steps, he abruptly left. Shortly after he left, Hank thought he saw movement in the trees.

Deciding it wasn't anything important, he laid down on a couch in the living room with his back to the fireplace. On each side of the fireplace was a window facing the side of a timbered hill. Suddenly with the shattering of glass, a shot rang out and a rifle bullet struck him in the back at the belt-line, paralyzing him from the waist down.

The next morning Jake Koch—on his way to Williamson's sheep-shearing plant in Dixie Meadow—stopped by the lower ranch and found his brother. For some reason Hank told Jake not to tell anyone he had been shot. Accustomed to obeying his big brother, Jake complied but finally Hank's fever got so bad that Jake headed for the upper ranch and met Ella on her way to find out why Hank hadn't come home. By the time she arrived Hank had lain on the blood-soaked couch for three days.

When Ella asked what happened and why he had told Jake not to tell anyone that he was shot, Hank sheepishly replied, "Oh, I guess I didn't dance fast enough. Besides, you would have probably thought I was on a drinking spree down here." Leaving little Vera with a neighbor, Ella, Jake and the hired man loaded Hank into a buggy and made a frantic 25-mile dash to Prineville.

Hank was still alive when the buggy careened into town but Dr. Belknap was unable to remove the .30-.30 bullet lodged beneath Hank's spine. He would mention to Ella that if Hank had been near The Dalles when the shooting occurred, doctors there had the facilities to perform the necessary operation for this type of bullet removal. Hank, who adamantly refused anesthesia in any form except for a big chew of tobacco, looked at Ella and quietly said, "Take me to The Dalles." Dr. Belknap was stunned. "My gawd man! The trip alone will kill you! And if by some miracle you should survive the trip, you'll never walk again." Anyway, they loaded Hank in a buckboard and headed for The Dalles 150 miles away.

In the interim an investigation of the attempted murder site disclosed enough evidence to link the shooting to the trapper and a sheep operation. Some were certain that Koch's unwavering determination to walk again was fueled by a desire to return the compliment. That may be so. Hank not only survived but walked out of The Dalles hospital under his own power.[10] However, the Shakespeare-quoting "King Lear" was never seen again.

Jake Koch didn't fair much better. While working with the sheep, he came down with spotted fever. Doc Belknap, experimenting with his new anti-fever serum, pulled him out of that. Then Jake walked into Matt Nolan's Occidental Saloon just as a cowhand and a sheepherder got into an argument. He stepped in to arbitrate the quarrel and took a .45 slug through his leg. Sometimes, diplomacy just doesn't work. Times were not peaceful in Crook County no matter what you did.

---

10 Henry Koch passed away in August 1962 as a direct result of internal damage caused by the old bullet wound, which in later years brought on short blackout periods. He was 87 years old at time of death. Hank is the author's maternal grandfather.

Sheep in the Ochocos (top), sheep shearers at Williamson Shearing Plant (middle) and the Williamson Shearing Plant on Dixie Meadow (bottom). Circa 1890.

Results of the Sheep and Cattle War in Crook County—dead sheep, 1895.

Courtesy of Steve Lent and The Crook County Historical Society

Crook County Journal Office in Prineville, 1905.

Courtesy of Steve Lent and The Crook County Historical Society

Wood Ranch near Ashwood, 1900.

Courtesy of Steve Lent and The Crook County Historical Society

Tom Houston sheep band on McKay Creek, 1890.

Courtesy of Steve Lent and The Crook County Historical Society

Howard, Oregon dance hall, 1890.

Courtesy of Steve Lent and The Crook County Historical Society

Howard, Oregon, 1910.

Courtesy of Steve Lent and The Crook County Historical Society

Howard, Oregon, 1910.

Courtesy of Steve Lent and The Crook County Historical Society

Ochoco Hotel at Howard, Oregon, 1910.

Courtesy of Steve Lent and The Crook County Historical Society

Klondike Kate, 1890.

Courtesy of Steve Lent and The Crook County Historical Society

Shaniko Saloon, 1900.

Courtesy of Steve Lent and The Crook County Historical Society

Bend, Oregon, 1885.

Courtesy of Steve Lent and The Crook County Historical Society

Bend, 1900.

Courtesy of Steve Lent and The Crook County Historical Society

George Senecal blacksmith shop at Suplee, Oregon, 1890.

Courtesy of Steve Lent and The Crook County Historical Society

Madras, Oregon, 1900.

Courtesy of Steve Lent and The Crook County Historical Society

Fire brigade at Millican. Circa 1910.

Courtesy of Steve Lent and The Crook County Historical Society

Skeletons of six horses near Burglar Flat in Ochocos. Believed to be the horses of robbers from John Day, 1940.

Courtesy of Steve Lent and The Crook County Historical Society

Fishing on Deschutes, 1909 (top), fish catch from East Lake, 1910 (middle).

Courtesy of Steve Lent and The Crook County Historical Society

Hungry cattle
waiting to be fed
in the upper
Ochoco Valley.

*Courtesy
Andrew Gale Ontko*

Interior of Prineville Saloon, 1890.

Courtesy of Steve Lent and The Crook County Historical Society

Ochoco Reservoir, 1918.

Courtesy of Steve Lent and The Crook County Historical Society

Ed Harbin in Prineville during smallpox epidemic, 1900.

Courtesy of Steve Lent and The Crook County Historical Society

Smith and Cleek Saloon in Prineville, 1890.

Courtesy of Steve Lent and The Crook County Historical Society

4th of July in Prineville, 1890 (top), the Prineville / Shaniko Stage, 1890 (middle), Steve Yancey's freight line loaded with Crook County wool leaving Prineville for Shaniko, 1890.

Ed White Saloon in Prineville, 1890.

Courtesy of Steve Lent and The Crook County Historical Society

Central Oregon Overland, 1890.

Courtesy of Steve Lent and The Crook County Historical Society

Wright log cabin on Ochoco Creek. Now Pioneer Museum in Pioneer Park in Prineville, 1880.

Courtesy of Steve Lent and The Crook County Historical Society

W.J. Schmidt house on Big Summit Prairie, 1890.

Courtesy of Steve Lent and The Crook County Historical Society

Bucket of Blood Saloon in Prineville, 1890.

Courtesy of Steve Lent and The Crook County Historical Society

Frank Elkins blacksmith shop in Prineville, 1880.

Courtesy of Steve Lent and The Crook County Historical Society

Blevins Ranch on Ochoco Creek, 1890.

Courtesy of Steve Lent and The Crook County Historical Society

Prince Glaze on horse below rim coming into Prineville, 1910.

Courtesy of Steve Lent and The Crook County Historical Society

Mecca Ferry near Warm Springs.

Courtesy of Steve Lent and The Crook County Historical Society

Hahn and Fried store in Prineville, general merchandise. They owned Big Muddy
Ranch, 1900.

Courtesy of Steve Lent and The Crook County Historical Society

Redmond's first school, 1900.

Courtesy of Steve Lent and The Crook County Historical Society

Ashwood, Oregon store, 1900.

Courtesy of Steve Lent and The Crook County Historical Society

Old Scout, first auto in Central Oregon, 1905.

Courtesy of Steve Lent and The Crook County Historical Society

Old Steady, second auto in Prineville, 1905.

Courtesy of Steve Lent and The Crook County Historical Society

Prineville Hotel, 1910.

Courtesy of Steve Lent and The Crook County Historical Society

Prineville Freight, 1910.

Courtesy of Steve Lent and The Crook County Historical Society

Jewish peddler in Izee, 1900.

Courtesy of Steve Lent and The Crook County Historical Society

Lava Butte in Central Oregon.

Prineville, 1900.

Courtesy of Steve Lent and The Crook County Historical Society

Constructing Ochoco dam, 1918.

Courtesy of Steve Lent and The Crook County Historical Society

Oregon Trunk Railroad Bridge, 1910.

Courtesy of Steve Lent and The Crook County Historical Society

A baptism taking place at the old bridge over Crooked River on Second Street in 1885.

Courtesy of Steve Lent and The Crook County Historical Society

Bridge over Crooked River in Prineville, 1885.

Courtesy of Steve Lent and The Crook County Historical Society

Hotel Shaniko, 1900.

Courtesy of Steve Lent and The Crook County Historical Society

Sisters, Oregon, 1910.

Courtesy of Steve Lent and The Crook County Historical Society

Antelope, Oregon, 1890.

Courtesy of Steve Lent and The Crook County Historical Society

Prineville High School, one of four in the state, 1905.

Courtesy of Steve Lent and The Crook County Historical Society

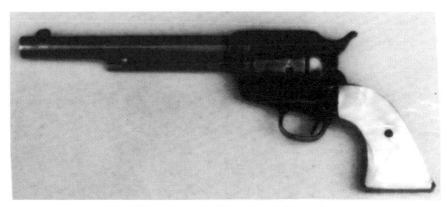

Hank Vaughan's single action Colt revolver.

Courtesy of the Oregon State Sheriff's Association

First train over Crooked River Gorge Railroad Bridge, 1911.

Courtesy of Steve Lent and The Crook County Historical Society

John H. Mitchell,
Oregon Senator.

George E. Chamberlain

Chamberlain is remembered
as genial, tactful and a master
politician. He also served 12
years in the United States Senate.

W.J. Sturdivan, frontier marshall and good friend of Frank Redmond. Central Oregon District Hospital in Redmond, Oregon is located on Sturdivan's homestead.

Marshall Sturdivan in his office in Ritzville, Washington. (Author's great grandfather.)

The Forestry Building was a favorite exhibit structure and was constructed with immense, unhewn logs cut from forests along the Columbia River. This building was the only structure to be left on its original site where it remained until destroyed by fire in 1964.

Louie Beirl, head sawyer, standing in front of sawmill that cut the logs for the Oregon Forestry Building in 1915.

Frank Redmond's house at site of present Redmond, 1900.

Courtesy of Steve Lent and The Crook County Historical Society

How a street scene may have looked in Prineville in the stylish 1880s. The sheriff is not about to arrest this lady. (The gentleman is Gale Ontko.)

BLUE AND GOLD
RAH! RAH!

To be truly free, and truly to appreciate its freedom,
a society must be literate.

Wm. F. Buckley, Jr.
Word Power

Oregon's population was approaching the half million mark and everyone was awaiting the dawn of the 20th century. Surprisingly, the 1900 census would reveal that Crook County had a growing Chinese population listing upwards to 50 families residing in and round Prineville.[1] To greet New Year's Day 1900, the *Portland Oregonian* would announce that Prineville had made telephone contact with the outside world. Either it had taken Prineville a couple of months to make use of their newly installed talking device; or it had taken *The Oregonian* that long to admit Prineville was just as up-to-date as Portland. Anyway, of equal importance, Oregon's fast-expanding timber industry was producing 500 million board feet of lumber annually . . . considered marvelous at that time. Within ten years, lumber production would grow to two billion board feet annually and the timber rush was on.

On February 23, 1900, the old Snake war chief—who in his youth had called the Ochoco his home—again made national headlines. Gourd Rattler, now blind and bowed with the weight of years, had died in a log cabin on the lonely banks of the Little Wind River. As the time approached for him to say farewell, the old dog soldier was beset with

---

1   Rhonda Hoover Dake, 1980 Crook County Pioneer Queen, would recall that Jim Lee—who had a laundry on West 5th Street—was the last of the Chinese to live in Prineville. Every Christmas he gave gifts of Chinese lilies, litchi nuts and silk handkerchiefs to the children who didn't tease him.

doubts. Having become a devout Episcopalian, he was now worried that he had offended the Sky Father by embracing the white man's religion. Not a pleasant thought for a warrior about to embark on the Sundown Train. A fellow convert attempted to explain that Dam Apua, the Sky Father, and God, the Creator, were the same spirit. Maybe so but that didn't give Gourd Rattler much comfort.[2] Perhaps the old chief remembered that day long ago when a budding missionary—eager to save souls from hellfire—asked for his permission to teach the Shoshoni about God. Gourd Rattler, in a testy mood, eyed the tenderfoot from head to toe and then snapped, "Young man, are you sure you know God yourself?"[3] Now that same question was being directed to his own troubled mind.

Two days after his death, followed by a mile and a half long procession, Gourd Rattler—for his service in the Sioux campaign—was buried with military honors at Fort Washakie, Wyoming. Has No Horse—still in pain from his last skirmish with the white brothers—was untouched by this display of hypocrisy. On that day in 1876 when Gourd Rattler made a near suicidal charge into Crazy Horse's amassed Sioux and Cheyenne shock troops, Has No Horse was riding by his side.

These men, so alike in their dedication to preserve Shoshoni heritage, were exact opposites when it came to attaining that goal. One believed that when struck by the advance of European culture it was prudent to turn the other cheek. The other held onto the ancient precept that civilized aggression demanded an eye for an eye and a tooth for a tooth. The Shoshoni themselves, condemned from the start, would gain little from either warrior's efforts.

The news of Gourd Rattler's death would barely cause a ripple in Crook County for a more ominous wave was crashing across the land. By mid-summer the smell of death hung like a curse over the central Oregon range. Out on the desert a great band of sheep lay dead and rotting in the sun—killed by the bullets of masked and silent men. It was now open war on the range. Less than fifteen miles east of Prineville, Allie Jones pushed his herds onto cattle range and experienced the first sheep slaughter on Mill Creek.

---

2   Talbot, *My People of the Plains*, pp. 38-39.
3   Joseph Breckaus, *Washakie, Chief of the Shoshoni*, p. 90.

Jones' herder, Tom Paine, rolled out of his tent at dawn only to be grabbed by masked riders who tied a piece of rag around his mouth; bound his hands to a tree; methodically shot his employer's sheep; and then rode off. Later, a masked woman on a spotted horse galloped up and cut him loose. In a low voice she warned, "Tell Allie when he wants to trespass on cattle land send a man big enough to handle the job." Paine did.

A few days later a new Ochoco landmark appeared . . . Dick Bluff, named for Dick Hinton, a sheepman who "lost a few sheep" in that area. It seems the foolish critters wandered too close to the edge of the rim and toppled to their death.

On the surface, Prineville was attempting to show a tranquil face by ignoring such crude actions while focusing on more mundane and less controversial issues. Apparently *McGuffey's Readers* weren't doing their intended job of keeping young minds occupied. Juvenile delinquency was running rampant which provoked many serious sermons and weighty announcements from public officials. In fact almost everyone had an opinion and most feared the younger generation was breaking the speed limit on the road to hell. There was now a new rage in dancing called the "Cake Walk" and Prineville's youth were eager to give it a try. Finally, one churchman after serious study, discovered the cause of teenage crime. It was tailor-made cigarettes!

Yes, smoking was the root of the entire evil problem. A heavy-set lady—who shall remain unnamed—heartily agreed with Pastor Bailey. She, being of the older generation, still wore a bustle (a sort of pad worn on the back below the waist to extend ladies' skirts). One day, while wearing a large model, she brushed past two young men puffing cigarettes on Main Street. An errant ash set her dress and bustle afire. The woman tried to outrun the blaze but a dozen men tackled her and extinguished her flaming attire. The news report of the day added, "She was not covered by insurance but a large shawl hid the damage."[4]

And so, 1900 faded into oblivion giving birth to the 20th century in 1901 with Oregon bemoaning the fact it had money problems. To increase the pain, eastern Oregon legislators inspired by the sheep industry, were proposing new financial methods for cleaning up the

4   The *Crook County Journal*, July 26, 1900, W.T. Fogle publisher and editor.

range. They wanted a scalp bounty law which paid hunters for killing coyotes, bears, wildcats and other predators (no mention of cattlemen) that preyed on sheep. Western Oregon was less than cool to spending tax dollars for that purpose but with high-powered politicians like Newt Williamson and John Mitchell rooting for the good old boys back home, the bounty apparently passed for Jim Dalton—operating out of Burns—collected over $1,000 for 490 coyotes and 63 wildcats trapped in the Paulina country that year.[5]

Education also got into the picture and debates were plentiful about the high cost of teacher's salaries and school taxes. Back in 1870, Bill Pickett did a good job for $34.25 a month while Miss Mary Douthit performed the same duty for $25.15. By 1901, male teachers were demanding $42.20 and ladies $38.66. Inflation was rearing its ugly head. To make matters worse—and students very unhappy—the Oregon Board of Education set a minimum school term of four long months. After all, it was a lot more fun to harass sheep then it was to tangle with *McGuffey's Readers*.

Since wages were so exorbitant, towns collected most of the men teachers while the women had to tough it out in the wilderness and it wasn't all that great. One lady assigned to Conant Basin, noting the lack of students, would lament, "Few babies have had the hardihood to be born here attended only by nature or by some rare soul among the resident women."[6] A shortage of pupils wasn't the only obstacle these pioneer educators faced.

Living conditions in the outback were always a problem for the teachers. One put up a cabin for herself beside the schoolhouse. Some rented vacant homesteads, others lived with some family kind enough to take them in. One schoolmistress, to augment her monthly salary, purchased a few straggly range cows only to see her livestock driven off by her bandit landlord and held for ransom in one of the mountain valleys from which it required the sheriff to rescue the herd. At least the resident

---

5   "Centennial Countdown," *The Oregon Journal*, May 8, 1959. Incidentally, to give an idea of how loyal Sen. John Mitchell could be when it came to big financial backers, he once said, "Whatever is (railroad mogul) Ben Holladay's politics is my politics, and whatever Ben Holladay wants I wants." The same could be said for whatever Hay Creek Co. or Big Muddy Co. "wants" they got.

6   Alice Day Pratt, a schoolmistress who homesteaded on Bear Creek.

bachelors sold hay on favorable terms. Many lady schoolteachers walked or rode horseback—if lucky—three or four miles daily to school.

Naturally, the bachelor who had obtained his 320 acres and wished to establish a home in a region of such rigors was reduced to descending "sheik-like" (as one damsel would put it) upon the lower settlements in hopes of stealing a maiden and schoolmistresses were fair game. One of these single gentlemen, having been employed by a venturesome homesteading teacher to cut fence posts, went to her house when the task was completed attired in his best town clothes and solemnly invited her to walk out with him to view the product of his labors.

Arriving upon the scene, he enlarged upon the length and breadth and height and depth of the pile of posts; marveled upon their form and quality and finally informed her that if she would be his, there would be no charge for the posts. His crafty proposition is a tribute to the business ability of Crook County bachelors since the posts in the event of consent would have been used to enclose a second 320 acres to be added to his own. No doubt it was a tempting offer.

When nearing the half-century mark, Bill Brown decided to marry. Not some old widow but a young strong healthily girl who could present him with a family. Brown, who hoped to raise seven sons, put it more bluntly, "Someday I shall marry a woman who will have a young one every year like the ewes in my flock . . . I'll breed her in the fall and lamb her in the spring."

With this in view, he built a large nursery on his Buck Creek house which already contained fifteen rooms. But "Old Man Brown" had waited too long. The young ladies simply were not interested. Then a buxom young school teacher arrived at Suplee and he found—so he thought—the girl of his dreams. He wined and dined her and even presented her with a brand new buggy complete with his best trotting horse. The answer was no! With the next lady to arrive, Bill tried a different tact. He presented this young lady with a gold necklace containing a diamond in the shape of his brand, the horseshoe bar. She wasn't interested. He then went so far as to offer $5,000 if she would marry. Even this didn't tempt her. Bill died a single man. So much for courting schoolteachers.

During these amorous interludes, the state was doing its best to keep teachers in the community a few months longer. The Board of

Education was no longer content with a four month school term. For that matter, they were not satisfied with an eight-year academic record and began pressuring for a high school education. William Boegli, county school superintendent, would remind his constituents that, "Those of authority in state educational matters have long felt the need of state and county schools in advance of the 8th grade." Others were not so mindful of the need but finally this sentiment took definite form in a bill introduced in the state legislature by Senator W. Kuykendull of Lane County, president of the Senate and a member of the Senate Education Committee. This bill which provided for the establishment and maintenance of high schools at county expense was passed February 26, 1901.

The citizens of Crook County were not overly eager to accept this new burden and by fall, Supt. Boegli was doing his best to convince the population that the county could well afford to establish a school of higher learning. Finally, a petition signed by 150 legal voters was presented to the County Court asking that funding of the questioned high school be submitted to the voters at the polls.

While the court was mulling the school issue around in its collective mind, the town of Howard circulated hand bills—printed in Prineville—inviting all comers to a 4th of July celebration. Promised entertainment included a dozen different kinds of races, a tug of war, fire works and an appearance by Captain Clume with "his celebrated plug uglies," the popular name for professional boxers and wrestlers. An added attraction was the chance to enter the Mayflower tunnel, then nearly a quarter of a mile (1,200 feet) into Gold Hill and it had taken over 10 years of hand labor to penetrate that far.[7]

.   By December 1901, the editor of the *Crook County Journal* had taken up the education battle. In his lead story, Bill Fogel stressed that the creation of a county high school should be brought before the people. "Undoubtedly many people in the county have felt the need of something of this kind heretofore, but no effort has been made to get such an institution. Years ago a few citizens of this town started an academy which failed for want of support for it."[8]

---

7   *Prineville Review*, May 11, 1901.
8   *Crook County Journal*, December 19, 1901. The *Journal* established in 1900 by A.G. Palmer and William Fogel had formerly been the *Mitchell Monitor*. Palmer was the owner of the *Crook County Journal* and Fogel the editor. Some sources incorrectly list their names as Parker

It was not as if the county was going broke. In spite of financial losses incurred by the range war, between June 20 and October 10, 1901, 83,200 sheep were shipped to market at an average of $3 per head; two-year-old steers were selling for $31 a head; yearling steers $22 a head; and heifers $24 a head. Henry Gray was offered $22.50 each for his yearlings and refused to sell.

Twenty-five thousand horses were slaughtered for meat export to Europe; another 250,000 horses and mules were bought by the British government for military service in South Africa with a life expectancy of two weeks as the bearers of English cavalrymen. These cavalry mounts brought $400 apiece on delivery. A wool scouring mill was established in Prineville for the purpose of washing wool to save weight in shipping by removing the dirt and grease; and this mill processed and shipped 150,000 pounds of wool in June and July bringing 12¢ a pound at The Dalles warehouse.[9]

Fortunately for students—or perhaps disastrous—homesteaders outnumbered stockmen and when the high school issue came up for a vote it passed 651 in favor to 223 opposed. A high school board was formed consisting of the County Court and it was decided to locate the school at Prineville, bringing on more complaints. Following this decision, Judge W.A. Booth resigned and M.R. (Dick) Biggs—rumored to be hiding out from a Missouri law warrant—was appointed county judge and chairman of the school board. It would be three more years before a high school was constructed.

In 1902 a room was secured in the Masonic Building and Prof. A.C. Strange of Portland took charge. Sixteen pupils enrolled of whom eight dropped out of school, three couldn't pass the exam leaving only five students to take up second year work. Meanwhile John Shipp, Prineville architect, submitted plans for a combined brick and stone building which was accepted. Bids were advertised and two Salem contractors took the bid for a cost of $20,400 and work began on April 25, 1904 and the building was opened for classes on September 15, 1904. Crook County High School had joined an elite scholastic group. At that

---

and Fogle or Fogler.

9   Files of the weekly *Crook County Journal*, June 20 through October 10, 1901.

time, there were only two other high schools in Oregon . . . one located at The Dalles and the other in Eugene.[10]

Admiring this new hall of higher education, Supt. Boegli was seized with rapture. "This building will surpass in architectural beauty any school of its size in the state and will be one which not only Prineville and Crook County, but the whole state of Oregon can justly be proud." It offered a three year course changing to a four year course in 1907. That was too much of a shock for local scholars. Not a student graduated that year.

---

10   *The History of Crook County, Oregon*, 1981 edition, p. 32.

CHAPTER 200

THE DESERT SHALL BLOOM

Instead of mountain men we are accursed with plagues of diggers, grubbers, over-grazers and clear-cutters whose object seems to be to make our mountains match our men . . . .

Edward Abbey
Disgruntled Environmentalist

Crook County contained over six million acres and at least five million of those acres were vacant public lands. This unclaimed resource—for years the unchallenged realm of powerful livestock men—was soon to become a threat in its own right. Living up to its Shoshoni heritage, the Ochoco was not making life pleasant for the invaders. With a range war raging across the country and education becoming a problem, another specter was slinking across the desert. This time it was water where nature never intended water to be. And it would be of little benefit to the livestock men who, like the trapper before them, were out to exploit what nature provided without any more capital outlay than was necessary to get the job done. Not only that, if successful, water would add to the woes of over population. Even the local newspaper would acknowledge that the overriding issue was the preservation of open range.

In an article entitled "Nature's First Law," a half-column was devoted to the law of self-preservation. Bemoaning the fact that stockmen were quibbling amongst themselves while the real threat was moving in, Editor Fogel would observe, "The human creature seems to be the most backward of all animals to avail himself of this law."[1] He was right. By

---

1 *Crook County Journal*, July 18, 1901.

the time the homesteaders began fencing off the open range, it was too late to react.

On one side, the county was trying to keep out all comers; on the other, speculators were doing their damnedest to lure people into the area. The Corvallis and Eastern Railroad was becoming a real menace. In 1900, it was extended to within 10 miles of the county's western boundary at the summit of the Cascades. If all went as planned, the tracks would cross Crook, Harney and Malheur counties with the route already surveyed. Based on locations of right-of-way stakes, the railroad would cross the Deschutes River at Pickett Island, 25 miles west of Prineville, proceed southeast past Powell Butte and continue across the high desert to Burns. However, the immediate concern was the incorporation of the Pine Falls Power Company whose aim was to build a system of electric railroads throughout eastern Oregon. According to one news reporter, "Such a scheme is not only feasible but a money-maker and the only thing necessary to bring about results is the right man . . . ."[2] For one reason or another, the right man didn't show up but the Edison Company's boast that "We will make the electric light so cheap that only the rich will be able to burn candles" was nearing reality.

Not only did Prineville now have electricity but as early as June 1901, Harvey Gates of Hillsboro made a coach trip through Mitchell en route to Burns with the view of establishing an electric light plant and "a new waterworks at that place."[3] The implication being that Harney and Malheur lakes could make the desert bloom from Burns to Hampton Butte.

However at the turn of the century it wasn't Harvey Gates' promise of electricity and water that was luring all the saddle tramps in eastern Oregon to the frontier town of Burns. A friendly young lady known as Malheur Nellie made the long, dusty ride to Harney Valley especially joyful. Nellie's business motto was "anything you want mister, anyway you like it mister" and her clientele adored her. A thrifty girl when it came to her own welfare, she planned to make a quick killing and then retire to a more prosaic occupation. Known to have no trust in the services of a bank, it was soon claimed that Malheur Nellie had a fortune in gold

2   *Crook County Journal*, August 15, 1901.
3   *Crook County Journal*, June 6, 1901.

coin—the proceeds from her many appreciative cowboy friends—hidden somewhere in or around her house and nearby shed. Sadly, Nellie died at an early age from one malady or another leaving a legacy in gold coins behind. Her retirement fund was never found and the suspected treasure shed is now gone, but Nellie's house is still standing in Burns, Oregon.

By September 1901 field work on another "big irrigation enterprise in Crook County" had begun.[4] The Oregon Development Company, organized by C.C. Hutchinson who had obtained 56,000 acres under the Carey Act, was gearing up to enter the water front. Three years earlier, the Deschutes Reclamation and Irrigation Company was formed by George Swalley and James Benham. The intention of the promoters was to select land under the Desert Land Act of 1877, then obtained financial backing through the Carey Act of 1884. The Carey Act offered certain states, among them Oregon, up to one million acres of public lands if occupying settlers would irrigate and cultivate the ground. Minimum size of these tracts were 160 acres with at least 20 acres under cultivation. This seemed simple enough to do and a sure-fire way to gain title to government land.

With this in mind, Swalley and Benham planned to encourage settlers to come to central Oregon, take claims under the Desert Land Act and for a fee, they would provide the water. This could be accomplished in two ways. A settler could acquire an interest in the canal by doing an equal amount of construction work or by purchase of water rights from the company. As it turned out, the Carey Act was a political failure but not the Swalley-Benham enterprise. It would lure hundreds of homesteaders into an already explosive situation and they would become the big losers. Most of the Carey Act lands reverted to government ownership and today are known as the Crooked River National Grasslands, under administration of the U.S. Forest Service.

But, in the summer of 1901, the Deschutes Reclamation and Irrigation Company was being challenged by the Oregon Development Company of Salem—with capital assets of $1 million—in separating gullible easterners from their hard-earned savings. The Salem company planned to bring water from the upper Deschutes to a point some thirty miles south of Prineville and irrigate the Millican Valley which covered

---

4 *Crook County Journal*, September 5, 1901.

65,000 acres of sagebrush supporting a few coyotes, rabbits, Bill Brown's horses and a hundred thousand trespassing sheep. By September, field work had begun and it was believed that at least 60,000 acres could be brought under irrigation.

The Deschutes Reclamation and Irrigation Company—with eight powerful stockholders—didn't take kindly to this competition. Chairman Swalley's opinion of Director Hutchinson was the same as that of the balladeer who cautioned "don't listen to him Dan, he's a devil not a man" for in Swalley's mind he was the chosen one to flood the burning sands with cool, clear water, and he would prove just that. The company owned a large section of unsellable land near Silver Lake containing some 8,000 acres along the course of a canal that needed outside capital to get dug. With a little imagination, company officials determined that seafaring men should be given some preference in acquiring a chunk of solid ground and went to work to remedy that situation. Working through a befuddled Congress over 46,000 acres near Silver Lake were thrown open to entry by sailors! Opening of this land for settlement was largely accomplished through political clout of the Deschutes Irrigation Company. By December the company was progressing satisfactorily on another tangent. This time their bait to sell people on desert living was the promise of a 65-mile-long canal into the low desert which would reclaim 165,000 acres of arid land in western Crook County between Bend and Powell Butte.[5] This worked great for the company but did little for the land-hungry populace who came from as far away as Pennsylvania, New York and Europe . . . only to starve on parched lands now used by the Oregon National Guard for armored tank maneuvers.

Within a year, another water speculator had entered the race. In August 1902, Alexander M. Drake—who acquired a sizable chunk of real estate boarding the east boundary of the Cascade Forest Reserve—announced that his Pilot Butte Development Company had applied for a contract with the state of Oregon to irrigate 85,000 acres in the vicinity of Bend. He also assured that an area of "between 400,000 and 500,000 acres of land could fall to ditches" if his project was approved.[6] Add these acres to the Deschutes Reclamation and Irrigation

5   *Crook County Journal*, December 5, 1901.
6   *Crook County Journal*, August 7, 1902.

Company plus the Oregon Development Company and the whole high desert from Farewell Bend to the Nevada border was to bloom like a garden on the northwestern rim of the Great Basin. It may not have been truthful but it was certainly a money-maker for the irrigation companies and thousands would take the bait. Towns like Imperial, Hemstad, Fife, Roberts, Held—to name but a few—would blossom only to wither in the desert sun. And fickle nature added a few rainy seasons to aid and abet in the folly of the oasis makers. Promoters would add such exotic names as Florida Springs, Chicago Valley, Flamingo Flat, the Golden Hole and Rhubarb Spring to local landmarks; but all too soon the Badlands, Hurricane Point, Cuckcoo Ridge, Dry Lake and Freezeout Flat would appear on central Oregon maps giving mute testimony to what really transpired. Perhaps the water specialists should have contacted old Doc Vanderpool who claimed back in 1882 to have discovered an underground river in the heart of the low desert. He also found—so he said—a free flowing spring in a cave three miles west of Horse Butte in a mighty dry area. For this betrayal of confidence, Doc was encouraged to don a life-preserver and abandon ship.

Beside a lack of water, the secretary of the Interior had, according to local sources, "Handed down a decision of great importance regarding land." This determination would affect many land owners both large and small. It stipulated that persons must actually live on their claim or their entry would be null and void. This was not pleasant news especially when coupled with the Forest Reserve Act of 1898 which fathered the sheep and cattle war. This act alone did much to irrigate the desert . . . not with water but with blood.

Seven days after Secretary Ethan Hitchcock's proclamation on land claims which dealt primarily with irrigation, Gifford Pinchot, chief of the Forest Service, entered the fray declaring that "The people of eastern Oregon cannot preserve their agriculture without keeping up their forest reserves." On arid land that was going to be somewhat difficult to do but an escape was provided when Chief Pinchot further declared, "The salvation of this country depends on the maintenance of its forest integrity."[7] Since no trees grew in the area of debate, it would be easy to maintain the "forest" in its aboriginal state of non-production.

---

7   *Crook County Journal*, September 12, 1901.

Not only were cabinet members issuing manifestos but Binger Hermann, Oregon's congressman from 1881 to 1897 and now commissioner of the General Land Office, was offering advice. Mainly because Hermann was a native son, a campaign started by eastern Oregon to have him recalled failed, thus dampening Prineville's 4th of July celebration. His supporters claimed Hermann was "a good citizen and a good officer."[8] Maybe so, but his Willamette Valley sponsors weren't facing stockmen's guns like the homesteaders were.

About this time miners entered the fray protesting Oregon's new "scalp law." Not that they were adverse to killing coyotes, bears and other outlaws preying on sheep but because some animal scalps belonged to badgers. According to these businessmen, badgers were extremely valuable to the mining industry. Some state politicians found this hard to believe but it was true. Often by examining the dirt excavated by badgers, pieces of gold-bearing quartz and cinnabar were found, thereby saving prospectors a lot of hard work.

No one seemed to be exempt from the unrest festering in Crook County. Frank Elkins, out to defeat Sam Smith for the job of county sheriff, found out the hard way. During the July 4th celebration his horse ran away with a buggy attached and in the process of chasing him all over town Frank's horse upset a freezer full of ice cream. That cost Elkins the election for the next four years although in 1904 Sam only beat him by three votes.[9]

In late May 1901, two petroleum companies set up headquarters in Prineville searching for oil. Indications of petroleum were found over a large territory to the east and south of Prineville causing more companies to file claim on several thousand acres of oil land. One, the Portland Oil Company headed by a Dr. Booth, was taking claims on Barnes Butte and as stated in the *Prineville Review*, would "commence drilling as soon as machinery can be brought in." The Cincinnati Oil Company, headed by Anne Frome, leased 1,000 acres on the head of Marks Creek and began drilling operations in September.[10] By 1902, crude oil was being used to

---

8   *Crook County Journal*, July 4, 1901. Hermann was re-elected to Congress in 1903 and served until 1907.

9   *Illustrated History of Central Oregon 1905*, p. 656; *Crook County Journal*, July 11, 1901.

10 *Prineville Review*, June 5, 1901.

fuel Portland's industry and it was speculated that oil could be used to power railroad locomotives.

The Cincinnati Oil Company was sinking its first test hole on Marks Creek when President William McKinley boarded a train to attend the Pan American Exposition in Buffalo, New York. While standing in a receiving line, the president was shot twice by a deranged anarchist. He died eight days later fulfilling an Indian curse.[11] As the nation reeled in shock, Crook County (used to violence) took the tragic news in stride.

With Prineville's stable population holding at 800, all this new activity was creating a boom. Perry Poindexter, who had opened his first restaurant and lunch counter in 1887, was an eminently successful businessman and he saw opportunity knocking. In the summer of 1900 he erected the Poindexter Hotel, one of the largest buildings in the city. Besides being a competent businessman he was also an "enthusiastic Nimrod and earnest disciple of Isaac Walton." His hotel became a national headquarters for hunters and fishermen. Since he preferred hunting and fishing, Poindexter turned over management of the establishment to Mrs. C.E. McDowell in 1901.

She changed the name to Hotel Prineville and advertised that the inn would be operated on the American Plan. In short, Mrs. McDowell charged different room rates ranging from $1 to $2 a day depending upon one's needs. Next, she installed a long distance telephone pay station and successfully took over Prineville's hotel trade with accommodations which "could not be surpassed in the city."[12]

Despite irrigation projects, railroad surveys and oil drilling, the range war was continuing quite well. In fact a public notice appearing in the *Prineville Review*, dated June 8, 1901—in the form of a warning to sheepmen—would suggest that hostilities were advancing full-bore.

---

11 For more on the Indian curse, see *Thunder Over the Ochoco*, Vol. 3, pp. 262-263.
12 *Crook County Journal*, October 7, 1901.

CHAPTER 201

COMIN' THROUGH THE SHEEP

*I will not allow any son of a bitch to go through
these sheep!*

Thomas Riley
April 4, 1901

When taking into account the first sporadic attempts at retaliation, the Crook County range war, now entering its tenth year of destruction, poses an interesting question. Who were the aggressors in this bloody conquest for grass? As the saying goes, it takes two to tango. Neither faction was as pure as holy water but the stereotype applied to both sides needs to be examined. The beef producers were not as sinful as conventional wisdom would dictate; nor were the wool growers as guiltless as they have been historically portrayed. An unbiased observer will have to decide for himself who was to blame in this pointless struggle for economic gain. Just bear in mind that prior to the enactment of the Forest Reserve Act in 1897 and the Taylor Grazing Act in 1934 there were no laws governing livestock use of the public domain.

In the spring of 1901 there were several lethal confrontations but the killing that made headlines was not cattlemen against sheepmen but sheepman against sheepman giving the impression that maybe it was the sheepmen instigating much of the trouble. In the fall of 1900, Thomas Riley—a tough young man fresh from the Emerald Isle—moved onto the narrow divide between Cherry Creek and Currant Creek and on October 18 filed a homestead entry in the middle of the Prineville Land and Livestock sheep driveway.[1] After erecting a 8' x 10' juniper log cabin

---

1   Prineville Land and Livestock owned by Henry Hahn and Leo Fried, Prineville merchants, was known throughout the region as Muddy Company because the main headquarters ranch was located on Muddy Creek in the extreme northeast corner of what is now Jefferson County. Riley's homestead claim was sandwiched between Muddy Company headquarters ranch on

in the Currant Creek drainage, he joined forces with John Creagan—a John Day sheepman—and they formed the Creagan and Riley Sheep Company with headquarters on Riley's claim. Sitting on the doorstep of Hahn and Fried's "Big Muddy Company," this was begging for trouble.

Riley's homestead was devoid of any vegetation except for a few juniper trees. In fact, the land wasn't worth the value of the filing fee. On the other hand, Creagan's ranch was located on some of the best winter and spring range in northern Crook County. Why the Riley-Creagan firm chose to move onto Riley's homestead with four men and all their sheep would indicate they were looking for a showdown. Tom Riley had made statements to the fact that he filed only for the purpose of harassing the Prineville Land and Livestock Co. and to break communications between their sheep camp and the headquarters ranch.

In less than a month after Riley filed his homestead entry, Prineville Land and Livestock bought the Black Rock Ranch and moved a thousand head of sheep onto it, establishing headquarters at the Brogan house. According to company officials negotiations for the purchase of the Black Rock Ranch were in progress long prior to the time Riley filed for homestead rights. Whatever, Riley and Creagan planned on using Black Rock Ranch and apparently they weren't going to let any technicalities like ownership get in the way and the battle lines were drawn.

Immediately, Muddy Company officials gave the order to obliterate every blade of grass on the Black Rock range and particularly any forage near the Riley homestead. And so, a systematic and persistent effort was made to drive Riley and Creagan off that range. It didn't work. Riley was handy with a rifle and he soon had Muddy Company herders so scared they refused to carry out company orders. Riley would meet them and warn, as he tapped his rifle, "I've go something here that will fix any son-of-a-bitch that herds sheep for the company."[2] It was then that Dave Bruner entered the scene. He knew little about sheep. Dave's specialty was guns.

---

the north and Phil Brogan, Jr.'s Black Rock Ranch on the south.

2   All information taken from the transcript of a murder trial in the Circuit Court of the State of Oregon for Crook County, May 13, 1901: State of Oregon vs. D.L. Bruner Defendant, Witnessed at Dalles City, Oregon this 11th day of December 1901, pp. 1 through 22, 52, 53, 391.

In the spring of the year it was customary to throw all the four and five year old wethers (castrated rams) into one band for a double purpose. Primarily it was done to get the wethers out of the way during lambing but of equal importance it was to fatten them for the summer mutton market. The mixing of wethers with ewes during lambing could cause a lot of unnecessary problems, not the least of which was trampling newborn lambs to death.

In late March 1901, Riley and Creagan moved onto the Currant Creek divide and began lambing out on Big Muddy's stock driveway. On April 3 things came to a head. Joe Dodlin and Hank Rodenhieser—both experienced hands with sheep—were to take a band of wethers through the divide to the company's Black Rock spring range. When they arrived at the pass, Riley and Creagan had sheep strung across the narrow canyon and Dodlin, not wishing to get the two bands mixed up, refused to go through when Creagan wouldn't move his ewes. When word of this stalemate reached headquarters, the ranch foreman—claiming that Dodlin and Rodenhieser weren't crowding the sheep enough—told Bruner to take the wethers through to spring pasture and on the morning of April 4, Bruner proceeded to carry out orders.

When Creagan saw the Muddy sheep approaching being herded by Bruner, he suspected that he and Riley's bluff had been called. Running forward, he yelled, "For Chris' sake Bruner don't drive your band of dry sheep through our lambs!" Prior to this confrontation, Riley, who had been looking for lambs, returned to the cabin where Joe Good was cooking breakfast. When they heard Creagan shouting, Riley came out with a rifle and followed Bruner up to the divide to show him where the property line was. Then, as John Creagan and Charles Campbell, witnesses to the event, would later testify: "Without warning, Bruner deliberately pulled out his six-shooter and shot two shots at Mr. Riley who dropped his rifle and started running back to the cabin. At that point Bruner picked up Riley's rifle and began chasing him firing as he went. He fired two shots missing both times. On the third shot he hit Riley in the back of the head and the bullet came out his forehead. Riley fell dead." According to Creagan, "Bruner pursued Riley for at least 55 yards up to the time he killed him. then walked down to make sure Riley was dead." One thing was certain, Riley was found some 180 yards from where

Bruner fired the first shot determined from empty shell casings. Tom Riley was killed with his own weapon, a .30-.30 Marlin.

Bruner would tell a much different story. When Dodlin couldn't make it through, the riding boss of Prineville Land and Livestock Co. told Bruner to take the sheep up on the hillside and move them to Black Rock Ranch. On the morning of April 4, Bruner discovered that Riley and Creagan had put a band of sheep within 200 yards of his camp on the west side of Muddy Creek draw making it impossible to get through with his band of wethers without great loss to the Riley-Creagan band of ewes and lambs. As Creagan yelled at him not to mix the bands, Bruner altered his course to the east side of the draw. In looking up, he saw Riley come out of the cabin with a rifle and start for him then disappear into a gulch. Meantime Creagan and Campbell stood out in the open like decoys. As Bruner reached the top of the ridge, Riley came up from the opposite side shouting, "I'm an Irishman!" implying he was a tough customer, "And I will not allow any son of a bitch to go through these sheep!"

Bruner calmly replied that if nationality was a factor he was of French descent. "I'm also an American citizen not born in a foreign country and if you don't want the sheep mixed fine, you turn 'em back."

At that, Riley drew down on Bruner with his rifle. As he did, Bruner grabbed the rifle barrel, threw it up, drew his pistol and fired two rapid shots. One bullet hit Riley in the hand, the other grazed his face striking him in the right arm causing Riley to drop the rifle. Throwing his hand to his face, Riley started running toward the cabin shouting, "I'll get a gun and kill you!" By then, men were coming out of the cabin so Bruner grabbed up Riley's rifle and fired two warning shots at them. The third shot—which Bruner claimed was an accident—hit Riley in the back of the head killing him instantly. Maybe it was unintentional but at 125 yards it also says something about Bruner's accuracy with a .30-.30 rifle.

After the fatal shooting, Bruner returned to Muddy Station where he was arrested by Sheriff W.C. Congleton, brought to Prineville and lodged in the county jail to await trial. Rushing to his defense, the Prineville Land and Livestock Company retained the services of Prineville's best . . . the law firm of Barnes, McGinn, Brink and Hopkins. However, it would appear that this battery of attorneys were more interested in protecting the company's good name than they were in defending hired gun David Link Bruner.

Representing the state of Oregon was District Attorney Frank Menefee assisted by N.J. Sinnoth. After a little legal haggling, "Twelve good and lawful citizens and tax-payers of Crook County were accepted and sworn as a jury."[3] Because of the hostile environment in Crook County, the trial was set to convene in The Dalles.

Presiding Judge Bradshaw was quick to caution the jury that although Hahn and Fried's names would be mentioned they were in no way connected with Riley's untimely death. Prosecuting Attorney Frank Menefee wasn't so sure of that. In his opening remarks, he bluntly stated, "I believe the slaying was a malicious and deliberate murder instigated by parties [he didn't mention Hahn and Fried] who were interested in driving Riley and Creagan off from the range."

Lawyer Brink instantly challenged that statement. "Whatever may have been the intention of the Prineville Land and Livestock Company . . . none of its officers are upon trial here today; the trial that you are called upon to sit in is one in which D.L. Bruner is charged with premeditated murder—it is not the Prineville Land and Livestock Company."[4] So, Dave would take the rap for following orders.

Even with the Hon. George Barnes acting as defense attorney, Bruner was found guilty of murder in the second degree—and hatred in war-torn Crook County continued to mount. An innocent bystander with no axe to grind would do an excellent job of putting this impasse into perspective. "It is," he noted, "hard to imagine, without seeing, what havoc a flock of three thousand sheep works as it eats its way towards its winter home. In that dry country of central Oregon every bit of grass and foliage disappears. Bad enough when range is wide and no competition in sight, worse when rival flocks dispute for feed, but worst of all when the cattle ranges are invaded by this swarm of locusts."[5] And there you have it in a nutshell.

---

3   Those accepted for jury duty were: J.C. Clemmens; J.H. Garrett; A.G. Kibbey; C.M. Lister; A. Fogel; J.B. Merrill; H. Grimes; S. Collins; James Cram; E.L. Bradford; D.H. Smith; and J.C. Rassmussen. D.S. Dufer, official court reporter for the 7th Judicial District, state of Oregon, witnessed at Dalles City, Oregon on the 11th day of December 1901, in the circuit court of the state of Oregon for Crook County.

4   Opening statement from Hon. M.E. Brink to the jury in the murder trial of D.L. Bruner.

5   Wallis Nash, a reporter assigned to cover the Crook County range war in "Feud and Foray on the Oregon Range," *The Pacific Monthly*, March 1906, p. 250.

CHAPTER 202

THE TIMBER RUSH

*. . . and the ugly spreading cancer of bare eroding
earth is the legacy that the Forest Service will leave
us for centuries to come.*

Howie Wolke
Save Our National Forests

About the same time Dave Bruner was taking potshots at Tom
Riley, the *Crook County Journal* was bemoaning the fact that the federal
government was doing the same to the county of Crook. It seems that the
Forest Reserve Act of 1898 was having its effect. Editor Fogel would
grumble, "Our county line on the west extends to the summit of the
Cascade Mountains but the government timber reserve only leaves a strip
from two to eight miles wide and about forty miles long, bounded by the
Deschutes River on the east." No big worry. The Paulina range east of
the Deschutes, the Maury Mountains, Grizzly and the Western Blues
were yet untouched. According to the 1900 timber industry prospectus,
cruisers estimated those timber lands alone would yield up to 2 million
board feet of merchantable lumber per acre. The area of all timber
lands—exclusive of government reservations containing an estimated
34.5 billion board feet of merchantable timber—amounted to some
691,000 acres which held another 6.7 billion board feet of lumber with
little of this timber being claimed or owned by individuals. This oversight
would soon be corrected.

By 1902, the county population had jumped to 7,500 and a new
concern was facing the Ochoco in the form of more timberland with-
drawals. In an effort to strengthen the 1898 Act, June 28th saw the
passage of the 1902 Forest Reserve Act which, among other things,
mandated government grazing allotments for both sheep and cattle. This

announcement was not favorably received by either faction in the range war. It would also bring on a frenzied rush to file claims on timber lands.

As a result of wholesale destruction occurring throughout many of the nation's forests, Congress passed the Reservation Act in 1891 which included the historic Forest Reserve Clause. Under the Reservation Act, the president was given authority to withdraw lands from the public domain in order to protect them from the ravages of uncontrolled logging and mining. Under the Reserve clause, presidents Benjamin Harrison and Grover Cleveland began to withdraw public lands that would eventually become the United States National Forests. The first large-scale forest withdrawal occurred on February 22, 1897 when outgoing President Cleveland moved 21 million acres of western forest lands from the public domain into the forest reserve system. This withdrawal included the Cascade Forest Reserve which ran the full length of Crook County's western boundary and caused the first angry shots to be fired in the Crook County sheep and cattle war.

Later that same year, under President William McKinley, Congress passed the Organic Act of 1897 which in essence forbid clear-cutting but encouraged small-scale selective logging in the forest reserves. The Act of 1902 would lay the groundwork for the formation of the Blue Mountain Reserve in central and eastern Crook County and a new round of fighting. Three years later in 1905, President Theodore Roosevelt signed an executive order creating the U.S. Forest Service. He then assigned the new agency to the U.S. Department of Agriculture and in 1907 withdrew another 99 million acres from the public domain thus creating the bulk of our national forest system.

The 1902 act was causing considerable anxiety in Crook County. Large eastern-based timber companies were rushing into the county to grab any and all available timber lands before the forest reserve boundaries could be established. And this sudden interest brought in a new breed of entrepreneurs calling themselves "timber cruisers." These professionals were making big money offering to locate timber claims for a cost of $150 each. For this fee, they would locate section corners showing where the claim lay and particularly whether that tract was open to entry under the various Homestead Acts and/or the Timber and Stone Act of 1878. Ironically, a special Public Lands Commission appointed by President

Roosevelt recommended repeal of the Timber and Stone Act in 1903. However, it didn't happen until 1955.

After the timber cruiser had done his job all the claimant had to do was visit each subdivision of land—in 40 acre plots—before making a filing to provide proof of his claim. After showing the claimant where the corner markers were located, the cruiser was entitled to his fee, collected it and paid no more attention to the gentleman who claimed the land. Actually, it was a good deal for all concerned but few local landowners took advantage of the opportunity offered them other than to sell their existing timber rights for 50¢ an acre.[1] For the timber companies, it was a different story.

In the spring of 1902, Jim Petrie with a party of timber cruisers charged into the village of Bend to lay claim to the eastern border of the Cascade Forest Reserve before it could be extended east of the Deschutes River and found claim hunters everywhere. These men were making fortunes locating claims at $100 a piece—not for local residents—but for the Shevlin-Hixon Company. One cruiser had filed as many as 200 claims netting him $20,000 and acquiring 32,000 acres of virgin timber for "the company."[2] The local contestants in the range war finally realized what was happening under their very nose only to find they had been overrun by investors from out of state. These old central Oregonians were made the butt of many jokes because they had no idea that timber land had value. Now too late, they resolved to get what was left.

On July 25, 1902 the *Crook County Journal* published proof of filing on 90 timber claims. A single claim was 160 acres but a single claim was very unusual. Entries ran from two or three up to as many as twenty-one for a lone claimant showing what a large amount of land was involved in the timber rush. But timber filings weren't the only thing making news.

For weeks the headlines were about Harry Tracey, a gentleman who once wore the infamous Oregon Boot and who swore he would never wear one again.[3] Serving a life sentence for murder, Tracey had escaped

---

1 If landowners received only 50¢ per thousand board feet of timber their standing merchantable trees were worth $1,000 an acre. In 1902, merchantable trees in the eastern states were selling for $10 per thousand board feet.

2 The *Crook County Journal*, July 25, 1902 and October 16, 1902.

3 For more on the Oregon Boot see *Thunder Over the Ochoco*, Vol. 3, Chapter 103, "The

from the Oregon state prison. Some range warriors were secretly hoping he'd put his gun up for hire and head for Prineville. He didn't. Shooting his way to freedom, Tracey escaped into the state of Washington where he roamed for 60 days leaving a trail of holdups and murders behind him. After killing his eighth man, Tracey was wounded by a volunteer deputy in a wheat field near Spokane. As the posse closed in, Tracey placed a .45 Colt against his head and escaped the Oregon Boot forever. With Harry no longer available, the local citizens could again focus their thoughts on pine trees.

With the passage of the timber reserve act, a special dispatch arrived in Prineville from Washington, D.C. signed by the acting secretary of Agriculture. It ordered the temporary withdrawal from settlement on all public lands in a 6,000 square mile section of the western Blue Mountains—the Ochoco—with the intent of its ultimate creation into a forest reserve. The order was to remain in effect until a presidential proclamation was issued. It was certain the lands withdrawn were heavily covered with commercial timber and included in the withdrawal were many small valleys affording good pasture land which according to the notice "may or may not be opened for grazing after the reserve is created."[4] As far as the citizens of the county were concerned, mining and grazing were the only industries to be curtailed by the creation of a forest reserve.

The town of Howard near the headwaters of the Ochoco River sat well within the boundaries of the government withdrawal. For Vic Blodget, who was losing money on the Scissors Creek placer mine, this notice provided sufficient incentive to close down operations. Selling out to Lew McAllister, Blodget with three of his brothers headed for Alaska. McAllister, who had been on the local hit list since the 1880's, should have accompanied them. His days were now growing shorter.

Timber cruisers were warning the ranchers not to "throw away" their timberlands; that forested acres held the potential for great commercial value; and furthermore, "The day is not in the too distant future when timber land owners will be in the same category as the millionaires." One truthful cruiser reminded the Ochoco ranchers that in Wis-

---

Outcasts of Whiskey Flat."

4   The *Crook County Journal*, July 31, 1902.

consin private timber companies were paying from $10 to $15 per thousand board feet for standing timber. "At one half this price," he foretold, "a fortune can be made by an owner who has a 160 acre timber claim. Fifteen years hence, I honestly believe that he will not have to worry about his financial future."[5] Few heeded this advice believing the timber cruiser's only aim was to collect his $100 location fee. Most were more than eager to accept the big timber companies offer of 50¢ an acre for permanent timber rights as their main concern was about grass not pine trees.

During the federal government's rush to conserve timber reserves, nature decided to take a hand in this high-stake game. A lightning strike near Mt. Hood wiped out 170,000 acres of prime timber—incinerating people as well as trees—then jumped the Columbia River and consumed another 1/2 million acres of virgin forests as it raged toward Mt. St. Helens. Obviously, the storm gods were unimpressed with congressional acts.

From time of settlement until 1902, 40 million acres of forest had burned in western Oregon due to settlers clearing land and burning logging slash, destroying an estimated 160 billion board feet of timber. The loss in eastern Oregon was unknown at that time but timber cruisers estimated it to be equally impressive. Beyond doubt, fire was as effective in removing trees as .30-.30 bullets were in removing sheep and both improved the range.

---

5   The *Crook County Journal*, August 28, 1902.

CHAPTER 203

BLOODY WOOL

"It's only Charlie Winnek, his wife and kid!"

Nameless sheepshooter
August 1902

In July 1901 an unidentified correspondent writing to the *Crook County Journal* would add a new dimension to the range conflict. "I notice an article in your paper of last week regarding a clipping in the *Fossil Journal* about some sheep being shot in our community." The writer was quick to note that he knew nothing about the shootings but . . . "it was done for the benefit of the Beaver Creek stock range and I would like to say a word about this if you can find space in your paper."

> For the past few years sheep from other counties have been coming here, a good part of them making their summer headquarters here. The result is that our stock are skin poor in the fall. The above mentioned article [*Fossil Journal*] says that the outside sheep men are prepared to meet force with force. The Beaver Creek settlement is small but if there are any outside sheep men hunting for game and think they can bring sheep here and herd on the South side of the mountain between the Grant County line and the North Fork of Crooked River, then let them come. A word to the wise is sufficient.[1]

The gauntlet had been tossed and a week after this publication, the editor of the *Crook County Journal* would add his thoughts to the conflict:

---

1   The *Crook County Journal*, July 11, 1901.

"... a few men fired on a band of sheep of another county which were eating up the grass on the range. While this was not the best manner in which to apply the law, it seems to have been the manner adopted at this time. At best it is but an example of a man striking out for no good accomplishment, yet these persons are to be pardoned for their impulsive efforts to protect themselves from others. These outside sheep men are bringing their sheep to the grass on which the local stockmen expect to winter their herds. They feed on the winter range in this county as they go to the mountains in the summer and run over it until there is not a vestige of grass left. Is the local stock man to blame under these circumstances? Or is he running outside the limits of the statutory law?[2]

These were thought-provoking questions. But sheep were not the only animals being gunned off the range. In early May, Lewis Taylor took it upon himself to shoot several mules, the property of Hubbard Bilyeu of Wheeler County. In s swift move for justice, Taylor was brought to trial on May 13, 1901. Judge Bradshaw, apparently fed up with livestock executions, sentenced Mr. Taylor to one and a half years in the Oregon State Penitentiary suggesting that mules were not as destructive to the range as sheep.[3]

Then on Sunday morning, July 21, Prineville was jarred when a telephone message came in urgently requesting the service of a doctor at Durham's sawmill on Lytle Creek. Emmet Eagan—a logger—had been shot by Andy Lytle. Lytle started for town immediately after the shooting, gave himself up to Sheriff Congleton and shared a cell with Dave Bruner of Muddy Company fame. The reason he gave for the shooting was that "Eagan was paying improper attention to Mrs. Lytle." Since he admitted to the killing, few witnesses were introduced at the hearing and after spending three months in jail, Lytle was found not guilty in the murder of Eagan.[4]

Come August, Joe Wagner—a Wheeler County sheepman—moved his herds onto Wolf Creek some two miles over the

---

2   The *Crook County Journal,* July 18, 1901.
3   The *Prineville Review,* May 16, 1901.
4   *Crook County Journal,* July 25, August 1 and October 31, 1901.

deadline. Early one morning nine men surprised one of Wagner's herders while he was asleep and took his weapons at gunpoint. Then they killed 60 sheep outright and wounded 70 more. Over on Big Log Creek—named for an enormous yellow pine, eight feet in diameter which had toppled across the creek—another 150 head of sheep were slaughtered.

For a year, at least by local standards, conditions were somewhat peaceful. Then in mid-summer 1902, the dissension again turned ugly. Charlie Winnek, who owned a Prineville furniture store and operated a drug store, was also one of the few county residents who had taken advantage of filing a timber claim before the 1902 Timber Reserve Act could take effect. One morning in August Winnek decided to ride out and check this claim which was located in Gray's Prairie some 30 miles east of town. Since this would take some time, he took his family along for a pleasant week of rest and relaxation. What happened on this summer outing can only be told through the memory of a young girl who saw more than she was ever intended to see. The following is her eyewitness story:[5]

> The three of us, Papa, Mama and I, had come up from Prineville to spend a few nights at the claim. It was required that a certain number of days and nights residency be established to prove title to the property. We had made the long trip by buckboard the day before and spent this day catching small but delicious trout from the stream, now called Gray's Creek. I was in overalls and Mama had on a pair of Papa's coveralls.

> All of us had rubber bands tight around our pantslegs at the ankle to keep the ticks out. We each carried our fishing rod and Dad had a .22 rifle in case we saw a nice rabbit to add to our larder.

> We came out of the creek-bed willows and saw the man across Gray's Prairie. He stood in front of the half-log cabin, half-soddy that was the sheep herder's summer

---

5   Although Lorene Winnek Lakin was 85 years old at the time of interview on July 22, 1976, what she saw that day in 1902 was still crystal clear. "Some things, you never forget."

home. As we started to cross the meadow to my folk's timber claim, three more men came out of the cabin, each with a rifle in the crook of his arm.

Being an 11-year-old youngster I gave no particular thought to the men at the cabin. In 1902 for a man in the mountains to have a gun in his hand was more normal than not.

My Father saw we were caught in a trouble spot and were committed to go ahead with no detour and no retreat. Our only course was to proceed and act unconcerned. We continued our steady pace through the tall grass. While still a good distance away, I recognized one of the foursome. He was an older teenager who was dating a girl in the next block and I had a crush on him because he was nice to me. I hollered to him and waved, calling him by name. The men had been spaced out in front of the cabin, and when I called, it was like seeing the sawdust drain out of dolls as they recognized us and wilted in relief before our eyes.

The brother of my friend dropped his gun and collapsed to the ground, screaming with hysterical laughter, "It's only Charlie Winnek, his wife and kid!" He cried and giggled, and repeated over and over, "It's only Charlie Winnek." I thought he was having a crazy fit and I guess he was. None of the others said a thing, just stood slack and dazed.

Papa spoke lowly to me, "Don't say anything!" His tone carried a stern edge that left no doubt in my mind. Then we saw the sheep! I don't know how many there were, they seemed spread out over acres and acres. It was a rank, raw-smelling mountain of bloody wool.

"Keep walking, don't look," Papa barely muttered. Then, "Hello fellows," in a loud, cordial voice. We marched single file, Mama firmly prodding me so I couldn't stop and visit. She nodded politely and acknowledged, "Gentlemen," as we passed the silent, shaken men. Everyone ignored the cowboy rolling and sobbing on the ground. Still in formation, the three of us marched the mile or so to our cabin also in silence.

We hadn't seen the body of the slain sheepherder. It was found later, along with his dogs' bodies among the carcasses of the slaughtered sheep. The band had been run off the top of a steep ridge. It was called Sheep Rock after this episode.

Of course, we knew the four men. They were local cattlemen who believed sheep ruined the graze. The factions had been squabbling for some time. There'd been much talk, occasional saloon brawls, harassment and threats from both sides. But this was murder!

In retrospect, we realized that through the eyes of the guilty, taut-nerved men, we were taken for armed avengers instead of a peaceful town merchant's little family. The fishing rods could have easily looked like rifles from a distance.

Now we knew the reason for the constant bleating of sheep and the popping sounds we had heard throughout the morning as we made our journey. It was the cries of the poor animals as they were shoved over the cliff. Those that survived the fall were shot or had their throats cut. My parents discussed the serious situation in great detail. I was rightly impressed, and I swore a solemn promise to never say a word about what we had seen. We carefully followed our planned schedule and didn't return to town until the day our neighbors and friends expected us.

It was some time before the killing of man and sheep was discovered by somebody else. The town buzzed and the Sheriff examined the sight for clues. There was a pause in the on-running battle while the fruitless search for the culprits trickled along. We had blundered into the middle of the violent, brutal war, and we observed the code of survival of the times: "Don't take sides and keep your mouth shut!" None of the men were ever caught.

All are gone, now, dead of unspectacular old-age diseases. One of them, my secret flame, spent some time in jail for one scrape or another, but the others were accepted members of our community. Their children and grandchildren were playmates of my children.

At the turn of the 20th century, life held more spice for the rowdy inhabitants of central Oregon than it did for the bland sophisticates on the west side of the Cascade range. Balanced on a tightwire between two raging bulls, daily survival was a memorable experience but not exactly what anyone would wish to encounter again.

CHAPTER 204

THE BLACK PLAGUE

*It has been circulated around the county that this
city has several cases of smallpox, which is entirely
false and has not been founded on fact.*

The Prineville Review
April 9, 1903

In the final days of March 1903, a timber cruiser en route to Portland got off the Prineville stage complaining that he felt feverish. He took a room at the Poindexter Hotel and that night became deathly ill. The man admitted to having been exposed to smallpox before coming to Prineville but claimed he was immune to the disease because he had already had smallpox. Whatever, he soon died of unknown causes. Shortly thereafter, Howard Dillon who also had been staying at the hotel, became sick as did Ed Harbin who was doing repair work at the hotel and Ronda Claypool, a hotel employee.

Soon Dillon had a rash on his body and head. Three local doctors—Van Gesner, Horace Belknap and John Rosenburg—were called in but they couldn't agree as to his ailment but all decided it was "utterly unlike smallpox." They based their judgment on the fact that there was no odor and the victim had no appetite. According to the attending physicians, "in smallpox, after breaking out, there is always a desire for food."[1]

In 1903 medical knowledge was a little less scientific than it is today. A man with an ulcer on his leg was sent to The Dalles for an amputation and a patent medicine advertised in the *Prineville Review* flatly stated: "All children have worms!" But, for the minor sum of 25¢,

---

1   Pearle Dillon Breeding, the *Crook County News*, August 4, 1939.

you could purchase a jar of Kickapoo Worm Medicine with a candy flavor that "all the kids like."

However, Dillon wasn't afflicted with worms and a week later, the *Prineville Review* was quick to report that he didn't have smallpox either. Nothing of the kind. Then it went on to explain that complications of colds and grip were prevalent everywhere during this season and that was the probable cause of the timber cruiser's sudden death and Howard Dillon's current illness.

Following this diagnosis Dillon got worse and both Harbin and Claypool contracted the sickness. Now concerned, Dr. Belknap called in Dr. Wood Hutchinson of Portland—the State Medical Examiner—who pronounced the disease as smallpox. In a state of panic, the three victims were removed to a small building on the north side of the Ochoco River and placed in isolation. The only people to see them was Dillon's father, Leander Dillon, his brother Frank and John Claypool, father of Ronda. Within a few days Dillon died. County Coroner Joe Crooks, Gus Lippman, the town undertaker and his assistant, George Meyers all refused to touch the body. In desperation, Leander and Frank wrapped themselves in sheets and transported Howard's remains to the cemetery.

Surprisingly, Ronda Claypool and Ed Harbin survived. Before a week had passed, both Dillon's and Ronda's father came down with the plague. The Dillons would also prevail but John Claypool became the next to die. Lawrence Dillon, another brother and owner of the Dillon Saloon, closed his place of business for fear of contamination.

During this moment of panic, little Lorene Winnek was alone in her father's drug store. Seven months ago she had witnessed a terrible sheep slaughter in Gray's Prairie. Now, a new threat was approaching. A man entered the store who was shaking all over and his face was covered with "carbuncles." He told Lorene that he was freezing cold. She would remember:

> I told him he could go back by the stove and Papa would be in directly. He wasn't anyone I knew, and as a twelve-year-old town kid, I recognized all 700 residents. I guessed him to be a sheepherder. He asked for a drink and I poured a glass of water and handed it to him. Papa came in the back door, took one look at the sick man and rushed out. Within seconds he came back with Dr. Belknap.

The doctor stared at the man briefly and then asked me, "Did he touch you, Lorene?" I didn't understand and answered no. The poor fellow mumbled through chattering teeth, "Our hands touched when she gave me water." Doctor Belknap vaccinated me at once and I was whisked home to Mama. She was frightened to the core and proceeded to fumigate me to kill the germs. I stayed on the back porch while she sprayed me with full strength formaldehyde. Any germs would have been seared to ashes. I dropped my clothes on paper and Mama burned them all in the back yard.

Lorene survived but the shivering stranger wasn't so fortunate.

The editor of the *Prineville Review* had been in Silver Lake when the symptoms first appeared and which his paper had emphatically denied that there was a problem. When he arrived back in town, he exploded. One week after the denial, the front page announced, "We fully believe that a newspaper should give all the facts in regard to any contagion. While absent in Lake County there appeared an article last week in our paper headed 'Not Smallpox' which was misleading and not correct and should not have been placed therein . . . there is smallpox in Prineville and has been for two weeks . . . ."[2]

By the time another week had passed and some fifteen people had come down with the pestilence. Ed Harbin, who recovered rapidly from the dreaded disease, was quickly drummed into service to aid the sick and dying. He and Ronda Claypool—now immune from infection—were two of the very few who could safely go into homes that were quarantined. While Ronda worked as a nurse, Ed spent most of his time carrying provisions into the restricted houses and performing other errands of mercy.[3] It should come as no surprise that the madam of Prineville's house of ill-repute (as the citizens called it) made her place available for hospital use, while others froze in fear. She and her girls stood by to help nurse the sick. The whole community was grateful but never publicly acknowledged its debt.

---

2   The *Prineville Review*, April 9 and April 16, 1903.

3   Dolly Hodges Fessler, *Central Oregonian*, February 21, 1935.

As the disease spread, Sheriff Sam Smith had a pest house designated on the far east end of First Street not far from Indian Town which sat on the south bank of Ochoco River near the present location of Les Schwab's retail tire shop. Those exposed but not yet subject for the pest house were taken to the race track south of the pest house, put under quarantine and housed in tents. Now the heavy betting was not on the favorite horse but on what person would win or lose in the grim contest for survival. No one was allowed to leave this area until their quarantine period was over. Food and water was left at a designated line and then taken from there by Ed Harbin into the restricted zone. After the epidemic had run its course, the tents used by those under quarantine and all their clothing were burned. Those having the disease who recovered were dipped in a vat of disinfectant before they were allowed to come into town.[4]

The Shoshoni, knowing something was terribly wrong, abandoned Indian Town and beat a hasty retreat to Big Summit Prairie but it was too late. They packed smallpox back to the remnant of Tobacco Root's camp and the final coup was counted. Nothing would remain. In a frenzy of fear, once friendly neighbors charged into the Shoshoni camp. Horses and dogs were shot as well as those who had not yet succumbed to the disease. The Indian lodges and everything in them were put to the torch to prevent further spread of the plague and thus, the last of the once powerful Big Lodge, White Knife and Bear Killer tribes were gone forever. Only Dave Black Buffalo (Chocktote) and his wife Evening Primrose—daughter of Bloody Antler—survived by hiding in the Ochoco Mountains until the smallpox scare was over.[5] Has No Horse had escaped by moving to his government land claim near Fort Bidwell.

At the same time the Shoshoni lodges were engulfed in flames, the Poindexter Hotel was quarantined by the state Board of Health

---

4   Pearle Dillon Breeding, the *Crook County News*, August 4, 1939; Millard Elkins interview, June 7, 1968.

5   The 1903 smallpox epidemic was still uppermost in everyone's mind 30 years later. At the old Howard schoolhouse, the author was inoculated for the disease by a county health nurse in 1933. A chunk of skin about the size of a dime was scraped from the upper arm with a piece of glass and the serum applied in the raw area by a series of pin-pricks. It was an enlightening experience. Some 60 years later, the scar is still visible. As early as 1796, Edward Jenner, an English physician, discovered the principle of immunization against smallpox. However, his discovery met with great opposition among the medical profession and it would be many, many years before smallpox vaccination was put into general practice.

because two new cases of variola—as they called it—were discovered there. Only one week had passed since Dr. Hutchinson had given the hotel a clean bill of health. All passengers coming in on the stage were taken either to Winnek's drug store or the express office and thoroughly fumigated, no doubt with formaldehyde. Within days, all scheduled stage stops were canceled and Prineville was virtually isolated from the rest of the world save for mail and needed supplies.

All businesses signed agreements to close their stores at 7 p.m. each evening to help prevent the spread of disease. All dog owners were notified that dogs must be kept chained or otherwise secured or they would be shot. Charlie Winnek and Gus Lippman, the town's two furniture dealers, closed their stores and no furniture was sold until the smallpox ran its course. And there were no funerals. Following Lawrence Dillon's example, the saloons moved all card tables, chairs and other furniture out of their establishments so as to prevent crowds collecting and if necessary were prepared to close down entirely. This brings up an interesting side-light.

The Occidental Saloon—owned by Matt Nolan—used tokens instead of money for the various games. Because they passed from hand to hand all were gathered and destroyed. Tokens were never again used in the Occidental and in time people forgot they ever existed. Nearly three-fourths of a century later in 1973 a visitor from the Willamette Valley brought a token marked "Occidental Pool Hall, Prineville, Oregon" into Jo Forrester's antique shop and asked her about it. Little information could be given but one can't help wondering how it ended up in the Willamette Valley. Perhaps a customer left town in a hurry with the token still in his pocket more concerned about smallpox than collecting his cash at the pool hall.

Public schools closed. Barber shops closed. Church services were canceled and no public meetings were allowed. Even the post office was fumigating all mail and the post office itself was closed and securely locked with disinfectant being used each day from 11 a.m. to 1 p.m. so strong that according to the media "no human can remain in the house while it is in progress."

The *Review* also took issue with *The Bend Bulletin* and rebuked the editor for an "inappropriate remark" concerning the epidemic in Prineville informing him that the state Board of Health was doing all in its power to stamp out the disease. It would also take a slap at *The Oregonian* for the manner in which that publication had reported the smallpox epidemic.[6]

Then the editor in a lively discussion of smallpox "as obtained from an encyclopedia" got embroiled in a clash with a local clergyman questioning "the wisdom of public funerals during an epidemic." Not to be outdone in this exchange of medical knowledge, a local expert plunged his pen into the ink pot and citing another "authority" came up with the inspiration that "The worst case of smallpox can be effectively cured in three days simply by applying cream of tartar to the affected areas." That remedy didn't appear to work too well either.

By mid-May, the *Review* would claim "there is no danger of anyone contracting the disease by coming into our city."[7] Apparently the pestilence had run its course as there had been no new cases in the past 18 days. Even so, no one was eager to head for Prineville to test the validity of that claim.

It seemed as if cattlemen blamed the smallpox epidemic on sheep for 1903 saw a momentous escalation in the range war. As the CBS journalist Andy Rooney once observed, "People will generally accept facts as truth only if the facts agree with what they already believe." That may have been the case in 1903. The way the beef producers saw it, if infected sheep could cause spotted fever it was reasonable to believe they were also carriers of smallpox. Wool growers were equally certain that the origin was with infected cattle, citing cowpox as the guilty culprit.[8] Therefore, tens of innocent shorthorns and thousands of equally sinless woollies were marked for destruction.

The epidemic year of 1903 would also take the old Alkali Flat Stage Station operator Christian Meyer along with it in passing. Meyer, who survived three Shoshoni wars, died at the home of his son in Spanish Gulch while prospecting for gold.

---

6   The *Prineville Review*, April 23 and May 7, 1903.
7   The *Prineville Review*, April 30 and May 14, 1903.
8   The vaccine used to immunize for smallpox is derived from cowpox, a disease usually associated with dairy herds.

CHAPTER 205

OLD ALLIES

He lit out for Buck Creek and
got his pockets full of chuck,
and he took his sheep to Hampton
where he thought he'd change his luck.
But the way the 30-30's came
a whistlin' down the draw
Bill was morally certain that the work was pretty raw.

A Cayuse Buckaroo
Ode to Bill Brown

Beside a smallpox epidemic to keep nerves on edge, the elaborate three-story home which John Edwards built at Hay Creek Ranch for his English bride burned to the ground. Sheepmen were quick to point accusing fingers at hired gunmen for the cattle association. Lynn Nickols, Hay Creek Company foreman, was not so sure about that. He openly suspected the firebugs were rival sheepmen. By now, the range war itself was reaching epidemic proportions.

In the fall of 1902, "Henry Snodgrass"—alleged organizer—rode into the Camp Creek area and formed the Crook County Sheepshooters Association. As soon as they were in operation, he continued on to Silver Lake where he spent the winter of 1902-03. While there, according to an informant, "The Silver Lake ranchers inquired about the sheepshooting methods used in Crook County and Snodgrass told them 'what little he knew' about it and by spring 1903, the Lake County association was organized and ready for business."[1] This gentleman spoke the truth.

Bill Brown, ex-vigilante and acknowledged "horse king" of the West, was to be the target. A millionaire, Brown—whose two-story Buck

---

1   W.D. Officer to Ochoco National Forest Supervisor Harpman, February 5, 1927.

Creek ranch headquarters was furnished with imported furniture and sported a general store and huge warehouse—owned 43 acres of deeded land and controlled over 100,000 acres of range. Besides running thousands of horses across central Oregon, Brown was running 22,000 head of sheep not only on winter range claimed by the 96, Q, GI, Jaggi and Pot Hook ranches but on summer range claimed by Lake County ranchers as well. The coming trouble between Brown and the cattlemen had been fermenting for several years based on two different issues. One was the depletion of range by his horses; the other, his seeming tolerance of homesteaders. Now, he was going to get a wake-up call concerning his lax ways.

Early spring rains had brought on a bumper crop of grass painting the high desert a soft hue of green. Scattered throughout the area between Hampton Butte and Benjamin Lake—nibbling the fresh shoots of grass into the ground—were several bands of Bill Brown's sheep. At daybreak May 17, three days after the *Prineville Review* declared the smallpox outbreak under control, five heavily armed men rode south out of Camp Creek to rendezvous with six members of the newly formed Silver Lake Sheepshooters organization. Their prearranged meeting spot was the Last Chance Corral (a juniper log enclosure on the Crook/Lake County line) some nine miles west of Yreka Butte.

The following morning, eleven riders with soot-blackened faces to mask their true identities, packing rifles, pistols and clubs, rode leisurely eastward toward Benjamin Lake. Five of the horsemen were professional sheep killers. The other six were along to learn the tricks of the trade. The sun was inching toward high noon as Brown's herder dozed under a juniper tree. Suddenly, the peaceful quiet was shattered by pounding hoofbeats as a gruff voice demanded: "Grab a handful of sky!" Before the startled herder fully realized what was happening, rough hands jerked him erect, lashed him to the juniper tree and jammed a burlap sack over his head.

It was just as well that he couldn't see what was to transpire but the sounds were unmistakable. The bleating of sheep and the explosion of gunpowder told it all. Like in a shooting gallery, the rhythmic crack of rifles was interrupted only to reload. When the sheep dispersed across the desert, the riders chased them into terrified bunches where they were shot with pistols or clubbed to death. As the day progressed a grisly scene unfolded. Dead or dying sheep were lying everywhere. To the herder it must have seemed that the butchery would never end but toward sundown, the gunfire stopped and the eleven trigger men rode away.

Bill Brown and his hired men would find the carcasses of 1,400 animals . . . and this count doesn't include the 900 sheep killed the next day! Sixty years later, the bleaching bones of sheep could still be found scattered through the sage and juniper from Stud Horse Butte to Brown's well; and from Wagontire Mountain to Hampton Butte. In the two day extermination, Bill Brown lost 2,300 head of sheep.

Bill Brown was a strange man. On one hand he was as tough and brutal as any big operator in the Old West. On the other he held a child-like trust of anyone he met thus sending two opposing signals. Ironically, this present conflict which pitted friend against friend had its beginning not with cattlemen but with another sheepman, adding fuel as to who was really agitating the division.

In 1888, Brown—foreseeing that winter range was already becoming critical—fenced off a portion of land to put up hay. Another sheepman ordered his herder, Bill Overstreet, to cut the fence and graze out the meadow which he proceeded to do. When Brown discovered what was happening, he explained to the herder why the meadow was fenced and ordered him off the property. When Overstreet refused to go Brown threatened to get his rifle and run him off. At this point, Overstreet drew his pistol, made Brown get off his horse then get down on his hands and knees and eat grass. At the time, Brown had left his rifle back in camp.

When Brown later returned, Overstreet began shooting. He missed three shots with his pistol before Brown fired, killing him instantly. Brown then rode to Canyon City and gave himself up. There, he spent the next three months in jail awaiting trial. A Grant County jury determined the shooting was self-defense and Brown was acquitted.

By this time, he started acquiring a horse herd, buying good mares and importing thoroughbred studs. When purchasing, he bought all horses of one brand; in other words, Brown paid a certain amount and then all horses wearing that brand belonged to him. Bill himself didn't know how many horses he ran but some records place the number at 12,000 head. His main market was the United States and French governments who were buying his horses for cavalry mounts. Horses he paid five to ten dollars for, he sold for $50 to $100 each. From two horse auctions during the Spanish-American War, Brown realized a total of $150,000. Between 1888 and 1893 he was also setting up a profitable business for Hank Vaughan and the McCarty brothers who stole hundreds of Brown's free-roaming horses.

No matter where he went, Bill never carried any money except for maybe a 50¢ piece or a dollar. He preferred to pay with checks written on anything handy from a can label to a chunk of wood and his checks were honored in any bank on the Pacific Coast.

Because of his vast horse herds trampling out the range, Brown became the victim of wholesale rustling that wouldn't have been condoned if it had happened to another stockman and much of the thievery came from within his own ranks. One of Brown's best horse wranglers, a man he liked and trusted, was stealing him blind. When Bill found out, he was not only angry but deeply hurt. However, instead of shooting him as was the custom, he had him arrested and sent to the state penitentiary. Bill missed the man for he was an excellent horseman and after about a year his anger cooled down. So Bill caught the stage to Salem, had a conference with the governor and got the horse thief paroled to his custody, "morally certain the man had learned his lesson." He then promoted him to ranch foreman with the power to buy and sell, hire and fire. All went well for a year, or so Bill thought. His "reformed" foreman made a fortune selling company horses and skipped the country.[2]

Neither did Brown always win his court cases against livestock thieves even though it was well known the accused were guilty. His own fiery speech during trials caused him to lose. During one court session in Prineville the judge warned Bill that he might be fined for contempt of court. "I'm morally certain that I can pay the fine," replied Brown and went on talking. He paid the fine and lost the case. At another trial involving an alleged horse theft, Bill, with his characteristic frankness, looked over the jury and then shook his head. He turned to the judge and respectfully addressed him saying, "Your Honor, there isn't any use of me testifying here before this jury. Half of them are horse thieves themselves."

---

2   All information on Bill Brown from Cecil Rannels, Frank Gibson, Andy Ontko, Bert Tolliday, Andy Hrivonak, Buck Roba and Floyd Senecal.

But horses and sheep weren't the only reason the cattlemen were out to make an example of Bill Brown. In their eyes his most heinous crime occurred at the turn of the 20th century when speculators with promises of watering the desert were luring homesteaders by the thousands. Neither sheepmen nor cattlemen were overjoyed with the prospect and to them, Bill Brown in his way was encouraging them to stay. In some respects this was true, for without Bill's compassion for people worse off than he was, many would never have survived the first year on their homesteads. Andrew Ontko—a widower with six small children—could vouch for that. During a summer flash flood, half of his small cow herd packing the 333 brand were drowned in Warm Springs Creek.[3] Bill gave him unlimited credit until he could once again get back on his feet financially.

With an outfit as large as his, Brown had freighters bring in supplies to his Buck Creek headquarters from The Dalles, over 200 miles away. Owning a large company store and warehouse, he soon began supplying homesteaders with provisions many times, depending upon them to pay him if and when they could. Even at best, he was losing money. For example, he had his own method for weighing bulk products. One day Andy Ontko, Jr. stopped in to buy 25 pounds of rice. Brown took a sack, put some rice in it then hefted it. The scales were nearby but he didn't bother to use them. He put in some more scoops of rice in the sack, hefted it again and handed the bag to Andy. "I'm morally certain," he said, "that this sack contains 25 pounds of rice." When young Andy got back to his father's homestead he weighed the sack and found that it held 37½ pounds of rice.

One time a drummer stopped at the Buck Creek company store and offered a sample of chocolate candy. Bill liked candy and kept eating until the sample was gone. This made the salesman angry. "Now that you've eaten all my sample I don't suppose you will be interested in buying any candy." Looking him in the eye, Bill quietly replied, "Make me out an order for a ton."

Once he sold calico by the pound and homesteader's wives made some good buys before he went back to selling by the yard. Another time,

---

3   The author had the 333 brand registered in his name for over 50 years. In 1997, he transferred the 333 brand to his son, John Ontko.

two young men stole a wagon load of groceries from his store. Brown caught them and decided they needed to learn a lesson. So he had them arrested and brought to Prineville where they stood trial and were given a stiff fine. Then Brown gave them a job so they could earn the necessary money to pay the fine.

Bill was losing money not only from operating costs and theft but he loaned thousands of dollars that was never repaid. A religious man, he loaned money to build the first Methodist Church in Prineville. He gave ten thousand dollars to build the Pendleton Academy. At least ten thousand was donated to a home for the elderly in Salem—some say it was more like fifty thousand. Ten thousand went to the Willamette University School of Mines and several thousand to his sister, Sarah Ann.

The depression of the 1930's ruined him. Creditors closed in and 1,300 head of horses sold in Portland for two¢ a pound. With the loss of his range empire, Brown applied for application in the Salem Old Folk's Home which he had so generously endowed. Even here, he was still tough. When the oldsters were constantly complaining, Bill went into town, bought a bunch of shovels and presented them to the home superintendent with this sage advice, "Here are some tools to put these old fellows to work. All they do is loaf around month in and month out. They fight and cuss. If nothing else have them dig holes and fill them up again." And so Bill Brown, once a millionaire, died a ward of the state in January 1941. This was the man the sheepshooters were now out to get.

It turned out to be a two-pronged assault. After the initial sheep slaughter at Benjamin Lake, the eleven men parted company the next morning with the Camp Creek enforcers moving north and the Silver Lake boys riding east hell-bent on more mischief now that they had mastered the killing technique. Near Hampton Butte, the Camp Creek wool prospectors struck more pay dirt. The herder—fortunately for him—was still sleeping in his tent when they arrived and shot several volleys through it. Because he was lying on the ground, the herder escaped injury. Then the Camp Creek enforcers proceeded to shoot 500 more head of Brown's sheep. It was not really malicious as one rider would later comment, "We just wanted to touch up old Bill for a few head." And they did.

At the same time the Hampton destruction was in progress, the Silver Lake shooters arrived at the foot of Wagontire Mountain where they killed another 400 head of Brown's sheep at the Lost Creek corral. According to them, this attack had nothing to do with Brown personally but was more of a warning to outside sheepmen to stay clear of the area and for the remainder of the year it worked; however, it also brought on the Wagontire Water War waged by Lake County ranchers against Brown.

Lakeview stockmen convinced a few drifters to take up homesteads on Lost Creek and South Creek where they fenced off the water in such a way cattle and sheep could go under the fence but not horses. Tempers ran high and blood was shed on both sides. It eventually involved the Humane Society causing even more trouble. Finally, the federal government settled the matter by setting aside a strip of land leading to the disputed water as government property with the stipulation it could not be fenced. Neither side was happy but to avoid more publicity they called a truce.

The southeast corner of Crook County wasn't the only area reeling from renewed vigor in the range war. On March 12, 1903, less than a month before smallpox stampeded onto the range, the *Crook County Journal* would report, "On last Saturday night the sheep shed of Billy Nelson, about a half-mile this side of Mitchell, took fire and was burned to the ground with about 500 head of sheep killed and about that many more badly injured, the majority of which will die. This is a severe loss to Mr. Nelson, whom we understand just recently purchased these sheep which were all young and splendidly bred."

Two weeks later, the *Prineville Review* reported that on Saturday a week ago (March 21), Dick Koopman—a small-time cattle operator—lost two 30-ton haystacks by fire on Newsom Creek along with his cabin and barn. "As the fires occurred on the same night and were four miles apart, no other conclusions than they were of incendiary origin can be arrived at. This seems to be the outcome of the war between the sheepmen and the cattlemen which, although quiescent now, breaks out virulently at times."

Three weeks later on April 16, a murder was reported near Spray. Dead was James Jones, a sheepman well known in the Prineville area. He had been killed the afternoon of April 10 on the South Fork of the John Day River about 15 miles south of Dayville. A man named John

Glick, who admitted to the killing, gave himself up to authorities. The trouble between the two men arose over the use of sheep range. In October 1902, Jones had pulled a gun on Glick. Glick had Jones arrested in Grant County where he was bound over to the state circuit court under a $250 bond which was still pending at the time of the shooting. The murder appeared to have been premeditated. Jones was apparently unarmed and Glick shot him through the head and body with a .30-.30 rifle killing him instantly. While Glick readily admitted his guilt, he refused to discuss his motive. The Ochoco was exacting a deadly toll from its restless new occupants.

Next on the hit-list was Aldon Knighten, a rancher in the upper Ochoco Valley. It seems that Knighten allowed the owners of transitory bands of sheep to use one of his ranch buildings—situated along the deadline—as a storage shed thus making it their base of supplies. This was not a wise move on his part. On July 9, 1903, Knighten found his barbed-wire fence cut between every post for half a mile.[4] Draped over every post was a fresh sheep carcass. Nailed to one post midway in the span was a scrawled notice informing Knighten that he best remove the sheepmen's supplies or suffer the consequences.

Knighten paid little heed to this warning refusing to comply with it until he received another notice a few days later. This message was blunt and to the point. "If you value your life at anything, you'd better move the supplies." He did. In a state of panic, Knighten immediately moved all the provisions to the general store at Howard. A short time later, he sold the ranch to Henry Koch who inherited Knighten's bad luck. But, instead of getting beefed by a cowman, he was shot by a man employed by the big sheep operators to rid the range of predatory animals. No matter what you did, you couldn't win in this struggle for grass.

The remainder of 1903 was relatively calm. And, in spite of local misconduct, the country as a whole was progressing. An automobile crossed the American continent from coast to coast in 65 days. More unbelievable, eight days before Christmas—December 17, 1903—a miracle occurred at Kitty Hawk, North Carolina. Orville and Wilbur

---

4   The *Crook County Journal*, July 16, 1903.

Wright made four successful flights with a motor-powered airplane. The space age had begun.

Closer to home, a Prineville call girl journeyed over to the village of Bend for some holiday cheer and was shot in the head with a .45 by her boss. He claimed she was running away with a sheep herder. To show that Crook County did have a little law and order, a grand jury investigated the case and in its wisdom returned a no-true bill. They apparently decided it was no crime to murder a lady of easy virtue. And so, 1904 was creeping in. Maybe to a more honorable scene, maybe not.

Shortly after 1904 blundered onto the landscape, a stranger was wandering around the mountains of southeastern Oregon. Otto M. Rosendale, a mining engineer checking for outcroppings of quicksilver bearing ore along the Oregon-Nevada border, would make a startling discovery which to this day has never been confirmed or disproved. At the time of the sighting Rosendale would make the following observation. "Outside the fact that the trip of last week was in Oregon, one might have felt himself transferred to the wilds of New Mexico again. The interior of southeastern Oregon affords a great field for the mineralogist, the explorer, the ethnologist and the admirer of good and weird scenery. Here [I saw] the first traces of cliff dwellers that have been found above the 42nd degree."[5]

This is a difficult statement to accept when weighed against current knowledge of the area in question. Looking at Rosendale's disclosure from another perspective perhaps it is not so farfetched. The Western Shoshoni in their oral history handed down for generations have mentioned that following the Spanish invasion of New Mexico in the late 1600's, a group of Hopi migrated hundreds of miles to the north where they settled in the hunting grounds of their Shoshoni kinsmen, the Snake war tribes. The Oregon-Nevada border easily fits that description.

Also take into account what a writer-historian of that time period had to say about the locality of Rosendale's cliff dwellings:

> So isolated is the Harney country of Oregon from all the usual courses of travel, and so non-communicative have been the stockmen and prospectors who alone have penetrated to its most remote region, that its topography, its

---

5   Shaver, *History of Baker, Grant, Malheur and Harney Counties*, p. 743.

mineral wealth and its scientific wonders are comparatively unknown to the general public. The day is already
dawning when ignorance shall be completely dispelled.
Knowledge and the building of railroads will bring an
influx of people to take advantage of its natural resources,
and the result will be development along many different
lines, such as few even dimly foresee.[6]

He was sadly wrong in his predictions of development. Ninety-
four years after Rosendale's monumental discovery, if indeed there was
such, the southeastern portion of Oregon is still as remote and underde-
veloped as it was in 1904, and ignorance of its "scientific wonders" have
not yet been dispelled.

It seems obvious that the mining engineer was not the first to
locate the Harney cliff dwellings but he was most likely the only one who
knew for certain what he was looking at.[7] Later in Portland, Rosendale
would confide to a news reporter, "I have every reason to believe that I
discovered traces of cliff dwellings. I was alone on horseback traveling
through the southeastern portion of Harney County when I made the
discovery." Apparently the day when Rosendale made the sighting had
started out in typical eastern Oregon fashion with a heavily overcast sky
which as the day wore on would become sparkling clear.

By his own admission, Rosendale had lost sight of all landmarks
and had been traveling for the past six hours without bearings before the
overcast lifted. As the visibility began clearing he found himself in "a
peculiar spot." In an area barren of vegetation, black basaltic cliffs rose
abruptly from the desert and formed a gloomy, narrow ravine. Dismount-
ing and leading his "worn-out horse," Rosendale worked his way up the
defile toward higher ground in an attempt to recognize some landmark
as the sky had now broken clear. As he ascended this bleak canyon the

---

6   Shaver, *History of Baker, Grant, Malheur and Harney Counties*, p. 743.

7   As early as 1863 a news item in the *Humboldt Register*, Unionville, Nevada, dated December
     5, mentions the discovery of the Pueblo mining district on Pueblo Mountain in what is now
     southeastern Harney County. This discovery was attributed to Major M.D. Herman of Carson
     City. From this one could guess that Pueblo Mountain was already well known before the
     location of the mining district. The location of Pueblo Mountain, Pueblo Butte, Pueblo Valley
     and Pueblo City again appear with considerable accuracy on Lt. Col. R.S. Williamson's
     railroad survey map published in 1866. Pueblo is the Spanish word for city or village. Also
     see, "Major M.D. Harmon," *Oregon Historical Quarterly*, June 1946, p. 210.

engineer noticed that many of the overhanging cliff crevices were half filled with wind-blown sand. Then, near the head of this windy gorge, he spied an unnatural formation for the Pacific Northwest.

"There before me were about sixty-five cliff dwellers' habitations, deserted but in a fair state of preservation. I was looking upon a picture of queer and very strangely formed small buildings [these were Kivas], roofless, bound together with no material whatsoever, but hewn [from rock] with all the skill of the ancient craftsmen. In the middle of the place was an upright stone, resembling the famous altar stone of the ancient Aztecs of Old Mexico." It was Rosendale's guess "that most probably on this stone the bloody rites of human sacrifice were performed by an extinct race."[8] It is worth noting that according to Shoshoni legend, the ancient—some say mythical—City of Aztlan was located about 200 miles southeast of Pueblo Mountain.

Now before skeptics get too overwrought with disbelief, maybe engineer Rosendale knew what he was observing. Maybe not, but in 1893 Rosendale was one of a select group sent out by the Smithsonian Institution to penetrate the almost inaccessible region of New Mexico known as the Goronda del Muerto or the Journey of Death. The purpose of this mission was to examine the extensive cliff dwellings in that area. This assignment was to obtain accurate measurements for the reconstruction of cliff dwellings to be exhibited at the Chicago World Fair. These reproductions later became a part of the Chicago Field Museum.[9] By 1904 some of these cliff dwellings were also constructed for the Louisiana Purchase Exposition in St. Louis, most likely by the same engineers who worked on the Chicago World Exposition in 1893, including Rosendale whom some critics claim never existed.[10]

Rosendale would explain that he was already behind schedule on his assigned project of inspecting quicksilver claims so he did not take time to make a thorough examination of the locality or an exploration of the walled-in depression in the basalt cliff. "Yet, I am thoroughly con-

8   Shaver, *History of Baker, Grant, Malheur and Harney Counties*, p. 742.
9   Ibid., 743.
10   The following information on O.M. Rosendale is taken from the 1900 census. O.M. Rosendale was born in Germany in June 1860. By 1899, at the age of 39, he was living at 211 6th Street, Portland, Oregon. Rosendale was the son-in-law of L. Rosenthal, who was also born in Germany in May 1829, and who had moved to Portland in 1870. (1900 census, Department of Commerce, Bureau of the Census, Oregon R253, Vol. II, Sheet 3, lines 5 and 9.)

vinced that the caves served at one time as the habitations of what are commonly known as cliff dwellers." And this was Rosendale's last known statement on the subject of Hopi pueblos.

Now let's see what further mischief the passage of time has stored up its sleeve for the year of 1904.

CHAPTER 206

THE RECORD IS BROKEN

Our annual report shows that we have slaughtered between 8,000 and 10,000 head during the last shooting season and we expect to increase this respectable showing during the next season providing the sheep hold out . . .

Corresponding Secretary
Crook County Sheepshooters
Association

While Jack London took time to write *The Sea Wolf*, and James Barrie created the ageless *Peter Pan*; the central Oregon range war raged on. Undisturbed by such frivolities, Sigmund Freud expounded on *The Psychopathology of Everyday Life*; Puccini's opera "Madame Butterfly" opened in Milan; the Czech composer Anton Dvorák—who taught American songwriters how to produce classical music with his "New World 9th Symphony"—was playing his final note when a New York policeman arrested a woman for smoking a cigarette in public, giving promise that 1904 was off to a good start.

Japanese gunboats had just laid siege to the Russian outpost of Port Arthur, China when the Lake County Sheepshooters, flush with their earlier success, were again on the prowl. Mid-winter 1904 found them riding toward Wagontire Mountain to torment Bill Brown when they stumbled upon an unexpected quarry in the vicinity of Christmas Lake. The Benham brothers operating out of Lakeview decided in late January to herd 3,000 head of sheep into Christmas Valley where some shelter from wind and storms could be found. Their goal was the Hampton area where they intended to swipe a little of Bill Brown's range. On the evening of February 3, they were spotted by the Silver Lake boys.

As soon as the herder bedded the sheep down, five masked men rode up on horseback, took him at gunpoint, placed a sack over his head and tied him to a juniper tree. Then, with rifles, pistols, knives and clubs dealing mayhem, these gentlemen proceeded to demolish a few sheep. During the course of the night, 2,200 head—setting a new one-day record—were killed and the remaining animals were stampeded onto the open range to fall prey to coyotes. When the masked gunmen completed their job, they returned to the herder and warned that any sheep found crossing the deadline would be shot. They also advised against "talking too much" and left.[1]

On February 5, the herder stumbled into Silver Lake and telephoned Lakeview—the Lake County seat—to report the incident. It was three days before officers reached the spot and no trace of the sheep slayers could be found. Nevertheless, a quiet investigation was carried on for some time. During this, men who were thought to be in possession of evidence received anonymous letters and warnings in various ways cautioning them about talking. One man found a piece of rope tied to his doorknob and a note advising him to keep quiet. Neither was it a sure bet that these threats were the sole responsibility of cattlemen.

All of these warnings came from mysterious sources. Some of the letters were mailed at distant post offices and no clue could be successfully traced. In northern Lake County it had generally been believed that sheepmen and cattlemen were on good terms. To most local people it was surprising that the range war which had broken out in Crook County had suddenly struck Lake.

A short time after the Christmas Lake sheepshooting, Creed Conn, A Silver Lake merchant lost a barn and some valuable freight wagons by fire. Town gossip had it that Conn not only sold ammunition to the sheepshooters but was working hand-in-hand with the Silver Lake Livestock Association. Whether or not he was is unknown but he made a bad mistake by going to visit his brother, L.F. Conn, the Lake County district attorney and was rumored to have told things which the district attorney might make use of to prosecute certain members of the livestock asso-

---

1   *Illustrated History of Central Oregon*, Spokane, 1905. *The Crook County Journal*, February 11, 1904, would claim that 3,000 sheep were slain and that they belonged to Guy McKune of Silver Lake. McKune was the Benham brothers' ranch manager.

ciation. The second time Creed went to visit his brother, his favorite saddle horse took unexplainably sick and died.[2]

Following Creed's return from this second trip to Lakeview, he was very nervous and uncommunicative and was reluctant to discuss the recent misfortune of losing his barn, wagons and horse. On a blustery Friday morning, March 4, 1904, with a snowstorm howling across the desert, Conn went to the store and after speaking to his clerk about mail, walked out, mounted his horse and headed toward his ranch in Christmas Valley. He never returned.

Search parties were unable to find any trace of him. On April 25, six weeks after Conn's disappearance, a rider found his body lying in a field less than a mile from town. Two bullet holes were found in his breast and one in his back. His own revolver which was still clutched in his hand, held two empty cartridges. The body was found face up with arms outstretched. A corner's jury brought in a verdict of suicide.[3]

Four days later on April 29, all hell broke loose north of Benjamin Lake on Crook County's southeast border eclipsing the 1903 two-day slaughter in the same area and the 2,200 head killed in February at Christmas Lake. To better understand what was to happen, it's worth examining the testimony of an outsider sent in to investigate the situation. He would note that he was not sent to Crook County to theorize about the outcome of the range war. Among other things, he found that "sheep belonging in Wasco County or Lake County are deep in the middle of Crook County eating up everything they can find. Generally speaking, the settlers show a good deal of self-restraint, but now and then a killing is made." He also discovered that in some sections the cattlemen were holding their own and in others the sheepmen were wining out. So all-in-all, it was a toss-up as to whom was being taken advantage of.

In his opinion, "There is no disguising the fact that the cattlemen often show a spirit of outlawry. They are open-handed and open-minded. But just as they slap a fly that buzzes around their head too lively, they drive off and sometimes slaughter the sheep. They generally look upon

---

2   Arno Dosch, "The War For Range," *The Pacific Monthly*, February 1906, p. 158.

3   Grover Blake, "Oregon Range Wars," *True West*, January-February 1965, pp. 20-21. Blake, who was herding sheep in Crook County when Conn's body was discovered, places the date as April 25, 1904. A reporter for *The Pacific Monthly* two years later would give the date as April 22, 1904.

the sheep as a kind of vermin that it is well to get rid of . . . .meanwhile the sheepherders carry automatics, ostensibly for use on coyotes."[4] Now back to April 29, 1904.

A large herd made up entirely of wethers belonging to three big sheep companies based at Silver Lake moved into Benjamin Lake, summer range of the powerful Camp Creek-Crooked River cow outfits. In a brazen show of defiance, the camp tender and herder sent word to Camp Creek that they were well-armed and unafraid. If the ranchers wanted trouble just come out and pay them a visit. Eleven masked riders accepted the invitation. On approaching the herd, two men went in search of the camp tender while the rest swooped in on the herder, a man named Wilcox employed by the Grube & Parker Livestock Company.

According to Wilcox, it was about 4 o'clock in the evening when they appeared and he was bedding the sheep down. "They said unless I removed the sheep in two hours they would kill them, and then they left me." The herder didn't think they would bother him that night so he went about bedding the flock down. Meantime, the Camp Creek committee located the camp tender about a mile away, disarmed him and tied a sack over his head. He begged them not to take him back to camp as the herder would laugh at him but the cowmen assured him not to worry as the herder would get a sack over his head also. This seemed to make the camp tender feel much better and he offered no further objections.

Wilcox would later report: "In two hours the men came back and, after placing a sack over my face and tying my hands, they told me they had come to kill the sheep. They also warned if officers came to arrest them, they would treat the officers the same as the sheep and if anyone offered a reward for their arrest, they would kill the parties offering the reward. They were very deliberate in their work and went about it just as if it were an everyday occurrence." When the crash of gunfire faded away it was found that out of 2,700 wethers—the money crop—2,400 were killed and the remainder wounded or dying. What happened that bloody evening in 1904 is recorded as the worst single sheep slaughter in the history of the West.[5]

---

4   Arno Dosch, associate editor, *The Pacific Monthly*, February 1906, on assignment to investigate the struggle between cattlemen and sheepmen in central Oregon.

5   This occurrence takes into account the range wars fought in Texas, Colorado and Wyoming, thus proving the Crook County Sheepshooters played second fiddle to no one.

Wilcox headed for Silver Lake and reported the sheep killing. Men were sent out to investigate with the same results as the February shooting. By now the word was out that perhaps Creed Conn had been murdered, stirring up speculation in Prineville that the disappearance of a local rancher might also have been a planned execution.

In the 1890's, a Greek immigrant who had taken the name of Elias Davis arrived in Prineville. Because of his small stature, everyone called him "Shorty." About the time he was naturalized a U.S. citizen, Davis began acquiring land in Crook County. On court records, he listed his birthplace as Montemegro, Greece but renounced all allegiance to his former homeland. His ranch was located on upper Crooked River some 20 miles southwest of Prineville.[6] Those who knew him said that Davis, a bachelor, "was a nice little feller who never bothered anybody. He worked at his ranch, saved his money, but nobody seemed to know anything about him." During the many years he lived in Crook County, he was known to have left the area only twice.

And this brings up another mystery. In 1883, a Peter Davis—also known as Shorty—who owned a ranch on upper Crooked River, disappeared without a trace.[7] Were Pete Davis and Elias Davis one and the same? The intervening years and the different background of the two men involved would make that appear unlikely but it is food for thought.

Whatever, one morning Elias Davis, packing a rifle and pistol and accompanied by his stock dog, rode north into the Ochoco Mountains and was never seen again. The afternoon of the day he vanished, an ominous black column of smoke drifted up from Rough Canyon on the North Fork of Crooked River . . . a fire which burned for several days. Was this a funeral bier intended to hide any trace of murder? Some believed that it was. A later investigation found no evidence to link this blaze to Shorty's absence. It's difficult to believe that a wood fire—if indeed it was Shorty's final resting spot—could burn hot enough to consume horseshoes, rifle and other metal objects let alone the bones of

---

6   The Davis house in the Post area has long been torn down and nearly all traces of his ranch obliterated by a housing subdivision. As late as 1942, the old rock fireplace and tall chimney remained as a reminder that Shorty once lived there.

7   See Chapter 186, "The Day of the Hunted," p. 81-82. Both disappearances are documented by eyewitness accounts of men who were known for their integrity and not prone to wild drifts of the imagination.

horse, man and dog. If a crime was committed it is certain the perpetrator would be aware of this.[8]

Davis' Crooked River neighbors put out the word that he was murdered by cattlemen who were afraid his knowledge of their sheep shooting activities might cause them trouble. One story has it that Davis—whose ranch was surrounded by local sheep operators—received a warning that if he didn't get out of the country, his life was in danger. Taking the threat at face value, Davis rode into the mountains that fateful morning, hid out until evening and then under the cover of darkness lit out for the open lands of Nevada. Investigators in the case were reluctant to accept this theory.

A few months after Creed Conn's body was discovered, a sheep-herder claimed he knew what had happened to Shorty Davis. In 1905, after being questioned by Sheriff Frank Elkins, this story came out implying that Joe Lister knew something about Shorty's whereabouts.

Apparently, Joe and the sheepherder had been drinking a bit. As the night drug on, Lister, knowing that the herder was somewhat super-stitious confided that in an old well not too far from the herder's small shack, the ghost of Davis had arisen and chased him all the way across the flat. The herder brooded over this sighting and decided he just couldn't live near that well any more as he figured the killing would be blamed on him. So he told the sheriff he knew where Shorty's body was stashed. After some questioning, Lister had to admit he was just trying to scare the old man and it certainly worked.

Since no one came forth to claim Shorty's property, A.J. Derby—a Hood River lawyer—decided to investigate and try to discover who Shorty Davis was. His search led him to Portland to a restaurant where

---

8 Many years ago, a person well acquainted with range war events took the author to the alleged spot where Shorty Davis disappeared. Supposedly, horse, rider and dog were deposited in a soap-hole (quicksand) less than 8 miles from the Davis ranch house. If so, this would answer why no trace of man or beast was ever found. Many years later a skeleton was found in a remote section of the Ochoco which was considered by many to be that of Davis but positive identification was never established. If the information given to the author was true, the bones were not those of Shorty Davis.

Another old timer revealed the name of a man whom he believed had killed Shorty Davis. According to him the murderer had boasted of the deed in later years, and it was known that this man had killed at least three other men. But the suspected murderer, who has been dead for a number of years, never publicly admitted the crime and as the saying goes, dead men tell no tales.

Shorty was known to have visited, and from there to San Francisco to a man named Saphos, who was a friend of Elias Davis (alias "Shorty").

Shorty's real name was Leonidas J. Douris, a Greek immigrant who came to the United States to get away from people who always wanted to borrow money but would never repay their debt. In tracking down the Douris family, Derby learned there were five brothers living in Athens. Constatine Douris was chosen to come and represent the family and settle the estate in Crook County.[9]

In May 1904 a message was sent to Salem informing the governor of the suspected murders in central Oregon. Within hours, Governor Chamberlain ordered the state of Oregon to post a $2,000 reward for information leading to the arrest and conviction of the slayers of either Creed Conn or Elias Davis. At this point, the Lake County wool growers formed an organization and offered a like amount for the conviction of anyone guilty of "maliciously killing sheep belonging to any member of the organization. The Lake County Court also offered a reward for the capture of parties who killed sheep. No arrests were made although information was filed against several suspects.[10] Even when the State Legislature passed a bill appropriating $10,000 for the same purpose, no one talked. Instead, the sheep slaughter intensified.

On June 4, 1904—less than a month after the various rewards were posted—1,000 sheep belonging to Morrow and Keenan were exterminated in a high mountain meadow known as Little Summit Prairie some 40 miles east of Prineville. Over in Wheeler County, Tom Fitzgerald lost 100 sheep when riders on a moonlight raid without warning opened up a bombardment into the animals as they lay on the bed ground. In this case the herder, Dick Bradshaw, was neither tied nor blindfolded. In fact, he knew nothing of the attack until awakened by gunfire. He dashed for cover and hid under a creek bank until the sheepshooters departed. The next move was to burn the Honorable Newt Williamson's sheep-shearing plant located in Dixie Meadows near the present Keystone Ranch.

A week after this excitement, 65 head of sheep belonging to Allie Jones were killed on Mill Creek the evening of June 13. This strike was announced by the *Crook County Journal* June 16, 1904 with the blazing

---

9 In May 1907, the Crook County Court ruled that the heirs in Greece would get the money received by the state for the Davis property, less debts and court costs.

10 *Illustrated History of Central Oregon*, Spokane, 1905.

headline: "Mill Creek Stockman is the First Loser this Week in Sheep Slaughter!" This was followed by a similar release in *The Dalles Times Mountaineer* on June 17, and the *Deschutes Echo* on June 18 which noted that herder Tom Paine was caught napping.

This onslaught prompted the State Organization of Wool Growers and the Antelope Wool Growers Association to follow in the footsteps of the Lake County Sheepmen and offer a $1,000 reward for information leading to the arrest and conviction of any person found guilty of "shooting or otherwise killing or maiming of sheep." This incentive didn't attract too many takers either.

For some reason Allie Jones blamed Tom Houston and another rancher for the Mill Creek sheepshooting. Beside publicly threatening to kill them, Jones offered a reward of $150 each to anyone else who would do so. Naturally both men were on guard. A few months later while riding for cattle, Houston saw what he believed to be the glint of a gun barrel in the brush and, being a dead shot, he swung his rifle over the saddle horn and fired from the waist. Without looking, he rode some 75 miles into Prineville to report that he had killed Allie Jones. It just so happened Jones had been seen at one of the local saloons just a short time before Houston's arrival. Now, the question was who had Houston shot? Sheriff Sam Smith and a posse returned with Houston to the scene of the shooting and found nothing but a single drop of blood.[11] Being unseasonably cold, it was believed that whoever was hit was wearing a heavy sheepskin coat which absorbed the shock of the bullet, perhaps causing no more serious damage than a sore chest and a slight flesh wound.

If anything, the range war was becoming more lethal caused—at least in part—by the Oregon Wool Growers' offer of huge sums of money to squeal on your neighbor. As 1904 struggled toward its final destination a new contender slinked into the arena . . . the range detective.

---

11 Interview with Lem Houston, son of John Thomas Houston, December 20, 1949. It was never determined who Houston may have shot.

CHAPTER 207

THE BOUNTY HUNTERS

In some instances the wool growers of Eastern Oregon have been so unwise as to offer rewards for the arrest and conviction of sheepshooters. . . . We have therefore warned them by publication of the danger of such action, as it might result in our organization having to proceed on the lines that "Dead men tell no tales."

Corresponding Secretary
Crook County Sheepshooters
Association

"This is not to be considered as a threat to commit murder," the secretary would continue, "as we do not justify such a thing except where flock owners resort to unjustifiable means in protecting their property." With statements like this a case was being built against the cattlemen through public sentiment. An indictment was launched in rhetoric which by 1906 would influence the federal government to offer sheepmen the pick of the choice grazing allotments. It now appears that the animosity generated was not by accident but a deliberate attempt to crush the Crook County cattle industry.

Some fifty years after the conflict, Grover Blake (a pioneer forest service ranger) would write in a national publication, "It will be noted that the so-called [Crook County] range war was being waged *only* by cattlemen."[1] It is interesting that Blake expressed a different view when he first arrived in Crook County in 1904. Working for the big sheep outfits—among others, the Prineville Land and Livestock Company—he

---

1   Blake, "Oregon Range War," *True West*, January-February 1965, p. 21.

would note that "sheep herders were killed by employees of rival sheep owners in order to get the best range."[2]

On April 1, 1905, the Western Division of the Blue Mountain Forest Reserve came under the administration of the United States Forest Service with A.S. Ireland as supervisor of the Ochoco National Forest. At this time Blake was assisting with the herding of 6,000 sheep for George Trosper of Antone and was camped on Spanish Peak, dangerously close to the Paulina deadline. Two years later he went to work for the Forest Service as an allotment enforcer.

Commenting on the loss of 500 sheep in Paulina Valley in the heart of cattle range, Blake would further observe, "The perpetrators of all this lawlessness showed little or no fear of reprisal and boldly spread the word that continuation of the sheep killing could be expected. Many communications from Prineville were sent to newspapers to that effect. They called themselves the Crook County Sheepshooting Association of Eastern Oregon and so signed their letters . . . ."[3] Obviously Blake believed those letters to be the work of the cattlemen as did everyone else.

Most of the criticism of the sheepshooters at that time, and carried through to the present, were based on the boastful, sometimes sarcastic and often threatening correspondence printed in local newspapers and given attention by the national press. With the exception of a few unsigned reports all bore the distinctive heading of Sheepshooter's Headquarters, Crook County, Oregon and were signed by the corresponding secretary of the Crook County Sheepshooting Association. Keep in mind that there were only five known sheepshooting associations operating in eastern Oregon and the only one using the Crook County designation was not based in Prineville but in the Camp Creek area south of the Maury Mountains.[4]

2   Blake, *Sowing the Seed*, p. 3, MS.
3   Blake, *Blazing Oregon Trails*, p. 19, a private publication printed in Bend, Oregon in 1969.
4   The sheepshooting associations were:

Name	Founded	Base
IZ Sheepshooters	1896	Izee
Central Oregon Sheepshooters	1898	Paulina
Inland Sheepshooters	1899	Prineville
Crook County Sheepshooters	1902	Camp Creek
Lake County Sheepshooters	1903	Silver Lake

One of the more hostile letters directed to Harvey Scott, editor of the *Portland Oregonian*, dated December 29, 1904 would begin, "Mr. Editor, seeing that you are giving quite a bit of publicity to the Sheep-shooters of Crook County, I thought I would lend you some assistance by giving you a short synopsis of the proceedings of the Organization during the past year. Therefore, if space will permit please publish the following report."

This is a brief summary of what *The Oregonian* was requested to print. After the customary heading it started:

> I am authorized by the Association to notify *The Oregonian* to desist from publishing matters derogatory to the reputation of sheepshooters of Eastern Oregon. We claim to have the banner county of Oregon on the progressive line of sheepshooting and it is my pleasure to inform you that we have a little government of our own in Crook County and we would thank *The Oregonian* and the Governor to attend strictly to their business and not muddle with the settlement of the range question in our province.

There followed several more paragraphs in the same vein and then the letter concluded:

> When sheepmen fail to observe these peaceable obstructions [the deadlines], we delegate a committee to notify offenders . . . these mild and peaceful means are usually effective, but in cases where they are not, our executive committee takes the matter in hand, and being men of high ideals as well as good shots by moonlight, they promptly enforce the edicts of the Association.

The corresponding secretary would end his report with the number of sheep killed during the "last shooting season" and promised to increase that respectable showing the next season provided that "the sheep hold out and *The Oregonian* and the Governor observe the customary laws of neutrality." As usual, the letter was signed by the corresponding secretary of the Crook County Sheepshooting Association of Eastern Oregon.

It would seem that someone might question as to why the cattle-men kept calling attention to their misdeeds. You don't challenge a respected newspaper editor, a state governor or for that matter, a powerful U.S. congressman and get away with it. It just so happened that the Hon. J.N. Williamson, one of the big wool growers in Crook County, was also losing lots of sheep. The above was a highly inflammatory message just begging for trouble and it got the desired result.

The federal government was gearing up to deal with the range crisis while the state legislature of 1904, through its passage of a bill appropriating thousands of dollars to be used by the governor for "the apprehension of persons guilty of killing livestock belonging to others," was speeding up the action. This brought on the so-called "Range Detectives" who only served to heighten the conflict. In reality, they were paid livestock killers sanctioned by the state and under the employ of the Wool Growers Association. The rewards offered by sheepmen, the counties and the state lured some tough customers into the area under the guise of U.S. Deputy Range Marshalls. One of them was Jesse Selkirk, who was involved in an incident given no publicity at the time.

To set the scene, the range feud had reached its bloodiest worst in 1904. No only did that year claim some 10,000 sheep but cattle were killed in bitter retaliation as the carcasses spread across the land like rotten tokens of the abnormal hatred that comes when men once close grow to despise each other. Caught up in the web of death were two men with close ties to the cattle industry and several sheepmen. Then in the spring of 1904 sheepmen met at Antelope with J.D. McAndie, H.C. Rooper and Joseph Bannon offering large rewards for information that would lead to the arrest of the raiders of their flocks. They might as well have offered a sheep hide. Locals were too afraid to step forward and claim the money. The sheepshooters answered by killing a thousand head of sheep in Little Summit Prairie. And the letter writing campaign gained momentum.

Shortly after the wool growers' meeting at Antelope, *The Dalles Times Mountaineer* would publish an inflammatory letter attributed to the Crook County Sheepshooters Association entitled the "Supplementary Report of 1904."

> The New Year was duly observed by our brave boys by the slaughter of about 500 head of sheep belonging to a gen-

tleman who had violated our rules or laws. The names of active participants in this last brilliant action of the Association have not yet been handed in. When they are, we will take pleasure in recording them on the roll of honor above mentioned.

The Crook County papers have recently said some uncomplimentary things about our order which may invite attention later on.

Our work is now of too much importance to justify a diversion from the regular order of business.

We have recently extended our jurisdiction to cover a large territory on the desert heretofore occupied by sheepmen and we expect to have to sacrifice a few flocks of sheep there this winter.

This letter was signed with the customary "Corresponding Secretary, Crook County Sheepshooters Association" and dated June 17, 1904.

The letters accredited to the sheepshooters association were written for the express purpose of bringing the Crook County range war to the public eye. Over 30 years after the last shot had been fired, a new light was focused on the subject. Roscoe Knox, who came to Crook County in 1885 and engaged in the sheep business had taken an active, though secret, part in the range war. He had gained the confidence of Gov. Chamberlain and corresponded with him regularly in regard to the conflict. By his own admission, Knox was also a frequent correspondent to *The Oregonian* pretending to be a sheepshooter in order to make public and "expose the cattlemen's depredations" as he called it. Then came the clincher: Knox signed those articles . . . the Corresponding Secretary, Crook County Sheepshooters Association of Eastern Oregon![5]

Against this backdrop the hired gunmen entered the picture and it was a vicious game being played. Bear in mind that Prineville—Queen of Oregon Cow Towns—was also headquarters for some of the largest sheep operations in the nation and perhaps even the world. These local wool growers held no more love for the outside sheep operators than the

---

5   *The Crook County News*, Prineville, Oregon, Friday, August 4, 1939.

beef producers did and they certainly held no respect for the cattlemen. What happens next leaves much room for speculation.

Jesse Selkirk—hired gunman—moved unobtrusively into Prineville and his job was simplicity in itself. His gun was hired to kill not men but livestock. Note the distinction—not sheep or cattle but livestock. In a secret meeting so he would not be identified, Jesse demanded and got $2 a head for the killing of grass eaters. Expensive but worth it. And so, for a handful of dollars, Jesse rode deep into the Ochoco to enforce some deadlines of his own.

Selkirk was an old pro . . . none of the newfangled modern weapons for him. When he rode into the Ochoco Mountains he was packing a .44-70, old and deadly. The cartridges were loaded with 470 grain .44 calibre bullets backed by 70 grains of black powder. This was the notorious "forty-four seventy" Sharps long range buffalo gun.

Interestingly, his destination was Big Summit Prairie where the deadline knifed through the area like a finely honed blade. Here, Prineville Land and Livestock's [Big Muddy Company] deeded land rubbed shoulders with the summer range of the big cattle outfits based in the Ochoco and Paulina valleys; and it was also the trespass zone where Morrow, Sherman and Wheeler county sheep outfits clashed with all concerned whether they be cattle or sheep operators.

The morning Selkirk arrived—Thursday, August 4, 1904—a sheep execution was already in progress some 18 miles to the east in Little Summit Prairie where 500 head of Morrow and Keenan's sheep were under fire. On reaching the Big Summit killing grounds, Jesse methodically set up camp at daybreak. First he unrolled a piece of canvas and carefully laid out a cleaning rod and rags. This was followed by a small can of water and 250 .44-70-470 cartridges laid out in neat rows within reach of his trigger-finger hand. Then he spread his rest sticks, uncased his Sharps rifle, slipped a cartridge into the chamber and settled down in a comfortable sitting position for some money-making shooting.

The rest is history. Already dozens of cattle were grazing when shortly after sunup another 500 head of Morrow and Keenan's sheep filed noisily across the deadline soon to be followed by a hundred head belonging to Tom Fitzgerald, a Wheeler County operator. Within the hour, the herders drifted back to their respective camps for breakfast.

Slowly it penetrated their brains that they could hear the dull rumble of a heavy calibre rifle's evenly spaced, unhurried shots.

Meanwhile Selkirk was seriously completing his job. He wasn't just dropping sheep, he was literally blowing them to shreds and any cow that got in his way shared the same fate. When the rifle began to heat up and the black powder residue harden fouling the barrel to such an extent that accuracy might be destroyed, he wet a piece of rag and with the cleaning rod did a swabbing job. With a cool and cleaned bore he continued to shoot until his predetermined quota of kills for the day had been made. Selkirk was a cold, calculating professional—a veteran of the Lincoln and Johnson County wars and never make the mistake that he was not as adept at killing men as he was livestock. The only difference so far as Jesse was concerned was the price.

Within a week, Jesse Selkirk was paid a reward of $2,500 by the sheepmen's organization for bringing about the conviction of "some of the men involved in the slaughter of Tom Fitzgerald's sheep."[6] It is interesting to note that Forest Ranger Blake would later admit that "as a matter of record, the killers of the Fitzgerald sheep were in no way associated with the Crook County group known as the Crook County Sheepshooters Association."[7] You can bet that Selkirk, the bounty hunter, didn't implicate himself.

Five weeks before Selkirk slipped into the Ochoco Mountains, Milt DeHaven—range detective, deputy U.S. marshall and gunslinger from The Dalles—received word from Antelope that his services were in demand. Six days later on July 4, 1904, when the stage rolled into Mitchell, DeHaven unloaded at the hotel. The rumor was already spreading that DeHaven was under the pay of sheepmen and the word went out to the cattlemen to take no chances.

There were six Puett boys living in Crook County at this time and all would die violent deaths.[8] One of the brothers, Monk Puett, a known

---

6   Blake, "Oregon Range Wars," *True West*, January-February 1965, p. 62.
7   Blake, *Blazing Oregon Trails*, p. 23.
8   Two of the brothers were gunned down at the old Redby Rooming House in Prineville in the 1930's. At one time, they had a hide-out cabin on Trout Creek about two miles east of Grindstone Creek in the Suplee area. They had dug a shaft under the cabin floor with a tunnel leading into a dry wash where they kept their horses tied. In the event that the cabin was surrounded by a sheriff's posse, they had an easy escape route. Remains of this cabin were still visible in the late 1950's.

horse thief, suspected killer and a dead shot was rumored to be on the payroll of the Central Oregon Sheepshooters Association. It just so happened that Monk was in Mitchell when the Antelope stage arrived. Speculation ran high that if DeHaven and Puett met there would be bloodshed. As a point of interest, Monk's brother—W.H. Puett—had recently served three terms as Mitchell town marshall and had just been replaced by John Stice.

When the stage arrived, the streets of Mitchell were awash with flood waters from a cloudburst that day. Seven days later the town would be destroyed by a flash flood but that was in the future and more pressing things were occurring this afternoon.[9] John Carrol, owner of the Carrol Saloon, had just kicked Puett out of the building for shooting off firecrackers. When the Antelope stage splashed to a halt at the Bethune Hotel, Monk and Roy Gray (a rider for the big Ochoco cattle outfits) were blasting away with .45 Colts at tin cans floating down Main Street. As the passengers stepped off the stage, Monk started an argument with DeHaven that would end in a shoot-out.[10]

It was obvious that DeHaven was loaded for action. When he stepped off the stage he was packing a .303 Savage rifle and a Winchester model 1873 forty-four forty loaded with 200 grain .44 calibre bullets and 40 grains of black powder interchangeable with the handgun now tucked away in his suitcase (which later was discovered to hold nothing but hundreds of rounds of .44 calibre bullets).

DeHaven checked into his hotel room, grabbed the .303 Savage and returned to the street. Anticipating trouble a crowd had already gathered and as DeHaven stepped off the hotel porch, Marshall John Stice jumped between the two gunmen and took Puett's .45 slug in the groin. As Stice went down, DeHaven leveled his rifle and both men fired simultaneously. Monk took a step backward as DeHaven attempted to lever another round into the rifle chamber but it was a futile effort. He had forgotten to load the .303 before coming out into the street. Milt calmly turned his back to Puett, climbed the porch steps and headed back into the hotel after more bullets. In the meantime, Puett pitched face down

9   For more on the 1904 flood, see *Thunder Over the Ochoco*, Vol. IV, Chapter 173, "Let's Build Towns."

10   Eyewitness account as told to the author by Roy Gray, March 22, 1956.

in the flooded street. As DeHaven reached his hotel room door, he too collapsed, shot through the tip of his heart.

By then, John Carrol—the saloon keeper—had arrived and De-Haven was placed on a bed. During this, Puett's sister dragged him out of the water and then entered the hotel. As she watched DeHaven die, she yelled, "Give me a knife and I'll cut his damn throat!"[11]

What agreement William Milton DeHaven made with the Antelope Wool Growers Association will never be known. The only certainty is that he never lived to carry it out.

Two weeks after the Mitchell shoot-out, the *Crook County Journal* posted a notice to sheepmen signed by the Crooked River and Beaver Creek Stock Association that no outside sheep would be permitted to graze in the territory south or east of Lookout Mountain, which also included the head of the Ochoco River. This was no idle threat. The same day the warning appeared in the *Crook County Journal* on July 21, 1904, a party of six men made an attack on Miles Lee's sheep camp on Spanish Peak. G.W. Brooks, the herder in charge, had just arrived in camp and was preparing to get supper when he was startled by several shots fired close to camp.

Brooks rushed out of the tent with his rifle and observed several men busily engaged in firing upon the band of 2,300 sheep scattered about the camp. The sheep were bedded down and the gunmen were firing as fast as they could pull the triggers.

Brooks hid behind some trees and opened fire on the sheep-shooters. At this point the entire party of raiders began shooting at him. Brooks had only eleven cartridges, all of which he fired at the men. He then tried to crawl to where he had more ammunition cached but the raiders made it so hot for him that he was obliged to run for his life. He managed to escape, bareheaded and coatless, by dodging behind rocks and trees until he was out of range of their bullets.

While the Spanish Peak sheep massacre was in progress, three wool growers from Antelope—H.C. Rooper, J.D. McAndie and Joe Bannon—met with 30 prominent cattlemen from the Ochoco and Mill Creek valleys and hammered out a solution to the range problem or so they thought. After a hearing, with concessions being made on both sides,

---

11   George Carrol, son of John Carrol, Sisters, Oregon, May 29, 1973.

deadlines were established which those in attendance thought were satisfactory for all concerned. It was their belief that if the deadlines were strictly observed the range troubles in the Blue Mountains would be over. That was wishful thinking. It was only 13 days after this meeting that Jesse Selkirk—based on his $2 a head bounty—shot 1,250 sheep and cattle in Big Summit Prairie on both sides of the deadline. Then, the wool growers took off on a different tangent.

By December, the north-central sheep owners were agitating the state legislature for a slice of Crook and Wasco counties to form a new province known as Stockman County; and it was feared by Prineville that The Dalles would lend its support to Antelope in the latter's effort to secure the seat of the new county. Efforts were also being made to divide Wasco County from north to south, giving the county seat of the western division to Hood River.

In spite of the good intentions expressed by the hostile stockmen who met in the Blue Mountains in July, the range war gave no indication of slowing down and the Deschutes Irrigation Company was pestering the State Land Board for a contract to reclaim 100,000 acres in the Powell Butte area. People hadn't learned yet that farming the low desert was no shortcut to wealth, but there was little else around to provide a living with the range war in full progress, so they agitated for water.

CHAPTER 208

BUSINESS AS USUAL

Construction of the Mayflower stamp mill is a red letter day in the commercial history of Crook County.

Crook County Journal
October 11, 1906

The winter of 1904-05 brought no respite in the range war. In fact, it started with a bang. On New Year's Day Fred Smith, a Paulina rancher based on Grindstone Creek, was greeted by six masked men who shot 500 head of sheep almost on his front doorstep. Another 500 head were stampeded into open country where they became wolf and coyote bait. Prineville, itself, was doing its studious best to ignore the range conflict but the old veterans like Jesse Selkirk and John Edwards knew the Crook County dispute was every bit as vicious as its predecessors—the Lincoln County and Johnson County range wars—with the death toll rising.

Meanwhile, the Church Workers Society of Prineville compiled and published *The Best Friend Cook Book*. Among other interesting recipes was one on "how to cook your husband." Now that may sound rather indelicate but the instructions were: "Keep 'em constantly in hot water; roast 'em; add a little sugar; maybe a little spice; do not stick sharp instruments into 'em to see if they're becoming tender . . . ." but you get the picture. Anything to take the mind off the uncertainties at hand.

Hay Creek Ranch was producing a half million pounds of wool each year boosting Shaniko into the world shipping center of wool. But like a stalking mountain lion, the range war was closing in. Although allocation of range would end the conflict it also spelled doom for the large stock ranches. Without unlimited summer range, Hay Creek Company had seen its peak.

Anticipating the loss of open range, a scheme promoted on May 14, 1905 by the Citizens Business League of Prineville to irrigate 40,000 acres of sagebrush land lying north of town was practically assured. It would see its fulfillment with the completion of Ochoco Reservoir in the summer of 1918 along with a $41,000 lawsuit filed by upset farmers who claimed that Twohy Brothers Construction Company, while building the dam, diverted water from their irrigation systems and caused loss of crops.

Town construction was again on the agenda. In April 1905, John Rush platted the townsite of Lamonta west of Prineville. At the same time, Frank T. Redmond, a school teacher from the Dakota country, homesteaded on the Deschutes River and before another year had passed was credited with platting the townsite of Redmond while awaiting the coming of water promised by the Deschutes Irrigation Company. Actually it was Col. Belcher, who had laid out Seattle, that platted and named Redmond. At the time, his son-in-law, John Hicklin Hall—U.S. district attorney connected with banking and power projects in what would later become Deschutes County—was removed from office on December 31, 1904, prosecuted and convicted on Oregon land fraud charges. He was later pardoned by President Taft.[1] Following Col. Belcher out of Washington in 1905 was the ex-frontier marshall, W.J. Sturdivan.

During this flurry of building activity, Monroe Hodges, who platted the townsite of Prineville in 1877, died of natural causes on July 4, 1905.[2] In Crook County at this time, anyone who wasn't shot to death died of "natural causes."

Adding to Crook County's woes, the promised Columbia Southern Railroad line from Shaniko was in default. So, in January 1905, the Central Oregon Transportation Co. was established with A.E. Hammond as president and D.P. Rea as general manager. The intent was to construct a 16-foot-wide roadbed from Cross Keyes Stage Station south of Shaniko across Crook County to the sister city of Bend, a distance of 75 miles. When completed, this road was the longest auto route on the Pacific

---

1   Belcher's grandson, John Hall, Jr., was governor of Oregon, taking office following the tragic airplane crash that took the lives of Governor Snell and other state officials in southern Oregon in 1947. Corning, *Dictionary of Oregon History*, pp. 104-05.

2   Monroe Hodges' wife, Rhoda Wilson Hodges—the mother of seven children—died in Prineville on July 12, 1898.

Coast, specially constructed by a machine firm in Portland. The roadbed was plowed, scraped, leveled and compacted with a 10-ton roller after which a layer of petroleum was laid down and again subjected to the roller. Quite sophisticated for that day.

Within six years, the Oregon Trunk Line—waging a relentless war in the lower Deschutes canyon—by-passed Prineville and entered Bend in May 1911. Seven years later, the City of Prineville Railway would connect with the Oregon Trunk Line on August 4, 1918.

By May 25, 1905, Crook County was entering the industrial age. On that day final arrangements were made to install a reduction furnace on the north slope of Lookout Mountain at the 6,000 foot level to separate quicksilver from cinnabar at the American Almaden Mine. The American Almaden Quick Silver and Gold Mining Company—better known as the Mother Lode—was located near the headwaters of Canyon City Creek (as it was called then). First discovered in the fall of 1899 by Carl Silterly and Henry Cram, the main ore producing vein was found in 1901 by a young prospector named Art Champion. Because of difficulty in the transportation of heavy machinery to work the mining property, the ore dump increased in size until the spring of 1905. Nevertheless, with the discovery of the glory hole, the Mother Lode was incorporated under the name of the American Almaden Mining Company with a capital stock of one and a half million shares.[3] However, the ore dump continued to grow so E.W. Elkins, a local investor, went to Portland to arrange financial backing for further development of the mining property. Charles Fitzgerald, a mining engineer who came from San Francisco to inspect the site, was convinced that there was sufficient high-grade ore in the mine dump to justify an expenditure of $8,000-10,000 for construction of a furnace which was completed in the fall of 1905.

Prior to Fitzgerald's survey, Henry Gould (a representative of California's New Almaden Mine, the United States' largest producer of quicksilver) inspected the Mother Lode and believed that the main ore deposit had not yet been reached. It was his opinion that the Lookout Mountain vein extended all the way to Round Mountain some five miles

---

3   The principal stockholders were Levi Tillotson, president; H.S. Cram, vice president; E.N. Wheeler, secretary; J.S. Silcox, treasurer; William Tillotson and John Combs, board of directors. For more on quicksilver mining refer to *Thunder Over the Ochoco*, Vol. IV, Chapter 179, "Liquid Silver."

to the northeast. Gould would express regret. "I have only one objection to offer and that is that someone else [other than the California New Almaden] has found this deposit."[4] This was high praise for the local mine.

The Oregon Mayflower Company at Howard on the Upper Ochoco River was also booming. Owned by a Washington corporation formed by the Thronson brothers, it had control of 27 placer claims, five lines of ditch, a large water storage reservoir and all available water rights.[5] The placer deposits—worked spasmodically and without system since the 1870's—were yielding large amounts of gold. It was the Thronson brothers intent in the spring of 1905 to begin installing hard-rock mining equipment which would put Crook County on the map as a major gold producer.

While investment money was flowing between the Mother Lode and the Mayflower, Virgil Earp—ex-marshall of Tombstone, Arizona and survivor of the celebrated gunfight at the O.K. Corral—ended up in Oregon. Earlier in the year, Virgil had joined his brother Wyatt in the rush to the Goldfield, Nevada strike. He died there on October 20, 1905. Wyatt sent word to Virgil's daughter Nellie in Oregon that if she wanted her father's body she best come get it. That's how Virgil Earp came to repose for eternity in Portland's Riverview Cemetery.

About the time Wyatt and Virgil Earp were headed for the Nevada strike, a sewing machine salesman named Bruce Gatewood visited the Mayflower Mining camp. Gatewood failed to sell any sewing machines but not being one to become discouraged by such setbacks, he switched careers and obtained an option to purchase the mine from the Oregon Mayflower Company. He then took the stage to Portland where he managed to organize the Gatewood Mining and Trading Company. The final agreement between Gatewood and the Oregon Mayflower Company was made on December 16, 1905. Gatewood must have been a pretty fast talker because he acquired the mines for nothing down with

4   *Crook County Journal*, June 16, 1904.

5   The main stockholders in the Oregon Mayflower Company were: J.A. Thronson, secretary; C.J. Thronson, treasurer; and Thron Thronson—an assayer, geologist and mining engineer of repute and reliability—was president and general manager of the corporation. For more on the Mayflower group of mines refer to *Thunder Over the Ochoco*, Vol. IV, Chapter 178, "Fire in the Hole!"

nine months before his first payment of $2,500 was due. (Thron Thronson may have been a sharp mining engineer but he certainly wasn't up on financial matters.) However, the contract did stipulate that Gatewood would pay 75% of the net value of any gold bullion extracted from the mine to the Oregon Mayflower Company; and that he would build a steam hoisting plant adequate for sinking a 600 foot shaft. It also required that Gatewood render to the Oregon Mayflower Company every thirty days accurate itemized accounts of the expenses and costs of mining, working and reducing all ores, together with the net value of the ore mined.

The only reason that this contract was recorded in the mining records is because Gatewood defaulted on it. In the language of the default notice he "wholly failed, neglected and refused" to honor any terms of the contract.[6] Despite this, Gatewood was able to raise sufficient money through the sale of stock and from the backing of a few Kansas City capitalists to enable him to install some formidable equipment at the mine.[7] He had a five-stamp mill constructed—capable of pulverizing hard-rock into gravel—to crush the Mayflower ore. A Wilfely concentrating table was set up to separate out the heaviest, and therefore the most gold-bearing of the crushed rock. Gatewood also put in a cyanide treatment plant which was intended to remove more gold from the crushed and concentrated ore.

The building of the massive stamp mill was met with great enthusiasm and extravagant hopes by the citizens of Crook County, and for the moment, overshadowed the traumatic effects of the Blue Mountain Forest Reserve Act. When the stamp mill began operating on October 8, 1906—a month before the clash between the federal government and the stockmen at Canyon City—residents from Prineville, Mitchell, Ashwood and the Ochoco Valley gathered at the stamp mill to hear Tom Baldwin of Prineville's First National Bank speak of the "brilliant prospects" of the mine. The crowd would cheer as Wilda Belknap broke a bottle of Ochoco River water across the face of the battery signaling Gatewood to engage the water wheel that powered the five 750-pound stamps. A reporter for the *Crook County Journal* would joyfuily pro-

---

6   *Crook County Mining Records*, Vol. III, pp. 326-29.
7   *Crook County Journal*, February 8, 1906.

claim: "The gold stamp mill is in successful operation not to stop until the Northwest comes to know that Crook County contains a gold mine that is a commercial success!"[8] Thirty years before, the autocrats of Crook County were doing their damnedest to keep it from being publicized.

Actually, the machinery Gatewood installed was never really in successful operation. According to Art Champion, who was in a position to know, it wasn't the fault of the mechanical device but a management problem as "a lot of drinking and gambling were going on."[9] Whatever the reason, the last step of the production process never functioned properly which meant that the long and costly trip to the Tacoma smelter was still a burdensome necessity.

During this, by one means or another, Lew McAllister regained control of the Mayflower mines. For some reason, McAllister felt the need to file a location notice on the Mayflower lode in April 1911.[10] This was rather curious since he already owned the mine and especially strange since a month after filing Lew was shot and killed at the mines.

The shooting took place on May 9 with the news hitting the Prineville newspapers two days later. The *Prineville Review* ran the story on the front page.[11] Following is its version of the altercation.

> Lewis McCallister, one of the pioneers of Crook County and a well known mining man and prospector of the Ochoco mineral belt, was shot and almost instantly killed at the mines by Ernest Robinson after a quarrel between the two and a move on McCallister's part as if to draw a gun. There was but one witness to the shooting, Miss Ruth Robinson, who corroborated her brother's testimony that McCallister opened hostilities by throwing a shovel at Robinson and then reached for his pocket. This act drew two shots from Robinson one of which penetrated both of McCallister's lungs and the other inflicted a flesh wound

---

8   *Crook County Journal*, October 11, 1906.

9   Arthur James Champion, June 1939.

10 *Crook County Mining Records*, Vol. III, p. 440.

11 *Prineville Review*, May 11, 1911. An account of the shooting appearing in the *Central Oregon Shopper*, August 4, 1949 places the date as May 28, 1911 which does not agree with any of the 1911 accounts.

in his forearm. McCallister ran forty or fifty feet and dropped to the ground, dying in a few minutes.[12]

The *Crook County Journal* was more cryptic and buried the story on an inside page.

> Killed was Lewis McCallister, a well-known rancher and resident of the Sisters country. The shooting occurred near McCallister's mine in the Ochoco near Prineville. McCallister found another man using water, the right to which McCallister claimed. McCallister reportedly attacked the other man with a shovel. The other rancher fired, killing McCallister instantly.

The *Prineville Review* made no bones about letting readers know where its sympathies lay in the matter and was most likely reflecting the views of the townsfolk. Robinson—according to *The Review*—was described as a quiet man not given to hunting trouble and highly respected by his neighbors. What the paper didn't mention was that Robinson—fresh from the Silver City diggings—was known at the Ochoco mines as "the Idaho Claim Jumper."[13] McAllister on the other hand was characterized as being obsessed by the mines and unable to stand having anyone at work anywhere near him. *The Review* called him "slightly mentally unbalanced" and suggested that although he was not a violent man, he would occasionally wave a gun at some intruder and order him away using strong language. Nevertheless, *The Review* admitted McAllister was not armed when he was shot by Robinson.[14]

When the Prineville coroner went to the mines to pick up McAllister's body he impaneled a jury and held an inquest. The jurors found that the killing was justifiable homicide because Robinson acted in self-defense. Back in Prineville, District Attorney N.W. Sanborn was dissatisfied with the findings of the coroner's jury and ordered Robinson's arrest. Robinson was indicted for murder on May 18, and it was said that he then "became the hero of a spectacular two-weeks trial held

---

12 A McAllister descendant says that the spelling of Lew's name as "McCallister," as it appears in most records of the time, is incorrect.

13 Arthur Champion, August 4, 1949.

14 *Prineville Review*, May 11, 1911.

in the cattle-sheep feud town of Prineville."[15] On May 28, after deliberating for ten hours, the jury accepted the testimony of Ruth Robinson and found the defendant not guilty. Oddly, the actual records from this case have been lost. Only the indictment and verdict were preserved in what was labeled Crook County Circuit Court Case 1780.[16]

It is interesting to note that at the time of Robinson's trial there were five murderers and one cattle rustler being held in the county jail. Four of the murderers were acquitted and the remaining one was sentenced to one year in prison. Although it was definitely proven that the cow thief stole in order to feed a starving family, he was convicted and sentenced to serve seven years in the Oregon State Penitentiary. In Crook County it would appear that rustling was more offensive than murder.

Now back to the fatal confrontation between Robinson and McAllister which took place as Lew was shoveling out a mining ditch. Vera Koch heard the two men quarreling some days before the shooting with McAllister accusing Robinson of jumping one of his gold claims. The families living in the upper Ochoco Valley always thought what occurred was premeditated murder.[17] It was their belief that Ruth Robinson was to engage McAllister in conversation and then shoot him using the alibi that Lew had tried to molest her. They further believed that she fired the first shot wounding Lew in the arm, then panicked and Ernie finished the job.

Be that as it may, it is difficult to understand why unarmed Lew McAllister would try to bluff the armed Ernest Robinson by acting as though he was reaching for a gun. As one person observed, the equivalent bluff in poker would be to bet heavily without having been dealt any cards. Also, it was Robinson's second shot that killed McAllister. One would think after the first shot it would have been obvious to Robinson, claimed by his lawyer to be "a quiet man not given to hunting trouble," that McAllister had no gun.

---

15 "Mayflower Mine Dates Back to Fall of 1871," *The Central Oregon Shopper*, Old Timer's Edition, Thursday, August 4, 1949.

16 *Crook County Circuit Court Records*, Vol. III, Case 1780.

17 Vera Koch Ontko, *Through the Golden Gate of Yesteryear: Life On the Upper Ochoco, 1907 through 1918*, p. 21. At the time of this writing, Vera was the only living witness to the Robinson-McAllister dispute.

It would later surface that Ruth Robinson was Ernie's girlfriend not his sister. A few years after the murder trial while Robinson was riding the rails he fell from a moving freight train and had to have a leg amputated. Residents on the upper Ochoco maintained it was just retribution and that he had received his punishment meted out by a higher judgment.

After Lew's death, his brother George and W.T. Davenport filed on the Mayflower lode. In March 1912 they entered into a rather unusual contract with two men. For the sum of one dollar they agreed to sell their interest in the Mayflower group of mines at any time within one year of the contract date for one million dollars in gold coin, "or such less sum as the parties hereto may hereafter agree upon."[18]

Yes, it was business as usual in the Ochoco with the range war still skulking in the shadows.

---

18   *Crook County Mining Records*, Vol. III, p. 507. One of the unnamed men in this contract was most likely Art Champion. By his own admission, in the fall of 1912 he purchased the McAllister interests from the estate and began prospecting. Within a year, he and Davenport granted a lease to three men from Canyonville in southwest Oregon and in four days beginning November 5, 1913, these men, working with mortar and pestle, extracted $6,000 in gold from the surface. By June 1, 1917, they had grossed $100,000 in gold dust.

Dr. Cass A. Cline, first dentist in Central Oregon. Cline Falls and Cline Butte named for him, 1880 (top). David Wayne Claypool, one of the earliest settlers in Central Oregon, 1880 (bottom).

J.N. Williamson, early
Prineville settler served in
Congress and was indicted for
land fraud at turn of century
and not convicted, 1880.

Courtesy of Steve Lent and
The Crook County Historical Society

Mr. and Mrs. Ike Ketchum,
early settlers in the
Prineville area, 1900.

Courtesy of Steve Lent and
The Crook County Historical Society

B.F. Nichols, early settler and
driving force in the legislation to
form Crook County in 1880.
Circa 1890.

Courtesy of Steve Lent and
The Crook County Historical Society

Francis Bernard Prine,
founder of the City of Prineville.

Courtesy of Steve Lent and
The Crook County Historical Society

John LaFollette, early settler
in Powell Butte area, 1890.

Courtesy of Steve Lent and
The Crook County Historical Society

Thomas LaFollette,
early settler in Camp Creek
and McKay Creek, 1890.

Courtesy of Steve Lent and
The Crook County Historical Society

Art Champion, early mine
operator in Upper Ochoco.
Married Gale Ontko's
divorced grandmother, 1918.

Courtesy of Steve Lent and
The Crook County Historical Society

John Taylor, early Central
Oregon photographer.
This is a self portrait
in Suplee, 1910.

Courtesy of Steve Lent and
The Crook County Historical Society

Cyrus "Cy" Bingham, early
Ochoco forest ranger and
Malheur National Forest
Supervisor, 1910.

Bingham was a tall man
and weighed 300 pounds.
(He was a good friend
of the author's father,
Andy Ontko.)

Courtesy of Steve Lent and
The Crook County Historical Society

Jim Blakely, first elected sheriff
of Crook County, 1895.

Courtesy of Steve Lent and
The Crook County Historical Society

George Churchill, first sheriff
of Crook County, 1884.

*Courtesy of Steve Lent and
The Crook County Historical Society*

Crook County Sheriff
Reub Booton and
Jim Blakely (age 94).

*Courtesy of Steve Lent and
The Crook County Historical Society*

William "Bill" Brown
in later years, 1925.

Courtesy of Steve Lent and
The Crook County Historical Society

Dr. Horace Belknap, early
Crook County doctor, 1885.

Courtesy of Steve Lent and
The Crook County Historical Society

Til Glaze, Prineville saloon
owner. Killed in a shootout
in Burns, 1885.

Courtesy of Steve Lent and
The Crook County Historical Society

Ann Glaze, wife of
Til Glaze, 1885.

Courtesy of Steve Lent and
The Crook County Historical Society

Col. William "Bud"
Thompson in later years.
Circa 1890.

Courtesy of Steve Lent and
The Crook County Historical Society

B.F. Allen, early sheepman on
Allen Creek and banker.
Circa 1890.

Courtesy of Steve Lent and
The Crook County Historical Society

Barney Prine, 1900.

*Courtesy of Steve Lent and
The Crook County
Historical Society*

Sam Hamilton,
stable keeper in
Prineville, 1890.

*Courtesy of Steve Lent and
The Crook County
Historical Society*

Farquar McRae, 1885.

Courtesy of Steve Lent and
The Crook County Historical Society

General George Crook,
namesake for
Crook County, 1875.

Courtesy of Steve Lent and
The Crook County Historical Society

Luther and Helen Claypool, Paulina Valley, 1900.

Courtesy of Steve Lent and The Crook County Historical Society

Ewen Johnson, early
Ochoco settler.
Circa 1880.

*Courtesy of Steve Lent and
The Crook County Historical Society*

Blakely family (left to right): Henry, Capt. James, William, George, Joe, and Jim. 1895 Oregon Sheriffs (top). Alice Day Pratt, early woman homesteader in the Post area, 1915 (bottom).

Courtesy of Steve Lent and The Crook County Historical Society

Edward Henry Harriman,
1848-1909, railroad
magnate and financier.

Reproduced from the Dictionary of
American Portraits, *published by Dover
Publications, Inc. in 1967*

James Jerome Hill,
1838-1916, railroad
promoter and financier.

*Photograph by Pach Brothers
Reproduced from the* Dictionary of
American Portraits, *published by Dover
Publications, Inc. in 1967*

Til Glaze Band in Prineville. Til owned the saloon in Prineville and Glaze Meadow at Black Butte is named for him, 1880.

Courtesy of Steve Lent and The Crook County Historical Society

Yesteryear scene shows Indian camp northwest of Prineville near Crooked River.

CHAPTER 209

THE BLUE MOUNTAIN FOREST RESERVE

If there is one section in the State of Oregon where a forest reserve should be established, it is the Blue Mountain region and my endorsement of the measure is strong and unqualified.

H.D. Langille
U.S. Forest Inspector, 1906

It was becoming increasingly obvious that there was a need for administration of the public domain and especially—in view of the escalating range war—a need for the allotment and supervision of grazing rights. Even so, community sentiment ran high against the creation of a federal forest reserve in eastern Oregon which had been authorized by the Act of July 28, 1902. Stockmen, miners and loggers believed the government was depriving them of their established rights and unjustly charging them for something that was already theirs. This opposition came at the height of the Oregon real estate swindle commonly known as the rape of the public domain.

Between 1903 and 1910 the U.S. District Court for Oregon presided over the most far-reaching and sensational series of trials in its history—the Oregon land fraud trials. Before they ended an incumbent U.S. senator, a local U.S. representative, a defrocked U.S. attorney and a cast of other colorful characters would be convicted of bribery and conspiring to defraud the government of its public lands. It got its start in 1891 when Congress passed legislation authorizing the president to set aside and reserve government lands as public reservations. In September 1893, President Cleveland established the Cascade Range Forest Reserve which knifed down Crook County's western border virtually cutting a continuous swath from the Columbia River to the California line.

By 1897, Congress would pass further legislation—The Forest Reserve Act—establishing additional timber reservations on the national domain. This act set the stage for the coming problem. It allowed bona fide settlers within the forest reserve to deed their land to the federal government in exchange for other federal lands outside the withdrawal area. Landowners who wished to participate in this land exchange submitted affidavits to their local land offices proving that they had settled the land, had lived on their claims prior to passage of the act and had built dwellings and made improvements. A simple arrangement, all fair and good.

Then in 1900, a three-man Portland land syndicate began under-cutting this enlightened piece of legislation by preparing a series of fraudulent homestead claims in collusion with government officials in several Oregon land offices. By bribing both settlers and land officials, the syndicate obtained affidavits and deeds for non-existent settlers. These fictitious entrymen or "straw men" would hold the lands and—under terms of the Forest Reserve Act—exchange them later for more valuable lands, subsequently transferring them to the syndicate. In desperation, Congress—vaguely aware that something was amiss—appointed a federal grand jury and hired a tenacious special prosecutor of whom it was said would "crucify Christ if the price was right" and the Oregon land fraud trials began.[1]

---

1   After finding the group guilty in December 1904, the court delayed sentencing and several members of the conspiracy skipped the country. Head of the so-called syndicate, Steven A.D. (Sad) Puter, a lumber assessor (who was living with Emma Watson, one of the groups bogus entrymen), went to Boston where he escaped at gunpoint from a federal agent only later to be recaptured in California. On May 24, 1906 the *Prineville Review* would report that Secret Service men learned of his whereabouts by shadowing a woman. Puter was on his way to keep an appointment with this woman when arrested. In July 1906, he was sentenced to two years in the Multnomah County Jail. Horace McKinley, a timber speculator, fled to Chicago and married Marie Ware, the Oregon land commissioner who prepared fraudulent homestead claims. McKinley then headed for Manchuria accompanied—according to reports of the day—by the notorious belly dancer "Little Egypt." After a 30,000-mile chase, U.S. Deputy Marshall Jack Kerrigan returned him to Portland for sentencing. Oregon's four-term U.S. Senator John H. Mitchell and the Hon. J.N. Williamson, Oregon's two-term U.S. representative from Prineville, refused to testify claiming congressional privilege. (Todd Peterson, "The 1903-1910 Land Fraud Trials," U.S. District Court for Oregon, the court's historical society publication, Portland, 1990.)

It was against this backdrop that on April 1, 1906—with Oregon's population edging over the 500,000 mark—the Western Division of the Blue Mountain Forest Reserve came under the administration of the United States Forest Service with A.S. Ireland placed in charge as forest supervisor and headquartered in Prineville. Ireland soon discovered that he faced a population that was extremely antagonistic to the new bureaucratic set-up. Ten days after his arrival in Prineville, Ireland received a letter from Washington, D.C. that wasn't going to help make his stay more pleasant or him more popular. The letter charged him with the responsibility of educating the public on the new scheme of things; the issuance of grazing permits on federally controlled lands; the establishment of allotment boundaries; and, above all, the enforcement of regulations handed down by the secretary of Agriculture.

The charge of enforcement was pretty much like commanding the wind to stop blowing since the forest service, in its wisdom, allowed Supervisor Ireland three men on a year-long basis and four men to be hired for a six-month period. His area of responsibility covered approximately what is now the Deschutes, Ochoco and Malheur National Forests.

What Ireland needed was a few men like Cyrus J. Bingham—a cowboy gold miner—who was hired as a ranger in 1903 to patrol the Cascade Reserve on Crook County's western border . . . soon to become the Deschutes National Forest. Standing well over six feet tall and weighing in at 300 pounds, Bingham wore a size 17 collar and a size 7¾ hat. He was a bear of a man who could grip a 100-pound sack of wheat in his teeth and swing it over his head. Irate stockmen, miners and loggers wouldn't give him much trouble.

One of the few forest rangers employed by the federal government at that time, Bingham like the others had the duties of lookout, fireman, ranger, trail builder and grazing supervisor all to himself. The men who took these jobs received no supplies from the government. They bought their own tools, provided their own food and purchased their own horses out of their $75 a month salary. Bingham was often joined by his wife in the mountains and she was known to be as tough as he was.[2]

---

2   As Cy's daughter, Frances Bingham Krechel of Hemet, California tells it, "Mother was undaunted by the tasks of killing and cleaning deer, tanning their hides and butchering their meat." Snow storms and heavy rains had little effect on her parents who camped out most of

Within a year after Ireland took charge of the Western Division of the Blue Mountain Forest Reserve, he received much needed help when in November 1907, Bingham was promoted to forest supervisor of the newly created Malheur National Forest and transferred to John Day. That didn't last long. When it came to forest fires, Cy believed in letting nature take its course. Like the Native Americans before him, Bingham believed that fires cleared brush and promoted the growth of nuts, berries and trees. When forest service philosophy changed, Bingham's non-interference attitude toward forest fires fell out of favor. As John Schraff (who worked with Bingham on the Malheur) told it, "Cy didn't quite fit the Forest Service because he was a believer in keeping the forest clean. Light burning was one of his hobbies and something that he pursued, but of course that was against the thought at that time." So in 1920, Bingham resigned his position as supervisor to run for sheriff of Grant County.[3]

Another federal employee, J.D. (Bert) Fine, who served as Forest Guard in 1906 on what later became the Ochoco National Forest, soon made contact with the enemy. This is the way Bert put it: "Yes sir, A.S. Ireland sent me into the Beaver Creek country on what is now the Ochoco the first year she was organized. The cattlemen showed me a deadline on their side of which sheep did not keep their good health very long, and the sheepmen inquired casual-like what would happen if I turned up missing some day. It made me an ounce or two nervous so I just got them birds together and says 'Now Boys, if you are looking for a fight, there is a company of soldiers down on the coast that Uncle Sam hires for that particular purpose and I reckon they will accommodate all comers, but as far as I am concerned, I want it understood that I am in the Civil Service and not the War Department.'"[4]

---

the year in the high Cascades.

3   As Grant County sheriff, Bingham viewed the newly imposed Prohibition Law with the same detached attitude as he used to greet forest fires. After holding that position for a dozen years and building a reputation as the "biggest sheriff in Oregon," he turned in his badge in 1932. According to John Schraff, the way Cy told it, "I was caught in the 1932 Democratic landslide and retired from office." He died from pneumonia on January 16, 1937 and is buried in the cemetery at Canyon City. The author met John Schraff in Burns, Oregon many years ago and Andy Ontko (my father) was well-acquainted with Cy Bingham.

4   *Forest Service Region 6 Publication, 6-26,* December 1920.

Fine didn't come back to tempt fate. He decided being a barber in John Day was a little safer occupation and Supervisor Ireland didn't push the matter.

Believing they could solve the range problem, department heads came up with the idea that Ireland might get the job done with college students. His few full time employees weren't so certain that was the solution. During a meeting at the supervisor's office to plan the next season's work the question of the distribution of college students came up. Ireland asked Jesse Allison—in charge of the Snow Mountain area—"How many college students can you use this summer?" Jesse was lost in thought for a moment and then replied, "Not very many, I'm going to be mighty busy this summer."[5]

In an effort to gain some local cooperation, Ireland advertised and held a public meeting November 15, 1906 in Canyon City with what was called the "Honest Forest Reserve Organization" composed of stockmen, miners and representatives of the timber industry. At this meeting Ireland would assign each stockman his 1907 grazing allotment (ballyhooed as the end to the Crook County range war). To back him up, Washington shipped in Henry Langille, U.S. forest inspector and trouble-shooter for the Department of Agriculture.

The meeting got off to a shaky start when the Crook County stockmen petitioned for the inclusion of several townships along the western end of the proposed Blue Mountain Forest Reserve—specifically the Maury Mountains—with the intent to have the federal government protect the local range from the migrating herds of sheep from the south. This proposal was strongly endorsed by Congressman Williamson. Langille vetoed the proposal because the lands lay outside the proposed forest reserve boundary. In his opinion the entire population of eastern Oregon was "dependent in a greater or less measure upon the natural resources of the lands in question and only by the forest reserve system can these resources be considered."[6]

In concert with the livestock men, the withdrawal of the proposed Western Division of the Blue Mountain Forest Reserve also met with strong resistance from the mining and timber industry both of which had

5   Jesse Allison told this story at the Ochoco National Forest Guard School, June 1942.
6   U.S.F.S. records of the April 1906 formation of the Blue Mountain Forest Reserve on file at the Supervisor's Office of the Ochoco National Forest in Prineville, Oregon.

added their fair share to the demise of the Ochoco's natural resources. An attorney representing the mining interests stated their case quite bluntly. "We are getting along very well as we are and want to be left alone."[7] End of argument.

The timber companies were equally adamant. Forested land was being secured under the mineral land laws and stripped of its cover. Many mining claims were held for timber rights with just enough assessment work being done to prevent their location by bona fide prospectors. Many of the large mining companies like the American Almaden and Oregon Mayflower which operated smelters, stamp mills and concentrators required large quantities of wood, not only to fire the furnaces, but for other purposes as well and they would file on or purchase other claims—even though no mineral in place could be shown—just to reserve the timber to the operating claims. And tamarack (Western Larch) was the timber in demand.

It was claimed by the protesting miners that tamarack—considered the most valuable component of the forest at that time—had little commercial value as saw logs but was an excellent timber for mining purposes and was needed as shoring in the development of present and prospective mining tunnels and shafts. Therefore, they were fighting to exclude any land supporting tamarack from the federal reserve system. Forest representatives would concede that at higher elevations, the trees had little commercial value as saw logs.

However, the great destruction of trees wrought by some mining companies was causing not only alarm with the timber industry but among other mining companies who consumed the material as well. Actually, the sawmill companies were working hand-in-glove with the mining industry as the mines were the prime market for lumber and they held the best chance to exclude timber land from the forest reserve act.

Langille had a good argument for including timberland in the withdrawal. "It is the only timber body between the Cascades and Rocky Mountains and the demand will be heavy and constantly increasing . . . ." He had no idea how true that prediction was. Unfortunately as Langille noted, "The withdrawal of these lands from entry was too long deferred and the sawmill companies and speculators have located the best

---

7   "Blue Mountain Reserve," the *Central Oregon Shopper*, Thursday, August 4, 1949.

and most accessible timber of commercial value." By the end of the 20th century, it would be questioned as to whether the Forest Service was indeed the guardian spirit of the woods or the dark angel who helped engineer its lingering death.

For years the federal government suspected that large amounts of merchantable timber were being stolen from the vast national forests of the Pacific Northwest, accounting for tens of millions of dollars in revenue lost to the treasury. By 1991, a special federal task force was created within the U.S. Forest Service to investigate and help prosecute the biggest thieves—believed to be lumber companies taking far more and better trees than they were paying for. Four years later the effort was in disarray. After bringing forth the biggest timber-theft case in U.S. history in 1993, the special investigative unit did not produce a single prosecution and by 1995 many members of the team were directing their critical attention toward another alleged culprit . . . their own agency, the government's care takers of the forest reserve![8] Back in 1906, if Forest Inspector Langille could have looked into the future, he would have resigned from the service.

As was, the 1906 withdrawal took effect in time to prevent wholesale location on extensive tracts of merchantable pine in Crook, Wheeler, Grant and Harney counties. There was a mad rush to file timber entries in these counties after it was learned that the withdrawal would be made and before official notice reached the local land offices but all filings were canceled. Seventy-five years later it would be the Forest Service denuding the Ochoco Mountains in a manner that would put the early despoilers to shame.

When the opposition squared off at the Canyon City meeting berating the intended timberland withdrawal, Inspector Langille would counter that "The protests which have been filed against the proposed Blue Mountain Forest Reserve are mostly based upon misunderstanding of the objects and purposes of the department . . . ." Whatever, other than granting permits (upon payment of a grazing fee) to all men whose livestock had previously grazed on the reserve, the Canyon City meeting adjourned without taking any action. For the 1907 season, it was stipulated that cattle could not enter the range until June 1 and sheep not until

---

8   "Theft Investigators Blast Forest Service," *The Bulletin*, Bend, Oregon, January 16, 1995.

June 15 but Supervisor Ireland—even with the arrival of Big Cy Bing-ham—had neither the men nor the means to enforce this directive.

The forest allotment ruling was publicized as ending the sheep and cattle war. Many stockmen were antagonistic to government control of the range but in a year or two it was apparent to most stockmen that the old free range was gone and perhaps it was the best for all.[9] However, it wasn't until 1934 when Congress passed the Taylor Grazing Act that legal machinery was actually provided to regulate and protect the remainder of the public domain in eastern Oregon by closing the open range to unauthorized use.

No one knows how far the range war would have gone, except Congress finally stepped in and set definite boundaries by federal law—not beneficial to the cattlemen—and like thunder slowly fading over the distant Blues the war came to an end. But in 1907, the guns of anger had not yet been silenced in the final conquest of the Ochoco.

---

9 Following are the events leading to the creation of the Ochoco National Forest:

September 25, 1893: Cascade Range Forest Reserve established by presidential proclamation.
April 29, 1898: Land removed from Cascade Range Forest Reserve by executive order.
June 2, 1905: Maury Mountain Forest Reserve created.
March 15, 1906: Blue Mountain Forest Reserve established.
March 2, 1907: The term "forest reserve" was changed to "national forest."
July 1, 1908: Deschutes National Forest created from parts of Blue Mountain, Cascade and Fremont National Forests. (This included all the land we now know as the Ochoco National Forest.)
July 11, 1911: Part of Deschutes National Forest designated Ochoco National Forest.

Information given by USDA Forest Service, Pacific Northwest Region 6, Portland, Oregon.

CHAPTER 210

LOCAL FOLLY

The city of Portland, Oregon as voiced through its press has wantonly, falsely and maliciously attacked the integrity and honor of the citizens of Crook County; and by aspersion and innuendo accused its city and public officials of crimes and misdemeanors too grossly false and ridiculous to be considered seriously . . . .

Crook County Journal
December 14, 1905

Before 1907 could get off to a running start, some old business had to be taken care of. The range violence may have declined in 1906 but it certainly wasn't over. Shortly before the Forest Service took charge of grazing allotments, sheepshooters were again on the prowl in Wheeler County. The latest victims of the war were the Butler brothers who lost 200 head of sheep 12 miles east of Mitchell in the vicinity of Buck Point. Soon thereafter, the rebuilt sheep shearing plant in Dixie Meadow owned by Congressman Williamson was again put to the torch. The only difference this time was that Sheriff Frank Elkins arrested two men on suspicion of arson. However, there is a strong possibility that this crime was politically motivated instead of being sheep oriented.

About the time of this incident, the Oregon Land Fraud Trials were heating up. Among those indicted and being tried in federal court in Prineville were Williamson, Dr. Van Gesner, ex-sheriff C. Sam Smith, Judge M.R. Biggs and a gentleman named Bates, a suspected agent for *The Portland Oregonian*. Two years before this investigation, Harvey Scott—editor of *The Oregonian*—made an unsuccessful run for the U.S. Senate. At the time, Williamson, a member of the state legislature, refused to support Scott's bid for national recognition. It appears that

Scott took this as a personal insult to his honesty and had been brooding about it since 1903.

Testimony brought out in the Prineville trail was described by the *Crook County Journal* as "sensational" and would "throw new light on Scott's famous gumshoe campaign for the United States Senate."[1] C.A. Duncan, who owned a ranch two miles downstream from Williamson's property on the upper Ochoco River and a witness for the government in the pending prosecution of Mr. Bates (Scott's emissary as the *Journal* put it), stated that someone from the *Portland Oregonian* threatened Williamson to the effect that if he would not back Harvey Scott for senator, *The Oregonian* would dig his grave. In short, the paper—through scathing editorials—intended to bring about his political and financial ruin. Based on this declaration local merchants threatened to boycott Portland wholesale houses which would stand to lose a half million dollars in trade annually from Prineville.

In a meeting between Scott and representatives of the Prineville Merchants Protective Association, the businessmen attempted to get Scott to retract some of the statements he had made in *The Oregonian* concerning things that happened at Prineville. Scott, referring to Williamson as "the political enemy of *The Oregonian*," refused to do so.

Meantime, Gesner and Smith were indicted by a federal grand jury on charges of conspiring to intimidate government witnesses and thereby prevent their testimony in the pending trial of Williamson, Gesner and Bates; and Judge Biggs was arraigned on timber fraud charges.[2] Williamson, Gesner and Bates were found guilty of perjury. Then, Charles A. Graves, county surveyor, Erwin M. Wakefield, a former partner of Williamson in the sheep business and two others were indicted

---

1   All information relating to the Prineville Land Fraud Trials are taken from the files of the *Crook County Journal* dated July 27, September 14, September 21, September 28, October 5 and October 19, 1905. It was during this period that D.F. Steffa and S.M. Bailey took over publication of the *Journal* and R.E. Gray, with 20 years service on different papers between the Atlantic and Pacific, took over as editor on June 7, 1906. Nine months later on March 28, 1907 the firm of Steffa, Bailey and Gray dissolved by mutual consent and Gray became the sole owner of the business.

2   It took 36 ballots to convince a majority of the jury panel that Judge Biggs wasn't totally innocent of wrong doing. Both he and Gesner served time in federal prison.

by the federal grand jury on charges of conspiracy to defraud the government of lands.[3]

During all of this legal activity, Percy F. McGargle of the Buffalo Automobile Club and his assistant driver, a mechanic from Lansing, Michigan pulled into Chicago on August 26, 1905 on their try at the longest automobile run on this continent . . . 9,000 miles from coast to coast and back again. The drivers expected to arrive in Portland 35 days after leaving New York to celebrate the Lewis and Clark Fair. No doubt, they hoped to cash-in on the 2.6 million sightseers who came to see the mammoth exposition which opened on June 1, 1905 in the old Guild's Lake area of Northwest Portland. They didn't make it. On November 9, 1905 the *Crook County Journal* would announce, "The two transcontinental auto tourers arrived in Prineville last Friday afternoon about two months behind the schedule which they announced when leaving New York City. The delay was caused by extremely heavy blizzards encountered on both sides of the Rocky Mountains." Their big 18 horsepower Reo—the largest car ever to be seen in the Pacific Northwest—didn't navigate too well in three-foot snow drifts. Apparently they were unaware that Dwight Huss reached Portland on June 21 in his 1903 Oldsmobile. He had left New York 44 days previously and won the first transcontinental auto race.

Among those to greet the victorious driver were the famed De Moss Lyric Bards now based at the family farm in Sherman County, Oregon. They too had arrived in Portland in June from a whirlwind concert tour of the Mid-West. Huss made one grand appearance but the eastern Oregon singers and musicians who had captured the hearts of Shoshoni warriors some 33 years in the past gave 142 performances at the 1905 Lewis and Clark Centennial Exposition.[4]

---

3   The specific charges against Graves and Wakefield were that they talked four women into making false proof of timber entry. The women in their claim affidavits stated that they had made no contract or agreement to sell land to anyone else; whereas, it was alleged that it was a fact that they had agreed to sell the land.

4   The De Moss family would perform in five great world fairs: The World Columbia Exposition 1893 in Chicago, Illinois; the Louisiana Purchase Exposition 1904 in St. Louis, Missouri; The Lewis and Clark Centennial Exposition 1905 in Portland, Oregon; the Alaska-Yukon Pacific Exposition 1909 in Seattle, Washington; and the Panama Pacific Exposition 1915 in San Francisco, California. (De Moss, *Sweet Oregon*, p. VII.)

Some of these concerts were held at the Forestry Building, a favorite exhibit structure constructed with immense, unhewn logs cut from forests along the Columbia River. Louie Beirl, hard-rock miner and discoverer of the Sunshine Mine on the upper Ochoco River, was head sawyer for the sawmill company which cut the logs for this architectural monument.[5]

Lewis and Clark Exposition or not, the land fraud trials dragged on, while the on-going battle between the *Portland Oregonian* and the *Crook County Journal* continued full-bore. The way the *Journal* saw it: "*The Oregonian* has shown no signs of relenting in its publication of unscrupulous falsifications regarding the residents of this city . . . we can hope for nothing better than to be the object of lying abuse." Apparently, Harvey Scott was not going to let up on the Hon. J.N. Williamson come hell or high water. In time, this personal vendetta would backfire. Two years later, on appeal, Williamson was found innocent on all charges.

By the time 1906 climbed into the ring, the old free-wheeling days in Crook County were coming to an end. On a blustery day in March, a federal grand jury indicted J.R. Eastwood and Jack Dee—who owned a sawmill in the vicinity of Grizzly Mountain—charging them with unlawful cutting of timber on government land. To make certain that they stood trial, U.S. Marshall Griswell rode into Prineville and placed both men under arrest with bond set at $500 each.[6]

Eighteen days after the Western Division of the Blue Mountain Forest Reserve came under the administration of the United States Forest Service, the *Crook County Journal* jarred its readers with this glaring headline: "April 19, 1906 — 2,000 dead — property loss in the millions — fires sweep through 50 blocks of buildings in the wake of the San Francisco earthquake!"

Perhaps addled by the earth tremor, a Crook County jury decided that George Miller (charged with the murder of Warren Curtis) was not guilty because Curtis stole a horse belonging to Miller. Just maybe, Crook County wasn't losing its Old West flavor.

Four months after this incident, B.F. Zell was shot and instantly killed (at his home two miles east of Prineville) by Fred Shepherd, his

---

5   This building was the only structure to be left on its original 1905 Exposition site where it remained until destroyed by fire in 1964.

6   *Crook County Journal*, March 29, 1906.

hired hand. This was not a smart move on Fred's part. Old Ben's roots ran deep. The Zell's had been in the territory since 1868 . . . in short, they were some of the founding fathers of what became Crook County. Brother Abe Zell had served as army scout for Gen. Crook during the Shoshoni war and it was rumored that Pete Zell had more than a nodding acquaintance with the vigilantes. Therefore, it is not surprising that Shepherd was given the death penalty . . . the first legal hanging in the annals of Crook County.[7]

So, 1906 ended with the hanging of a local gentleman in Salem and the fatal shooting of a logger in the Three Creeks area nine miles south of Sisters.[8] Upholding its end of the bargain, 1907 hurdled onto the central Oregon plateau with citizens in the western part of Crook County clamoring to be separated from their kinsmen in the eastern section of said county. It seems that County Commissioner Alexander Drake—taking his cue from Wheeler County—wanted to annex everything west and south of Prineville to the aspiring hamlet of Bend. If the residents of Madras would support his proposed county division, Drake promised they could inherit all the Crook County lands north of Prineville. That heresy got nipped in the bud before it could bear fruit.

A Prineville delegation headed by the Hon. Newt Willliamson, descended on Salem to take care of the matter in the state legislature. On February 21, 1907—the same day the vessel *Bessie K.* sank at the mouth of the Coquille River with the loss of nine lives—they reported that "Deschutes County hasn't a ghost of a chance to become reality." And that was final. Of more importance to the rest of Oregon, ice floes jammed the Columbia and communities dependent on the river steamers for fuel and food supplies were hard pressed.

---

7   Fred A. Shepherd was hanged at 12:55 o'clock at the penitentiary in Salem on November 30, 1906. The execution was witnessed by about 40 persons. *Crook County Journal*, December 6, 1906.

8   On Sunday, December 2, 1906 at 1:30 p.m., H.A. Melvin, a rancher, shot and killed S.H. Dorrance of the firm of the Dorrance Brothers (who ran a sawmill in the vicinity of Three Creeks Butte). The fatal shooting was the aftermath of a lawsuit. (*Crook County Journal*, December 6, 1906.) Five months later a grand jury reported that they could find no true bill against H.A. Melvin who last fall "shot and killed Dorrance in self-defense." (*Crook County Journal*, May 9, 1907.)

By the end of February—overshadowing the proposed Deschutes County schism—the word was out that Edward Harriman's Oregon Railway and Navigation Company (with strong ties to Union Pacific) would soon be coming to Crook, Lake and Klamath counties. In fact, it was hoped that the rails would extend into Harney County. The mere thought of twin bands of steel bisecting the Ochoco caused the value of timberlands to sky-rocket. Pushed by eastern capitalists, forested claims in eastern Oregon were being sold for $4,000 to $8,000 each. By January 1908, timber claims were in such great demand that even in mid-winter eastern Oregon was overrun with claim hunters. Not only men but women, frequently traveling alone, could be seen wandering the forests searching for claims.

There was only one drawback to this exciting railroad news. The Government Reclamation Service was blocking access to the lower Deschutes Canyon. However, by April 1907, with ice still blocking the Columbia, the Reclamation Service had a change of heart and withdrew its petition opposing construction of the OR&N line and work was expected to start up the Deschutes Canyon at any time.

Why the railroad companies decided upon the narrow Deschutes Canyon to gain access into central Oregon is difficult to understand. A much easier route south from Shaniko into the Crooked River Valley was rejected because of "troublesome hills." Apparently the low-level route following a water grade up the Deschutes gorge, while formidable, no longer appeared to be impassable—just costly. And so, this area was destined to become the battleground for progress.

The lifting of the construction ban would introduce another contender into the transportation field. Great Northern, the parent company of what became James J. Hill's Oregon Trunk Line, would enter the race into central Oregon in direct competition to Edward H. Harriman's Oregon Railway and Navigation Company (again backed by Union Pacific). Within days of this announcement, two automobiles bearing Harriman officials slipped into town and took apartments at the Prineville Hotel.[9] It was hinted their errand had special significance. Shortly after their departure a party of OR&N surveyors and engineers arrived in Prineville looking for a gasoline for their automobile. While the members

---

9   *Crook County Journal*, March 29, 1906.

of the party were very secretive about the purpose of their trip through Crook County it was generally believed that their object was to block the efforts of the Oregon Trunk Line through central Oregon.

The iron horse was closing in but as yet it hadn't replaced the hay-burner when it came to frontier passenger service and shipping. The Cornett Stage and Express Company serving the area between Shaniko and Silver Lake by way of Prineville, Bend and Rosland was the longest stage line in the United States under one management. George McIntire (Mack) Cornett operated more than 500 miles of stagecoach route with 360 head of stage horses and more than 100 vehicles. With changes of drivers and horses, the coaches traveled the distance from Shaniko to Silver Lake—over 200 miles—in 50 hours. Rain or shine, the stage left Shaniko at 6:00 p.m. daily. Twice during the night horses were changed at relay stations and by 8:00 a.m. the following day, the coach would rumble into Prineville, the distribution center for all points into the interior. During the 1905 Lewis and Clark Exposition in Portland, the Cornett Stage Company was offering two-day passenger service from Prineville to The Dalles railhead for those who wished to attend.[10]

Of all the commodities coming into Prineville by coach and freight wagon, liquor was running a close second in popularity behind mail. In fact, it so disturbed the blue-noses in the southwestern portion of the county that they brought prohibition to a vote in 1906. Out of a population of 5,754 (according to the latest county census) 579 ballots were cast with the outcome being 205 for prohibition and 374 against prohibition. This vote would soon change but not exactly for the reason it should have. In short, consumption of booze can be hazardous to your well-being.

For example on January 31, 1907 the *Crook County Journal* would make the following observation. "Leander Dillon, an old timer in Crook County and well known throughout eastern Oregon met with a horrible death Sunday morning." He certainly did. Mr. Dillon was literally roasted

---

10   Mack Cornett was a pioneer of the auto industry. He was the first of the early stagecoach operators to use motor vehicles in his business and by 1910 had 13 automobiles in operation using White Steamers, Chalmers and Studebakers. The hard service his cars were subjected to on the Shaniko-Silver Lake run soon exposed their weaknesses and early auto makers kept in contact with Cornett who helped correct these defects. (*Crook County Journal*, August 29, 1907; *The History of Crook County, Oregon*, 1st Ed., 1981, p. 88.)

alive. There was no mention as to whether or not Leander had been visiting his brother Lawrence's Main Street Saloon. What the article did reveal was that Leander was in the habit of sleeping in a wagon at the Dillon feed yard. This wagon, covered with a double tent to make it warm and comfortable, was equipped with a bed and camping outfit. On Sunday morning, January 27—sometime between midnight and 1:00 a.m.—Dillon went to the wagon intending to go to bed. He was more or less intoxicated and it was supposed that he lit a candle before retiring. The candle burned low setting fire to the bread box on which it sat and the rest is history.

Four months later—again on a Sunday morning—Prineville citizens were awaked by the clanging of the fire bell to find the home of Johnny Prior in flames. Prior—found lying face down on the floor near the front door—didn't make it out. It was believed that he tried to escape but "being intoxicated was overcome by the smoke and flames."[11] Such shenanigans went on for a year but the straw that would tip the scales in favor of temperance was fast approaching.

One evening Jack Kitching, George McVey and William Stroud were tipping a few at Matt Nolan's Occidental Saloon. The talk drifted around to the Rev. C.A. Housel, pastor of the First Methodist Church, and a loud-spoken supporter of prohibition. Apparently the conversation got a little boisterous as the city marshall accused Stroud of disturbing the peace and arrested him on a charge of disorderly conduct. Once the marshall hauled Stroud off to jail, Kitching and McVey went looking for further mischief. Around midnight they found what they were looking for and open-fired with their six-guns on the stained glass windows of the First Methodist Church. Unfortunately for the two target shooters, seconds after the shots were fired, they were spotted by Anna Winnek and Judge William Bell who later tried their case.

It was of small consequence that old Leander Dillon and Johnny Prior were taking up space on Boot Hill but the breaking of church windows was nothing short of profanity at its evil worst and it brought on prohibition in 1908. Enforcement of this new county ordinance got Sheriff Frank Elkins and Deputy John Combs into big trouble.

---

11 *Crook County Journal*, May 22, 1907.

After confiscating all intoxicating beverages in the local saloons, they dutifully seized the first wagon load of booze that rolled into town—destined for the Bennett Saloon in Bend—and stashed it in the old courthouse.[12] (Amidst protests from the city of Bend, the new stone courthouse was still under construction.) With the courthouse rapidly becoming overstocked with contraband whiskey, Elkins—as any well-thinking county official would do—posted notice in the local papers that he would auction off the troublesome stock of liquor to anyone interested in buying. When District Attorney Fred W. Wilson at The Dalles got wind of this it sent him into a state of trauma. According to the district attorney's office it was not exactly legal for a sheriff to sell booze in a dry county when it was his duty to arrest anyone else for doing the same thing which brought on the problem in the first place. However, that was just one of the sheriff's worries. The circuit court then issued an order demanding him to sell the attached items to the highest bidder with cash in hand and the remainder of the distilled spirits held at the court—meaning Bennett's wagon load of 90 proof bourbon—to be disposed of in a like manner.[13] Acting on Wilson's advice, Sheriff Elkins and Deputy Combs quietly hauled all the offending liquor up to the rim south of town and irrigated the sagebrush which seemed to suffer no ill effects from this shot of liquid plant stimulant.

To encourage non-alcoholic participation in its services, the Poindexter Hotel barber shop was making some unique offers. If a person brought in up to five dollars worth of any kind of produce—eggs, fruit, butter, cabbage, potatoes, parsnips, onions—the produce could be exchanged for haircuts. And, in defiance of Congress and the Federal Reserve Act, the livestock business was booming. Cattle were selling for $30 a head; sheep for $5 a head and Prineville was becoming noted as the best horse market in the Pacific Northwest. A million pounds of wool sold at Shaniko for $210,000 and the Prineville creamery constructed in

---

12 The old two-story wooden courthouse, built by Dr. H.A. Belknap at the cost of 5,474 dollars, stood on the same location as the present courthouse. At this time, the wooden structure had been moved to East Third and Fairview streets to make room for the construction of the new stone courthouse which cost 48,590 dollars at completion in 1909. The old wooden courthouse was used as a school annex for many years.

13 *Crook County Journal*, November 19, 1908.

1907 was advertising that one man could turn out 1,200 pounds of butter a day.

The Prineville creamery wasn't the only business touting its wares. Sponsored by Prineville merchants, the Superb Medicine Company show was making quite an impression on the townsfolk in the summer of 1908. Not only was the medicine show furnishing free entertainment in the form of Nikinia, a beautiful exotic dancer and her cohorts Lew Emerson (a comedian) and Jack Vance (who performed in black face) but between acts it was also offering tooth extractions, cross eyes straightened and skin operations free of charge. All of this was paid for by the Prineville Merchants Association. Now this was advertising at its best.

Also in 1908, the first outdoor advertising sign, "Chew Mail Pouch Tobacco," was displayed on a barn in Wheeling, West Virginia. Two years later, progressive Crook County merchants were making good use of such means to publicize their merchandise. Strategically placed on sandstone cliffs overlooking the Lower Bridge area west of Terrebonne and Trail Crossing on Crooked River, they can still be seen 85 years later. The words painted on the rocks: "Go to Lynch and Roberts Store of Better Value, General Merchandise, Redmond," are bright and easy to read with the date 1910 emblazoned on the unfurled scroll. Mike Lynch and J.R. Roberts were determined Portland businessmen who believed that Redmond, with the Bend-Madras-Prineville roads passing through it, was the hub for tourist traffic.

But in 1908 the range problem as the *Crook County Journal* would put it, "still remains a difficult nut for Congress to crack." Even so, Forest Supervisor Ireland was confident that stockmen would like the grazing permit plan and it was his hope that grazing permits would eventually do away with the range war. Based on this expectation, the most important livestock meeting yet held in Prineville was called to order on December 10, 1908. Following a week of discussion during which Supervisor Ireland announced that a fence would be built dividing the Deschutes National Reserve into two districts—one for cattle and one for sheep—the cattlemen and sheepmen reluctantly agreed to this allotment of grazing lands. Thus, another crisis was averted in the semi-dormant range feud.

As 1908 drifted into mid-stream, free enterprise in central Oregon was also flowing with the current. In July, a 64-year-old entrepreneur named Robert Grant, who happened to be the Bend postmaster, hit upon a sure-fire way to make some money. The one thing he neglected to take into consideration was the method he chose to gain that end. The local residents were pretty liberal when it came to making a buck and could accept most shady deals with no qualms. But when it came to tampering with the U.S. mail, they got a mite touchy. When apprehended, District Court Judge Woolworth fined old Bob $3,361.76, the exact amount he had embezzled from funds entrusted to the U.S. Postal Service. Grant pleaded poverty. No problem. In lieu of the fine, Judge Woolworth sentenced Grant to serve 3½ years in the federal prison on McNeil Island in Puget Sound. Apparently the judge figured that Grant's hard labor was only worth about $2.63 a day, which was probably about right.

And this was the way prosperity evolved in the first decade of the 20th century on the central Oregon frontier. It was certainly in step with the pattern set forty-one years in the past when the first westsiders trickled over the Cascade range to settle in the verdant Ochoco and Crooked River valleys.

CHAPTER 211

THE IRON PONY

I saw women become hysterical and sob as they came near the train and appreciated that they were finally in close communication with the rest of the world.

A.C. Jackson
R.R. Official, Redmond, Oregon,
September 30, 1911

In 1900 when the Columbia Southern Railroad—supported by Harriman's OR&N—was completed to Shaniko that town became the shipping point for interior Oregon. Even so, Prineville was the real dispersal center for all passenger and freight service. Seven regular stage lines based in Prineville operated daily to Shaniko, Silver Lake, Lakeview, Sisters, Madras and the Warm Springs Agency; three times a week to Paulina and Burns; and twice a week to Mitchell, John Day and Canyon City.[1] Then in 1909, after years of speculation, rail service into Crook County was close to becoming reality. As one observer would put it: "This event is one of the most interesting episodes in central Oregon history . . . perhaps without parallel in the history of railroad building."[2] It would match two corporate giants—James J. Hill and Edward H. Harriman—in a no-holds-barred contest to open central Oregon to the outside world.

As noted earlier, the big livestock producers were not eager to have steel tracks laid into the area. Prior to 1909 several railroad builders had made attempts to reach central Oregon but for various reasons (mainly political and financial) these efforts were fruitless. Now with

---

1   *Crook County Annual*, 1902, p. 6.
2   William Tweedie, *Some Aspects of the Early Development of Crook County*, p. 109.

agriculture, mining and timber interests holding sway and needing an outlet to market their products, a rapid transit system was a necessity. This was especially true when taking into account that there were billions of board feet of yellow pine timber along the eastern front of the Cascades, the Paulinas and the Ochocos ready for harvest with nowhere to go. Adding to the urgency insofar as farmers were concerned, Portland was second in the world only to New York as an exporter of wheat and flour. Yet in mid-April 1909, five sailing vessels from England lay idle in the Willamette River, waiting for a grain cargo and it wasn't financially worthwhile to transport wheat from Crook County to Portland by horse and wagon. For purely selfish reasons, western Oregon was leading the fight to bring the railroad into central Oregon and the target of abuse was Edward Harriman and his Oregon Railway and Navigation Company which, under the name of the Deschutes Rail Line, had been doing preliminary road surveys in the lower Deschutes Canyon for several years.[3]

As usual it was *The Oregonian* complaining that Portland was being denied access to the big money being generated in Crook County. This agitation took root four years earlier in a blistering editorial by Harvey Scott under the date of October 30, 1905. "This newspaper takes upon itself to remind Mr. Harriman that Oregon looks for important things under his immediate initiative." After three paragraphs of trashing Mr. Harriman it would conclude, "Above all, specifically, we want a railroad connecting Portland as a terminus with the highly potential but sparsely settled central and southeastern Oregon." In short, so Portland and the Willamette Valley could tap central Oregon's lucrative economic resources.

Mr. Harriman replied to Mr. Scott's editorial on November 17, 1905 stating in essence that he was aware of Oregon's need for a rail line into the interior but because of the obstacles in constructing a road grade in the Deschutes Canyon it was impossible "to proceed with the promptness and speed demanded by a press which makes light of these difficul-

---

3 For an in-depth study of the major railroad companies and their subsidiaries involved in central Oregon see Due and Rush, *Roads and Rails South From the Columbia*. This is the most comprehensive history on central Oregon railroad operations published to date.

ties."[4] Harriman was not exaggerating about the challenging, in fact nearly impassable terrain encountered in the lower canyon.

As early as 1854, Jefferson Davis—then Secretary of War—sent a survey party headed by Lt. Robert Williamson into the West to locate a possible rail route between the Mississippi and Sacramento valleys with a connecting line from the Sacramento Valley to the Columbia River. On this segment of the survey Davis instructed Williamson to check a possible route up the Willamette Valley or "the valley of the Deschutes River near the foothills of the Cascade chain." Lt. Williamson was soon told by road locators like Sam Barlow and Steve Meek who were familiar with the area that he would be wasting time in studying the Deschutes Canyon. Upon receiving this information from Williamson, the Secretary of War advised Congress on May 1, 1855 that "the character of the country along the Deschutes River is such as to render it impossible that a practical route can be found."[5]

Again in 1899 the Deschutes Canyon was considered as a possible route to interior Oregon. In that year Harriman's Oregon Railway and Navigation Company made a survey from The Dalles through Dufur, Tygh Valley and down White River to the Deschutes; thence up the Deschutes to Madras and Bend. This route was also given up as impractical.[6] Then in 1906, Hill's Oregon Trunk Line made a survey up the Deschutes to Madras via Willow Creek and by 1907 construction crews working the west side of the river began grading a road bed. At the same time, Harriman's Deschutes Line made another survey on the east side of the river and it began to look as if central Oregon was going to have a railroad.

Nearly two years would pass while various surveys were being conducted by both Hill and Harriman but no iron pony galloped into central Oregon. Finally the Portland Chamber of Commerce decided to take a hand in the matter and sent a delegation to the state legislature with a unique proposal. This enlightened group recommended that the state of Oregon amend the Constitution whereby it would empower the legislature to go into the railroad business. The chamber of commerce

---

4   Scott, *History of the Oregon Country*, Vol. IV, pp. 378-79.

5   Lt. Abbot, *Exploration for a Railroad Route*, 1854-55, Vol. VI, p. 9.

6   Engineer's Report, Spokane, Portland and Seattle Railroad Files, Portland, Oregon.

was smart enough to know this proposal wouldn't fly but it was thought that it would serve as a bluff to force Harriman interests—namely Union Pacific—to start construction into central Oregon.[7]

During discussion of the Portland recommendation, Harriman's attorney, William Cotton, explained that the reason no work had been done in the Deschutes Canyon was because Union Pacific's survey maps of the road grade had not been approved by Congress. There were a number of men present who took exception to that statement among them W.F. (Billy) Nelson representing Great Northern's Oregon Trunk Line. Later, evidence would surface proving that Cotton was telling the truth.[8]

By May 1909 the citizens of Redmond—claiming they had lost faith in both Harriman and Hill—were pushing for an electric railroad to be built from The Dalles running through Madras and "at some point branching, one fork going to Prineville and the other to Bend."[9] What they had in mind by an "electric railroad" is anyone's guess. However, it didn't seem likely that Harriman's Deschutes Line was going to pass through Prineville. Six months prior to Redmond's wishful thinking, J.P. O'Brien (general manager of the Deschutes Line) in a Prineville meeting bluntly stated, "I haven't heard that people of Prineville have any affection for the railroad. They haven't taken up the matter with me but we [Harriman and O'Brien] do not contemplate running the line into Prineville."[10] Apparently Union Pacific was well aware of Prineville's earlier opposition to any rail lines being extended into Crook County. O'Brien's statement would cause the *Crook County Journal* to complain, "We can't stand to have a railroad built 20 miles away nor can we afford to build a sub-line 20 miles." Before the railroad battle was over, that thinking would change, at least in regard to constructing a sub-line.

Meanwhile, to keep the pot boiling, Louis Hill—son of James J. and president of Great Northern—visited Prineville in an effort to soothe raw nerves. In a public speech he would comment, "I do not see how it would be possible for a railroad to come within 18 or 20 miles of Prineville and stay out of it." Perhaps not, but Hill made no promises that it would come to Prineville either. Sheriff C. Sam Smith reported that in

---

7   *The Bulletin*, Bend, Oregon, February 17, 1909.
8   *Federal Railroad Report*, No. 172, p. 738.
9   *Crook County Journal*, May 13, 1909.
10 *Crook County Journal*, December 2, 1908.

a private conversation Louis Hill told him that Prineville residents should not be impatient about a railroad. The way Hill put it, "We've got to build the backbone before we build the ribs." Former congressman Newt Williamson expressed a more favorable attitude on the part of Hill:

> I had many conferences with Mr. Hill when he was here, and he indicated to me that if these people wanted a railroad they would get it. Prineville is and always will be the distributing area for a vast district. The railroads are bound to recognize this and in time give proof of it in a substantial way.[11]

However, these hopes were soon blasted for in the early part of 1909 the reclamation service, after lifting its earlier ban on railroad construction in the Deschutes Canyon in 1907, decided that the railroads would have to build above a proposed dam-site in the vicinity of Sherar's Bridge. According to railroad engineers this change of grade alignment would make it inconceivable if not impossible to use the Deschutes Canyon and this was the opinion of such men as Great Northern's Chief Engineer John Stevens, who designed the Panama Canal. Within a month political pressure was applied and the reclamation department modified its requirements and railroad interest was again revived.[12]

Of equal importance to railroad construction was the implementation of a grazing permit system and management of timber sales on the Western Division of the Blue Mountain Forest Reserve. The first timber sale on what would become the Ochoco National Forest was made to the Pioneer Telegraph and Telephone Company of Prineville on August 30, 1909. However, selling trees was of minor concern when compared to the problem of enforcing grazing regulations. Allotment boundaries had been placed on maps but without a survey it was anyone's guess as to where they were on the ground. This lead to trespass both intentional and unintentional. Unfortunately, the Forest Service whose eager young rangers packed a new manual of federal regulations in their saddle bags saw all infringements in the same light . . . deliberate, at least on the part of the cattlemen. The outside wool growers backed by such men as Newt

---

11   *Crook County Journal*, May 12, and June 9, 1910.
12   *The Bulletin*, Bend, Oregon, March 17, 1909; April 28, 1909.

Williamson, who had given up his congressional seat in 1908, packed political clout.[13] The Forest Service—right or wrong—tended to favor their interests and many beef producers weren't taking kindly to this show of favoritism. One new-fledged forest guard flatly stated that "Trespassing was common on the part of cattle owners. Little or no effort was made to hold the cattle or horses on the range allotted to them."[14] Apparently horses were now involved in the range conflict but sheep were too virtuous to offend.

It was strongly believed by the range watchdogs that most cattlemen were not only antagonistic to government administration but some were openly defiant. According to one allotment enforcer, Fred Light, who ran a large cow operation on Upper Crooked River, had several hundred head of cattle on forest range and it was not uncommon to find upwards to 200 head of his stock on sheep range on any given day. Warning letters were ignored and Light openly boasted that he would continue to graze his cattle where he had always ranged them and no government appointee was going to stop him from doing so. It was generally understood that Light had been an active member of the sheepshooters and would not yield to anyone—including the federal government. Some believed that if Fred was pushed too hard "a certain forest guard would disappear." Light himself publicly announced that he intended to maintain his right to graze cattle on the forest and if necessary "had money to fight the government in court." He soon got the chance.

With three trespass cases pending against him, Light carried his legal battle to the U.S. Supreme Court and lost all the way. When eventually summoned to defend his claim in Federal Court in Portland, he gave up the fight and paid the damages in full both actual and punitive.

Stubborn ranchers like Fred Light were not the only ones in trouble. Some local sheepmen were also getting shoved off the range. The migratory flock owners were out to secure Crook County grazing allotments by any means possible and with Washington and local politi-

---

13   John Newton Williamson, publisher of *The Prineville Review*, owned one of the largest sheep operations in Oregon. He served as state representative, speaker of the House of Representatives, state senator, and was twice elected to the Congress of the United States.

14   Blake, *Blazing Oregon Trails*, p. 28. Blake, who became district ranger of the Big Summit District would later admit that some sheep herders took pride in committing trespass and stole grass from other allotments not assigned to them.

cians in their back pockets they would get the job done. The new range war would not be fought with rifles but with federal regulations, and slow strangulation by government red tape would be infinitely more effective than a stray .30-.30 bullet. So, it wasn't just local operators with a preference for beef or those who favored mutton, but both who would suffer in the long haul.

John Edwards, tough old veteran of two range wars and owner of Hay Creek Company (the largest sheep breeding station in the world) was next on the hit list. By September 1909, reductions in forest reserve rangeland allotted to the ranch forced Edwards to sell most of his flocks. In all, Edwards was running 70,000 head of sheep but his original government allotment of 30,000 head had been slashed to 12,250 head to make room for Sherman, Morrow and Wheeler county sheepmen. Within three months, the Portland *Oregon Daily Journal* would announce the event. "Huge ranch forced on market . . . . The famous Hay Creek sheep breeding plant to be sold because government curtails grazing privileges in forest reserves." Edwards sold some 20,000 head of sheep and in 1910 sold the 70,000 acre ranch to L.B. Menefee and Henry L. Pittock, publisher of the *Portland Oregonian*. At the time of sale, the sheep were valued at $350,000 and ranch improvements at over $75,000.[15]

At the same time John Edwards was being regulated off federal range, another high-stake gambler cashed in his chips. Edward Harriman, a good friend of Edwards who sometimes visited Hay Creek Ranch, died, throwing Deschutes railroad plans into a state of confusion.[16] Two months before Harriman's death it appeared that railroad construction would actually start in the Deschutes Canyon. On July 7, Twohy Brothers (construction contractors for the Deschutes Line) accompanied by Harriman's chief engineer, G.W. Boschke (who built the Galveston sea wall)

---

15 *Prineville Review*, January 6, 1910. In 1922, Menefee and Pittock sold out to W.V. Sanderson who in turn traded the ranch to Fred W. Wickman in 1937 for an island in Hawaii. Wickman sold the holdings to A.J. Smith and Sons of Kalispell, Montana, who were owners from 1952 until 1954 when Wickman again resumed operations. Later, a group of Texans purchased the ranch for a reported $4.7 million. Besides cattle, they did run about 2,000 head of sheep on the ranch.

16 At the time of death on September 9, 1909, Harriman controlled over 60,000 miles of track and estimates of the value of his estate ranged between $200 and $300 million. *Dictionary of American Biology*, Vol. VIII, p. 296.

moved considerable equipment and several carloads of laborers into the area. A supply base was established in Grass Valley and work began on a 12-mile access road into the lower Deschutes Gorge. This was an expensive undertaking as the final grade down to the canyon floor dropped nearly 1,600 feet in elevation in a distance of two miles. This section of the supply route was so steep that it required special cleated shoes for the draft horses to maintain their footing.[17]

Shortly before Harriman's forces set up camp in Grass Valley, Hill's agents were at work and things began to happen with great rapidity. In 1908, the obscure Central Oregon Railroad was incorporated on June 18 and soon thereafter filed maps for a right-of-way from Madras to Bend passing over the Crooked River Gorge. No one seemed to know who owned the new railroad but it would hold an important role in the forthcoming battle. On July 23, 1909—just sixteen days after Twohy Brothers moved into Grass Valley—Porter Brothers, another contracting firm, suddenly appeared on the scene and began unloading heavy equipment at The Dalles. At the same time, John Stevens—one of the world's greatest engineers—slipped into central Oregon disguised as a fisherman. Traveling under the name of James Sampson, he quietly scouted out the Central Oregon Railroad survey across Crooked River. It was believed that Stevens had met secretly with Billy Nelson (a Seattle railroad promoter) and bought the controlling stock in the Oregon Trunk Line before the Harriman system knew what was occurring.[18] During this period of speculation, Porter Brothers purchased the Central Oregon Railroad survey which they immediately sold to Great Northern for the identical price they had paid for it.[19] At this point, Hill publicly announced that Great Northern owned the Oregon Trunk Line and named

---

17 Starting near the head of Rattlesnake Canyon this wagon road, called Reckman Grade, clung to the face of the almost perpendicular canyon wall between Rattlesnake and Gert Canyon, reaching the Deschutes River a mile south of what is now the Beavertail Recreation Area. From this point supplies were transported both up and down the canyon to the work sites. At the mouth of Mack Canyon a blacksmith shop was constructed and as late as the 1960's it was not uncommon to find dozens of the special made horseshoes. Before the BLM opened access into the lower Deschutes Canyon following the old Deschutes Rail Line roadbed, I made several trips up and down Reckman Grade. It was not something you would care to do on a daily basis.

18 *The Bulletin*, Bend, Oregon, July 7, July 21 and July 28, 1909.

19 The reported sale price for the Central Oregon Railroad survey amounted to $170,352.50. Brogan, *East of the Cascades*, pp. 240-41.

John Stevens as its new president. Of greater significance, by acquiring the Central Oregon Railroad Company's rights for the crossing of Crooked River, Hill had virtually blocked Harriman's move to build a parallel line to Bend.

This transaction was regarded as the first step in a titanic struggle for control of the Deschutes Canyon. The conflict would now shift from legal skirmishes in the courtrooms to open warfare in the field. Within a few days after the news broke that the Hill and Harriman people were engaged in a multimillion-dollar race into central Oregon, contractors established camps up and down the river. On the west side more than 1,000 men, working under 20 different subcontractors, were on the job for Porter Brothers three days after the battle lines were drawn. At the same time, Twohy Brothers moved 26 flat cars loaded with laborers to various camps on the east side of the river.

A Union Pacific surveyor recorded in his diary that crews from the opposite sides of the river were lobbing bullets at each other. "Fortunately," he added, "no one seems to be much of a shot." *The Dalles Chronicle* would report:

> Harriman has begun work on the disputed route through the canyon and is prepared to seize the strategic points without waiting for the courts to settle the condemnation suits now pending with the Oregon Trunk. Camps established at various points between the mouth of the Deschutes River and Sherar's Bridge are reported determined to repeat tactics which have proved effectual in the past in an effort to secure any desired route against a possible rival.

In other words, Winchester rifles were now accepted as bona fide construction tools.

It was now very evident that the Porter Brothers meant business when it came to building a railroad. In preparation for the actual laying of track, the first dirt was moved at the mouth of the Deschutes shortly before midnight July 16, 1909. Some 30 miles up river, under the cover of darkness, other Porter crews were moving into combat position. When the Harriman forces awoke the next morning, crews found that not only were they cut off from the wagon road they had built from Grass Valley, but that the line of construction they had mapped was covered with Porter Brothers men.[20]

The wagon road passed through the Gert ranch and Union Pacific had received permission from the owner to construct the vital supply line into the Deschutes Canyon. Now Twohy Brothers found the railroad iron gate at the head of the grade locked and guarded by a Porter Brothers employee. R.G. Calvert, staff correspondent for *The Oregonian*, would report in the *Grass Valley Journal* on July 30, 1909, "The sentry is not armed but the pockets of his coat bulge conspicuously." Johnson Porter (president of Porter Brothers) had stepped in and bought the land from Gert.[21] Within hours, Harriman's attorneys swung into action, and a temporary restraining order was granted against Porter Brothers blockade. Ignoring the court order, they stationed more guards at the gate. Meanwhile Twohy Brothers gathered a large force of laborers and four days later started for the gate fully intending, if it became necessary, to remove both gate and guards with a stick of dynamite. This caused the Porter Brothers to remove their gatekeeper and a conflict was narrowly averted.[22]

By September preliminary bouts were over and all concerned were ready to settle down to the serious business of building railroads. This alone would demand a tremendous amount of manpower.[23] The

---

20 As late as the mid-1960's, there were abandoned railroad box cars sitting beside the stretch of road where Porter Brothers employees blocked the passage of Twohy Brothers crews. These box cars served as quarters for Union Pacific surveyors and construction foremen. Some were conspicuously labeled WAR OFFICE. These railroad buildings were destroyed because they might pose a safety hazard to recreationists.

21 Tweedie in his master's thesis refers to the Gert property as the "Gurtz ranch." Grass Valley, located on the Columbia Southern Rail Line into Shaniko, was the main supply depot for railroad construction in the lower Deschutes Canyon. Until the parallel rail lines reached Sherar's Bridge both Great Northern and Union Pacific were dependent upon the wagon access road down Gert Canyon to get supplies to the crews working the lower Deschutes Gorge.

22 *Portland Oregonian*, August 3, 1909.

23 During the peak construction period, Porter Brothers had 3,800 men working on the Oregon Trunk Line and Twohy Brothers an estimated 4,000 laborers strung out from Free Bridge in the lower canyon to Crooked River Gorge. Common laborers received 20-30¢ an hour; carpenters and concrete men from 35-40¢; and well drillers were paid $7 a day. Teamsters received $6 a day. Camp lodging was furnished and meals were 25-30¢ Interview with Phil Brogan, May 1959, based on Brogan's earlier interview with John L. Stevens, president of the Oregon Trunk Line. The *Crook County Journal* in August 1910 would place the total number of workers in the Deschutes Canyon at "about nine thousand."

normal labor supply came out of Portland and Spokane but with labor in strong demand in the timber and mining industry and wages high, men were hard to hold in the sweltering heat of a rocky canyon infested by rattlesnakes. So, with the exception of several hundred Chinese, most of the workers were immigrants from southern Europe who were about to receive a more liberal education than they had bargained for. These native Greeks and Italians would soon find out that work in the narrow Deschutes Gorge was not only spectacular, costly and dangerous, but it would mark the end of an era in railroad building. The back-breaking toil required to surface a roadbed and lay twenty-pound iron rails from the Columbia River to the frontier town of Bend was—for all practical purposes—done by hand. Breathtaking wooden trestles soaring over side drainages; 16-foot wide ledges chiseled across the face of sheer bluffs; tunnels blasted through solid rock where balls of rattlesnakes were jarred from subterranean dens; and an awesome steel arch spanning Crooked River Gorge were accomplished with equipment consisting mostly of picks, shovels, spike hammers, wheelbarrows, hand-drills, hand cars and black powder. It was definitely no task for the faint-hearted.

The struggle for control of the Grass Valley wagon road and the stationing of armed guards at the strategic crossing of Crooked River was just the start of many fights between Oregon Trunk and Union Pacific over railroad right-of-way. The Oregon Trunk survey, after staying on the west side of the river for over 70 miles, was forced to cross the Deschutes at North Junction because of an impassable bluff at the mouth of Antoken Creek. This river overpass brought on a major conflict between the two contractors.[24] Despite Oregon Trunk's legal access to a river crossing at North Junction, Union Pacific held the land physically and a crisis situation was developing. During more playful interludes, rival laborers were detonating each other's dynamite caches. Oregon Trunk, being more civilized, filed suit in federal court and by August 1909, Judge Robert S. Bean decided that Oregon Trunk's right-of way survey predated that of Union Pacific's Deschutes Line, which would clear the way for Porter Brothers to proceed. There was just one major problem. A short distance south of North Junction, Oregon Trunk's

---

24   Engineer's Report, Spokane, Portland and Seattle Railroad Files, Portland, Oregon. The SP&S was jointly owned by Great Northern and Northern Pacific.

survey crossed the Smith homestead on Davidson Flat and Frank Smith proved to be a stubborn barrier.[25]

Although the Oregon Trunk survey maps were approved at Washington, D.C. before Smith secured title to his homestead, he had filed on it while approval of the survey was still pending thus giving him prior rights. In a swift move to wipe out this obstacle, Johnson Porter offered to buy the homestead for $2,500. Smith refused to sell. The next day, Twohy Brothers upped the ante to $3,500. Apparently Frank thought he had run his bluff to the limit and sold, giving them a controlling segment of the right-of-way. Again Oregon Trunk went to court in an effort to oust Union Pacific from the North Junction bottleneck but all this accomplished was the posting of armed guards on the Smith homestead and outright gun battles between survey and construction crews.

Shad Krantz, a reporter assigned to cover the railroad conflict, graphically describes the rivalry of the two warring camps:[26]

> The almost perpendicular cliffs towered up fifteen hundred feet above the angry rushing water. Along a narrow trail on the east side of the canyon a legion of Greeks and Italians, armed with drills, pickaxes and dynamite, were hewing and blasting a forty foot shelf out of the rock wall. Suddenly a big boulder, falling apparently from the clouds, struck close to them. The men scattered like frightened quail. A whole rain of falling rocks struck where they had been standing. An unseen and desperate enemy was rolling boulders over the edge of the cliffs.
>
> A few nights later a rival camp of aliens on the other side of the river were thrown into a panic by the discovery of a plant of dynamite close to their sleeping quarters.

In this war of attrition each side placed lookouts on rims overlooking the gorge. These spotters watched for places where their opponents stored powder. On dark nights, a crew of five or six men would slip across the river and detonate the caches. The result was that both sides faced delays because powder was not always available when needed and the

---

25 *Federal Reporter*, No. 172, p. 738.
26 Shad O. Krantz, *Technical World* (a railroad magazine), Vol. 18, September 1912, pp. 27-28.

stalemate at Smith's homestead threatened to stop construction altogether.

Since Oregon Trunk was already hamstrung, Porter Brothers in a fit of anger built a grade across the Deschutes Railroad's survey line at North Junction, blocking Harriman's crews from further progress into central Oregon. Three days later on September 9, 1909, Edward Harriman died bringing inner contentment to Great Northern officials. They hoped that Union Pacific under new management would be willing to compromise. No such luck. The outcome was that the federal government stepped in and enforced the Canyon Act, resulting in a joint track usage agreement covering eleven miles between North Junction and South Junction. On May 17, 1910, Porter Brothers and Twohy Brothers signed a "cease fire" agreement which was to last for "a period of 999 years."[27] Perhaps that was how long they thought it would take to reach Bend.

The minute the North Junction barrier was ruptured, ranchers as far away as Grizzly, Prineville and Ashwood could hear the rumble of blasting in the rocky canyon assuring them that the railroad was coming. Meantime, Porter Brothers stationed guards at the Crooked River bridge site in order to hold the right-of-way as this area continued to be a source of contention.

The spot chosen was the narrowest place on the gorge and the only practical approach for a railroad crossing. Even so, it was 350 feet across the gorge from rim to rim and 320 feet straight down to water level. When completed, the steel arch bridge was one of the highest in the world. It would be over a year and a half before a work train reached the gorge and another two months before actual construction of the bridge itself was begun on June 4, 1911.

During this period and after leaving South Junction, the two railroads took separate routes. Union Pacific left the river at Mile 88 and came up Trout Creek staying on the high ridge west of Madras before descending into Metolius. On its course up Trout Creek, Union Pacific blasted its way through five tunnels; constructed two major bridges across Trout Creek; and spanned Willow Creek Canyon with a trestle 1,050 feet long standing 275 feet above the ground.

---

27   Engineer's Report, SP&S Railroad Files, Portland, Oregon.

At the same time, Oregon Trunk continued upriver to Mecca; came up Willow Creek crossing under Union Pacific's trestle at Madras; then stayed east of Union Pacific's line to Metolius.[28]

By now, Oregon Trunk was advertising sight-seeing tours into central Oregon. A month after bridge construction began over Crooked River Gorge, a trainload of Portland tourists rumbled up the canyon in July to witness the spectacular undertaking. The southbound passenger train, running at full steam on track that was still not fully ballasted and tamped, derailed and plunged into the river north of the Warm Springs Reservation near the railroad siding at Dant. Six people, scalded by steam from the locomotive's ruptured boilers, died in the accident.[29] A coroner's jury was rushed to the scene and concluded that the accident was due to excessive speed as the train was running at 53 mph on a track restricted to 10 mph. This investigation determined that the conductor and assistant superintendent of maintenance were guilty of negligence. Perhaps it was just as well that the passenger train didn't get farther at the speed it was traveling.

A few months later in January 1912 another tour train was making a winter run up the canyon which in itself was not too smart as snow was causing a problem in the middle canyon. One train was snowbound at Maupin for two weeks and another trapped between Gateway and North Junction for three days. As the January visitor train crept across the Deschutes at North Junction the temporary bridge began to give way. Fortunately the train was able to stop but the passengers had to crawl to safety on the swaying bridge. To make the situation worse, it was a blustery winter night and the survivors were lucky that they didn't die from exposure. Riding the iron pony into Crook County may have been an adventure but it was also hazardous to your health.

On February 11, 1911—just four days before the last great Indian hunt in history began at the Denio ranch a few miles south of the Oregon-Nevada border—an Oregon Trunk work train, preceded by

---

28 On July 10, 1923 an agreement was reached for Oregon Trunk to use Union Pacific's line between South Junction and Metolius.

29 This mishap occurred at Mile 69 some 22 miles south of Sherar's Bridge. Among those killed were the train's engineer and Louis Rising, member of a prominent Illinois family, who was storekeeper at the Warm Springs Indian Agency. Due and Rush, *Roads and Rails South From the Columbia*, p. 79.

horsemen, gunshots and wild cheering, chugged into Madras in a swirling snowstorm. By September 30, the first passenger train to span the awesome Crooked River Gorge braked to a stop at Redmond. The fact that a railroad, which had been talked of, hoped for and dreamed about for so long, had actually become a reality seemed almost too much for some to endure as hysteria and sobbing ruled the day. The following morning, the celebrated train rolled into Bend where already some 2,000 spectators had gathered to commemorate Railroad Day.[30]

On October 5, 1911, James J. Hill drove a golden spike at the end of the rails in Bend. Unlike Leland Stanford, president of Central Pacific and Thomas Durant, vice-president of Union Pacific, who took turns missing the famous golden spike which connected the transcontinental railroad at Promontory Point, Utah on May 10, 1869, Hill pounded slow and deliberate. Watching Hill drive the historic spike were William McMurray, a Union Pacific official and Hill's longtime friend William Hanely, cattle king of Harney County.[31] The golden spike, immediately withdrawn, was passed around for inspection and last seen in the hands of Jim Hill. Some claim that Hill gave it to Hanely saying as he handed it over, "Here Bill, I was building the railroad to come and see you."[32]

The driving of the spike marked the end of the bitterest and most expensive struggle in railroad history. This battle for a right-of-way in a rugged canyon where a saddle horse could hardly get a footing lasted for two years and cost $25 million mixed with blood, sweat and grief.[33] Yes, the iron pony had finally bolted into central Oregon but in so doing it had bypassed the Queen of Oregon Cow Towns, the matriarch of Crook County and the acknowledged trade center of interior Oregon. Obviously

---

30 Engineer's Report, SP&S Railroad Files, Portland, Oregon; *Redmond Spokesman*, October 5, 1911; Bend *Bulletin*, October 11 and 12, 1911.

31 Hanely, a would-be eastern Oregon politician who ran several times for governor and once for the Senate—losing all races—owned several large ranches north of Harney and Malheur Lakes totaling almost 25,000 acres. The 6,700-acre Bell A ranch, 3½ miles from Burns was considered one of the best in Oregon. The Double O ranch 35 miles southwest of Burns was eight miles from gate to front door. Hanely laid the cornerstone for the new Bend railroad station.

32 Brogan, *East of the Cascades*, p. 245.

33 For more on the railroad battle in Deschutes Canyon see: Oregon Guide, *Oregon: End of the Trail*, Portland 1940; Scott, *History of Oregon*, Vol. IV, p. 375; *The Oregonian*, Sunday Magazine, December 30, 1951, pp. 6-7; Holbrook, *A History of American Railroads*, pp. 184-85.

Great Northern and Union Pacific bore a grudge against certain Prineville citizens and now they would pay for their sins. But, in true Ochoco fashion, the intended victims fought back to set another milestone in railroad history.

CHAPTER 212

THE GALLOPIN' GOOSE

Ordinance 231, authorizing the city to build a railroad and to issue $100,000 of bonds to aid in its financing was approved unanimously by the Council for submission to the voters.

Minutes of the Prineville City Council
March 7, 1916

By 1910 Prineville was beginning to lose its Wild West image but not very much. On April 6, 1910 *The Bend Bulletin* would report (no doubt quite gleefully) that: "Last Saturday evening George Estes of Prineville shot and killed A.R. Randall on the range near the county seat. Randall worked for Allie Jones, whose sheep, it is alleged, were trespassing on the range rented by Estes despite the latter's repeated warnings that he would protect his rights. But five minutes were required by the coroner's jury to reach a verdict of justifiable killing exonerating Estes from blame." With all its fanfare, the Federal Reserve Act hadn't suppressed the guns of war.

On the lighter side, you could buy a 1910 Model T Ford from Charley Shattuck, Prineville's car salesman. The sport model came complete with top, side curtains, windshield, gas headlamps, speedometer, gas generator, side and tail oil lamps all for $1,050 delivered to Portland. The only problem being that there weren't all that many roads to travel on. Maybe that's why Stonewall Whiskey advertised in three grades was selling at $4, $5 and $6 dollars per gallon.

The forest ranger at Beaver Guard Station, some twelve miles southwest of Mitchell, was complaining that if he wished to communicate with the supervisor by telephone, it was necessary to cross the Blue Mountains—a distance of 20 miles—to the newly constructed Ochoco Ranger Station. This could seldom be accomplished by horseback in winter due to deep snow. And because of snow, for seven months out of the year the mail between Prineville and Mitchell had to be carried some 130 miles by horse stage through Shaniko while the actual distance between the two post offices was only 60 miles.

The *Prineville Review* would report that "another flour famine threatens Prineville" owing to the mill being out of commission. It seems that merchants were limiting their supply to one sack per customer to keep anyone from cornering the flour market in Crook County. Apparently, they had little faith that any supplies would be arriving by freight train in the near future.

Of questionable importance, stocks were being sold by an experienced hustler in a "mythical project" to irrigate northwestern Crook County with water from Crescent Lake. This had the Madras citizens quivering with excitement and they tended to ignore the fact that Crescent Lake was 85 miles from the area it was intended to flood with water and the ditch would have to cross a range of mountains to get there.

Even with railroad construction crews now blasting their way up Deschutes Canyon, access was still a major problem for watchdogs of the newly created Ochoco National Forest. In 1910, the only passage across the Ochoco forest, other than game trails and a few Indian and trapper trails, had been constructed in 1908 along the summit of the Blue Mountains in an effort to connect the various ranger districts and it wasn't an easy route. In September 1909, it took Grover Blake over ten days to pilot 17,000 sheep some 30 miles to the Ike Mills ranch in Beaver Creek Valley on this so-called stock driveway. In the same amount of time, cowboys drove a herd of cattle from Prineville to Portland over the Cascade range.

With this in mind, Blake, Clyde Hon, W.A. Donnelly and Henry Zevely got together on August 4, 1910 with intent of improving the Summit Trail. About the only thing of interest on this project happened the first night out. The road gang set up a base of operations under the north rim of Mt. Pisgah where a small meadow provided horse feed. Shortly after making camp, Blake and Hon killed a deer. Taking what meat they could carry in the darkness back to camp, they hung the remainder of the carcass in a tree. Early the following morning the four headed out to retrieve the rest of the meat. Hon and Donnelly were the first to arrive and while waiting for Blake and Zevely a "very huge bald-faced grizzly bear reared up on a nearby log." Old Silver-Tip, scenting the fresh venison, proceeded to have breakfast while the road warriors—with only three cartridges for their rifle—were afraid to move. When Zevely and Blake finally arrived the big grizzly had wandered off into the Lodgepole thickets. Although his huge footprints were seen on several occasions, the grizzly was never seen again.[1]

Lack of a railroad wasn't slowing cattlemen in getting to market. As mentioned earlier, on March 1, 1910, Sam Smith started over the snow-drifted Cascades with 125 head of 3-year-old shorthorn steers. Ten days later, he sold them to the Burke Commission Company of Portland for $76.80 a head . . . the highest price ever paid in the Pacific Northwest for beef on the hoof. Fourteen days later, Smith sold his big Keystone Ranch to George Russell for $55,000 in the largest single real estate transaction to take place in Crook County. Russell, a horse buyer headquartered in Tacoma, Washington, would run horses on the Keystone. He would also do something else unheard of in the livestock business.

Years ahead of his time, Russell was gambling that the domestication of elk was a money maker. The massive elk harvests of the 1870s and '80s, mainly for their teeth and hides, nearly depleted the Oregon elk population. The 1903-04 annual report of the Oregon Game and Forestry Warden reflects just how serious the elk situation had become. In this report, the game warden would note: "The law protecting the killing of elk expires September 15, 1904 and should be reenacted as soon as possible. If not, only a few years will pass by when the elk of Oregon will be an animal of the past."[2]

Russell was going to solve this problem by stocking the Keystone Ranch with 30 elk imported from Idaho. It didn't work. The elk escaped

---

1   Blake, *Blazing Oregon Trails*, pp. 31-32. Thirty-five years later in May 1945, Gale Ontko, Kenny Osborn and Sid Lowery were opening the road to Pisgah lookout and camped in this same meadow. One evening, about 9 p.m., a cougar screamed and smelling fresh meat, charged into camp hoping to grab a handout. There was no sleep that night as we kept the campfire blazing like a major forest fire. At daylight cougar tracks could be seen in the snow where the big cat had paced back and forth around the camp looking for food. Obviously the cougar was starving as game was very scarce for there was still three and four foot snow drifts under the north slope of Mt. Pisgah.

2   The elk law was extended to 1910 but actually lasted until 1933.

and were promptly shot by neighboring ranchers who had developed a taste for elk steak.

Elk weren't the only thing disappearing in central Oregon. The arrival of a railroad in Bend was having the same effect on once thriving towns which were bypassed by the iron pony. No longer did passenger stages operate from Prineville to Shaniko and hotel business in Shaniko virtually vanished. Population fell from 495 in 1910 to 120 in 1920 and continued the plunge to a ghost town in the 1960's. Prineville did not actually decline in the 1911-1916 period but it didn't grow either. On the other hand Bend was expanding rapidly, gaining almost 4,000 in population between 1910 and 1920 while Redmond had taken away Prineville's interior trade.

When it became obvious in 1910 that the railroad terminal would be Bend not Prineville, things began to happen at the county seat. To have a rail line 20 miles away was worse than having one a hundred miles away because Bend, Redmond and Madras were certain to take over wholesale distribution and attract lumber mills for timber harvest, packing plants for farm products and provide opportunities for other industry. Not only was a railroad necessary for development but by 1900 there was ample evidence nationwide that a town without rail service could not survive as a trade center.

The first hint that Prineville wasn't going to take this annoyance lying down appeared in the *Crook County Journal* September 1, 1910. As stated in the *Journal*: "If it comes to the very worst, some of the conservative citizens of Prineville assert that they will themselves build a branch railroad line up Crooked River Valley in order that Prineville will not be left off the map." Some in the western section of the county who would be served by the railroad thought this article was quite hilarious until it became evident that this was no idle threat. The mother town was preparing to play hard ball with her wayward step-children and would soon receive some welcome help.

H.A. Kelley, who had been a civil engineer with the Oregon Trunk Line, settled in Prineville and soon took over as city engineer. Kelley made some preliminary surveys of a railroad route via the town of Lamonta and estimated the cost to build at half-a-million dollars. The line was to run along the base of Gray Butte and across Poverty Flat to Prineville with a branch going up Willow Creek to tap timber resources at Grizzly.[3] By early 1911, Tom Baldwin (Prineville banker) and C. Sam Smith joined the railroad battle. Along with Kelley and other local residents, articles of incorporation were filed to form the Prineville & Eastern Railway Company. Other stockholders included some of the heavyweights in county administration.[4] Now all they had to do was raise some working capital. Its worth noting that one socially prominent name doesn't appear on the articles of incorporation . . . lawyer George Washington Barnes, ex-vigilante and publisher of the *Prineville (Ochoco) Review*. It seems that Barnes saddled his favorite mount; rode over to Canyon City to visit his girlfriend; got into a gun-fight; and was killed on June 26, 1911. Barnes did marry his sweetheart—Mrs. Alex Bowsman—before her ex-lover, George W. Anderson, let daylight into his chest with three .45 calibre slugs.[5]

About the time George got gunned down, some modern conveniences did come to Prineville when concrete sidewalks were installed—but not without controversy. The two banks on the opposite corners of Third and Main each had sidewalks installed about three inches different on grade. The argument was not about money, but about whose sidewalk survey was correct. This kept the townsfolk's mind off railroad operations for several days. However, the idea of a city-owned railway system was making news.

The minute word got out that Prineville—looking for financial support—was serious about building a branch line many outside groups were showing interest in the project. Representatives of the L.M. Rice construction firm visited Prineville showing great optimism; H.H. Skewes representing the St. Louis firm of Stanger & Co. promised to

---

3   *Crook County Journal*, September 28, 1910.

4   Stockholders in the Prineville & Eastern Railway Co. were: Charles M. Elkins whose family had been active in the Willamette Valley and Cascade Mountain Military Wagon Road Company; Robert A. Booth, a prominent Eugene lumber man with vast timber holdings in the Ochoco Mountains; George M. Cornett, who for three decades had been the principal stagecoach operator in central Oregon; E.J. Wilson, who had been an agent for SP&S and the Columbia Southern Railroad; Granvel N. Clifton, stockholder in the Ochoco Gold Milling Company on Scissors Creek; David F. Stewart, mayor and prominent Prineville businessman; Thomas H. LaFollette, big sheep operator and pioneer nurseryman; and George W. Noble, vice-president of the First National Bank.

5   The body of George Barnes was taken to Prineville and laid to rest beside the remains of Ginevra Marks, his first wife. (June 29 and July 6, 1911, *Prineville Review*; July 6, 1911, *Crook County Journal*.)

have a line in operation within eight months; H.P. Sckeel, owner of a sand and gravel quarry in Tenino, Washington said he would finance and build the line provided Prineville would give a $75,000 bonus plus right-of-way and land for terminals; Robert Strahorn, promoter of the Oregon, California & Eastern Rail Road (who had spent two years in the Ochoco as a war correspondent covering Crook's Shoshoni campaign) offered to build a network of lines connecting Bend, Prineville, Burns and Lakeview; Twohy Brothers, railroad builders who constructed the Ochoco Dam eight miles east of Prineville, also submitted a bid but none were making firm commitments in the way of doing anything.[6]

On his four-day trip through central Oregon there is little doubt that Strahorn was driving the hardest bargain. Businessmen, cattlemen, bankers and homesteaders who pledged support to his Oregon, California & Eastern Rail Road were bluntly told:

> Let it be understood clearly that I will not pay 1 cent for rights of way or terminal sites. I do not care how you get them, but they must conform to my specifications and be turned over to me all in shape, without my having to conduct any of the negotiations or be burdened with any expense in connection with obtaining them.[7]

Even under these stringent conditions cash, labor, terminal sites and rights-of-way were offered and the railroad builder was assured that the terms he exacted would be complied with. He did nothing.

Prior to and during these negotiations a new figure, Mrs. L.B. Kerwood, entered the picture in November 1911. She had recently bought a large farm in the Prineville area and immediately indicated interest in seeing a railroad built. Working independent of the Baldwin group—but not hampering its efforts—Mrs. Kerwood publicly announced in the *Crook County Journal* that the need for a railroad into the Prineville area could not be ignored and she believed she could interest Boston capital in building it.[8] Mrs. Kerwood then contacted both Great

---

6   *Crook County Journal*, January 4, October 3 and October 10, 1912; October 14, 1915 and March 29, 1917.

7   *The Bulletin*, Bend, Oregon, November 24, 1915.

8   Undoubtedly, Mrs. Kerwood contacted Thomas W. Lawson, described by his daughter as a "thirty-times millionaire." Wall Street financier and owner of a 1,000 acre estate in Cape Cod,

Northern and Union Pacific to determine what they intended to do, if anything, in the way of serving Prineville. Further discussion with Great Northern followed and in March 1912, she prepared a statement of freight potentialities of Crook County for Louis Hill, stressing the agricultural output. While nothing directly came of Mrs. Kerwood's efforts, the *Crook County Journal* gave her credit for "stirring things up."[9]

During railroad negotiations time was running out on a few old-timers. The four year period between 1911 and 1915 would see the passing of some of the more colorful figures to shape the destiny of the Ochoco. In 1911 the old vigilante George Barnes was gunned down in front of a Canyon City saloon. In 1912 Lorinda Kerwood who harassed the railroad giants in an effort to gain financial support to fulfill Prineville's dream for economic expansion, quietly disappeared into obscurity. In 1912 Has No Horse stalked into a Fort Bidwell boarding school and calmly knocked the daylights out of an overbearing schoolmaster. For this reckless behavior, he died in a Nevada prison in 1914. Then in 1915 Henry Wheeler, who took a Shoshoni bullet in the face when he drove the first stagecoach across the Ochoco, died peacefully at his home in Mitchell, Oregon.

Meanwhile, the Prineville City Council kept searching for investors but private firms were reluctant to put up money due mainly to limited traffic in the immediate future. Finally in 1916, the city council voted to finance a municipal railroad by selling bonds and obtaining contributions. Still unable to get reasonable bids for construction, the city decided to lay track with its own labor force and on May 30, 1917 the work began.

A year and a half later, Locomotive No. 1—known to the local citizens as "The Gallopin' Goose"—rumbled up the Crooked River Valley in a December snowstorm and, with whistle blowing, ground to a stop at the new City of Prineville Railroad Depot. This 1918 Christmas

---

Massachusetts, Lawson purchased 640 acres of farmland in the lower Crooked River Valley in 1911 and gave it to his daughter and son-in-law—Hal and Dorothy Lawson McCall- as a wedding present. The proposed Prineville Railroad would have to cross through their property. Hal McCall's father, Samuel W. McCall, a U.S. congressman and governor of Massachusetts, was also a prospective investor. One of Hal and Dorothy's sons, Tom McCall, served as governor of Oregon from 1967 to 1975.

9   *Crook County Journal*, November 9, 1911 and April 19, 1912.

present gave Prineville instant recognition for operating the only city-owned railroad in the United States.

CHAPTER 213

A COUNTY IN DISTRESS

The Bible tells us to love our neighbors, and also to love our enemies; probably because they are generally the same people.

G.K. Chesterton
An Innocent Bystander

In 1911 with railroad access to the outside world, the inhabitants of western Crook County were becoming somewhat arrogant, especially those in the northeast section where agriculture held sway over livestock and timber production. Now that Prineville was cut-off from the rail line and frantically trying to get connected, county division was again in the wind stirring up memories of Bend's 1907 attempt to split Crook at the seams. Suspecting strong opposition from the county seat, Bend came up with a new tactic. Spearheaded by Robert Sawyer, a young Harvard law student who was the protégé of George Putnam, editor of *The Bulletin*, Bend formed a citizen's committee whose sole purpose was to incite Madras farmers into a state of political unrest.[1] To Prineville's detriment, it would work.

It also appears that conduct in the county's railroad towns was getting out of hand. So much so that it was attracting statewide attention. By 1912, in an effort to quell more adverse publicity, Governor Oswald West suggested that the citizens of Bend, Redmond and Madras raise "less hell and more hogs" if they desired to stay out of trouble. He further

---

1   In 1915, Putnam became personal secretary to Oregon's governor, James Withycombe, and was married to Amelia Earhart, the first woman to cross the Atlantic in an airplane. In an attempt to fly around the world, Earhart's plane disappeared over the western Pacific on July 3, 1937 and was never seen again. Putnam edited and published *Last Flight*, a book consisting largely of her diary of the last ill-fated journey transmitted from the various stopping places on the way.

warned local authorities that if they didn't enforce the law, the state of Oregon would.

Shortly thereafter, the governor lived up to his word. He sent an undercover deputy to sit in on an illegal poker game run by Redmond's mayor, H.F. Jones, in a back room of the Redmond Hotel. When the special deputy arrested Jones and Z.T. McClay (the local marshall), West asked for, and got, resignations from both men. For this foolishness, the governor was voted out of office in 1914.

Over in Madras, Grace Shugert—in her tireless crusade for cleanliness—was running for mayor on a platform of "more water for wash day!" Madras residents were not convinced of the need for that reform and rejected Ms. Shugert's bid for public office.

Throughout these preliminary bouts, Bend was in training for the main event. City fathers were plotting to revive the Deschutes County issue but not looking forward to a rematch with Prineville. Most likely, they were reluctant for good reason. Aware of the conspiracy, it is certain—in view of what was to transpire—that Prineville backers rushed to the defense and some closed-door deals were made in Salem. In any event, the state legislature passed a unique law in 1913 whereby—instead of a simple majority—it would require 65% of the voters living within the proposed boundaries of a new county and 35% of the voters residing in the original county to be in favor of a change before it could be effected.[2] Keep in mind that the areas clamoring for county separation were the Agency Plains west of Madras and the High Desert east of Bend, both of which were overflowing with newly arrived homesteaders who held no love for the big livestock outfits in the Ochoco country.

Even with the help of new legislation, the Prineville title holders would suffer a body blow delivered by the Bend citizen's committee. Guided by the Harvard lawyer Robert Sawyer, an arrangement was made by the political leaders of the two proposed new counties to vote in favor of each other's proposal. In short, the residents of intended Jefferson County would vote in favor of the planned Deschutes County and the latter would vote in favor of creating Jefferson County in the northern third of Crook County. They were gambling that the death of Crook County's pagan saint Has No Horse in March of 1914 and the outbreak

---

2   *General Laws of Oregon 1913*, p. 21.

of World War I four months later would overshadow their covert action and it almost worked.

Under these conditions an election was held in November 1914 and the vote was sufficient to create Jefferson County but an uncommitted contender had entered the ring. Loyalists in the Redmond area had no desire to be placed under the governing fist of Bend and their anti-division sentiment was strong enough to block the formation of Deschutes County. Redmond was now on Mr. Sawyer's hit list and *The Bulletin* was not kind in its reporting of Mr. Redmond's municipality.

With Bend smarting in defeat, nothing more was heard about county division for the next two years. Then the issue, which had been slumbering since the 1914 election, came to life again. This time the motivaters in the south end of Crook County were determined that nothing would stand in the way of their plans. On July 6, 1916, a petition bearing several hundred names was filed with the secretary of state, containing an interesting proposal. It requested that a motion be placed on the ballot at the coming fall election which—if passed—would transfer the county seat of Crook from Prineville to Bend.[3] This appeal got the desired reaction.

Whether or not this was intended as a bluff to force those who opposed county division into line is hard to determine but it had the effect of scaring the Crook residents into thinking that if Bend wasn't allowed to be the seat of a new county, voters might remove the county seat from Prineville to Bend. This was no idle threat. Bend was growing rapidly in population and with two major sawmills having been recently established, the city could probably muster enough support to accomplish this transfer of power.

Prineville officials were now thoroughly aroused and a committee was appointed July 20th to confer with a delegation from Bend.[4] After two weeks of squabbling, the negotiators came to an agreement concerning the county lines. There was some controversy over the Terrebonne and Powell Butte precincts but a compromise was reached whereby

---

3   *Crook County Journal*, July 6, 1916.

4   The men appointed to serve on the Prineville committee were: George Russell, Columbus Johnson, Isadore Meyers, Luther Claypool, C. Sam Smith and Hugh Lister. (*Crook County Journal*, July 27, 1916.) The Bend committee names are too numerous to mention.

Powell Butte was to remain in Crook County and Terrebonne would be included in the new county.[5]

Shortly thereafter the residents of Crook County were notified that the two appointed groups representing west Crook County and east Crook County had arrived at a compromise. Spokesmen for the western area agreed to use their efforts to defeat the measure to transfer the county seat to Bend if the citizens of the eastern end would agree to vote for the division of Crook County according to the lines agreed upon by the committees. However, the Prineville delegation emphasized that the promise would not be binding unless a majority of the citizens of the northwest end of the county (the Redmond area) would agree to vote against the county seat removal.

Meanwhile Warren Brown, Crook County Clerk, was facing a problem on how to hold an election in a split precinct. When the arbitrators drew the proposed boundary lines on a map subdividing Crook County, the non-existent landmark placed the Fife precinct partly in present Crook County and partly in the proposed county of Deschutes.[6]

Because of the unusual 1913 law governing the formation of counties it would be necessary for the people who lived in the Fife area to vote separately on the split-off issue. After consulting several local lawyers, and not arriving at any satisfactory conclusion concerning the election, Brown took the matter up with the county court. After lengthy deliberations, the court instructed the county clerk to prepare two ballot boxes. Although all the voters lived in Crook County, one ballot box was to be used by the electors who resided north of the division line in Crook and the other by the voters living south of the line in anticipated Deschutes County.

On October 30, 1916—a week before the election—Brown attempted to clarify this confusing issue in a letter sent to the election judges of the Fife precinct. It stated in part: "Owing to the fact that the county division line divides your precinct, it has been necessary to

---

5   *Crook County Journal*, August 3, 1916.

6   Fife was located in southeast Crook County on the headwaters of the South Fork of Crooked River approximately three miles southwest of the GI Ranch and six miles due north of the present Crook-Deschutes County line. It was established as a post office on May 17, 1890 and named for the Scotland county of Fife, former home of Thomas Balfour, the first postmaster.

prepare two boxes for ballots; one being marked Deschutes and the other Crook. All voters should state whether or not they live in the proposed Deschutes County, or in the part that will remain in Crook County . . . . If the elector resides in the proposed Deschutes County, his ballot should be placed in the box marked Deschutes. If he resides in the part that will remain in Crook County, his ballot should be placed in the box marked Crook. Then, when the count is made, the ballots should be counted from the Deschutes box first . . . . After counting all the ballots from the Deschutes Box, count the ballots from the Crook box . . . . This will be necessary to get the required percentage for county division under the present law . . . ."[7]

Brown thought that the election judges would have no difficulty in carrying out instructions but apparently they did. Whether by accident or by design, only one ballot box was used which could alter the way the vote was being counted in the Fife precinct. It didn't take long for news of this oversight to reach Bend.[8] When word was relayed to the Bend precinct that the Deschutes County measure was going down in defeat it was met with disbelief. In a state of confusion Robert Sawyer, accompanied by Clyde McKay and several Bend businessmen, jumped into an automobile and headed for Prineville to see what was going on. What they found out caused them to launch injunction proceedings against Warren Brown to prevent him from certifying the election returns from Fife. Because the election board had used only one ballot box, the 40 votes cast in the Fife precinct were counted as though the voters all lived in the proposed new county, whereas the registration book showed that only five of them lived in the proposed Deschutes County.

The vote was so close in the other parts of Crook County that had the vote been allowed to stand in the Fife precinct as first voted, the county measure would have failed, but if the votes were counted according to where the voters lived, the measure could carry. Following the injunction against certification of the vote, opponents of county division entered a demurrer, the legal way of admitting that the facts stated in the injunction were true but not sufficient to constitute a good defense in law.

7   This letter signed by Warren Brown, county clerk, appears in the 1916 Crook County Clerk Files dated Prineville, Oregon, October 30, 1916.

8   Robert W. Sawyer in his interview with William Tweedie which was later presented to the Department of History, University of Oregon, August 1939.

Based on this argument no corrections were necessary as all of the voters resided in Crook County. The matter was finally taken into Circuit Court where a suit—unique in legal records—was filed naming Clyde McKay of Bend as the plaintiff and Warren Brown of Prineville as the defendant.[9]

Judge T.E. Duffy, who had ruled on the county seat of Jefferson and was a supporter of Deschutes County, handed down a decision on December 12, declaring the election board at Fife was in error and allowed the vote to be counted according to which county the voters lived in. Bear in mind, at the time of preference all voters resided in Crook County. Judge Duffy then ordered the county clerk to certify the returns to the proper authorities and, on December 13, 1916, Deschutes was officially proclaimed a county by Governor James Withycombe.[10] Thus, through a legal technicality, the citizens of Bend gained what they had coveted since the turn of the 20th century.

Not all Deschutes residents were aware of their current status. Some news speeds ahead while some just drags along. Four months after Governor Withycombe's proclamation, a curious Bend property owner received a tax notice from "Deschutes County." Somewhat confused, she sent a note along with her tax payment expressing displeasure. "I am enclosing a draft and addressing it to the sheriff of Deschutes County. I do not understand this, but suppose it is all right although I supposed Bend was in Crook County. If the name has been changed, all okay, but think Crook is a very appropriate name and very applicable to some [in Bend] who sold lots here."[11] And that was the opinion of one disgruntled tax payer.

The creation of Deschutes County saw the Ochoco—Land of the Red Willow—at last whip-broken and harnessed to the plow of progress. Reduced in size from a vast wilderness empire that once stretched from the Cascade range to the Snake River plateau, it was now nothing more than a small island in the heart of Oregon. Yet, as the Crook-Deschutes battle raged, a native son let the world know that those born to the freedom of the Ochoco would not and could not be tamed.

---

9   Judgment Roll Crook County No. 2757, Conclusions of Law, pp. 1-3.
10   *General Laws of Oregon*, 1917, p. 6.
11   *The Bulletin*, Bend, Oregon, April 19, 1917.

CHAPTER 214

THE LAST DOG SOLDIER

When the posse found Shoshoni Mike and his raiders, a bitter gunfight took place. His ammunition exhausted, Shoshoni Mike led his people, now armed with bows and arrows, in a suicidal charge.

Humboldt Star
March 2, 1911

For all practical purposes the epic of the Ochoco ended in 1911 when the iron pony wandered into Bend. Although still in its death throes, the days of open conflict in central Oregon were a thing of the past and it seems fitting to end this saga with a native son born to the old way of life. A man who called the Shoshoni Ochoco home and rode the trail with great warriors like Has No Horse, Paulina and Pony Blanket . . . a dog soldier to the end.

During the latter course of his life this man was known as Mike Daggett. It was claimed that no one ever knew his Indian name. Is it possible that he was Dave Chocktote's friend Dead Deer, the man—according to Chocktote—who was called "Mike Deer Gut" by the whites? We will never know. The name Mike Daggett was probably given by an Indian agent who found his Shoshoni name hard to spell.[1] Also, after the hysteria of the second Shoshoni uprising (the Bannock War), a Christian name gave the Indian some protection. Whatever, "Mike Daggett" was the name officially used by the Office of Indian Affairs.

---

1 If indeed this was Dead Deer his name in Shoshoni would have been spelled something like *Masiduedeeheah*. Mike Daggett was also known as Salmon River Mike; Indian Mike; Idaho Mike; Rock Creek Mike; and Shoshoni Mike. At the start of the Bannock War in 1878, the Snakes raided Duck Valley and ran off all the Shoshoni defectors. A man named George R. Daggett was superintendent of the Western Shoshoni (Duck Valley) Reservation and may have been the unnamed Indian agent who gave Mike his name. It was common practice at that time to give Indians Christian surnames which had no bearing on their real names.

335

James Bascomb, who built the Rock Creek Stage Station east of Silver City, Idaho in 1865 and was later killed by Buffalo Horn, believed Shoshoni Mike was about 33 years old at the time of the Bannock War. This would fit with his suspected birth in the 1840s, placing the date about the time of the 1845 emigrant train's passage across the Ochoco when the Shoshoni nation was in a state of upheaval with a split between the western war tribes and the eastern peace-lovers already in progress. This is mentioned only to help determine Shoshoni Mike's true identity.

Mike was described as being short, slender, and thin-faced with a light complexion who wore his hair in two long braids indicative of his Snake heritage. Dayton Hyde—Mike's biographer—believed he was a Bannock and not a Shoshoni because he "clung to the old way of life." Hyde was on the right track but, in keeping with the prevailing concept that the only Shoshoni were the passive disciples of Gourd Rattler, he forgot—or perhaps never knew—that the western supporters of Wolf Dog were the elite of the Shoshoni nation. . . the dreaded Snake War Tribes and as such were not inclined to accept white domination at any price. After the first Shoshoni war, the only Snakes given any recognition were the Robbers, who were mistakenly classified as a separate group called Bannocks. Mike himself said he was a Shoshoni . . . an Ochoco Shoshoni, not an Eldahow Shoshoni.

There is little doubt that Mike served with honor in the Shoshoni war. In 1868 when Has No Horse and his dog soldiers surrendered at Fort Harney, they were accompanied by a young brave wearing the headdress of a war chief. This war bonnet made of deerskin, eagle feathers and split cow horns was identical to the one worn by Mike some forty years later in·his last defiant charge against the Nevada militia. It is recorded that Shoshoni Mike, along with other war criminals (including the Snake war chief Yellow Jacket), was sentenced to life on the Fort Hall Reservation in 1869. Before nine years had passed, Mike and Yellow Jacket were again mounted and riding with Has No Horse and Pony Blanket in their last violent attempt to purge eastern Oregon of American settlers.

In the aftermath of the Bannock War, the few remaining hostiles were not accepting reservation life gracefully. Has No Horse refused to stay on the Klamath Reserve and was roaming eastern Oregon but staying out of sight. Yellow Jacket escaped from the Yakima Reservation and was eventually placed on the Nevada Western Shoshoni (Duck Valley) Reservation in 1886.[2] Shoshoni Mike, again placed on the Fort Hall Reservation, deserted and was hiding out on Rock Creek in the Idaho Sawtooth range, the old hunting grounds of the Snake war chief Tuanna. Here, Mike often wintered in a sheltered cove on the Crockett's Rock Creek Ranch.

Somewhere during this period—perhaps at Fort Hall—Mike met and married a Ute girl named Jennie. During their life Mike and Jennie had ten children (five boys and five girls) which was a large number for a Shoshoni family. Although the children were known by a mixture of English and Shoshoni names, their Indian names were used when not conversing with white people.[3] Sky, one of their daughters who was also called Mike, died when she was quite young. When speaking of her to his friends the Crocketts, Mike would sadly remark, "Girl him just lay down and die." The Crocketts would describe Mike Daggett as an honest, hard-working man.

There was good reason why Snake warriors and their families avoided government housing like the plague, which in reality it was. Children were separated from their parents and being unused to the new life many died. In 1883, the Salt Lake City *Desert News* would report that out of the Snake children herded onto the northern Ute reservation that year, there were 15 deaths from measles, 13 from whooping cough and five from other diseases.[4] The loss of children was just one of the hardships these wards of the United States had to face. Reservation Indians were slaves not only to alcohol but to opium brought in by Chinese laborers. To make the situation more unbearable, Indians dying from hunger were forced to adapt to a life of peace while their white landlords still lived by the gun and though they preached God, law and the courts, they settled their own differences with fists, clubs, knives and guns and that arrangement would include any Indian who got in the way.

By 1890, the civilized intruders of eastern Oregon, Idaho and Montana were bemoaning the fact that free-roaming Indians (Snakes) were interfering with their lifestyle. Concerned citizens of Malheur

---

2   Descendants of Yellow Jacket's band comprised about 50 percent of the Duck Valley Reservation population in the 1960s. Frenholm and Carley, *The Shoshoni*, p. 267; Canfield, *Sarah Winnemucca*, p. 212.

3   The Daggett boys were named Jack, Jim, Catchum Charlie, Eat-em-up Jake, and Cleve. The Daggett girls were named Lizard, Heney, Sky (Mike), Snake, and Hattie. The girl's Christian names are unknown.

4   *Desert News*, Salt Lake City, Utah, February 9, June 18 and November 27, 1883.

County, Oregon circulated a petition requesting that the Shoshoni in eastern Oregon be returned to a reservation, any reservation just so long as they were taken out of Oregon. Fred Brown, a Butte, Montana butcher, complained that Indians from Fort Hall were raiding his slaughter house for scraps of meat. Yellowstone Park officials were grumbling that Indians from eastern Oregon and Idaho were killing game south of the park and some miners from Caraboo, Idaho charged the Indians with starting forest fires which supposedly destroyed timber needed for mining purposes.[5] Most of these complaints were a deliberate attempt to force the starving Indians back onto a reservation and the complaint from Yellowstone Park got the desired results. The distinguished members of the Boone & Crockett Club of New York City, in a meeting at the Knickerbocker Club, resolved that any Indians still on the loose should be rounded-up and suggested military force if it became necessary.[6]

When the dragnet was cast, the few remaining Snake hold-outs—including Mike Daggett—kept on the move eluding all efforts to place them on a federal reserve. American society, then and now, could neither understand nor tolerate individuals who failed both to depend upon it and follow its rules. After the remnants of Has No Horse's followers died in Big Summit Prairie during the 1903 smallpox epidemic, Shoshoni Mike and his family became unique in that they were probably the last band of Indians in North America living the old life in the ancient way. If their lot was a hard one of extremes of weather and food it was theirs by choice to be preferred over life on the reservation. With starvation or execution ever on the horizon it was a more difficult and dangerous life than their ancestors had known, for at the dawn of the 20th century a non-reservation Indian had about as much chance for survival as a lone sheep in wolf territory.

---

5   Malheur petition from D.D. Munger and others to Secretary of Interior, April 29, 1890; Fred Brown to Indian Department June 3, 1890; S.G. Fisher to Commissioner of Indian Affairs September 3 and 29, 1890; W.S. Dalliba to Secretary of Interior September 13, 1890; U.S. National Archives Records, Office of Indian Affairs.

6   The memorial signed by Theodore Roosevelt—president of the Boone & Crockett Club—included such other intrepid frontiersmen as Carl Schurz, Secretary of the Interior 1877-1881 and George Bird Grinnell, considered to be one of America's earliest and greatest interpreters of the American West and Indian culture. (See Grinnell's letter to John W. Noble, Secretary of the Interior, April 12, 1889, U.S. Archives, Records of Office of Indian Affairs.)

Mike was now disappearing for months and no one knew where he went. For years, as their family increased in size, the Daggetts roamed throughout southeast Oregon and northern Nevada hunting in the Owyhee country once claimed by the White Knife Snakes; sometimes going as far north as the southern Blues to make contact with Has No Horse's family; ranging through the Steens Mountains westward to Paulina's old hideout on Hart Mountain; south into northern California to visit Little Rattlesnake's descendants on the Round Valley Reservation; and then east across northern Nevada on their return to the winter camp at Rock Creek on the Idaho-Nevada border. On these wide-ranging forays, Mike was often joined by the Chocktotes, a young Shoshoni couple who periodically left the Klamath Reservation to live like the Daggetts.

Mike's requirements from the civilized world were few . . . some coffee, a little flour, maybe some sugar and lots of ammunition. To pay for this, Mike made and sold buckskin gloves, moccasins and rawhide ropes. The older boys were well known as experienced horse-breakers and they too were bringing in money. During haying season, the girls worked in the ranch kitchens and did laundry. While thus employed, Lizard—the oldest daughter—met and married Lige Harris, a Negro cowboy from Texas. Following her marriage to Harris, Lizard no longer traveled with her family on their extended trips into the back country.

In an effort to escape reservation life, sons and grandsons of the old Snake dog soldiers were working as ranch hands for the big cattle outfits in eastern Oregon and northern Nevada. According to Dave Chocktote, the Daggetts were camped on Bill Hanely's 18,000 acre Double O Ranch southwest of Burns, Oregon in the fall of 1909. One of Hanely's Shoshoni buckaroos began visiting camp and it wasn't to see old Mike. He had fallen in love with Snake and one evening, with Mike and Jennie's blessing, they pledged their love near a blazing bonfire in traditional Shoshoni manner. However, unlike Lizard, Snake decided to spend the winter with her parents on Rock Creek and return to her husband the following spring. As the old saying goes, the best laid plans of mice and men often go astray.

It's worth noting that as Snake and her cowboy lover enjoyed a brief interlude together, wedded bliss was not so joyous on the Umatilla Reservation. Johnson Chapman, a Umatilla brave, galloped into Pendleton and filed for divorce from his Indian wife. At the hearing, Chapman nearly lost his suit when he admitted to the judge that he didn't know his wife's name[7] We can hope that a Shoshoni cowhand remembered Snake Daggett's name to his dying day for in the spring of 1910, the Daggett's world disappeared in a halo of gun smoke.

Frank and Guy Tranmer, the sons of a prominent Idaho judge, had turned to cattle rustling and were roaming over the same area that Mike traveled. In April 1910, Jack Daggett was bringing some horses into Mike's camp when he blundered into the Tranmer gang altering brands. Caught in the act, the rustlers open-fired, killing several of Daggett's horses. In the running gun battle which followed, Jack was wounded in the leg and Frank Dopp, a 14-year-old gang member, was killed. Now in a state of panic that Jack would expose them, the Tranmers decided to lay the blame of cattle rustling on Mike and his boys. Their original plan was to wipe out Mike and his family but with the fatal shooting of Dopp they came up with a new idea. Returning to the dead horses, they buried them along with Dopp in a dry wash to keep them from being detected by buzzards which in turn could lead a curious ranch hand to the scene of the crime. Next, they spread word that they had caught Shoshoni Mike butchering cattle. The first to report this rumor with blazing headlines was the *Twin Falls Times* and it would get the desired results.[8]

After the Tranmer encounter when Jack Daggett—clinging to his horse's neck—galloped into camp with his shattered leg spouting blood like a miniature geyser, Mike knew his medicine had gone bad. For weeks during the winter of 1909-10, he had observed an ominous sign in the sky . . . a fiery object which approached ever closer with each passing night. Mike sensed it was a messenger of doom and now he was certain when, despite all of her efforts, Jennie was unable to stop the flow of Jack's blood and that evening he bled to death.

Mike wasn't alone in his anxiety. The bright streak he had witnessed in the winter sky was Halley's Comet and it had put the fear of God into mankind as a whole. Some civilized "experts" were making wild predictions of things to come including one that claimed "cyanogen in the comet's tail might combine with hydrogen in the atmosphere to

---

7   "Centennial Countdown," *Oregon Journal*, Portland, Oregon, May 15, 1959.

8   "Indian Mike and his band altering brands," *Twin Falls Times*, Twin Falls, Idaho, May 9, 1910.

produce deadly hydrocyanic acid" and destroy the world.[9] For Mike and his family, no matter what Halley's Comet did, their days on earth were numbered.

The ranchers who knew Mike didn't believe the Tranmer's story but Elko County Deputy Sheriff Grim with eight men headed north towards Mike's camp to bring him in for questioning. By the time they arrived, Mike had vanished and it was believed that Lizard Harris had warned him that he was wanted for cattle rustling. Mike knew he had just as much chance of proving his innocence to a white jury as he did of convincing a judge that water ran uphill so he was running for his life. Meantime, the pose stumbled upon the dry wash where the horses were buried and found Frank Dopp's body.[10] The *Twin Falls Times* was quick to jump on this startling news and on May 12, 1910 under the banner "Cattlemen Out for Bad Indian" announced that "the roaming Shoshoni Indians rustling cattle in Nevada killed Frank Dopp."

Now operating like a Snake war chief, Mike—instead of heading northwest as expected—swerved southwest toward Pyramid Lake living mostly on wild game. When crossing the Santa Rosa range, he passed a Washoe encampment but the Washoes (recognizing Mike as a Snake warrior) refused help. That night, in true Shoshoni fashion, the Daggett boys raided the Washoe camp stealing food and fresh horses. By morning, Mike and family were again on the run pushing north into the bleak Black Rock desert. From here, Mike again turned west coming almost into Oroville, California before veering northeast toward Fort Bidwell, Has No Horse's old safety zone where California, Nevada and Oregon meet. During this heartbreaking journey, and facing possible death at every turn in the trail, 19-year-old Snake—six months pregnant when their flight began—kept the family going with her bright outlook and unwavering good spirits.

On this push to the north, perhaps in an effort to make contact with his old war chief Has No Horse, Mike hid-out in the Warner Mountains a few miles from the Oregon border and just south of what is now the Sheldon National Antelope Range. He was taking refuge in Little High Rock Canyon less than 50 miles east of Alturas, California where another Ochoco refugee, Bud Thompson (editor of the *Alturas Plaindealer*), was

---

9   "Centennial Countdown," *Oregon Journal*, Portland, Oregon, May 16, 1959.
10 *Elko Independent*, Elko, Nevada, April 25, 1910; *Humboldt Star*, May 11, 1910.

writing *Reminiscences of a Pioneer* . . . the memoir of his early escapades in Crook County and the Bannock War, where Thompson and Shoshoni Mike most likely tried to kill each other.

Mike was now in sheep country and he wasn't enjoying it. It was no secret that Mike hated sheepmen. The central Oregon range war which raged southward to the California line was still fresh in his mind and Mile's allegiance had been with the cattlemen. Some claim that his animosity was fueled by lusty young Basque herders who attempted to molest his daughters which may have some basis in fact. Snake, even though pregnant, was a very attractive woman and 18-year-old Heney was described as an untamed beauty ripe for picking. Whatever, Mike was now raiding sheep camps for food. One herder losing supplies slipped back to camp only to have Mike appear pointing a shotgun at his head and motioning him back to the sheep. That evening when the herder returned he found camp had been cleaned out of groceries and the Daggetts had disappeared.

In late June 1910, Mike left his fortress in Little High Rock Canyon and moved along the edge of Surprise Valley where he and the young men went to work in the hay fields along Pit River. Jennie and the older girls hired out to do cleaning, cooking and other household chores for the ranchers' wives. In mid-July, Snake gave birth to a little girl . . . Mike and Jennie's first and only known grandchild. This attempt at leading a normal life would soon be interrupted.

Meantime up in Oregon more exciting news than a few Shoshoni cow thieves was making headlines. On July 14, about the time Snake Daggett went into labor, a 21-year-old Portland landmark, the Exposition building—largest public building on the Pacific Coast at the time it was constructed—went up in flames. This fire also claimed the lives of two men and many horses stabled in the big frame structure.

Portland ladies were also competing with the Daggett girls for news coverage. In 1910, a group of Portland women held a mass meeting to protest high steps on streetcars which, according to them, led to "leers by loiterers." The streetcar company immediately took action to lower the steps.

But the news of importance would come from a small town south of the Fort McDermit Indian Reservation. Jean Quillici, a Nevada bartender, and his wife were shot in a hold-up. Immediately the word went out that Mike and his renegade Shoshoni were responsible. A few months later, Nimrod Urie, a member of the Tranmer gang, confessed to the crime and was sentenced to death.[11] Frank Tranmer got life in prison but later was found guilty of killing Mrs. Quillici and received the death penalty. Unfortunately this confession came too late to do the Daggetts any good.

News of the Quillici murder drifted into Surprise Valley and again Mike vanished in Little High Rock Canyon. By the end of October, Mike had killed the few mountain sheep in the area. Facing starvation, he and the boys butchered a couple of stray cows. Shortly thereafter, the worst winter storm since the blizzard of 1889-90 howled off the Pacific and slammed inland on January 15, 1911. During the storm, the Daggett boys got careless and killed three more cows hoping that would feed the family until spring. They had just finished skinning them when a passing sheepherder's dog smelled the blood and led the herder, Bert Indiano, to the fresh carcasses. Indiano immediately headed for Will Denio's ranch to report that rustlers were in the area.[12]

Heading into a blinding snow storm, Indiano didn't arrive at the Denio ranch until the next day. Harry Cambron, a Nevada cattleman who was engaged to Mattie Denio's sister, Laura Murphy, had also just arrived at the ranch. With five days to kill before his wedding on Saturday, January 21, he talked Indiano into returning to the scene of the crime to determine if the slaughtered cows were packing Will Denio's brand. The following morning, January 17, just as they were leaving, Peter Errampouspe and John Laxague—French partners in a big ranch operation who were running sheep in Modoc County, California, Washoe County, Nevada and Lake County, Oregon—arrived at the Denio ranch looking for Indiano, their missing herder. They too volunteered to go along with Cambron and Indiano. On the morning of January 18, they entered Little High Rock Canyon and were spotted by Jim Daggett. When Jim told

---

11   "Urie Makes Complete Confession of the Foul Murder of the Quillicis," *Humboldt Star*, Winnemucca, Nevada, January 11, 1911. Nimrod Urie was sentenced to hang but at the start of World War I—at the request of his mother—Urie was pardoned by Nevada Governor Oddie on the condition that he would enlist in the Canadian Army. After the war, Urie became a sheep herder in the Snake River area.

12   The little town of Denio in southeast Oregon was named for Will Denio's father, Aaron Denio. Aaron, who engaged in milling, ranching and mining, settled in the extreme south edge of Harney County, Oregon in 1885. He died there in 1907. (McArthur, *Oregon Geographic Names*, p. 214.) The Denio's big cattle operation straddled the Oregon-Nevada line stretching from Washoe County, Nevada into Harney County, Oregon.

Mike that armed ranchers were approaching their hideout, the old warrior in an effort to protect his family from further torment, made a desperate decision. Gambling that severe weather would provide an avenue of escape, Mike and Jim ambushed the ranchers in a narrow gorge and shot them. For a Snake warrior who had raided wagon trains on the Applegate Trail and fought in two Shoshoni wars, the killing of four white men was no big deal.

As the killing shots reverberated down canyon, it was snowing so hard that trains couldn't move. Knowing the storm had tied up the West and it would be weeks before anyone came looking for the missing men, Mike holed up for three weeks in his winter camp before a 10 man search party went out to look for the missing men on February 8, 1911. Two days later the *Humboldt Star* would announce: "Believe sheepmen were murdered . . . the rumor is that a bunch of outlaws from across the border in Oregon attacked and killed them."[13] This was a reference to the notorious Pat Russel gang operating out of Harney Valley.

Again on the run, Mike found the Black Rock desert blocked with a record four feet of snow. Forced out of his intended escape route into southeast Oregon, he turned south passing within eight miles of Winnemucca. Had the Daggetts separated, they would have gained freedom but family ties held them together. Meantime the search party stumbled upon the four bodies when they spotted Cambron's frozen arm sticking out of a snow drift. Finding Mike's winter camp, they put two and two together and spread the word that this was the work of Indians.

A special train out of Lakeview, Oregon was chartered to bring state and county officials to the Denio ranch to inspect the murder scene and a wire was sent to the Secretary of War requesting that federal troops be sent to Nevada to quell an Indian uprising. Washington must have taken the request for what it was—an act of hysteria—as no soldiers were dispatched. The War Department had more pressing matters to contend with. Mexico was undergoing one of its periodic revolutions in 1911 and U.S. intervention was expected. In fact, the Oregon militia was now on stand-by for quick response.

Even so, a news-hungry media envisioned another Custer massacre and four days after the Oregon Trunk Line reached Madras, Oregon

---

13   *Humboldt Star*, Winnemucca, Nevada, February 10, 1911.

on February 11, 1911, the last great Indian chase in history began. The Nevada State Police were now in the act and rewards totaling $15,000 were being offered for the capture—dead or alive—of Shoshoni Mike and his band.[14]

After the initial uproar, the volunteer Indian fighters dropped to 22 because most of the white warriors didn't want to share the reward but there were plenty working in individual groups hoping to beat the authorized force to the kill. It was now one predator after another. In an effort to follow Mike's trail, word was sent to the Warm Springs Reservation in central Oregon asking for help. Jim Teham and Henry Barr, experienced Indian trackers who were more than willing to count coup on some Snake warriors, were brought in for the job.

Time was of essence. If Mike, making about 12 miles a day, could reach the Owyhee he would be safe forever in that jumble of inaccessible canyons. Along the way, he was butchering Miller and Lux cattle to stay alive. Up on Willow Creek Sheriff Ralph Lamb, a famous lawman from Humboldt County, his brother Kise Lamb and Skinny Pascal, a Paiute tracker, were attempting to cut Mike off from the Oregon border.

Sheriff Ferrel of Washoe County in a February 23 news release would state, "Trail of murders leads through Humboldt County evidently headed for Owyhee country. The murder was committed by a band of Shoshoni Indians composed of one old man, three young braves, two old squaws, one young one and three children."[15] When trackers found where Mike turned south some thought he had joined with Jim and Jerry Winnemucca, Bad Face's nephews. This caused further panic. Jim had a bad reputation and was considered a highly dangerous man. On the other hand, Jerry was easy-going but if it came to war, he was apt to forsake his peaceful ways and fight until the battle was over. However, the Indian hunters had little to fear from the Winnemucca boys. Jerry had the good sense to stay clear of trouble and most likely Jim was taking advantage of this diversion to rustle cattle.

---

14   The rewards offered were:
State of Nevada: $5,000; Mrs. Errampouspe: $2,500; Mrs. Laxague: $2,500; citizens of Surprise Valley: $2,000; Humphrey-Cambron Cattle Co.: $2,000; state of California: $1,000. As usual, Oregon was ignoring the fact that an Indian revolt was in progress on their back doorstep.

15   *Winnemucca Silver State*, February 23, 1911.

By now, Snake's infant daughter was starving and Mike's medicine was weak. On February 26—200 miles and 16 days from the start in Little High Rock Canyon—the feared band of renegades which had inspired another Indian killing craze throughout the western states, were one day's journey away from freedom. In reality, this dangerous group of hostiles—a little family of Shoshoni—were the last holdouts of their native culture. Their cheeks hollow and eyes dull from malnutrition; the feet of children and adults wrapped in sagebrush bark and rags against the bitter cold; the hooves of their horses bleeding; they stumbled in near-exhaustion down a snow-covered ravine. It was near dawn and ahead lay an open flat some ten miles wide. They dared go no farther in daylight for fear of being detected. Mike was well aware that isolated ranches with telephones were helping in his defeat. Bone-weary, the Daggetts camped under a protective overhang in the Rabbit Creek wash to await nightfall and dozed off without posting a guard. Indian police had already set up patrols along the southern boundary of the Duck Valley Reservation straddling the Idaho-Nevada line to prevent Mike from slipping onto the reservation and many sheriff posses were organized along the Oregon-Nevada border.

On Sunday—the white man's Sabbath—Heney went out to check on the horses. Hearing hoofbeats, she looked up and saw 21 men riding down Rabbit Creek draw toward her.[16] It was now high noon, February 26, 1911. In a panic, Heney tried to move the horses down to camp as the posse charged killing three horses, one of which fell on Heney knocking her to the ground. Their appetite whetted for blood, the cheering posse thought she had been shot.[17] Heney would later testify that the Daggetts were given no chance to surrender. Each posse member had to be aware that if Mike gave up peacefully there would be no battle, no

---

16 The posse members were: Capt. J.P. Donnely, Nevada State Police; Sgt. Buck, Nevada State Police; Pvt. Stone, Nevada State Police; Pvt. Newgard, Nevada State Police; Sheriff L.C. Smith, Modoc County, California; Sheriff Ferrel, Washoe County, Nevada, Henry Hughes; William Parsons; Ed Hogle; George Holmes; Joseph Reeder; Jack Ferguson; Ben Cambron; Warren Fruits; Mort West; Frank Perry; O.D. Van Norman; Charley Demick; Sid Street; Fred Hill; Gilbert Jackson; Jim Baty; and Skinny Pascal, Paiute tracker. Other posse leaders not in on the kill were: Sheriff Ralph Lamb, Humboldt County, Nevada; Deputy Merrick Prussia; Constable Dean H. Young; Constable Charlie Byrnes; and Jim Teham, Warm Springs Oregon tracker.

17 The *San Francisco Examiner* in a 1936 interview with Mort West, one of the posse members.

satisfaction of revenge for the murders at Little High Rock Canyon and no stories to tell.

At the start of the onslaught, Sheriff Ferrel tried to keep the Nevada State Police from joining the fight mainly to keep them from sharing in the reward. Joe Reeder quickly settled this argument when he shouted: "Oh Hell! Let 'em have their way. The Injuns are just as apt to shoot a sonuvabitch of a state policeman as one of us." On this happy note, the attack began.

Sheriff Lamb, who arrived later, would dryly comment that three average men armed with .30-.30 rifles—even cowardly ranch hands—could have stood on top of the bluff overlooking Mike's camp and should he have refused to surrender could have wiped out him and his family without exposing themselves to danger. Such was not the case.

Mike, hearing gunfire and seeing Heney running toward camp, charged the posse on foot trying to lure the attackers away from his children. He was packing a .40-.52 Henry black powder rifle, most likely the same weapon he packed in the battle of the upper Ochoco River Valley when Has No Horse was brought to his knees in 1868.[18] Jim had a .38 Savage automatic pistol with only one clip of bullets. Jake carried an ancient Colt cap-and-ball handgun and Charlie was armed with a black powder shotgun shooting a charge of small rocks or anything else that would fit down the barrel. The women would fight with bows, arrows and spears. This against a posse equipped with new high-velocity repeating rifles and sidearms.

Shoshoni Mike, with his body half shot away, was the first to fall but he refused to die. Propping himself up on one elbow he encouraged his family to fight. In the three hour battle which followed hell itself was unleashed. Led by the Nevada State Police, the posse made no attempt to distinguish between woman, child or man but instead fired on anything that moved. Jennie was shot as she tried to crawl to Mike's side. As the Ute woman fell, Heney ran to her screaming. Ignoring danger, she held her mother's face to her breast until Jennie's eyes dimmed forever.

Little by little the Indians gave way down Rabbit Creek draw. Eighteen-year-old Heney, now armed with a spear, was crawling down

---

18 For more on this fight see *Thunder Over the Ochoco*, Vol. III, Chapter 147, "The Land You Left Me—I Have Lost!".

the dry wash when she found her brother Jim with one bullet left in the .38 automatic he had taken from Harry Cambron. Posse members running wild, galloped past their hiding spot blasting away at Jake and Charlie who were desperately trying to escape. Sneaking down the wash on foot, Ed Hogle spotted Jim. Instantly Heney stood up in front of her brother and faced the approaching gunman. With a provocative smile, she pulled up her torn skirt to expose her womanhood and moved toward the astonished cowboy with a weaving shuffling dance holding her ragged dress above her waist as she advanced. Stopped in mid-stride, Hogle stared in fascination. Suddenly, Heney dropped to the ground and Jim fired his last shot before being cut to ribbons by a snarl of bullets. Hogle staggered back clutching his arms to his chest yelling, "My gawd! I've been hit!" No one believed him until he stumbled backward some forty feet and toppled over dead.

In the aftermath of Hogle's death, the posse went berserk. Eat-em-up Jake and Catchum Charlie were wounded in a frenzied charge. Although both were hit many times, they managed to crawl to cover and continue firing until their ammunition was gone. At that point, Jake—a 13-year-old boy who had never been a warrior—panicked and was literally shot to pieces as he ran. Charlie, his 14-year-old brother with three bullets already in his body, jumped up crying, caught Jake in his arms and was shot in turn. Later when the frozen bodies were collected, the two boys could not be pried apart and were buried together.

As the posse raked the sagebrush with bullets, Snake—once a joyful girl—was crouched under an overhanging bank with the baby strapped to her back. In an effort to protect her child, Snake stayed out of the fray but when the sound of rifles ceased for a moment she raised her head only to be caught in a crossfire. Snake pitched backward and lay still, the baby's head hanging in the bloody snow and muck. This crying infant would never know the mother who died to save her life.

Even little Hattie and Cleve took part in the battle throwing rocks and even fistfuls of gravel at the rampaging horsemen before Heney slipped in and took them down the rocky arroyo. Unfortunately, she was seen. Heney tried to defend the children with a short spear tipped with the blade of a sheep shear but a Nevada State Policeman slipped up behind her, threw a coat over her head and wrestled her down. The Shoshoni girl was then hog-tied. Cleve was roped while Hattie huddled by the trussed-up body of her sister, too young to understand what was happening.

During the one-sided battle, the Indians had managed to retreat nearly a mile down the snow covered gulch. When the bounty hunters rode back up to where Mike had fallen they were due for a shock. He was trying in vain to reach his rifle which brought on another round of shots. Every cowboy who rode by emptied his gun at Mike. One observer claimed Mike was so riddled with bullets that his stomach was shot completely away but the old dog soldier—still propped up on one elbow—his eyes glistening with hatred, stared them down. His head-dress, once so proudly worn in battle, lay dirty and disheveled on the ground stained with blood and mire. When his attackers saw that he was still alive but unable to move, Ben Cambron walked up and pried Mike's mouth open with his rifle barrel to see how old he was by looking at his teeth. He then asked, "What kind of damn Indian are you?"

The Sundown Trail was beckoning as Mike glared at Cambron and snarled: "Shoshoni! I am Shoshoni Mike!" And with that remark, given almost like a war-chant, the last Snake dog soldier turned his head away and greeted his old comrades in the Milky Way.[19]

Two days after the brutal assault on Mike's starving family—bal-lyhooed as the last Indian war fought in the United States—the *Nevada Silver State* would headline: "Band of Murderous Shoshones Wiped Out By Posse."[20] And so they were. Blasting a hole in the frozen ground with a case of dynamite brought in by buckboard from the Golconda Mine, the Indian bodies were dragged in with horses and dumped into a mass grave. Onlookers by the hundreds from Jordan Valley, Winnemucca and surrounding country came to see the bodies and were angry that they hadn't been left on the desert for public display. Cheated of one spectacle, they thronged around the living captives making their survival even more miserable.

Heney, Cleve, Hattie and the baby were placed in the Winnemucca jail where Heney covered her face with a blanket to avoid the stares of

---

19 The Nevada Historical Society has a picture of Mike's body and grave marker in Rabbit Creek wash. This is the only known photo ever taken of Shoshoni Mike.

20 *The Silver State*, Winnemucca, Nevada, February 28, 1911. The battle site was within 60 miles of the Oregon border and freedom in the Owyhee Canyon, ancient hunting grounds of the White Knife Snakes.

the curious. Paiute women were permitted in the cell corridor and through them, Heney signaled for a pair of scissors so that she might cut her hair to mourn her dead properly. The request was refused for fear she would kill herself and the children. Oddly throughout this ordeal, Lizard Harris—with the blood of warriors cruising through her veins—never once visited her sisters and brother and refused to care for the younger ones, including Snake's baby. The blame for this lack of compassion can be placed on Lige Harris' fear of adverse public opinion and Lizard being a dutiful wife submitted to her husband's demands.

Others were adding their comments to the tragic event. Harry Preacher—leader of the Eastern Shoshoni—was giving interviews in which he confirmed that Shoshoni Mike was a Snake and he was glad Mike had been killed because he made life more complicated for the reservation Indians by roaming free which was probably true.[21] Only World War I stopped the media craze over Mike and his refusal to conform to government regulations. All of Mike's possessions after being held for evidence were given over to the posse as souvenirs. The $50 cash found on the bodies of the dead Indians was used to pay for their inquest.

Supposedly for their safety, the captives were taken to the Reno jail in a closed carriage. Meanwhile, the posse members returned home heroes, wined and dined by all, chased by pretty girls previously unavailable, slated for fame and glory the rest of their days. The only thing they didn't receive was the promised reward money.

On May 1, 1911, Heney, Hattie, Cleve and the baby were transferred to the Carson City Indian School. *The Reno Gazette* would marvel: "The squaw was resplendent in a late model black hat, cream puff dress and red ribbons galore." A far cry from the bloody rags she was wearing when captured. Four months later, Heney again made headlines when she and her best friend, Ida Best—a Shoshoni girl—vanished without a trace. Ida did return to Carson City a short time later and Heney eventually did too. Immediately upon Heney's return, the four captives were taken under guard to the Fort Hall Indian Reservation. Here, they all—with the exception of the baby—contracted tuberculosis and died in 1912. Snake's child was then adopted by a white couple and given

---

21   Statement of Harry Preacher appearing in *The Wells Herald*, Elko, Nevada, March 22, 1911.

the name of Mary Jo.[22] End of story . . . but not quite.

On October 1, 1910—three months before Shoshoni Mike made his final bid for freedom—Evan Estep took charge as superintendent of the Fort Hall Reservation, a job he held until the spring of 1914. Cut from the same mold as Sam Parrish, the former superintendent of the abolished Malheur Reservation, Estep was a tough administrator who believed in the integrity of the Indians placed under his care and looked upon them not as government wards but as equals to their white neighbors. This was not a popular concept in the American West and Estep no doubt believed that Shoshoni Mike was no more guilty of wrongdoing than his white accusers. Five days after Mike was killed, Estep warned all whites, who had a habit of poaching on Indian lands, not to stray across the reservation boundary. If they ignored his warning, he would order the Indian police to arrest them with a resultant confiscation of arms, fishing gear and possible maximum fine of $200.[23] This notification didn't sit well with the local offenders, especially when he began arresting trespassers.

Like Shoshoni Mike, other Indians were accused of rustling. Estep again shocked everyone when he defended the Indians claiming the rustlers were white men led by the notorious "Six-shooter Sal." According-ing to Estep, this woman gang-leader had stolen at least 1,000 horses and 3,000 cattle from the Indians over a 10-year period. He tried, but couldn't get a conviction. As Estep out it, "The average white jury does not appear to regard it as much of an offense to steal from an Indian.[24] This was the man who adopted Shoshoni Mike's infant granddaughter, the sole survivor of the last Indian battle fought on the North American continent . . . 21 years after the massacre at Wounded Knee, South Dakota.

Mary Jo Estep was raised in white society and lived in Montana and New Mexico before the family settled on the Yakima Indian Reservation in 1924. The Shoshoni girl, who never married, eventually became

---

22 Hyde in his *Last Free Man*, p. 239, would state that the baby was adopted by Harry Eastep at Chemawa, Oregon where there was an Indian school similar to the one at Carson City, Nevada. He obtained this information from Effie Mona Mack's *The Indian Massacre of 1911*. This is beyond doubt a misspelling of Evan W. Estep's name. I could find no record of a Harry Eastep (or Evan Estep) at an Oregon Indian school. However, Mary Jo Estep was a school teacher and may have been the "Eastep" referred to.

23 *Pocatello Tribune*, March 4, 1911.

24 Evan W. Estep to Commissioner of Indian Affairs, March 21, 1912, Records, United States Indian Service, U. S. National Archives.

an elementary school teacher. In a 1988 interview with the Associated Press, Mary Jo told of how she was taken off the cradle board on her dead mother's back and raised by the Esteps. "The white people [my adoptive parents] treated me just like one of them." She would also note that "most of my friends are non-Indians."

Mary Jo never sought many details about the massacre of the Daggett family. She didn't know Shoshoni Mike was her grandfather until she read Dayton Hyde's *The Last Free Man*, published in 1973. At that time Mary Jo would have been 63 years old.

In 1992, Estep—then 82—entered the Good Samaritan Health Care Center in Yakima, Washington complaining that she felt tired. On the morning of December 19, she was accidentally given three doses of prescription medicine intended for another patient.[25] The error was discovered within a half hour but Estep's attending physician ordered that no corrective measures be taken. That was because Mary Jo had signed a form barring "heroic measures" to keep her alive. It said nothing about treating reversible conditions. Estep was informed about the incorrect medicine but was not told the severity of her condition or given any treatment options. A nurse who had power of attorney over Estep's health matters declined the nursing home's offer to have the patient rushed to a hospital. According to the nurse, she felt it was too late to be of any benefit to Mary Jo.[26]

Several of Estep's friends arrived at the nursing home that afternoon to pick her up for a Christmas party. She remained alert for much of the day, but her heart rate and blood pressure fell in the evening and she died around 11:30 p.m.[27] Esther Jarnecke, a friend from Wapato, would comment, "All we could do was stay at her side until the end." Louis Jarnecke put it more bluntly. "You look at what happened here, and you could say she died at the hands of the white man, too." Snake Daggett, who died with a bullet in her head at the age of 19, would have

---

25 According to the Washington Department of Social and Health Services, the incorrect medicines were Tenormin and Apresoline for hypertension and Procordia XL for heart problems.

26 For more on this tragic accident see "Probe deepens in death of Indian massacre survivor," *The Bulletin*, Bend, Oregon, March 17, 1993.

27 Two separate death certificates were issued for Estep. Two days after her death, her attending physician wrote "age-related" for contributing factors to the cause of death. On December 23, a new death certificate issued by the Yakima County Corner listed "accidental ingestion of prescription drugs" as a contributing factor.

been proud of her daughter born on the edge of a Surprise Valley hay field during that hot summer of 1910.

After Shoshoni Mike Daggett was gunned down in 1911, only Dave Chocktote remained of the men who rode with Has No Horse in their youth. Has No Horse himself would die in a Nevada prison three years later. Shoshoni control of the Ochoco was blotted out forever but it is debatable as to whether American administration was any better. About all that can be said for the white invaders is—to paraphrase the old Roman warrior Julius Caesar—they came, they saw, they conquered. With that, I leave it to writers more gifted than I to narrate the outcome of the 20th century.

> *The west is dead my friend*
> *But writers hold the seed*
> *And what they saw*
> *Will live and grow*
> *Again to those who read.*
>
> **Charles M. Russell**
> Western Artist, 1917

Appendices

LIST OF SETTLERS
BIBLIOGRAPHY
INDEX

THE FIRST SETTLERS

A partial list of 5,000 plus residents of Crook County at the turn of the 20th century. At the time of creation in 1882, Crook County included present Deschutes County, Jefferson County, the southern third of Wheeler County and the extreme southwest corner of Grant County. Information taken from Wasco County files prior to 1882; Crook County files after 1882; Portland Oregon Journal, March 31, 1927; Illustrated History of Central Oregon, Spokane, 1905; the History of Crook County published by the Crook County Historical Society in 1981; and personal journals covering a 40 year period from 1868 to 1908. Although some accounts name people living in central Oregon prior to 1868 they were merely searching for a place to establish a land claim. The true settlement didn't occur until the late spring of 1868. Names appearing in parenthesis are those of wives and the year of marriage if known. Most certainly this list is incomplete and children have not been recorded. Most married couples could account for an average of five children each. Each settler's name is followed by the year in which they came.

Abbot, John (single)	1880	Atterbury, John (single)	1880
Abbott, Joel (family)	1892	Awbery, Marshall (single)	1880
Abbott, John (single)	1880	Bailey, Love (single)	1870
Adams, William		Bailey, S.M. (Fay Hodges, 1905)	1902
(Nancy Maupin, 1867)	1871	Bailey, Zeke (single)	1870
Adamson, D.P.		Baldwin, David (family)	1874
(Tillie LaFollette, 1898)	1895	Baldwin, Tom (family)	1879
Alchul, Charles (single)	1871	Balfour, Thomas (family)	1882
Aldridge, Dave (family)	1879	Balsby, Charles (single)	1884
Allen, Albert (single)	1868	Barnes, Elisha (Suzanna Glenn)	1868
Allen, Andy (single)	1868	Barnes, George	
Allen, B.F. (Matilda Tate, 1862)	1871	(Ginevra Marks, 1870)	1868
Allen, Hardy		Barnes, William (single)	1868
(Daisy Davidson, 1900)	1874	Beamer, _____ (single)	1868
Allen, James M.		Bedewell, Charles (single)	1884
(1. Hanna Riggs		Beeler, Ferrel (Mary Cattwell)	1870
2. Cynthia Butler, 1871)	1868	Beirl, Louis (single)	1899
Allen, William (single)	1871	Belieu, Anthony (single)	1868
Ammons, Richard (Nora Birdsong)	1900	Belieu, Collit (single)	1868
Anderson, Billie (family)	1868	Belknap, Horace	
Anderson, Hallie (single)	1868	(Wilda Ketchum, 1888)	1884
Anderson, William		Bell, M.H. (family)	1873
(Lucinda Crain, 1860)	1871		

Bell, Wells A.
   (Effie Vanderpool, 1895)   1894
Bennett, John
   (Mary Elizabeth, 1857)   1885
Bernard, Charles
   (Rosa Delore, 1891)   1887
Bernard, Henry (Ethel Drummond)   1904
Biggs, Richard
   (Laura Starclift, 1894)   1889
Birchtorf, Henry (single)   1880
Birdsong, Henry
   (Emma Farthing, 1878)   1888
Black, Addison (family)   1880
Blakely, James (single)   1868
Blakely, Joe (single)   1869
Blevens, Pendleton
   (Julia Ann Welch, 1860)   1882
Blodgett, Victor (single)   1897
Boegli, William
   (Amanda Adams, 1901)   1889
Bolsby, Charles (Lily Delore, 1892)   1884
Bolter, Edward (family)   1882
Booth, William (Lucy Corey, 1877)   1871
Bosher, Henry (single)   1884
Bosko, D. (family)   1882
Boss, Jack (single)   1884
Bostwick, Issac (single)   1868
Bostwick, Neum (family)   1882
Bostwick, William (family)   1880
Boyce, A.W. (Mary Weber, 1869)   1881
Boyle, Sofronia (family)   1880
Breese, Collit (family)   1884
Breese, John (Mary Rooke)   1884
Breese, Richard
   (Charlotte Gray, 1878)   1889
Brennan, Thomas
   (Polly Hinkle, 1889)   1882
Breyman, A.H. (family)   1873
Brotherhead, Charles (single)   1868
Brown, Michael
   (Jennie McCullough, 1908)   1881
Brown, S.S. (family)   1879
Brown, W.W. (single)   1882
Brummer, Hanis
   (Beatrice Welburn, 1909)   1880
Buchanan, T.F. (Miss Hale, 1890)   1887
Burkhart, George (single)   1868
Burkhart, Raymond (single)   1868
Burmeister, Henry (family)   1882
Burnham, A.J. (single)   1880
Bushnell, C. (family)   1882
Bushnell, C.L. (Bess Cates, 1915)   1908

Bushnell, Johnson (family)   1880
Cadle, William
   (Margaret Johnson, 1882)   1880
Calavan, Joel (Aver Spear, 1879)   1895
Calbreath, Clarence (family)   1876
Calbreath, John (family)   1868
Calbreath, Thomas (family)   1868
Campbell, Edward
   (Sarah Rodman, 1882)   1878
Campbell, John (family)   1878
Cannon, Anthony (family)   1869
Carey, E.R. (family)   1868
Carey, F. (family)   1873
Carey, Louisa (family)   1873
Carmichal, Richard (family)   1880
Carroll, Samuel (Margaret Scott)   1869
Carson, Mark
   (Elizabeth, _____, 1849)   1884
Cartwright, Charles (family)   1868
Castle, Ike (family)   1882
Castle, Lem (family)   1882
Cattrell, James (family)   1868
Cecil, Lige (family)   1880
Cecil, W.C. (family)   1871
Cerry, G.N. (family)   1880
Chamberlain, Jasper (family)   1878
Champion, Arthur (single)   1898
Childers, Ben (single)   1874
Chitwood, Pleas (family)   1868
Christiani, Michael (family)   1873
Churchell, George (single)   1880
Circle, Vince (family)   1882
Circle, W.C. (single)   1880
Circle, William (family)   1873
Clark, H. (family)   1868
Clark, William (family)   1868
Clarno, Charles (family)   1870
Claypool, John (family)   1868
Claypool, Wayne
   (Louisa Elkins, 1857)   1868
Cleek, Henry (family)   1876
Cline, Chaste (family)   1887
Cline, Dr. Cass (Emily Marchfork)   1887
Cline, George (family)   1872
Cline, Meta (family)   1882
Coff, Fannie (single)   1880
Coffelt, James (Mary Pickem, 1900)   1899
Collver, O.G. (Annie Fields, 1886)   1885
Colman, Henry (family)   1868
Combs, James (Jane Dyer, 1847)   1870
Combs, John (family)   1871
Compton, Sam (Jane, _____, 1876)   1878

Conant, Edward (single) — 1869
Congleton, William (single) — 1880
Conklin, Bessie (single) — 1899
Connell, Lawrence (single) — 1883
Cornett, George (Effie Toney, 1893) — 1881
Cornez, Julius (single) — 1887
Corum, Sam (family) — 1883
Cox, James (family) — 1880
Crabtree, John (family) — 1868
Crain, A.J. (Mary Lytle, 1865) — 1880
Crain, A.J. (family) — 1880
Cram, Perry (family) — 1883
Crandall, Jesse (single) — 1876
Cranston, Bill (single) — 1868
Crooks, Aaron (family) — 1872
Crooks, Joseph
    (America Warren, 1873) — 1872
Culver, O.C. (family) — 1880
Curl, Gove (family) — 1878
Curtis, Jack (family) — 1890
Cyrus, Enoch
    (Mary Sutherlin, 1869) — 1882
Darling, Charles (family) — 1891
Daugherty, Lou (family) — 1868
Davenport, Alec (single) — 1898
Davenport, William
    (Mary Hassler, 1891) — 1898
Davis, Elias — 1893
Davis, Harry (single) — 1880
Davis, John (family) — 1868
Davis, Peter (single) — 1876
Daw, Frank (single) — 1870
Delore, Alex (single) — 1880
Delore, Augustine (Zoe _____) — 1882
Delore, Peter (family) — 1880
Demaris, Enoch
    (Almeda Roberts, 1863) — 1880
Demaris, John (Jane O'Kelly 1883) — 1886
Dillard, Henry (family) — 1880
Dillard, Horace (single) — 1880
Dillon, L. (family) — 1880
Dixon, Harve (family) — 1880
Dobbs, Eli (Sara Davis, 1883) — 1885
Dodson, George (family) — 1880
Doon, Ah (single) — 1878
Doon, Moy (Single) — 1878
Dorsey, John (single) — 1870
Dorsey, Robert (single) — 1870
Douthit, J.H. (family) — 1876
Driggs, Katrina (single) — 1882
Drips, Jesse (single) — 1880
Dunston, Jack (single) — 1880

Edmondson, William (single) — 1885
Edwards, Henry (Mattie Zell, 1899) — 1900
Elkins, Collins (Mamie Johnson) — 1870
Elkins, James (Helen Millard, 1862) — 1870
Elliott, Dause (family) — 1885
Elliott, Jim (family) — 1880
Elliott, John (Frances Backus, 1891) — 1876
Elliott, Kinman (Nancy Pickrell) — 1876
Ellis, M.R. (single) — 1888
Estes, Ben (single) — 1885
Estes, George (single) — 1885
Evans, H.P. (family) — 1885
Ewell, Jim (single) — 1870
Ewell, Ples (single) — 1870
Faulkner, John (family) — 1878
Fogle, Anton (family) — 1876
Foley, Lige (family) — 1876
Foren, Thomas (family) — 1876
Foren, William (single) — 1878
Forest, Francis
    (Rebecca Rodman, 1885) — 1876
Foster, Jasper (single) — 1871
Foster, William
    (1. Mary Marks, 1869
    2. Mary Faulkner, 1879) — 1869
Foster, William (Mary Allen, 1876) — 1871
Foster, William H.
    (Josephine Brown, 1897) — 1887
Fought, James (family) — 1882
Fowler, Lark (single) — 1880
Frazier, Sarah (family) — 1884
Freeland, Ed (family) — 1880
Fried, Leo (family) — 1880
Friend, Columbus
    (Henrietta Crooks Hale, 1888) — 1875
Fry, A.B. (single) — 1868
Fryrear, John (family) — 1876
Fuller, James
    (Irene Demaris Hereford, 1901) — 1897
Gage, John (Frances Price) — 1877
Gaines, Charles (family) — 1881
Garner, J.O. (single) — 1885
Garret, Harlan (Mary Hash, 1873) — 1869
Gates, George
    (Olive Johnson, 1893) — 1905
Gates, William (Mary _____) — 1869
Gee, Hugh (Merlie Wilkins, 1906) — 1904
Gerardo, Joe
    (Josephine Rossi, 1902) — 1905
Gerow, Arnold (family) — 1877
Gessner, Van (Annie Fields, 1886) — 1883

Gibson, Hiram
    (Margarete King, 1875)   1885
Gilchrist, John
    (Nellie Parrish, 1879)   1878
Gillenwater, Luther (family)   1888
Gird, Nathan (single)   1881
Glaze, Tillman (Ann _____)   1877
Glenn, Edward (single)   1869
Goulett, Fred (single)   1884
Graham, Dick (family)   1877
Graham, Robert (single)
Grant, Alfred (Bertie Hazen, 1900)   1900
Graves, Charles
    (Annie Fields, 1886)   1883
Gray, Henry
    (Rebekah Hunsaker, 1875)   1876
Gregory, James (Maud Troth, 1897)   1901
Grimes, Henry
    (Samantha Elliott, 1871)   1877
Gulliford, Jacob
    (Elizabeth Vanderpool, 1872)   1878
Gulliford, Jasper
    (Elizabeth Hodges, 1872)   1878
Gulliford, William
    (Ellen Haptonstall)   1869
Hackleman, Abram
    (Eleanor Davis, 1862)   1878
Hale, D.H.
    (Henrietta Crooks Brown)   1869
Hale, John (family)   1869
Hale, W.S. (family)   1876
Hamilton, Sam (family)   1878
Hamilton, Thomas
    (Lorenda Crooks, 1889)   1873
Hamilton, Tom (family)   1878
Hamilton, William (family)   1876
Hamilton, William (Jane Gholson)   1876
Hamlin, Reason (family)   1868
Harbin, Almire (family)   1881
Hardman, William (single)   1868
Haresty, Charles (family)   1876
Harmon, John (family)   1876
Harrington, R.P. (Ada Crane 1891)   1882
Harrison, John (family)   1881
Harrison, William (family)   1881
Hash, John (Elizabeth Edwards)   1878
Hawkins, James
    (Mary Thomason, 1893)   1894
Hearing, Amos
    (Elizabeth Nye Hon Thompson)   1876
Hedgepath, Manford (single)   1873
Heisler, Jeff (single)   1873

Heisler, Monroe (single)   1876
Heisler, Susan
    (William Vanderpool)   1870
Heisler, William
    (Martha McConnell, 1851)   1870
Hendrickson, Rufus (single)   1873
Henkle, Joe (family)   1878
Henry, Allen (single)   1876
Hensley, Edward (Mary Dow, 1905)   1904
Hereford, Franklin
    (Irene Demaris, 1887)   1876
Hereford, John
    (Emily Morgan, 1860)   1876
Hill, Taylor (family)   1873
Hindman, Samuel (single)   1869
Hinkle, M.A. (family)   1876
Hinton, Alex (Bessie Anderson)   1876
Hinton, Ben (Mary _____)   1880
Hodges, Alexander
    (1. Abigail Zumwalt, 1850
    2. Dulcina Tomlinson, 1853)   1869
Hodges, Arthur
    (Stella Gesner, 1900)   1870
Hodges, Monroe
    (Rhoda Wilson, 1855)   1871
Hodges, Silas
    (Susannah Hearing, 1883)   1870
Hogan, Willam (single)   1876
Holman, Hardy (single)   1869
Holman, John (single)   1869
Hon, Clyde (Daisy Zevely, 1894)   1886
Hon, John
    (1. Olive Cayle
    2. Ida Klum)   1886
Horsell, William
    (Martha Mertsching, 1912)   1900
Houston, Charlie
    (Sara _____, 1888)   1889
Houston, Floyd
    (Alva Allen, 1897)   1886
Houston, James
    (Sarah Gregory, 1887)   1888
Houston, Thomas
    (Sallie Ammons, 1894)   1886
Howard, Howard (family)   1873
Howard, James (family)   1880
Howard, Joseph (family)   1873
Howard, Lytle (family)   1873
Hrivnak, Andrew
    (Anne Ontko, 1909)   1910
Hudson, Harry (single)   1878
Humstead, Gid (family)   1890

Hunsaker, Joe
    (Elizabeth Campbell, 1854)   1873
Huston, Knox
    (Victoria Childers, 1866)   1878
Huston, Sid (single)   1871
Huston, William (family)   1871
Hyde, Edwin
    (Elizabeth Evans, 1873)   1898
Isinhort, S. (single)   1881
Jackson, Oliver (family)   1876
Jaggi, John (single)   1876
James, T.B. (family)   1868
Jayne, Andrew (family)   1876
Jinkins, Tom (family)   1869
Johnson, B.F.
    (Jennie McPheeters, 1898)   1872
Johnson, Bill (Mary Street)   1886
Johnson, Columbus
    (Frances Ketchum, 1893)   1873
Johnson, Ewen
    (Nancy Stinson, 1854)   1868
Johnson, Jasper (family)   1876
Johnson, William (single)   1873
Jones, (Allie) Alvis
    (1. Ora Powell, 1896
    2. Mary Carter, 1904)   1889
Jones, Ben (family)   1876
Jones, Watt (family)   1876
Jory, Stephen
    (Melinda Crooks, 1880)   1873
Judy, George (family)   1868
Kester, Arnold (Delia Baker, 1880)   1889
Ketchum, I.L. (Sarah Dingee, 1886)   1878
Kinder, W.H. (Elizabeth Pollard)   1878
King, Samuel (single)   1897
Kirkham, William (family)   1882
Kizer, George (family)   1876
Knighten, Aldon (family)   1878
Knox, Roscoe (Matilda Buoy, 1861)   1887
Koch, Henry (Ella Sturdivan, 1899)   1906
Koch, Jacob (Annie _____, 1901)   1904
LaFollette, Jerome
    (Sophia Howard, 1851)   1869
LaFollette, Thomas
    (Margaret Allen, 1876)   1871
Lambert, Nick (single)   1882
Lampshire, Steve (family)   1880
Landgon, Perry (single)   1881
Langdon, George (single)   1881
Langdon, Luke
    (Emma LaFrancis, 1875)   1880
Larson, Lars (Helga _____)   1904

Lattie, John (single)   1882
Lawson, James (family)   1868
Lawson, John (Rose Miller, 1873)   1874
Leach, Nancy (single)   1869
Lee, Columbus (family)   1880
Lee, Jim (single)   1892
Lee, John (family)   1869
Lewis, Charles (single)   1885
Liggett, Leander
    (Catherine Cowan, 1878)   1880
Lillard, Charles
    (Grace Bedell, 1894)   1880
Lister, Thomas (Mary Geter)   1870
Little, Andy (family)   1880
Logan, Cecil (single)   1871
Logan, Lysander (single)   1870
Logan, Sam (single)   1882
Logan, Thomas (family)   1868
Long, Charles (single)   1882
Long, Joel (single)   1882
Long, Thomas
    (America Calavan, 1849)   1868
Loughlin, Edgar
    (Elizabeth Darnielle)   1898
Lowery, Russell (family)   1884
Luckey, James
    (Eunice Robbins, 1881)   1868
Luckey, John
    (1.Ella S. Miller, 1864
    2. Sallie Hodges, 1881)   1868
Lucky, Eugene
    (Molly Guilliford, 1872)   1868
Luster, Charles (single)   1881
Lytle, Andrew (Sarah Romp, 1868)   1870
Mackey, James (family)   1880
Mailing, Charles (single)   1873
Markam, Barney (Harriett _____)   1882
Marks, Attwood (single)   1869
Marks, Bluford (family)   1869
Marks, James (single)   1869
Marks, William (family)   1868
Marshall, James (single)   1868
Marshall, W.B. (family)   1885
Martin, John (single)   1880
Martni, Joe (single)   1885
Matley, Ruben (single)   1882
Maupin, Garret (single)   1879
McAllister, George (single)   1873
McAllister, Lew (single)   1873
McCabe, William (family)   1882
McCaffery, Frank
    (Minnie Truax, 1895)   1905

McCall, Henry (Dorothy Lawson) 1911
McClun, James
    (Carrie Berry, 1900) 1905
McCoin, William (family) 1880
McCord, Gus
    (Amanda Gulliford, 1885) 1885
McDonald, Frank (family) 1882
McDowell, George (single) 1868
McDowell, H. (family) 1882
McDowell, James (single) 1868
McDowell, Oswald (family) 1880
McDowell, William (single) 1868
McFarland, W.R.
    (Lucy Jane Masterson, 1874) 1882
McKenzie, Charles
    (Johanna Farrel, 1885) 1906
McLerson, _____ (family) 1882
McMath, Mike (family) 1882
McMeekin, William (family) 1882
McMeen, James
    (Emma Williams, 1884) 1884
McNeer, James (family) 1885
Mealey, (Star) C.J. (single) 1879
Merritt, Ed (single) 1883
Meyer, Isidor
    (Philippina Berz, 1894) 1882
Mickel, Isadore (Blanche _____) 1900
Miller, George
    (Estella Walton, 1861) 1871
Miller, Grant (Sally Hinton, 1900) 1884
Miller, James (Katherine Pringle) 1868
Miller, John
    (Lillie Chambers, 1890) 1904
Miller, Nelse (family) 1882
Miller, Richard
    (1. Nancy Jane Lawson, 1871
    2. Celestine Johnson, 1878) 1868
Millican, George (family) 1868
Milligan, Cornelius
    (Elsie Dollar, 1901) 1876
Milligan, V.H. (Anna _____) 1883
Milliron, William
    (Sarah Lemley, 1859) 1880
Mills, Ike (Ann Loughlin, 1883) 1882
Modie, Lee (family) 1885
Mogan, Frank
    (Martha Mogan 1883) 1880
Mogan, Mike
    (Martha McLeod 1878) 1882
Monroe, Thomas (Mary Snedeker) 1869
Montgomery, Cam (family) 1880
Montgomery, J.M.(family) 1885

Montgomery, Kennedy
    (Ellen Blakely, 1856) 1871
Moore, M.A. (family) 1882
Moore, Zeth (family) 1880
Morgan, Orange (single) 1869
Mulvahill, Mike (single) 1897
Narcross, Jake (family) 1869
Neese, Clay (family) 1881
Nelson, Preston (single) 1873
Nelson, Rufus (single) 1883
Newsome, Sam
    (Sarah Simpson, 1876) 1871
Nicely, Walter (Marie Ontko 1916) 1908
Nichols, B.F. (family) 1871
Nichols, Lyn
    (Florence Grimes, 1902) 1876
Nickolas, B.F. (family) 1871
Nickolas, Larch (family) 1870
Noble, Andrew
    (Varina Shelton, 1892) 1871
Noble, George (single) 1870
Noble, John (family) 1868
Noble, William
    (Sarah Sultzberger, 1864) 1871
Nye, Granville (single) 1885
Nye, Manford
    (Adell Yancey, 1892) 1884
Nye, Michael (Harriet Pike, 1842) 1871
O'Dell, Bob (Nancy Hinton, 1891) 1880
O'Dell, Clint (single) 1880
O'Dell, Henry (single) 1880
O'Kelly, C.J. (Lydia Elliott, 1885) 1880
O'Kelly, Joseph (family) 1880
O'Neil, C.C. (Mary Clarke, 1894) 1882
Offit, Z.B. (single) 1880
Ontko, Andrew, Sr. (family) 1910
Osborn, G.H. (family) 1880
Osborn, Robert
    (Ida Gulliford, 1887) 1880
Osborne, George
    (Ella Rogers, 1877) 1878
Palmehn, Charles (single) 1881
Palmer, A.C. (family) 1880
Palmer, J. (family) 1895
Parker, Edmund
    (Gertrude Richards, 1895) 1885
Parrish, Zan (family) 1881
Pattee, George (single) 1880
Peck, William
    (Mary Newman, 1872) 1881
Pengra, B.J. (family) 1881
Pengra, Billy (single) 1883

Perry, E.R. (family)	1881	Riqua, Charles (single)	1868
Perry, Lawrence		Riser, _____ (single)	1884
(Rosella White, 1863)	1888	Roba, George (Mary Soijka, 1886)	1887
Pett, Charles (single)	1877	Robbins, Abner (family)	1868
Philaber, Richard (single)	1880	Roberts, George	
Pickett, William (single)	1868	(Josephine Roberts, 1906)	1905
Pitcher, Billy (single)	1871	Roberts, Hughes (Phoebe _____)	1891
Poindexter, James		Roberts, Joseph	
(Elvira _____, 1850)	1896	(Sophronia Rice, 1886)	1887
Poindexter, Perry		Robinson, James (single)	1895
(Isabella Wilson, 1884)	1881	Robinson, John	
Pollard, W.R. (family)	1880	(Malinda Rush, 18780	1899
Polly, John (single)	1871	Rodgers, Clark (family)	1879
Porfily, Ralph		Rose, Jack (single)	1868
(Bertha Maben, 1909)	1889	Ross, Morgan (family)	1882
Porter, Tom (family)	1881	Rush, John (family)	1884
Post, Wallace (Lucy, Herbert, 1866)	1885	Schmidt, William	
Post, Walter (single)	1885	(Sarah Lowery, 1900)	1885
Pough, Bill (single)	1881	Schoolin, Jerry (single)	1882
Powell, Daniel (family)	1870	Senecal, Dedron (family)	1876
Powell, John (Millie York)	1870	Senecal, Marcell	
Powell, Marion (family)	1870	(Mary Delore, 1874)	1900
Powell, Mark		Settle, I.M. (family)	1868
(1. Victoria Thompson, 1880)		Shelly, Troy (family)	1884
2. Aver Zeverly Gerow, 1894)	1870	Shepard, Ben (Annie Picket, 1901)	1882
Powell, Oliver (family)	1870	Sheperd, Ben (single)	1882
Powell, Thomas (Amanda Ritter)	1870	Sichel, Mose (family)	1868
Powell, William (single)	1883	Sites, Dr. J.B. (family)	1868
Powers, Buckskin (family)	1880	Sizemore, John (family)	1868
Prantz, Charles (family)	1890	Slater, James (single)	1868
Price, Bruce (family)	1881	Slayton, James (family)	1882
Price, R.S. (family)	1881	Slayton, Samuel	
Prine, Barney (Elizabeth _____)	1868	(Eliza Savery, 1858)	1869
Prine, Dave (single)	1869	Smith, Albert	
Prine, Frank (single)	1868	(Martha Yancey, 1872)	1870
Prine, William (single)	1868	Smith, Alex (single)	1898
Pringle, Clark (family)	1881	Smith, Harry (single)	1869
Pringle, Octa (single)	1881	Smith, Henry (family)	1870
Province, _____ (family)	1885	Smith, J.J. (Olive Forrest, 1897)	1884
Puett, W.H. (family)	1885	Smith, Robert (family)	1868
Quinn, William (Mary Porter, 1864)	1870	Smith, Sam (family)	1868
Rannells, Ed (Stella _____)	1882	Smith, William (single)	1868
Ray, William (family)	1884	Snoderly, Hugh (family)	1884
Read, Perry		Snoderly, James (single)	1869
(Hatie Montgomery, 1873)	1871	Soloman, C.L. (family)	1868
Ream, Charles		Sommerville, John (single)	1868
(1. Ida Dowell, 1873)		Sparks, Aliya (family)	1868
2. Elizabeth Wade, 1895)	1900	Spear, Isaac (Martha Zevely, 1879)	1884
Redmond, F.I. (family)	1905	Splaun, S.S. (single)	1880
Rhodes, Riley (family)	1880	Springer, Barney (Ann Todd, 1883)	1879
Richards, D. (family)	1880	Springer, Guyon	
Richardson, _____ (single)	1884	(Nora Gaucher, 1883)	1887

Sproul, Andy (family)	1868	Thorp, John (single)	1874
Staats, W.H. (Emma Turpen, 1885)	1879	Todd, Johnny (family)	1877
Starr, Samuel		Toms, John (single)	1869
(Anna Williamson, 1870)	1879	Turner, George (single)	1877
Statts, William (family)	1868	Turner, Henry (family)	1877
Stearns, Sydney		Tye, Ng Ah (single)	1884
(Frances Day, 1887)	1883	Uren, Tom (single)	1879
Steers, Lee (Nellie Laughlin, 1890)	1886	Valpey, Edward (family)	1891
Stephenson, Tom (family)	1871	Van Houten, J.P. (family)	1873
Stevens, George		Vanderpool, Dr. Larkin	
(Fannie Cobb, 1898)	1896	(Mary Turnage)	1869
Stewart, David		Vanderpool, James (family)	1873
(Grace Plummer, 1875)	1879	Vanderpool, William Meadows	
Stewart, H.B. (family)	1884	(Elizabeth Templeton, 1874)	1869
Stewart, John (family)	1868	Vanina, Fulgenzio	
Stewart, William (family)	1868	(Catatina Rivera, 1877)	1884
Stone, Milo (single)	1884	Vaughan, Henry (Rose Ruby, 1874)	1881
Street, James (family)	1885	Veazie, Edmond (Harriet Lyle)	1868
Street, Joseph (Nettie Best, 1884)	1886	Venton, Mort (single)	1880
Streithoff, R. (single)	1870	Vining, Daniel (single)	1868
Stroud, Jake (family)	1885	Volrath, _____ (family)	1884
Sturdivan, W.J.		Volrath, R.H. (family)	1881
(Magdalene Brehm, 1879)	1905	Wagner, _____ (single)	1882
Sumner, Ann (family)	1868	Wagner, _____ (family)	1882
Sumner, Anne (family)	1884	Wagonblast, John	
Sumner, John (Eliza Yantis, 1858)	1871	(Mary Payne, 1873)	1904
Sumpter, Alex (family)	1869	Wall, Archie (single)	1874
Sutton, Penelope (single)	1881	Warren, Andy (family)	1868
Swalley, Edward (family)	1884	Webdell, Anthony (family)	1869
Swank, Helen (family)	1885	Wells, W.C. (family)	1869
Swartz, Al (family)	1868	Wheeler, Henry (Dorcas Monroe)	1873
Swartz, Dave (single)	1879	White, Newton	
Swartz, Ike (single)	1872	(1. Catherine Burkhart, 1848)	
Tallman, Annette (single)	1880	2. Anna Woodside, 1852)	1868
Taylor, James (single)	1879	Whittaker, W.H. (family)	1880
Taylor, Joseph		Wichizer, James (single)	1868
(Isabell Rizear, 1876)	1878	Wigle, William	
Templeton, David		(Martha Spalding, 1859)	1886
(Lavina Pell, 1855)	1870	Wiley, Bob (single)	1868
Tetherow, Jack		Wiley, George (single)	1868
(Sophronia Crowe, 1854)	1879	Wilhoit, W.M. (family)	1868
Thomas, Daniel		Williams, Josiah (single)	1869
(Candice Smith, 1870)	1869	Williamson, J.N.	
Thomas, David (single)	1877	(Sarah Forrest, 1882)	1869
Thomlinson, William (family)	1879	Willoughby, Dr. (family)	1872
Thompson, Amos		Wilson, Albert (Ida Hunsaker, 1887)	1887
(Elizabeth Nye Hon, 1852)	1874	Wilson, J. (family)	1880
Thompson, J.M. (family)	1876	Wilson, Robert	
Thompson, John (single)	1880	(Chasity Sutton Lytle, 1863)	1877
Thompson, Riley (_____ Hinton)	1874	Wilt, Marcus	
Thompson, S.G. (single)	1878	(Katherine Creamer, 1879)	1883
Thompson, William (family)	1878		

Windom, James
    (Rebecca Leach, 1884) — 1884
Winkler, Gus (single) — 1878
Winnek, Charles
    (Anna Wallace, 1879) — 1899
Winters, Dave (single) — 1874
Winters, Jerry (single) — 1874
Wood, James
    (Ada Belle Rush, 1902) — 1875
Wood, Joe (family) — 1874
Wood, John (single) — 1874
Wood, Lee (Lena Robinson, 1901) — 1875
Wood, S.S. (family) — 1868
Woods, Lin (family) — 1868

Woods, W.T. (family) — 1880
Wright, Jasper (Rhoda _____) — 1878
Wyman, Charles
    (Makala Hamilton, 1880) — 1879
Yancey, J.P. (Susannah Hegler) — 1881
Yancey, Stephen
    (Sarah Adams, 1893) — 1881
Young, Jerry (family)
Zell, Abraham (family) — 1868
Zell, John (single) — 1870
Zell, Peter (family) — 1881
Zevely, James (Elizabeth Boyle) — 1886
Zevely, John
    (Hannah Walker, 1843) — 1868

BIBLIOGRAPHY

(combined bibliography for volumes 4 & 5)

Books and Articles

- Adams, James Truslow. *The Epic of America*. Washington, D.C., 1931.
- Ade, George. *The Old Time Saloon*. New York, 1993.
- Angel, Myron. *History of Nevada with Illustrations and Biographical Sketches of Its Prominent Men and Pioneers*. Oakland, 1881.
- Amundson, Carroll. *History of the Willamette Valley and Cascade Mountain Military Road Company*. University of Oregon thesis Series #17, 1928.
- Armstrong, David A. *Bullets and Bureaucrats: The Machine Guns and the United States Army 1861-1916*. Westport, New York, 1982.
- Bailey, Paul. *Walkara, Hawk of the Mountains*. Los Angeles, 1956.
- Ballantine, Betty and Ian Ballantine (Eds.). The Native Americans, Atlanta, 1993.
- Bancroft, H.H. *History of Oregon*, Vol. II, 2 vols. San Francisco, 1888.
- ———. "Scrapbooks." Vol. 93. Bancroft Library, Berkeley, California, N.D.
- Blake, Grover C. *Blazing Oregon Trails*. A private publication printed in Bend, Oregon, 1969.
- ———. *Sowing the Seed: The History of the Ochoco National Forest*. Ochoco National Forest, Prineville, Oregon. M.S., 1957.
- ———. *Harney County and Its Rangeland*. Portland, 1950.
- Bourke, Captain John, G. *On the Border with Crook*. New York, 1891.
- Brady, Cyrus Townsend. *Northwest Fights and Fighters*. New York, 1907.
- Breckous, Joseph. *Washakie, Chief of the Shoshoni*. New York, 1927.
- Brimlow, George Francis. *Bannock War of 1878*. Caldwell, Idaho, 1938.
- Brimlow, George Francis. *Harney County and Its Range Land*. Burns, Oregon, 1980.
- Brogan, Phil E. *East of the Cascades*. Portland, 1964.
- Brown, Dee. *Bury My Heart at Wounded Knee: An Indian History of the American West*. New York, 1971.
- Campbell, Arthur. *Antelope: The Saga of a Western Town*. 1990.
- Canfield, Gae Whitney. *Sarah Winnemucca of the Northern Paiutes*. Norman, Oklahoma, 1983.
- Corles, Hank. *The Weiser Indians: Shoshoni Peacemakers*. Salt Lake City, 1990.
- Corning, Howard McKinley, (ed.). *Dictionary of Oregon History*. Portland, 1956.
- Dana, Samuel Trask. *Forest and Range Policy*. New York, 1956.

- DeMoss, Elbert Oliver. *Sweet Oregon: The DeMoss Family Lyric Bands*. Bend, Oregon, 1995.

- Due, John F., and Francis Juris. *Rails to the Ochoco Country*. San Marino, California, 1968.

- DuPont, Henry A. *The Campaign of 1864 in the Valley of Virginia and the Expedition to Lynchburg*. New York, 1925.

- Farrell, Allie M. *Jefferson County Reminiscences*. Portland, Oregon, 1957.

- Fee, Chester Anders. *Chief Joseph, the Biography of a Great Indian*. New York, 1936.

- Forsyth, George A. *The Story of a Soldier*. New York, 1905.

- Foster-Harris. *The Look of the Old West*. 1955.

- Freidel, Frank. *The Presidents of the United States of America*. Washington, D.C., 1981.

- Fussner, F. Smith, (ed.). *Glimpses of Wheeler County's Past*. Portland, 1975.

- Ganoe, Col. William, A. *The History of the United States Army*. A private publication by Eric Lundberg, 1964.

- Garcia, Andrew. *A Tough Trip Through Paradise 1878-1879*. New York, 1967.

- Gaston, Joseph. *Portland, Its History and Builders*. 3 vols., Chicago, 1911.

- Glassley, Ray Hoard. *Pacific Northwest Indian Wars*. Portland, 1953.

- Gregg, Jacob Ray. *Pioneer Days in Malheur County*. Los Angeles, 1950.

- Haines, Francis. *Nez Perce and Shoshoni Influence*. Great American Series. Berkeley, California, 1945.

- Hamersley, T.H.S. *Complete Army and Navy Register of the United States of America*. N.D.

- Hanley, Mike. *Owyhee Trails: The West's Forgotten Corner*. Caldwell, Idaho, 1974.

- Harney, Corbin. *The Way It Is,* Nevada City, California, 1995.

- Harris, Jack. "The White Knife Shoshoni of Nevada." *Accumulation in Seven American Indian Tribes*. New York, 1940.

- Harvey, A.G. *Douglas of the Fir*. Cambridge, Massachusettes, 1947.

- Hasley, John. *The History of Idaho*. Boise, 1910.

- Hatton, Raymond R. *High Desert of Central Oregon*. Portland, 1977.

- Hawthorne, Julian. *The History of the United States: 1846-1912*, Vol. III. 3 vols, New York, 1912.

- Hayes, Rutherford B. *Diary and Letters of Rutherford B. Hayes*. 5 vols. Columbus, Ohio, 1922-1926.

- Hebard, Grace R. *Washakie: An Account of Indian Resistance of the Covered Wagons and Union Pacific Railroad Invasion of Their Territory*. Cleveland, Ohio, 1930.

- Heline, Theodore. *The American Indian*. Los Angeles, 1952.
- Helms, Irene H. *Remembering School Days of Old Crook County*. Prineville, Oregon, 1980.
- Henley, Burr. *Gold from the Grassroots Down: An Historical Profile of the Ochoco Mining District*. Prineville, Oregon: pamphlet, 1980.
- Highsmith, Richard M., (ed.). *Atlas of the Pacific Northwest*. Corvallis, Oregon, 1973.
- Hodge, Fredrick Webb, (ed.). *Handbook of North American Indians North of Mexico*. 2 vols., Bureau of American Ethnology, Smithsonian Institution Bulletin 30. Washington, D.C., 1907.
- Holbrook, Stewart. *A History of American Railroads*. Portland, 1951.
- ———. *Burning an Empire*. New York, 1943.
- ———. *The Rivers of North America: The Columbia*. Portland, 1955.
- Hooper, Albon W. *Indian Affairs and Their Administration, 1849-1860*. University of Pennsylvania Thesis, N.D.
- Hopkins, Sarah Winnemucca. *Life Among the Piutes: Their Wrongs and Claims*. Privately printed, 1883.
- Hosmer, Paul. *Holy Old Mackinaw!* (the timber industry), New York, 1939.
- Howard, Gen. O.O. *Autobiography*. 2 vols., New York, 1907.
- ———. *Famous Indian Chiefs I Have Known*. New York, 1908.
- ———. *My Life and Personal Experiences Among Our Hostile Indians*. Hartford, 1907.
- ———. *Nez Perce Joseph*. Boston, 1881.
- Hunter, George. *Reminiscences of an Old Timer: The Bannock War*. San Francisco, 1887.
- Hyde, Dayton O. *The Last Free Man: The True Story Behind the Massacre of Shoshoni Mike and His Band of Indians in 1911*. New York, 1973.
- Jackman, E.R. and, R.A. Long. *The Oregon Desert*. Caldwell, Idaho, 1969.
- Jackson, Helen Hunt. *A Century of Dishonor*. Boston, 1901.
- Jackson, Royal and, Jennifer Lee. *Harney County, an Historical Inventory*. Burns, Oregon, 1978.
- Josephy, Alvin M., (ed.). *The Great West*. New York, 1965.
- Karolevitz, Robert F. *Newspapering in the Old West*. New York, 1965.
- Kimerlin, H.B. *History and Geologist's Report of the Mayflower Group of Mines*. Berkeley, California, 1926.
- Knight, Oliver. *Following the Indian Wars: The Story of the Newspaper Correspondents Among the Indian Campaigners*. Norma, Oklahoma, 1960.
- Klapthor, Margaret Brown. *The First Ladies*. Washington, D.C., 1981.

- Kimerlin, H.B. *History and Geologist's Report of the Mayflower Group of Mines*. Berkeley, California, 1926.

- Kopper, Philip. *The Smithsonian Book of North American Indians*. Washington, D.C., 1986.

- Lefarge, Thomas H. *Memoirs of a White Crow Indian*. New York, 1928.

- Liljeblad, Sven. *The Idaho Indians in Transition,* 1805-1960. Pocatello, Idaho, 1972.

- Longstreet, Stephen. *War Cries on Horseback*. Garden City, New York, 1970.

- Landrum, Francis S. *Guardhouse, Gallows and Graves,* Klamath Falls, Oregon, 1988.

- Lyman, William D. *The Columbia River*. Portland, N.D.

- Lyon, Juana Fraser. "Archie McIntosh, the Scottish Scout." *Journal on Arizona History* Vol. VIII, (1966).

- Mack, Effie Mona. *The Indian Massacre of 1911*. Caldwell, Idaho, 1968.

- Madsen, Brigham D. *The Northern Shoshoni*. Caldwell, Idaho, 1986.

- McArthur, Lewis A. *Oregon Geographic Names*. Portland, 1952.

- McCall, Dorothy Lawson. *Ranch Under the Rimrock*. Portland, 1968.

- McCoy, Keith. *Melodic Whistles in the Columbia River Gorge*. White Salmon, Washington, 1995.

- McLoughlin, Denis. *Wild and Wooly: An Encyclopedia of the Old West*. New York, 1975.

- McNeal, William H. *History of Wasco County*. The Dalles, Oregon, 1953.

- Meacham, A.B. *Wigwam and Warpath: Or the Royal Chief in Chains*. Boston, 1875.

- Meier, Gary and Gloria. *Those Naughty Ladies of the Old Northwest*. Bend, Oregon, 1990.

- Miller, Joaquin. *Shadow of Shasta: The Modoc War*. Chicago, 1881.

- Miller, May. *Golden Memories of the Paulina Area*. Prineville, Oregon, 1974.

- Monaghan, Jay (ed.). *The Book of the American West*. New York, 1963.

- Mooney, James. *The Ghost-Dance Religion and the Sioux Outbreak of 1890*. Washington, D.C.: Bureau of American Ethnology, 14th Annual Report, 1896.

- Moorhouse, Major Lee. *Souvenir Album of Noted Indian Photographs*. Pendleton, Oregon, 1906.

- Morgan, Thomas. *My Story of the Last Indian War in the Northwest*. Portland, Oregon, 1953.

- Ontko, Vera Koch. *Through the Golden Gate of Yesteryear: Life on the Upper Ochoco 1907 Through 1918*. Prineville, Oregon, 1973.

- Payne, Doris Palmer. *Captain Jack-Modoc Renegade*. Portland, 1938.

- Puter, S.A.D. *Looters of the Public Domain: Oregon Timberland Fraud*. New York, 1909.
- Reiter, Joan Swallow. *The Women*. New York: Time-Life Books. New York, 1978.
- Riddle, Jefferson C. *The Indian History of the Modoc War and the Causes That Led to it*. San Francisco, 1914.
- Rothchild, Samuel. *Reminiscences of Oregon Pioneers: The Indian War of 1878*. San Francisco, N.D.
- Ruby, Robert H. and John A. Brown. *A Guide to the Indian Tribes of the Pacific Northwest*. Norman, Oklahoma, 1986.
- Schmitt, Martin F. (ed.) *General Crook: His Autobiography*. Norman, Oklahoma, 1946.
- Schmitt, Martin F. and Dee Brown. *Fighting Indians of the West*. New York, 1968.
- Schuette, C.N. *Quicksilver in Oregon*. Salem, Oregon: State Department of Geology and Mineral Industries Bulletin No. 4, 1938.
- Scott, Harvey W. *History of Oregon Country*. 6 vols., Cambridge, Massachusetts, 1924.
- Shaver, Fred (ed.). *The Illustrated History of Central Oregon*. Spokane, 1905.
- Shinn, Charles Howard. *Land Laws of Mining Districts*. New York, 1884.
- Slattery, Charles Lewis. *Felix Reville Brunot 1820-1898*. New York, 1901.
- Southworth, Jo Smith. *Millican Memories*. Bend, Oregon, 1977.
- Sprague, Marshall. *Massacre: The Tragedy at White River*. Boston, 1957.
- Stenberg, Millie P. *The Peyote Cult Among Wyoming Indians*. Laramie, Wyoming, 1946.
- Stewart, Patricia. *Sara Winnemucca*. Nevada Historical Society Quarterly 14, No. 4, 1971.
- Swift, Ernest. *The Glory Trail: The Great American Migration and Its Impact on Natural Resources*. Washington, D.C.: The National Wildlife Federation, 1958.
- Talbot, Ethelbert. *My People of the Plains*. New York, 1906.
- Thompson, Erwin N. *Modoc War: Its Military History and Topography*. Sacramento, 1971.
- Thompson, Col. William. *Reminiscences of a Pioneer*. San Francisco, 1912.
- Trenholm, Virginia Cole, & Maurine Corley. *The Shoshoni: Sentinels of the Rockies*. Norman, Oklahoma, 1964.
- Tuby, John E. *Sam Hill: The Prince of Castle Nowhere*. Beaverton, Oregon, 1983.
- Vestal, Stanley. *Sitting Bull*. Boston, 1936.

- Villard, Henry. *Memoirs of Henry Villard, Journalist and Financier*. 2 vols, New York, 1904.

- Voegelin, Erminie Wheeler. *The Northern Paiute of Central Oregon: A Chapter in Treaty Making*. Indiana University: Ethnohistory No. 2, Spring, 1955.

- Wallace, Robert. *The Miners*. Alexandria, Virginia: Time-Life Books, 1976.

- Webb, Todd. *The Gold Rush Trail and the Road to Oregon*. Garden City, New York, 1963.

- Wentworth, Edward Norris. *America's Sheep Trails: History Personalities*. Ames, Iowa, 1948.

- Wilkinson, W.D. *Geology of the Round Mountain Quadrangle*. Salem, Oregon, 1937.

- Winningham, Berylalee (ed.). *The Oregon Blue Book 1977*. Salem, Oregon, 1977.

- Wolke, Howie. *Save Our National Forests*. Kalispell, Montana, 1988.

- Yenne, Bill. *The Encyclopedia of North American Indian Tribes,* Greenwich, Connecticut, 1986.

- Ziegler, W.H. *Wyoming Indians*. A private publication by the Episcopal Church of Laramie, Wyoming, N.D.

Government Documents, Legislative Reports and Other Official Records

- Adjutant General of Oregon. *Annual Reports,* 1869-1880.
- Bureau of American Ethnology. *Annual Reports,* 1869-1880.
- Bureau of Indian Affairs. *Annual Reports,* 1869-1880.
- Circuit Court of the State of Oregon for Crook County. 1883-1916.
- Commission of Public Docks Reports. 1867-1880.
- General Laws of Oregon. 1866-1880.
- Grant County Mining Records. . Canyon City, Oregon.
- *Historical Highlights of Public Land Management 1498-1962*. Washington, D.C.: United States Department of Interior, 1962.
- Letter, Commanding General, Military Division of the Missouri to Commanding General, Military Department of the Platte, March 16, 1877. (Concerns over a Snake uprising in eastern Oregon.)
- Modoc War Official Correspondence. Bancroft Library, Berkeley, California.
- Ochoco National Forest Files, 1906-1927. Prineville, Oregon.
- Office of Indian Affairs. *General Files, Oregon, Idaho and Nevada,* 1869-1880.
- O.I.A. *Special Files, Oregon, Idaho and Nevada,* 1869-1880.
- O.I.A. *Oregon Superintendency, Letters Sent and Received,* 1869-1880.
- O.I.A. *Idaho Superintendency, Letters Sent and Received,* 1869-1878.

- O.I.A. *Nevada Superintendency, Letters Sent and Received,* 1869-1878.
- Oregon House of Representatives Journal. 1870-1880.
- Oregon Supreme Court Library. *McKay Verses Campbell Case No. 8839 and 8840, District Court D, Oregon, September 26, 1870; November 7, 1871.*
- Records, Department of Medicine. Willamette University, Salem, Oregon.
- Schuette, C.N. *Quicksilver in Oregon.* State Department of Geology and Mineral Industries, Bulletin No. 4. Salem, 1938.
- U.S. Adjutant General Office. *General Orders, Special Orders and Circulars,* 1869-1880.
- U.S. Army Department of the Columbia. *Commands and Annual Reports,* 1869-1879.
- U.S. Army Division of the Pacific. *General Orders, General Court Martial Orders, Special Orders and Circulars,* 1869-1879.
- U.S. Army Department of the Platte. *Military Correspondence,* 1876-1878.
- U.S. Court of Claims, Case No., H219. *Shoshoni Tribe of Indians, Petitioner v. the United States of America, Defendent.*
- U.S. Court of Claims, Case E-344. *The Yahuskin Band of Snake Indians v. the United States of America.* Peter Paulina Petitioner.
- U.S. Department of the Interior. *Bureau of Indian Affairs Report,* 1873.
- U.S. Department of the Interior. *General Files, Oregon,* 1869-1880.
- U.S. Land Office Documents. *The Dalles City, Oregon.* Series No. 2896.
- U.S. National Archives Records. *Office of Indian Affairs,* 1869-1880.
- U.S. Secretary of the Interior. *Annual Reports to Congress,* 1869-1880.
- U.S. Secretary of War. *Annual Reports to Congress,* 1869-1880.
- U.S. House of Representatives. *Executive Documents,* 1869-1880.
- U.S. Senate. *Committee Reports and Executive Documents,* 1869-1880.
- U.S. Senate. *Bill 695.*

Miscellaneous Publications, Magazine Articles and Letters

- *Army and Navy Journal,* Vols. XII-XV. June 1875-June 1878.
- Blake, Grover C., "Oregon Range War," *True West,* January-February 1965.
- Blakely, Jim, "When the Juniper Trees Bore Fruit," *The Sunday Oregonian,* March 12, 19, and 26, 1939.
- Brimlow, George F. "The Life of Sarah Winnemucca." *Oregon Historical Quarterly.* June, 1952.
- Burdette Ochiho to Gale Ontko, letter dated Klamath Falls, Oregon. August 4, 1956.

- Champion, Art, "The Mayflower Mining District," *Wheeler County Chronicle*, December 1938.
- Champion, Art, *Mining World*, Vol. 2, No. 8, August 1940.
- Chinn, Lt. Col. George M. *The Machine Gun*, Vols. I and IV, Navy Bureau of Ordinance.
- *City Directory*. Portland, Oregon, 1875.
- Clark, Keith and Donna (eds.). *Daring Donald McKay: Or the Last Trail of the Modocs*, Oregon Historical Society. Portland, Oregon, 1971.
- Collier, A.J. *A Geologist With the Oregon Bureau of Mines and Geology*. Salem, Oregon, 1914.
- Colorado Governor's 1887 Report of the Ute Difficulties.
- *Corrine Idaho Record*, Vol. 13, No. 1. August 25, 1877.
- Crook County Mining Register. *Ochoco Mining District Records*, 3 vols. Prineville, Oregon.
- Dickinson, Fred, "The Five Dollars Worth $50,000," *This Week Magazine*, March 8, 1964.
- *Dictionary of American Biology*, Vols. VIII and XIV.
- *Dictionary of the Chinook Jargon*. J.K. Gill & Co. Portland, Oregon, 1889.
- Dosch, Arno, "The War for Range," *Pacific Monthly*, February 1906.
- Dunnington, Jean, "Chief Ochiho," *The Journal of the Modoc Historical Society*, No. 12, 1990.
- Engineer's Report, *Spokane, Portland and Seattle Railroad Files*, Portland, Oregon 1910.
- Evan W. Estep to Commissioner of Indian Affairs, march 21, 1912, *Records, United States Indian Service*, U.S. National Archives.
- Federal Railroad Report, No. 172, Washington, D.C.
- *How to Kill a Nation: U.S. Policy in Western Shoshone Country Since 1863*. Western Shoshoni National Council, P.O. Box 210, Indian Springs, Nevada, 89018.
- Judgment Roll Crook County No. 2757, *Conclusion of Law*.
- Juris, Frances, *North from Prineville Over the Old Dalles State Road*, letter dated December 23, 1902.
- Kuehnelt-Leddihn, "Utopia and Idealogies," *Chronicles*, Vol. 12, No. 12, December 1988.
- Krantz, Shad O., *Technical World* (a railroad magazine), Vol. 18, September 1912.
- Lundgren, Walkema, "The Gold Belt of the Blue Mountains of Oregon," *U.S. Geologic Survey*, 1901.
- McKay, William C. *McKay Papers*. Umatilla County Library, Pendleton, Oregon.

- Matthew Cullen to Gale Ontko, letter dated Portland, February 5, 1971. *Oregon Historical Society List of Warm Springs Scouts Serving in the Snake and Modoc Wars.*

- Minutes of the Prineville City Council 1882-1917.

- Nash, Wallis, "Feuds and Forays of the Oregon Range," *Pacific Monthly*, March 1906.

- National Archives Publication No. 2598, Military Department of the Platte, July 3, 1878 (concerning the Bannock War).

- O'Callaghan, Jerry A. *The Disposition of the Public Domain in Oregon.* Washington, D.C. 1960.

- Ochoco Mining register, *Articles of Confederation*, Crook County Clerk's Office, Prineville, Oregon.

- Oliver, Emery, *Mineral Survey No. 411 of the Mayflower Group of Mines*, Bureau of Land Management files, Portland, Oregon.

- Oregon Council for the Humanities, *A View of Gold Mountain: Letters from the Kam Wok Chung Trading Company*, Portland, Oregon 1994.

- Oregon Guide, *Oregon: End of the Trail*, Portland, Oregon 1940.

- *Oregon Historical Society. Oregon Historical Quarterly*, Vols. III, IX, X, XI, L, LXVIII, LXXIX.

- *Oregon Wildlife*, Vol. 37, No. 4, April 1982.

- Padgett, Keith W. (consultant), *History of Crook County, Oregon*, Dallas, Texas 1981 and 1994.

- Potter, Miles F. and Harold McCall, "The Golden Years of Eastern Oregon," *The Ore Bin*, Vol. 40, No. 4, April 1978, State of Oregon Department of Geology and Mineral Industries Records, Department of Medicine, Willamette University, Salem, Oregon.

- *Reid, _____. Progress of Portland for the Year Ending 1877-1878*, a pamphlet published in 1879 by the Secretary of the Portland Board of Trade.

- Rinehart, W.V. *Unpublished Manuscript.* Bancroft Library, Berkeley, California, N.D.

- Rinehart, W.V. "War in the Great Northwest." *Washington Historical Quarterly.* April, 1931.

- Rock Creek Mining District. *Articles of Operation*, filed in Grant County Records, Canyon City, Oregon.

- Santee, J.F. "Egan of the Paiutes." *Washington Historical Society Quarterly.* January 1935.

- Schaefer, _____. "President Grant Plays Samaritan When Wild West Show Goes Broke." *WPA Oregon Historical Records Survey for Umatilla County, Oregon.* State Archives, Salem, Oregon.

- *Smithsonian Magazine*, Vol. 24, No. 12, March 1994.

- Southworth, Jack (ed.). *Grant County in the Beginning.* John Day, Oregon, 1990.
- Stearns, Frances E., "Indians and Rattlesnakes are Feared by Pioneer Women," *Crook County News*, August 4, 1939.
- Steward, Julian H. "Basin-Plateau Aboriginal Sociopolitical Groups." *Bulletin 120*, Bureau of American Ethnology. Washington Printing Office, 1938.
- Steward, Julian H. "Changes in Shoshoni Culture." *Scientific Monthly*, Vol. XLIX. Washington D.C., American Association for the Advancement of Science, 1939.
- Steward, Julian H. and Wheeler-Voegelin, Erminie. *Paiute Indians,* Vol. 3. New York, 1974.
- Throckmorton, Major. "Shoshoni Must Die." *East Oregonian.* Pendleton, Oregon, July 27, 1878.
- Turby, J. David. "Hailstorm of Death." *VFW Magazine.* February 1972.
- Tweedie, William, "Some Aspects of the Early Development of Crook County," *Thesis Paper*, August 1939.
- Veazie, A.L. *Address to the Dedication of a Monument to the Pioneers of Crook County.* Prineville, Oregon, August 7, 1939.
- Washakie, Letter to Hank Brownson dated February 25, 1892, *Herford Collection*, University of Wyoming Library.
- Western Shoshone Defense Project, Vols. 3-4. 1995-1996.

Newspapers

- Antelope Herald (Oregon)
- Ashland Tidings (Oregon)
- Ashwood Prospector (Oregon)
- Blue Mountain Eagle (John Day, Oregon)
- Carson City News (Nevada)
- Central Oregon Shopper (Prineville, Oregon)
- Central Oregonian (Prineville, Oregon)
- Cline Falls Press (Oregon)
- Corinne Reporter (Utah)
- Crook County Journal (Oregon)
- Daily Alta (San Francisco, California)
- Daily Bulletin (Portland, Oregon)
- Deschutes Echo (Bend, Oregon)
- Desert News (Salt Lake City, Utah)
- East Oregonian (Pendleton, Oregon)
- Elko Independent (Nevada)
- Evening Gazette (Reno, Nevada)

- Evening Post (San Francisco, California)
- Evening Press (Asbury, New Jersey)
- Humboldt Register (Winnemucca, Nevada)
- Humboldt Star (Winnemucca, Nevada)
- Idaho Enterprise (Boise)
- Idaho Statesman (Boise)
- Jacksonville Reporter (Oregon)
- Madras Pioneer (Oregon)
- Nevada State Journal (Carson City)
- New York Times (New York)
- Ochoco Review (Prineville, Oregon)
- Omaha Herald (Nebraska)
- Oroville News (California)
- Oregon Journal (Portland)
- Oregonian (Portland)
- Owyhee Avalanche (Silver City, Idaho)
- Owyhee News (Owyhee, Nevada)
- Pocatello Tribune (Idaho)
- Prineville News (Oregon)
- Prineville Review (Oregon)
- Redmond Spokesman (Oregon)
- Reese River Revielle (Austin, Nevada)
- Ritzville Times (Washington)
- The Bulletin (Bend, Oregon)
- The Chronicle (San Francisco, California)
- The Dalles Mountaineer (Oregon)
- The Dalles Optimist (Oregon)
- The Dalles Times (Oregon)
- The Silver State (Winnemucca, Nevada)
- The Tribune (Salt Lake City, Utah)
- Twin Falls Times (Idaho)
- Virginia City Union (Nevada)
- Washington Chronicle (Washington, D.C.)
- Wells Herald (Elko, Nevada)
- Wheeler County Chronicle (Mitchell, Oregon)

INDEX

THUNDER
OVER THE OCHOCO

VOLUME I: *The Gathering Storm*

Covering hundreds of years from pre-Columbian times to the collapse of the world fur trade in 1840, Volume I meets the Shoshoni Indians before the arrival of the Europeans and tracks their rise from peaceful eastern Oregon agriculturists to the aggressive Snake war tribes, rulers of the Pacific Northwest. By 1812, they had clashed with every major world power in their jealous guardianship of a land they called Oyerungun. Their undisputed hunting grounds beyond the setting sun would soon become coveted by white foreigners searching first for precious metals and later for valuable fur-bearing animals. The gathering storms of hatred would hover ominously on the distant horizons. Volume I chronicles the events which inevitably would lead to war.

VOLUME II: *Distant Thunder*

The twenty-year period between 1840 and 1860 would see overland migration across the land known to the Shoshoni as the Ochoco—Land of the Red Willow. The Americans would call it eastern Oregon. Never on friendly terms with the white invaders, the Shoshoni tolerated passage across their ancestral hunting grounds only so long as the American homesteaders stayed strictly on the dusty thoroughfare called the Oregon Trail. When they transgressed, the distant thunder of gunfire reverberated across interior Oregon like the tolling of a death knell. Volume II narrates the suffering, heartache and death of those unfortunate souls who dared to venture into the Ochoco; and it covers the first brutal Indian wars fought west of the Mississippi River.

VOLUME III: *Lightning Strikes!*

Between 1860 and 1869 rich deposits of gold were discovered in eastern Oregon, and the citizens of the Willamette Valley were out to claim their share at any cost. Shoshoni dog soldiers were equally determined that they keep to their side of the Cascade barrier. War was officially declared. The opposing forces went for each other's throats locked in a death struggle that seemed endless. The crashing crescendo of thunder was accompanied by lightning strikes of destruction which ricocheted into four western states—and the military campaign they thought would last but a few weeks stretched into years. In flashing raids, Shoshoni dog soldiers humiliated the Oregon Cavalry, taking a deadly toll on mining settlements, homesteads, stagecoaches and wagon trains. It would take a battle-hardened army baptized in the carnage of the Civil War four years to bring the Shoshoni to their knees: an aggressor with unlimited resources pitted against a foe that was undermanned, undernourished and outgunned—but desperately fighting for survival. Volume III is the story of the first violent Shoshoni outbreak, which would again erupt in the 1870s.

VOLUME IV: *Rain of Tears*

The thirteen year interval between 1866 and 1879 would witness monumental changes in the Ochoco. With the surrender of Has No Horse's battered army, western Oregon had free rein to exploit the Ochoco as it saw fit. In a blind daze, the Shoshoni would witness frontier towns springing up where their lodges had once stood. As thousands upon thousands of bawling cattle and sheep trampled their ancestral hunting grounds to dust, the proud warriors of a by-gone year again rebelled. And, for a fleeting moment, shook the state of Oregon to its very foundations. Then it was over. Stripped even of reservation rights, the few survivors drifted between the four winds on their final journey into the bitter rain of tears.

VOLUME V: *And the Juniper Trees Bore Fruit*

Between 1880 and 1916, the birth of industry would give vent to new bloodshed in the Ochoco. Six-shooters roared in the night, ranchers disappeared never to be seen again. . . and the juniper trees bore fruit: the dangling bullet-ridden bodies of men whose only crime was to oppose the land barons who ruled old Crook County with a Winchester rifle and a rawhide rope. As the 19th century staggered to a close, a Shoshoni visionary born in the Ochoco foretold the rebirth of Indian supremacy. His wondrous dream was buried in a common grave at Wounded Knee, South Dakota. By the time the 20th century blundered onto the scene, saddle-blanket blazes hacked into the Ochoco pines marked the deadlines between sheep and cattle range and woe unto him who crossed these barriers. Rifle shots echoed the length and breadth of the Deschutes canyon as the Hill-Harriman railroad giants battled to link central Oregon to the outside world. Ironically, the last Indian war fought in the United States would explode on the Oregon-Nevada border in 1911 when a Shoshoni chief led his followers, armed only with bows and arrows, in a suicidal charge against a group of stockmen. Thus ended the *Thunder Over the Ochoco*. Would the new owners do a better job of managing the land they had wrenched from the Shoshoni? I leave that to other writers to decide.